Child Labor
in America

MW00614785

Child Labor in America

THE EPIC LEGAL STRUGGLE TO PROTECT CHILDREN

John A. Fliter

 UNIVERSITY PRESS OF KANSAS

© 2018 by the University Press of Kansas

All rights reserved

Published by the University Press of Kansas (Lawrence, Kansas 66045), which was
organized by the Kansas Board of Regents and is operated and funded by Emporia
State University, Fort Hays State University, Kansas State University, Pittsburg State
University, the University of Kansas, and Wichita State University

Library of Congress Cataloging-in-Publication Data

Names: Fliter, John A., 1959–, author.
Title: Child labor in America : the epic legal struggle to protect children / John A. Fliter.
Description: Lawrence, Kansas : University Press of Kansas, 2018. | Includes
bibliographical references and index.
Identifiers: LCCN 2018004639
ISBN 9780700626304 (hardback)
ISBN 9780700626311 (paperback)
ISBN 9780700626328 (ebook)
Subjects: LCSH: Child labor—Law and legislation—United States—History. | Child
labor—United States—History. | BISAC: HISTORY / United States / 19th Century. |
HISTORY / United States / 20th Century. | LAW / Child Advocacy.
Classification: LCC KF3552 .F55 2018 | DDC 344.7301/31—dc23.
LC record available at https://lccn.loc.gov/2018004639.

British Library Cataloguing-in-Publication Data is available.

Printed in the United States of America

10 9 8 7 6 5 4 3 2 1

The paper used in this publication is recycled and contains 50 percent postconsumer
waste. It is acid free and meets the minimum requirements of the American National
Standard for Permanence of Paper for Printed Library Materials Z39.48-1992.

CONTENTS

Acknowledgments *vii*

Introduction *1*

1 From Public Good to Moral Evil: State Laws and Child Labor in the 1800s *12*

2 Divided, We Fall: The Beveridge-Parsons Bill *43*

3 Regulating Child Labor as Interstate Commerce: The Keating-Owen Act and *Hammer v. Dagenhart 69*

4 Taxing Profits of Companies Using Child Labor: *Bailey v. Drexel Furniture Company 95*

5 Congress Proposes the "Children's Amendment" *123*

6 The Great Depression and the Renewed Fight over the Child Labor Amendment *157*

7 The Fair Labor Standards Act and Final Victory in *United States v. Darby Lumber 191*

8 Contemporary Child Labor Issues *221*

Postscript: Those "Truly Stupid" Child Labor Laws *231*

Chronology of Events *241*

States Ratifying the Proposed 1924 Child Labor Amendment *247*

Cases Cited *249*

Notes *251*

Bibliography *287*

Index *309*

ACKNOWLEDGMENTS

I have been teaching undergraduate students the three landmark child labor cases—*Hammer v. Dagenhart, Bailey v. Drexel Furniture Company,* and *United States v. Darby Lumber*—in my constitutional law course for twenty-five years. Like many people who considered the cases involving federal institutional powers and constraints, I tended to view the child labor precedents as historical examples, involving long-settled constitutional issues, where the Supreme Court worked to define the scope of the congressional Commerce Clause and taxing powers. After observing some contemporary interest groups and elected officials criticize child labor laws and the *Darby Lumber* decision, which upheld federal child labor restrictions, I wondered whether my generation had failed to learn the lessons of history. I decided to study the origins of oppressive child labor and the protracted state and federal legal struggle to regulate the practice. This book is the result of that investigation. The project has led me to a better understanding of the role child labor has played in the nation's social, political, and legal development. My hope is that students, teachers, and general readers will be enlightened by the story as well.

Several staff members at the University Press of Kansas contributed to the publication of this book. I would like to thank former editor Charles "Chuck" T. Myers for his enthusiasm and early support of the project. I am grateful to Editor-in-Chief Joyce Harrison for managing the initial stages of the review process. My editor, David Congdon, shares my interests in political science, law, and history. I appreciate his work supervising the reader reports, subsequent revisions, and final stages of manuscript review. I also want to thank Michael Kehoe for his efforts in marketing the book, my production editor, Larisa Martin, for her work in coordinating the later stages of the book-making process, and Martha Whitt for her meticulous copy-editing. Finally, I want to thank the various reviewers who read all or portions of the manuscript, including Robert Macieski, David S. Tanenhaus, and my friend and former coauthor Derek Hoff. Although the manuscript benefited greatly from the comments of these reviewers, I take full responsibility for any errors or omissions in the book.

This book would not have been possible without the support of my department, the College of Arts and Sciences, and the Provost's Office at Kansas State University. My department head, Jeff Pickering, offered encouragement throughout the process, and I appreciate his assistance in securing grant funding and sabbatical leave. The semester of leave provided much-needed quiet time for writing. I am grateful for my political science colleagues who supported me as I dealt with some health issues while writing the manuscript. It is a pleasure to work with such a fine group of people. Several political science graduate students assisted with various aspects of the research, including Chelsey Eimer, Madushika Nadeeshani Weerasinghe Pathiranage, and Derek Shaw. I appreciate their help tracking down books, obscure reports, and other materials.

A University Small Research Grant supported a week of field research at the Library of Congress's Manuscript Division. The staff in the Manuscript Reading Room provided valuable assistance and access to several paper collections, including those of Albert J. Beveridge, Felix Frankfurter, Alexander J. McKelway, National Child Labor Committee, National Consumers' League, Theodore Roosevelt, and Harlan Fiske Stone. My research also benefited from the resources available at K-State's Hale Library and access to the Edgar Gardner Murphy Papers in the Southern Historical Collection, Wilson Library, at the University of North Carolina, Chapel Hill.

Projects like this one often demand a lot of time away from family. My wife, Leah, deserves praise for her patience and support over the years. I also want to thank our two boys, David and Eric, for giving me the joy of being a father. Around the time that I completed the manuscript, Leah and I helped move David, our youngest son, into the dorms for his freshman year in college. Now officially an empty nester, I miss having the boys (who are now fine young men) around the house. Although I'm sure I will learn to relax and enjoy my newfound freedom, perhaps another book project will make the transition easier.

John A. Fliter
Manhattan, Kansas

INTRODUCTION

The archives of the Library of Congress house thousands of photos of working children taken by Lewis W. Hine over a century ago for the National Child Labor Committee (NCLC).[1] One famous photo shows a ten-year-old girl taking a momentary glimpse out the window while tending a spinning machine in a textile mill. She had already been working for over a year. The picture is just one of more than one thousand images showing children at work in the cotton and silk mills. Another photo depicts a group of boys, between ten and fourteen years old, working the breaker rooms in a coal mine. Covered in coal dust, the boys are hunched over a conveyor belt as they separate the dull slate from the sharp, glistening coal deposits. A "breaker boss" with a large stick stands behind the youth, keeping them on task. Another image shows a group of two dozen breaker boys with blackened faces posing for a photo after a day's work. Most of the boys are under fifteen, but they look like little men.

More than three hundred photos in the NCLC collection capture children between five and fourteen working as oyster shuckers or shrimpers for canning companies. In one picture, a group of children stand in front of a mound of shells over three times their height. Another photo features Manuel, a bare-footed five-year-old shrimp picker, with a bucket in each hand and a face that looks years beyond his tender age. In a 1911 photo, Mary, an eight-year-old girl, stands over a wooden bin shucking oysters. She started at 3:00 a.m. and by the time she quits at 5:00 p.m., she will earn five cents for a four-pound bucket of shelled oysters. Another image shows three boys, all appearing younger than fourteen, making cigars. One has a large "stogie" stuffed in his mouth and all the boys reportedly chewed tobacco and smoked. These photos, available online, are visual reminders of a time in American history when many children worked long hours, often in unhealthy and dangerous conditions, in a daily struggle for subsistence. Poverty, greed, weak state labor laws, and nonexistent federal regulations permitted this kind of child labor exploitation.

Most Americans today do not give child labor laws much thought. Child labor, however, was a prominent policy issue in American politics for nearly one hundred years, especially during the first few decades of the twentieth century. Children had worked since the first settlers arrived on the shores of America. Their labor helped families survive and contributed to the community. During the 1800s, however, public attitudes about working children changed from viewing labor as a personal and public good to a moral and social evil. In *Child Labor: An American History*, Hugh Hindman uses data from the National Child Labor Committee archives to document the growth of child labor as a social problem.[2] Hindman argues that industrialization both created the problem of child labor and provided the impetus toward its eradication. The evolution of public opinion on child labor paralleled the transformation of the American economy from its local agricultural base to a national industrial juggernaut. The turning point was a shift in household economy from production for domestic consumption to production for markets where children worked outside the family in factories and mills.

Regulation of working children began in the 1840s at the state level in a haphazard and inefficient way. Weakened by legislative compromises and lack of enforcement mechanisms, early state laws combating child labor were limited and ineffective. Reformers consistently lobbied for tougher regulations. After the American Civil War (1861–1865), a growing number of people sensed that child labor was a problem, but accurate information on the scope of the practice was unavailable. Data from the 1870 Census revealed a significant portion of child workers, thus spurring reform efforts. As part of the Progressive Era (1890–1920), numerous individuals, interest groups, and politicians devoted a substantial amount of their time, talents, and resources to the issue of working children. Federal attempts to curb child labor started in 1906 and resulted in several laws, four major Supreme Court decisions, an (ultimately unsuccessful) Child Labor Amendment proposed by Congress in 1924, and landmark legislation such as the Fair Labor Standards Act of 1938. Along the way, there were contentious constitutional battles over states' rights under the Tenth Amendment to control local labor conditions versus federal power to regulate interstate commerce and levy taxes to restrict child labor. There is a rich and illuminating legal and political history to be told about the struggle to regulate child labor in America. This book attempts to tell that story.

Before we proceed much further, a definition of child labor is in order. Many people have different ideas about the nature and scope of child labor, and the concept has changed over the years. At its most basic level, child labor may be defined as the commercial employment of children age seventeen and under for their labor. But it is much more than that. As used throughout this book, child labor is mostly a pejorative term. A social reformer writing almost a century ago defined child labor as "the work that interferes with a full living of the life of childhood and with the best possible preparation for adulthood."[3] Another commentator defined the term in its legal meaning as "the gainful labor of children at unfit ages, for unreasonable hours or under unwholesome conditions."[4] Walter I. Trattner, the author of the first comprehensive history of child labor reform, defined child labor as "the work of children under conditions that interfere with their physical development and their education."[5] In contemporary legal terms, these definitions describe what is called "oppressive child labor."[6] All three definitions suggest a difference between children's work, which is constructive, and child labor, which is exploitative.

Proponents of child labor regulations did not attempt to eliminate all work performed by minors. Reformers recognized the educational and developmental value in children's work. Child labor legislation does not prevent children from working part-time during the school year or extended hours over the summer. Regulations do not prohibit children from performing odd jobs for neighbors or doing chores around the house, such as washing dishes or taking out the trash, although some children may mildly protest such tasks. As strange as it seems, however, those arguments became part of the debate over the failed Child Labor Amendment. For various reasons that will be explained in the pages that follow, the text of the amendment used the phrase "child labor," rather than "child employment," which implies payment for work. Opponents of the amendment used the broad language to claim that the proposal would give Congress the power to regulate chores around the house or family farm and even homework assignments for school. It was a rather specious contention because reformers never sought such invasive restrictions. For some citizens concerned about the growing concentration of federal power, however, this was an effective argument against the amendment.

There are several key historical observations involving child labor and society that are important for understanding the development of child labor laws. First, child labor has always been a problem of poverty, both cause and effect. For most of American history, economic necessity compelled children of the poor to start work at an early age in order to contribute to the family income. This was especially true during the second Industrial Revolution of the late 1800s, which saw and with the influx of millions of immigrants from Europe. Prior to the development of a welfare state and public assistance programs, a child's income was often essential to the survival of his or her family. Alternatively, children of wealthy families were never sent to work in coal mines, glass factories, or textile mills. Because the working poor had few options, low-income parents often opposed and evaded child labor laws. Once committed to a life of labor at an early age, however, few children advanced out of poverty. Child labor was always cheap labor.

Second, child labor and public education are inextricably linked. As the government restricted their labor, children needed something productive to do with their time. Learning filled the gap. The first compulsory school laws were enacted in the 1850s but few children were covered by them, and they mandated only three months of schooling a year. In 1870, less than 5 percent of children were subject to compulsory attendance laws; by 1908, that number climbed to 72 percent. A system of state-funded public schools, however, was not widely available for most of American history. Consequently, the expansion of public schools, compulsory school attendance, and improved educational standards became some of the most effective child labor reforms.

A third key observation is that reformers have always viewed child labor as both an individual and community problem. When children are sent to work at an early age for long hours under harsh conditions, they often grow up illiterate and physically and socially degenerate. Those individual disabilities had consequences for society. Some of the earliest critiques of child labor expressed concern that the practice undermined democracy and social order. Child labor was viewed as a threat to the foundations of representative government. Middle-class reformers envisioned a generation of uneducated working poor who would grow up to be ignorant and angry adults vulnerable to the radical doctrines of anarchism and communism. Other reformers warned that the physical toll on child workers created a population unfit for war and American imperial ambitions. These instincts were inherently conservative yet they informed some of the Progressive arguments against child labor.

Finally, child labor reform encompassed class and racial dimensions. Many of the social reformers were educated middle- and upper-class citizens from midwestern and northeastern cities. Progressive-Era crusaders were wealthy philanthropists, university professors, journalists, clergy, and community activists from such centers of social reform as Hull House, a settlement house in Chicago cofounded by Jane Addams and Ellen Gates Starr. These social reformers sought restrictions on the labor of working-class immigrant families, many of whom resented their efforts. Additionally, the story of the child labor reform movement is really a narrative about white reformers seeking regulations on labor performed by primarily white children. This was especially true in the post-Reconstruction New South. Because racial segregation excluded black children from manufacturing jobs, many poor white children labored for long hours in the textile mills. Historian Shelley Sallee has demonstrated that to promote even minimal reforms in southern states, northern and southern Progressives used a "white supremacy" strategy to build support for reform among the southern middle-class.[7]

Many law journal articles and book chapters have examined state and federal attempts to regulate child labor, but no scholar has provided a comprehensive analysis and balanced treatment of the legal arguments, economic issues, and broader constitutional history involving the efforts to limit oppressive child labor. Few books on the market adequately describe the constitutional conflict over child labor in America, and the books in print have several limitations.[8] As the title implies, this book is primarily a legal history of the decades-long struggle over child labor in America. Emphasis is placed on the doctrinal development of state child labor and school attendance laws, the debates in state legislatures and Congress, the development of administrative powers to enforce the laws, the political battle over the Child Labor Amendment, judicial review of child labor laws, and legal commentary on important cases. While a detailed analysis of every state child labor law is not practical, this work provides summaries of state laws at important historical junctures and highlights conflicts in several battleground states, such as Massachusetts and New York, critical in the development of child labor laws. I also incorporate throughout the book the most recent legal and political science research and analyses on the four federal child labor laws, interest group tactics and strategies, and the major Supreme Court decisions.

Dozens of interest groups campaigned for and against child labor laws across decades. The primary reform groups were the National Child Labor Committee, the National Consumers' League, the American Federation of Labor, and the National Federation of Women's Clubs. Opponents of child labor regulations included the Southern Textile Committee, the National Association of Manufacturers, the American Farm Bureau Federation, and the Catholic Church. Each side had its share of defections. Some early child labor reform advocates, such as New York governor Alfred E. Smith, became vocal opponents of the Child Labor Amendment, while groups like the American Farm Bureau ultimately switched their position in support of the amendment. Like other policy areas in which interest groups are active, child labor law opponents used three strategies to defeat regulations: (1) lobbying to secure votes in a legislature, at both the state and congressional levels; (2) challenging the constitutionality of child labor laws in state and federal courts; and (3) influencing the substance of the laws so that the administrative provisions surrounding them were so inadequate as to make the regulations unenforceable.[9] All three tactics involve important features of interest-group politics and public policymaking.

In examining the long struggle over child labor, several conclusions regarding the relationship between law and society are warranted. First, law is a social institution that both shapes and is influenced by social forces. Legal change is often incremental and slow. Society must work through an experimental process of trial and error in developing laws to address social problems.[10] Public attitudes on child labor evolved across decades, influenced by personal observation, empirical research, interest-group advocacy, and the media. Also, technological developments in manufacturing altered the apprenticeship system and work environment, and economic conditions influenced the nature and prevalence of child employment.

Age limits for child labor are a good example of this legal dynamic. Many of the early laws (1840–1890) fixed the minimum age for factory and mill employment at ten to twelve years. By modern standards, that age range is too early to stop being a kid attending school and begin a life of labor. As society progressed, reformers recognized that the age limit should be higher because children need more room for mental and physical development. The next generation of child labor laws (1890–1910) set thirteen or fourteen as the minimum for employment and recommended compulsory education through that age, albeit only for three months a year. Eventually, fifteen and then sixteen became the standard minimum age for industrial and manufacturing work. By the time reformers proposed the Child Labor Amendment in 1924, eighteen was the recommended minimum for employment in dangerous job categories. Each incremental increase in the minimum age generated intense opposition from many employers, parents, and interest groups who benefited in some way from child labor. For instance, when in 1886 Connecticut set the minimum at thirteen years for employment in mechanical, mercantile, or manufacturing establishments, critics claimed that the law was too sweeping and would give children a "perpetual Fourth of July" the entire year.[11]

Second, mere enactment of child labor laws was not enough to solve the policy problem. Some citizens and officials believed that once a law was on the books, the social evil of child labor was resolved and thus additional laws were unnecessary. The reality, however, was much more complex. Around the turn of the twentieth century, Roscoe Pound, dean of Harvard Law School, developed a sociological jurisprudence that emphasized the impact of social forces upon the law and noted the differences between the law on the books and the law in action. For Pound, "the life of the law is in its enforcement."[12] By 1900, twenty-eight states had child labor laws on the books. Reformers, however, consistently complained that both child labor and school attendance laws were "a farce," "inoperative," or "dead letter," and that more effective laws were needed to improve administration and enforcement.

When the first child labor laws were enacted in the mid-1800s, a professional administrative system did not exist at the state or federal level. Massachusetts pioneered the first state bureau of labor statistics in 1869, which, according to the US Department of Labor website, was the first such department in the world.[13] By 1900, only twenty-one states had an administrative agency devoted to labor issues. At the national level, a Federal Bureau of Labor was established in 1884 and placed within the Interior Department, but the US Department of Labor was not formed until 1913. The federal Children's Bureau, the first agency of its kind in the world to focus on child welfare, was created in 1912. A system of bureaus and commissions provided much-needed statistical information on the nature and scope of child labor, and administrative officials were essential to rigorous enforcement of the laws. Once established, however, bureaus often lacked necessary personnel, resources, and administrative powers to investigate and force compliance with the law. Factory inspectors were needed to enforce child labor laws and truant officers were necessary to compel school attendance. Over time, those tools were provided, but it took decades to develop an effective administrative structure.[14]

Finally, the history of child labor laws informs our understanding of courts, public policy, and social change. State supreme courts upheld early state legislative efforts to restrict child labor under broad police powers to promote public health, safety, and welfare. Meanwhile, federal courts, especially the US Supreme Court, prevented social reform by striking down three congressional attempts to regulate child labor. From the time Senator Albert J. Beveridge introduced the first federal bills to restrict child labor in 1906, to the Supreme Court decision in *United States v. Darby Lumber* (1941), where the Court upheld child labor provisions in the Fair Labor

Standards Act, thirty-five years had passed. *Darby Lumber* was an important expansion of congressional power, but it arrived after the worst forms of child labor exploitation had ended. Unlike other policy issues of the twentieth century, such as civil rights, religious freedom, and the rights of criminal defendants, the US Supreme Court was not a catalyst for constitutional and social change on the issue of child labor.[15]

Probably more than any other factor, competing visions of the nature of the federal system, called dual and cooperative federalism, influenced the legal struggle over child labor.[16] Since the earliest debates over the practice, dual federalism adherents claimed that the US Constitution created a strict division of powers between the national government and the states, with the federal government limited to its enumerated or delegated powers. Those enumerated powers, they argued, said nothing about regulating local labor conditions. Reformers contended that Congress has both enumerated and implied powers to regulate child labor as interstate commerce and to tax products made with child labor, especially to prevent unfair market competition. Under cooperative federalism, federal and state governments share responsibility for policy problems, and the US government may intervene to bring about needed uniformity in child labor laws to serve national interests. States may still regulate, but if state law conflicts with federal requirements, federal law is supreme. These contrasting views of federalism affected every major congressional debate and federal court decision on child labor.

Child labor laws have been in place at the state level for over 170 years, and the major federal legislation governing child labor, the Fair Labor Standards Act (1938), has been on the books for 80 years. Following *Darby Lumber*, a social consensus developed around child labor issues. For decades, the conventional wisdom has been that children should be restricted from working certain dangerous jobs and excessive hours because education, recreation, and personal development are more important to child welfare than any wage contribution a child can make to the family budget. Consequently, few major conflicts involving child labor laws have erupted since the 1940s. Federal and state laws have been amended to cover areas still ripe for reform, but few child labor issues generate much public interest. Several subjects remain contentious, however. Children of migrant farmworkers are laboring long hours picking crops, and policymakers continue to debate the roles played by children in agriculture, such as kids operating machinery on family farms. These areas are noted for weak regulations and enforcement.

Following the Republican Tea Party victories in Congress and state legislatures in the 2010 midterm elections, some newly elected libertarian and
conservative representatives openly questioned the wisdom of child labor
and compulsory education laws and argued for their repeal or reform. More
recent, President Donald Trump's cabinet pick for secretary of education,
Betsy DeVos, generated controversy in part because of her association with
the Acton Institute, a conservative think tank that favors free market principles over public institutions. An article on the organization's website advocated a return of child labor, characterizing the practice as "a gift our
kids can handle."[17] Some of these modern critics of child labor laws take
the extreme laissez-faire position that the government should stay out of
the field of child labor altogether, while others simply want to allow kids
more freedom to work, often at much cheaper wages than adults. Republican senator Mike Lee of Utah, for example, argued that the federal government has no authority to regulate child labor, even though that power was
unanimously affirmed in *Darby Lumber*.

These attacks on child labor restrictions represent just one front of a
broad-based ideological assault on the welfare state and government regulations of the economy that originated during the Progressive, New Deal,
and Great Society periods. Everything from Social Security, the minimum
wage, and Medicaid to welfare programs and child labor laws are under attack. These policy battles have existed for decades but they intensified after
the Republican ascendance in state and federal government. One liberal
commentator suggested that Republicans were trying to "repeal the Twentieth Century."[18] The contemporary critique of child labor laws presents an
opportunity to revisit the history and rationale for such legislation. As this
book demonstrates, there are good reasons why our society has chosen to
restrict child labor and compelling arguments against efforts to weaken or
repeal the laws.

Children still work in America, and they will continue to do so into our
future. Across the United States, teens work in fast-food restaurants and
movie theaters, staff retail stores at local malls, bag groceries in supermar-
kets, and work numerous other jobs. But they no longer perform those tasks
to the detriment of their health or education. The worst forms of child labor
have been abolished. Some economists dismiss reform efforts and give the
market and technological change all the credit for eliminating oppressive
child labor. Others emphasize the activism of humanistic social reformers.
The truth lies somewhere in between. No single interest group or event is
responsible for bringing an end to oppressive child labor. Over many de-

cades a combination of factors all worked to end the evil of child labor exploitation: advocacy by the National Child Labor Committee and labor unions for effective child labor laws; technological improvements that displaced children from some jobs; higher wages for adult workers so their children do not have to prematurely enter the job market; and the development of programs like Social Security and unemployment compensation, which provided support for family members. Of course, child labor is still a serious global problem that warrants attention and reform, but that issue is beyond the scope of this book.[19]

As much as possible, the following chapters and discussions are organized chronologically to help the reader understand the historical development of child labor laws. Chapter 1 examines the British experience with child labor, colonial and early American attitudes regarding working children, the impact of industrialization on child workers, the shift in public opinion on child labor from a social good to a moral evil, and early state child labor and compulsory school attendance laws. Chapter 2 covers the reform spirit of the Progressive Era, the formation of the National Child Labor Committee, and the unsuccessful initial efforts to pass federal child labor legislation. The next chapter reviews the legislative debate over the first federal child labor law, the Keating-Owen Act, and analyzes the Supreme Court decision in *Hammer v. Dagenhart*. Chapter 4 describes the interest-group battles and congressional debates over the second federal law, the Child Labor Tax, and the decision in *Bailey v. Drexel Furniture Company*.

Frustrated with the Supreme Court's invalidation of the first two federal child labor laws, reformers turned to amending the Constitution. Chapter 5 covers the intense political battle during 1924 and 1925 over the proposed Child Labor Amendment. It appeared that opponents had defeated the amendment within a few years, but the Wall Street stock market crash in October 1929 and resulting Great Depression breathed new life into the proposal. The following chapter discusses the second round of the struggle over the amendment, from 1933 to 1940. Although the amendment was not ratified, Congress enacted the Fair Labor Standards Act (FLSA) as one of the last major legislative victories of Franklin D. Roosevelt's New Deal. Chapter 7 examines the congressional debate over the historic labor legislation, including the child labor provisions, the legal challenge to the FLSA, and the final victory over child labor in *United States v. Darby Lumber*. The last chapter covers the post–World War II amendments to the Fair Labor Standards Act and contemporary child labor issues. Finally, the Postscript reviews the libertarian and conservative attacks on child labor laws following the Tea Party victories in the elections of 2010. Some state child labor laws have been weakened, but no major changes have occurred to federal regulations. With Republicans in control of Congress and the presidency and comprising a majority in many state legislatures following the 2016 elections, the social and legal consensus on child labor laws may be seriously challenged in the coming years.

From Public Good to Moral Evil

STATE LAWS AND CHILD LABOR

IN THE 1800S

Anyone who studies child labor acknowledges that throughout history, in every region of the world, children have labored. The history of the United States offers no exception. From the colonial period through the present, kids in America have always worked. Youth have labored as members of a household economy, as slaves, indentured servants, apprentices learning a trade, and as wage laborers in factories and mills or doing industrial "homework." The nature of work performed by children has certainly changed and so have public attitudes about the proper role of work in a child's life. This chapter describes the British experience with child labor under the Industrial Revolution, the evolution of child labor in American culture, and initial attempts by state governments to regulate the practice.

Three factors contributed to the widespread use of child labor in early America: the pressing need for workers in settling a new country; fears over the societal burden of pauperism; and a moral belief in the virtue of work.[1] During the early American colonial period, child labor was considered a public good and something to be encouraged. The Puritans and Quakers viewed idleness as a sin and valued the discipline of work for children. John Wesley, the founder of Methodism, believed that work was virtuous and advocated child labor to prevent youth from idleness and vice. Court records and provincial laws document the attempts to promote a Puritan work ethic among children. As early as 1640, the Great and General Court of Massachusetts directed town magistrates to explore "what course may be taken for teaching the boyes and girles in all towns the spinning of yarne."[2] A year later the court expressed its desire and expectation that heads of families see to it that their children and servants were industriously employed "so as the mornings and evenings and other seasons may not be lost as formerly they have bene." In order to promote the textile industry, a 1656 decree prompted local officials to consider whether women, girls, and boys should be employed as spinners. Similarly, the Great Law of the Province of Pennsylvania provided that all children "of the age of twelve years shall be taught some useful trade or skill, to the end none may be idle."[3] The aptly named Boston "Society for Encouraging Industry and Employing the Poor" formed in 1751 to "employ our own women and children who are now in a great measure idle."[4] Other writings of the period encouraged the employment of poor women and children in early manufactories because it provided a means of support and lessened the community burden of caring for them.

In the pre-Revolutionary period, women and children were put to work making textiles. Most households had a spinning wheel and loom. From Massachusetts to Virginia, there are accounts of young children spinning and carding in their homes or spinning schools. If not busy with textiles, many children worked family farms. Children milked the cows, fed the chickens, planted seed, gathered water, chopped wood, and did other chores to contribute to the family agricultural economy. Usually performed under parental supervision, these tasks were essential to family survival, especially on the frontier. Agricultural labor was viewed as beneficial because it instilled a strong work ethic and kept children out of trouble.

After the American Revolution, prominent leaders endorsed the employment of children. Impressed by machinery and its potential to promote industry, George Washington observed a new threshing machine in operation and recounted in his diary: "Two boys are sufficient to turn the wheel, feed the mill, and remove the threshed grain. Women, or boys of 12 or 14 years of age, are fully adequate to the management of the mill or threshing machine."[5] In his famous report to Congress in 1791 on manufacturing, Secretary of the Treasury Alexander Hamilton marveled at the invention of the cotton mill in England and noted how it contributed to progress in the manufacturing of cotton fabrics. Hamilton, seeing the potential of manufacturing institutions to employ persons who would otherwise be idle and a burden on the community, commented that "in general, women and children are rendered more useful, and the latter more early useful, by manufacturing establishments, than they would otherwise be."[6] He estimated that four-sevenths of those employed in the cotton mills of Great Britain were women and children, "of whom the greatest proportion are children, and many of them of a tender age."[7] As the British people would soon discover, however, there was a dark side to the widespread use of children in the mills.

In Europe during the Middle Ages, the primary method of training and regulating child workers was the apprenticeship system. Various trades were organized under associations of craftsmen known as guilds. In order to maintain a monopoly on production and ensure the quality of work (and to please the king), access to the guilds was tightly controlled. Young learners were trained by master craftsman for a fixed period, usually seven years, and paid fees for the duration of training. Apprentices often worked long hours at difficult tasks, but rules protected them. Detailed regulations for the condition of employment and training were enforced by the guild and backed by the state. After learning the trade, the new journeymen were admitted into the guild, and as free men they enjoyed certain economic, social, and political privileges.[8] The apprenticeship system provided education to young workers, helped prevent the worst forms of child exploitation, and ensured employment in a skilled trade. Children outside the apprenticeship system, however, received no training or protection.

In the eighteenth century, the monopoly of the guilds was challenged by new political economy theories of free trade, laissez faire, and freedom of contract. These concepts advocated a limited role for government in market transactions. As free trade ideas gained prominence, the introduction of machinery in the production of goods fueled the growth of child labor and altered the apprenticeship system. The Industrial Revolution began in England in the middle eighteenth century, and children were soon used as a source of cheap industrial labor. In 1769 Richard Arkwright developed a machine for spinning cotton yarn, and the invention revolutionized the production of cotton. The manufacturing of cotton yarns and fabric moved from the cottages and farms of England to mill factories. The first rural textile mills, built near rivers for a source of power, used child apprentices as the main workers. Children were sought after for their small and nimble fingers and dexterity in working the machines. Unlike the apprentices of the guild system, these new child apprentices often did not enjoy the benefits of an education, skilled trade, or social standing. The concept of child labor changed as thousands of children were forced to work far from home with little or no protection for their well-being from employer, parents, or the state.

Although the exploitation of child labor occurred in other fields, such as agriculture, mines, and domestic industries, conditions in the late eighteenth-century factories in which cotton was spun and woven were horrendous and soon attracted public attention. The mill factories were damp, dingy, and unsanitary. Children, many under ten years old, were removed from the poor houses in London, Birmingham, and other cities to work the machines in the textile mills. After the invention and application of James Watt's steam engine in the 1770s, mills did not have to be located near water, and factory towns emerged. Eventually, poor parents sent their children to toil in the parish factory mills under the same terrible conditions. Some bound their children to shop owners to repay debts. Larger parishes used agents to find factories willing to take on pauper apprentices. In factory districts, nearly all the children became apprenticed to strangers who showed no concern for their welfare.[9]

By 1810, an estimated 2 million school-age children worked in the mills and factories. Charles Dickens called these establishments the "dark satanic mills" and helped publicize their evils in his novel *Oliver Twist*. With a seemingly inexhaustible supply of paupers from the city, few at first noticed—or at least focused on—the appalling sickness and death rate among the child workers. Poorly clad children as young as four or five worked from twelve to sixteen hours a day, around dangerous machinery, under brutal supervision.[10] Many were lodged in overcrowded and filthy houses and fed just enough to keep their frail bodies functioning. Through the abuses of this kind of "pauper apprenticeship" came the first child labor laws.

Public outrage over the cruelty and horrendous conditions led Parliament to establish a Royal Commission of Inquiry to investigate child labor. Introduced by Sir Robert Peel, an MP and wealthy cotton mill owner (and father of the future prime minister), Parliament passed the Factory Act of 1802, the first child labor legislation. The law made mill owners responsible for the health and morals of pauper apprentices, limited work to twelve hours a day, banned night work, and required employers to provide adequate clothing.[11] The original law was largely ineffective, however, because it lacked enforcement mechanisms. Over several decades, a series of factory and child labor laws were enacted that improved conditions, shortened work hours, and set a minimum age for employment. For example, the Cotton Factories Regulation Act of 1819 prohibited the employment of children under nine years and restricted the hours for children under sixteen years to twelve a day. Limited to cotton mills, the law did nothing to help child workers in other industries.

In 1833, Lord Ashley, a member of the House of Commons from Dorchester, became a leading advocate for the welfare of child laborers. He initiated investigations of factories, workshops, and mines and worked for passage of new laws. Ashley, later given the title of Seventh Earl of Shaftesbury, discovered that conditions in the mines were much worse than the mills and had probably been going on for a century. He was shocked and disgusted by the accounts he read. One-third of those employed in the coal mines were children under eighteen, and more than half of those were under thirteen. Nearly naked and chained to a harness, the children worked from fourteen to sixteen hours each day, driven by brutal miners to the point of exhaustion.[12] Other laws soon followed. The Regulation of Child Labor Law of 1833 prohibited children under nine from working in the textile mills, limited children between nine and thirteen to eight hours a day, and established a system of paid inspectors to enforce the child labor laws, although only four inspectors were assigned to the entire country. The employment of children under ten in mines was prohibited in 1835. The Ten Hours Bill of 1847 limited women and children to working ten hours a day, with children under thirteen restricted to six and a half hours a day. With the enactment of several other laws in 1878, Great Britain had effectively eliminated the worst practices of child labor.[13] Under Britain's unitary system of government, the Parliamentary laws applied to every region in England and were backed by enforcement provisions.

From Great Britain, the Industrial Revolution spread throughout Western Europe and the United States. The United States lagged behind England in the industrialization of its economy and was thus slow to learn the lessons about child labor exploitation from the British experience. By the time many Americans began to view child labor as a serious social problem in the 1870s, Great Britain had been addressing the issue for almost a century. Whether out of greed, ignorance, or indifference, the United States repeated many of the same mistakes faced under British industrialization. In 1825, an investigation by the Committee on Children in Massachusetts Factories concluded that it was unnecessary for the legislature to intervene to regulate child labor and therefore did not make any specific recommendations. The committee did note that "young persons" were working "twelve or thirteen hours each day, excepting the Sabbath."[14] In other words, children worked seventy-two to seventy-eight hours per week. The long hours left little time for schooling, and the committee acknowledged that legislation might be necessary in the future so that children were not exploited for financial gain at the expense of their education.[15] What little schooling existed for mill children was often provided by the companies themselves.

Some of the earliest critiques of child labor in America came from foreigners or foreign-born Americans. A French visitor to the United States in the late 1700s observed manufacturers employing children "from their most tender age," and he criticized the men who "congratulate themselves upon making early martyrs of these innocent creatures."[16] In 1829, Scottish-born Frances "Fanny" Wright, an abolitionist, feminist, and free thinker who became a US citizen in 1825, sternly warned an American audience: "In your manufacturing districts you have children worked for twelve hours a day and . . . you will soon have them as in England, worked to death."[17] But even some native-born Americans were noticing the harsh conditions of child labor. In 1838, the Senate of the Commonwealth of Pennsylvania investigated the use of children in the cotton mills. One witness who had worked in four different factories since he was nine testified that the "greatest evils known are, first, the number of hours of labor, and the number of young children employed."[18] In some establishments, fourteen hours was the norm, with work commencing as early as 4:00 a.m. during the summer season. Most children were employed at spinning and carding, with carding being the hardest work. Carding involves the disentangling, cleaning, and mixing of fibers for further finishing. Punishment by whipping was frequent, and children were docked for being late. The younger children under twelve were usually fatigued when leaving the factory and fell asleep when getting home, often without dinner. Another witness stated: "A great many of the parents who employ their children in the factories are honest, poor people; but there are some, who are idle and worthless, who live on the labor of their children."[19]

Over time, the dominant public perceptions of child labor in America changed from viewing it as a social good to recognizing it as a moral and social evil. The transition in public attitudes toward working children, however, came slowly. During the early Industrial Revolution, many employers and citizens seemed oblivious or indifferent to the impact of mechanization on working conditions and the growing use of children in factories and mills. According to Hugh Hindman, the turning point in public opinion followed a shift in the household economy from production for family consumption to production for markets where children worked outside the home.[20] Before industrialization, the entire household made things in or around the family home using hand tools and basic machines. The introduction of the factory system transformed the production process, changed the apprenticeship system, made wage labor the norm outside the farm, and increased the use of child laborers.

We may roughly date the early American Industrial Revolution from 1790, when Samuel Slater opened the first industrial mill in the United States, through the 1830s. Something closer to the modern corporation emerged during this time, and technological advances in transportation and communication spurred what many historians label the "Market Revolution," which vastly expanded the integration of national markets. A key labor change during the Industrial Revolution was the transition from an outwork system, in which small parts of a production process were conducted in individual homes, to a factory system, where work was performed on a large scale outside the home in a building, sometimes called a manufactory.

In the early mechanized stages of the cotton industry, the spinning machines were so simple to operate that only young children were used to tend the looms. Samuel Slater, the "father of American manufacturing," initially employed nine children between seven and twelve years old to work at his Rhode Island mill, and by 1800 he employed over a hundred children in his factory. In the main, in other words, the first industrial workforce in the United States was composed of children younger than thirteen years.[21] Some mills employed dozens of children under an adult supervisor. When the local supply of young hands was exhausted, mill owners advertised in newspapers for families with multiple children to come live near the mills. An 1820 editorial in the *Manufacturers' and Farmers' Journal* anticipated that families would choose to live in New England rather than western states because they could easily find employment for their healthy children seven years of age and older.[22] Thus mill towns were born, and the lives and fortunes of many children and families were connected to the local mills.

With the introduction of the power loom, young children were not sufficient to operate the machines. In 1814, a group of Boston businessmen recruited thousands of young, unmarried New England farm girls to work the machines in their factories. One of these men, Francis Cabot Lowell, started the Boston Manufacturing Company in Waltham, a small village along the Charles River. The Lowell mill produced cloth using machines powered by the river. Some of the young girls brought in to work the mills were as young as ten, but most were in their late teens and early twenties. The Boston associates preferred young girls because they could pay them less than men, although the wages were generally good for the period. As an incentive to sign a yearlong contract, the girls, who were called operatives because they operated the machines, were paid in cash daily. The most well known of these mill towns was Lowell, Massachusetts, established in 1823 and named after Francis Cabot Lowell, who had passed away in 1817. Known as "Lowell Girls" or "Mill Girls," the young women lived in company boarding houses under the supervision of matrons. A dress code, curfew, etiquette training, and religious services were part of the rules set by the company. Although they worked more than seventy hours a week, many of the girls enjoyed their freedom from parental authority and an opportunity for education. By 1840, as many as eight thousand girls worked the textile factories in Lowell. As the number of mills increased, overproduction led to pay cuts and rent increases, and the Lowell girls "turned out," as a strike was called then, in 1834 and 1836. These were some of the first strikes of cotton factory operatives in the United States.[23]

As with other customs and practices, American colonists brought with them the English apprenticeship system as they settled throughout New England and the South.[24] The Industrial Revolution, with its characteristic competition, machine production, and division of labor, fundamentally altered the American apprenticeship system, just as it had in England. In 1828, journeyman mechanics complained that master mechanics employed only apprentices in their manufacturing establishments. After an apprentice completed his six- or seven-year training, he was dismissed by the master rather than being hired as a journeyman. The desire for cheap labor undermined the traditional apprenticeship relationship. Forced to look for employment elsewhere, the journeyman often found that shops only employed apprentices. By 1888, a New York State factory inspector, who had a duty to enforce apprenticeship rules, found that the old form of apprenticeship had become virtually obsolete. A seven-year apprenticeship was not needed to tend a machine. Young boys (and girls) were now assigned to a machine at one stage of the production process. They were not taught any other branch of the craft or the use of other machines. Employers explained that there was no need for an apprentice to learn how to do the labor by hand; the machine performed the task.[25]

In part because the conflict over slavery dominated American politics in the first half of the 1800s, child labor reforms were few and far between. There are no statistics available that accurately measure the scope of child labor during this period. Occasionally, governmental and interest-group reports provided estimates of the numbers of women and children employed. But these sources often did not specify the age of children or separate women from girls. In 1816, the Committee on Manufactures identified twenty-four thousand "boys under seventeen" and sixty-six thousand "women and girls" out of an estimated one hundred thousand cotton mill employees.[26] Rhode Island employed the most children in the first few decades of the nineteenth century. The *Digest of Manufacturers* reported in 1820 that "children (age not defined) constituted 43 percent of the labor force of textile mills in Massachusetts, 47 percent in Connecticut, and 55 percent in Rhode Island." A cotton report from 1831 counted 3,472 children under twelve working in 116 mills in Rhode Island compared to 439 in Connecticut with 94 mills, while the numbers for Massachusetts were unavailable.[27] The percentages were much lower in all three states by 1832, with Rhode Island dropping to 41 percent.[28] In Rhode Island, which still had no child labor regulations as late as 1853, a legislative committee identified over eighteen hundred children under fifteen years old working in the factories twelve hours a day for eleven to twelve months a year. In 1836, the Massachusetts House Committee on Education cited an account reporting that various manufacturing establishments in 1830 employed no less than two hundred thousand females. Six years later, that number was estimated to be half a million females with most of them young and tender in years. These vague and unreliable estimates provide only a glimpse into the extent of the problem. At the time, no common definition of child labor existed. In the first few decades of the nineteenth century, the phrase "child labor" often meant the labor of children under fourteen years old, but for some, only those twelve years and younger were considered child workers. Typically, girls fourteen to sixteen years old working in textile mills were viewed as young women and not counted as child laborers. The mills in Lowell, Massachusetts, for instance, could claim that they used no child laborers.

In antebellum America, New England trade associations were the first social groups to express concern about child labor on the basis that long hours at arduous tasks injured the health and education of future citizens. The tradeoffs were obvious. When children worked twelve to fourteen hours a day, six days a week, they had no time to attend school. Some of the earliest calls for reform noted that child labor resulted in masses of illiterate children who, when grown to adulthood, would not be able to contribute to representative democracy. In May 1813, Connecticut enacted what is considered to be the first child labor regulation in the United States. Instigated by General David Humphreys, a former officer in the Revolutionary War who owned a mill, the law required employers to provide schooling for their young employees and made factory owners responsible for the moral education of their workers, including attending church services. The law, however, was rarely enforced, and it did not address the minimum age for employment or maximum work hours, two features considered essential to child labor reforms. In 1818, the governor of Rhode Island spoke about factory children in a message to the legislature. He said: "It is a lamentable truth that too many of the living generation, who are obliged to labor in these works of almost unceasing application and industry, are growing up without an opportunity of obtaining that education which is necessary for their personal welfare as well as for the welfare of the whole community."[29] In 1832, a convention of the New England Association of Farmers, Mechanics, and Other Working Men reported that children were working over thirteen hours a day in the mills and factories, and the organization expressed concern for their welfare.[30]

Although they did not seek an end to child labor, trade unionists urged restrictions on the excessive hours children were employed and campaigned for universal education. Their efforts helped secure the first compulsory school attendance laws. School programs and facilities, however, were inadequate at the time. In the 1830s, the system of common schools did not reach the masses of poor working children. A cultural preference for individualism, suspicion of state paternalism, and concern over the teaching of sectarian religious values slowed the development of free common schools and allowed child labor to continue unabated. As common or public schools became more widely available, opponents of child labor argued that children should be in school rather than working.

Reformers recognized early on that no single solution to the problem of child labor existed. It was a multifaceted issue that had to be attacked from different angles: (1) a minimum age below which children should not be permitted to work; (2) a maximum number of hours of employment; (3) a minimum education as a prerequisite for starting work; and (4) some regulations prohibiting children from dangerous and unhealthy occupations.[31] Over time, these four requirements resulted in detailed laws specifying occupations from which children were banned, compulsory school attendance laws, and provisions for documenting proof of age and issuing employment certificates. All four elements were related and necessary for successful child labor reform, but they were not easy to achieve. Opposition from employers, parents, and politicians, combined with an often apathetic public, necessitated a decades-long struggle to secure effective standards in law.

In 1836 the National Trades' Union, a collection of skilled tradesman formed two years earlier, proposed that states establish a minimum age for factory work, and by 1860 several states had responded with legislation. In

1848, Pennsylvania set a minimum age for factory and textile mill workers at twelve and a legal working day of ten hours. Violators could be fined $50, half of which would go to the employed child and the other half to the Commonwealth. The law was the first US statewide ban of child labor based on age; the following year the minimum age was increased to thirteen years, and the prohibition was extended to silk, flax, and paper mills.[32] Enforcement required a lawsuit filed by private citizens. New Jersey established a minimum of ten years for manufacturing in 1851, and Rhode Island followed in 1857 with a twelve-year minimum for factory work. In 1855, Connecticut set the age minimum at nine years in manufacturing and factory establishments, and a year later, increased it to ten years.[33]

By the start of the Civil War in 1861, seven states had fixed maximum hours for working children. Typically, children worked twelve- to thirteen-hour days, six days a week, with Sunday off. In an age with no electricity, children in factories and mills worked from sunup to sundown, or as long as they could see. In 1842, Massachusetts limited children twelve years and under to ten hours. Other state maximum hour laws varied depending on the age of the child.[34] These few laws enacted prior to the Civil War were limited in scope and generally ignored and ineffective. The laws applied only to factory work and textile mills, and the minimum age standards were low. Moreover, they lacked enforcement mechanisms; for example, no proof of age was required in factories. In Massachusetts, New Jersey, and Rhode Island, employers could be punished for child labor abuses only if they "knowingly" violated the law. This placed a difficult burden of proof on local officials in obtaining prosecutions.[35] Employers and parents consistently evaded the laws. In many states, children could legally work if underage or beyond maximum hours if their parents consented, which they often did. For example, Pennsylvania limited children between fourteen and sixteen to ten hours a day, but with permission from the parents, those limits could be, and often were, exceeded. Consequently, in both states with rudimentary laws and those with no protective legislation, children were employed at a young age and worked long hours, including overtime and at night.[36]

Requiring school attendance was a direct and early method to reduce the prevalence of child labor. Compulsory school laws date back to the 1640s and the Massachusetts Bay Colony. Motivated by religious and economic concerns, the colonial laws ensured that children could read the Bible and would have the skills necessary to avoid pauperism. It was not until the development of common schools in the 1800s, however, that public education, compulsory school attendance, and child labor become linked. The principle of compulsory school attendance began in Massachusetts in 1852 when the Commonwealth enacted a law that required children between eight and fourteen to attend school for twelve weeks a year.[37] By 1895, more than half of the states and the District of Columbia had compulsory school attendance laws.[38] Like Massachusetts, most required only three months of schooling per year as an alternative to ongoing attendance; sometimes, an ability to read and write exempted one from school. For the latter requirement, in some jurisdictions, writing one's name on a form was sufficient proof of literacy! Factory inspectors described New York's compulsory education law as "dead letter" because it practically made it everyone's business to enforce but "what is everyone's business is nobody's business."[39] Enforcement problems and recognition that three months in school were not long enough for academic progress led to demands that children be required to attend for the full length of the school year. New York enacted the first such law in 1894, but it only applied to children under twelve years. With a minimum age of fourteen for working in factories, a gap existed between school attendance and child labor laws. Massachusetts, Connecticut, and Maine eventually eliminated that gap by requiring school attendance up to fourteen years, and nine more states followed in subsequent years. No southern state, however, had enacted similar compulsory school attendance laws by 1900.

The problem of child labor became more salient as industrialization intensified in the last decades of the nineteenth century. Powerful national corporations emerged and dominated in railroads, steel, oil, mining, meat packing, and agricultural production. The United States became the leading industrial nation of the world. Industrialization created opportunity and wealth for some, but working conditions were often harsh and labor conflicts increased. Mass immigration also brought millions of poor Irish, French Canadians, Germans, Poles, Italians, and other ethnic groups into the industrial cities of the Northeast and Midwest as a cheap source of labor.

During the Gilded Age from 1870 to 1900, many business owners and stockholders favored the use of child workers in the name of greater profits. Children were paid less than women, who were paid less than men. Children under the age of sixteen were employed as miners, messengers, mill workers, and factory employees and were often forced to work long hours under unsafe conditions for meager pay. A report from the period indicates the wide variety of occupations children participated in. Children labored as tinsmiths, paint scrapers, blacksmith shop assistants, breaker boys, errand boys, engravers, cigar makers, porters, office boys, finishers for dresses and coats, and wagon drivers. They worked at sewing machine, insect powder, ink, and twine factories, staffed paper stands and fruit carts, tended oyster saloons, made artificial flowers, cut feathers, picked rags, and colored maps.[40] These were just some of the hundreds of jobs performed by children in New York City.

By the 1870s, recognition grew that child labor was a serious social and moral problem that damaged the physical and intellectual development of children. In numerous publications and speeches of the period, child labor is explicitly described as an "evil," and the practice of employing boys and girls of "tender years" is characterized as "child slavery." Granted, some commentators used the word "evil" to describe child labor before the Civil War, but the term was not as ubiquitous as in the 1870s, when the issue increasingly seemed to provoke people's passions. In the South, child labor was often called "white child slavery," given that segregation prevented many young black children from working in the mills and factories.[41] Consequently, southern reformers appealed to racial prejudices by claiming that white children were being worked to death in the mills while black children attended school.

An 1871 *New York Times* editorial noted that nearly two thousand children under fifteen, with some as young as four, were found working in tobacco factories. "These and other facts presented," the piece commented, "should at once arouse the conscience of our people concerning this great evil. There is something in this tyranny of capital and greed of parents, exercised on helpless childhood, which should stir every honest man's blood."[42] The *Times* argued that the welfare of the children was a concern of the state. "A great class of youth is growing up in this City enfeebled in body and only partially educated." The paper warned that poor working children will "swell the great mass of ignorant voters who now threatens the very structure of our society."[43]

Reports from factory inspectors revealed a level of ignorance among child laborers that was almost inconceivable. Many young workers were children of foreign-born immigrants and illiterate. Some factory inspectors, however, found that children born in Europe who recently came to the United States were better informed than children born and raised in this country.[44] Most of the children were between twelve and fifteen years old, and the average age at which they started work was nine years. What little they had learned in school before going to work was long forgotten. Thousands could not write anything other than their name, and most could not read. Many lacked even a rudimentary understanding of the world beyond their factory and homes, some believing that the world might be a hundred miles long.[45] The New York Labor Bureau found that "at least thirty percent could not name the city in which they lived. Sixty percent had never heard of the United States or Europe, and ninety-five percent had never heard of the Revolutionary War or Abraham Lincoln."[46]

In 1873, the *New York Times* editors described the vicious struggle for survival that ensnared the "little slaves of capital." They wrote: "The employers and capitalists want all the work they can get, and the parents are only too ready to offer up their children for the sake of profit, though the employment may be at the expense of both education and health to the little ones— The boy or girl grows up thus chained to constant toil, and reaches maturity ignorant, careworn, weakened in mental and physical power, and utterly unfit for the real burdens of life."[47] Market competition, the *Times* continued, discouraged more socially enlightened employers from doing much about child labor. Some shop owners who personally opposed the practice employed children because they realized that parents would simply take them to another employer who might not treat them as well. "If one manufacturer refused to employ children in his works," the editors explained, "another would use them, would produce more cheaply, and soon undersell his competitors. . . . Whatever is done in the reform of this matter must be done by all employers."[48] It was impossible, however, to get all employers to voluntarily reject child labor. Only the coercive power of the state could bring about needed reforms.

The 1870 Census counted just over 12.5 million workers in the United States. Of that number, 739,164 were children ten to fifteen years old. Roughly one out of every seventeen workers was a child under fifteen years old. The 1880 Census, more rigorous in its data collection, identified the American workforce at 17,392,099. This statistic included 1,118,356 children ten to fifteen years old, which represented one out of every sixteen workers. The statistics do not measure the number of children under ten who were employed, so the number of child laborers was acknowledged to be much higher. Whether out of shame or fear of being caught, some employers underreported the number of child workers, and parents "raised" the age of their laboring children. Accounting for the population increase and excluding children working in agriculture, the number of child workers grew during the decade by 66 percent.[49]

Several minor political parties recognized the dangers of child labor and took a stand against the practice during this period. In 1872, the Prohibition Party became the first political party to include a clause in its platform condemning child labor. Several years later, the Working Men's Party, one of the first Marxist-inspired American labor parties, called for laws prohibiting the employment of children under fourteen in factories. At its national convention in 1880, the Greenback Party, formed in response to the depression following the Panic of 1873, also supported a ban on the employment of children under fourteen in manufacturing establishments.[50] None of these parties had much electoral success, however, so their impact on child labor laws was limited.

Economic recessions or depressions tended to swell the ranks of child laborers as people struggled to make a living. In the post–Civil War period alone, a series of depressions in 1869, 1873, 1882, and 1893 made life difficult in an era with little to no social safety net.[51] The Panic of 1873 lasted over five years, and about 3 million Americans lost their jobs. The depression caused by the Panic of 1893 was the worst in American history until the Great Depression.[52] More than sixteen thousand businesses failed, and one in six male workers lost his job. During this period, the Ohio commissioner of labor noted a connection between child labor, economic conditions, and school attendance. "Annual reports of the state superintendent of public instruction," he commented, "prove one thing conclusively, that under a depressed condition of trade, the school attendance rapidly decreases, and with every improvement in business comes an increase in the number of scholars."[53]

For the masses of poor concentrated in cities, child labor was often a matter of basic survival. With a surplus of labor and intense competition for jobs, wages for a workingman with a family were often insufficient to meet the cost of living. One economist estimated in 1889 that a man with a family had to earn at least $600 a year to meet essential needs. Many adult workers fell below that standard so child labor supplemented the family income.[54] A ten-year-old child working all day sewing buttons on trousers could earn twenty cents, and for that labor, the family was twenty cents richer. It was a vicious cycle. Child labor depressed adult wages, but the income from working children was crucial to make ends meet.[55] The social costs were steep, however. Early factory reports noted that a type of role reversal often existed: children and wives were employed while the father, unable to find work, remained idle, performed household chores, or took jobs with less pay. Children were being worked to death at an early age while adults, at the peak of their earning potential, could not find employment.[56] Kids were not only denied a natural childhood but also their physical and educational development significantly suffered.

Many dangers in the mines, factories, and mills degraded a child's health and sometimes resulted in loss of limb and life.[57] Those who defended the practice claimed that industrial labor kept children off the streets, toughened them, and gave them skills needed for adult life. To a certain extent, those claims were valid. Reports from factory inspectors and doctors, however, present a different, more complex picture. Children who began work at an early age and labored more than ten hours a day, often at repetitive tasks for years, were commonly described as "undersized," "delicate," "worn," and "puny."[58]

The first report of the Illinois Bureau of Labor Statistics, published in 1893, noted the transitory nature of child labor and how that instability might be a blessing in disguise because it would help save kids from the poisons inherent in many jobs: "The child who handles arsenical paper in a box factory long enough becomes a hopeless invalid. The boy who gilds cheap frames with mercurial gilding loses the use of his arm and acquires incurable throat troubles. The tobacco girls suffer nicotine poisoning, the foot-power sewing machine girl is a life-long victim of pelvic disorders."[59] Inspectors, social workers, and clergy who investigated and studied child labor often discovered that the largest numbers of child workers tended to be in occupations that presented the greatest danger to life and health.

In the anthracite regions of Pennsylvania and West Virginia, large numbers of boys, many under twelve years old, worked in the mines as door tenders, slate pickers, and mule drivers. Older and stronger boys drove the mules. The younger ones, known as breaker boys, sorted slate from the broken coal, which flowed like a black river down several chutes. A report from the period provides a vivid description of the back-breaking and dangerous work:

> The slate pickers sit in rows astride these chutes, their eyes fixed steadily on the broken coal that brushes past them down the steep incline, and their fingers nimbly at work picking out the black dull pieces of slate that are mixed with the glistening anthracite. During this flow of coal down the chutes, no shirking is tolerated. The boys must keep their eyes constantly on the chutes and see to it that all the bits of slate are taken out. . . . Some of the saddest accidents connected with coal mining have occurred in the breakers among the children who pick the slate. Little fellows have been ground to death in the massive machinery, and many of their comrades have lost their lives in the efforts to save them. . . . Sitting in a stooping position amid clouds of coal dust is painful, and tiny fingers are cruelly cut and bled by contact with the pieces of coal which are as sharp as bits of broken glass.[60]

Child labor laws were sometimes skirted by having boys go into the mines as "helpers" for their fathers. The name of the boy would not be on the payroll, and he would thus avoid detection while the wages of the father would be enhanced because of increased production.[61] At times, a child replaced his father who had been killed in a mining accident in order to support his widowed mother.

Cotton, wool, and silk mills, in both the North and South, employed large numbers of children. A Catholic investigator, who in 1886 personally observed two thousand children in the cotton and woolen mills of eastern New England, described the environment and dangers of the spinning rooms:

> The atmosphere of the spinning-rooms might be easily boxed and expressed to Australia without losing a particle of its peculiar strength. The fresh air could not absorb it. It is composed of equal parts of cotton, tallow, machine-oil, and human expirations. . . . Ears, eyes, mouth, and nostrils are assailed by it. Sickening and offensive, heavy and palpable, it is the atmosphere breathed by the children for half their unnatural lives. The oil from the flying machinery falls like fountain-spray through the room. It saturates the clothing and plugs every pore of the body with the aid of the cotton dust. The machinery is heavy, armed with dangerous gearing, belting, and pulleys. Simple accidents are common. First joints of little fingers often disappear in the cruel irons, a whole finger sometimes, at long intervals a hand or arm. Too often a little body is seized by the powerful mass and flung back to its horrified fellows lifeless, shamefully mangled. The children do not mind these things since they are risks common to all, and their friends and advocates will not see the sinfulness of exposing the naturally heedless child to risk of mutilation.[62]

Irene Ashby, an upper-class Englishwoman who became a passionate advocate for the poor, was hired in 1900 by Samuel Gompers, president of the American Federation of Labor, to come to America and investigate southern textile mills. Finding conditions "too horrible for belief," she described how working in the mills imperiled the health of the children. Some "suffer a horrible form of dropsy," she reported, an old term for the swelling of soft tissue due to excessive water. A doctor informed her that 10 percent of the children who started work before twelve years of age contracted consumption after five years of working in the mills. "The lint forms in their lungs a perfect cultivating place for tuberculosis, while the change from the hot atmosphere of the mill to the night chill or morning air often brings pneumonia, which frequently, if not the cause of death, is the forerunner of consumption."[63]

The tobacco trade was another industry extremely detrimental to the health of the child worker. The 1890 Census showed at least 8,158 children employed in the tobacco mills, but the real number was certainly higher. Children prepared the leaf for cigar makers, packed chewing tobacco, and made cigarettes. Nicotine poisoning found many victims. In cigar factories, the air was heavy with tobacco because the need to keep the leaves damp prohibited the introduction of fresh air. Novice tobacco factory inspectors often fell ill for several days after spending a few hours on the factory floor. Children inhaled the factory air all day, and some chewed tobacco or smoked cigars.[64] Respiratory illnesses and cancers were common.

The Children's Aid Society was one of the few organizations during this period that advocated for child labor reforms. Best known for the "orphan train movement," the Children's Aid Society was founded in 1853 by Methodist minister Charles Loring Brace and a group of social reformers at a time when orphanages and almshouses were about the only social services available for poor and homeless children. The society supported compulsory education, provided lodging houses, investigated the conditions of child employment, drafted and lobbied for child labor laws, and established numerous schools in New York City.[65] In 1872, Brace published *The Dangerous Classes of New York*, devoting a portion of the book to the problem of child labor. Commenting on the early laws passed by Massachusetts, Connecticut, and New York, Brace suggested that they "arouse conscience and awaken consideration, even if they cannot be fully executed."[66] By 1873, the society had established twenty-one day schools and thirteen night schools for working children.

Another organization, the New York Society for the Prevention of Cruelty to Children (NYSPCC), formed in April 1875 as an offshoot of the American Society for the Prevention of Cruelty to Animals. As the first child protection agency in the world, the society's agenda focused on the welfare of children and preventing abuse in its many forms, including child labor exploitation. Society members lobbied for laws, alerted officials to child labor practices, accompanied factory inspectors, and assisted with investigations. In many states, the organization was delegated state police powers to issue arrest warrants and prosecute cases.[67] By 1879, however, only seven states fixed a minimum age for employment of children, and twelve set maximum hours for working children.[68]

The Order of the Knights of Labor became the most prominent—and perhaps the most radical—organization advocating child labor laws in the 1880s. Formed in 1869 in Philadelphia as a secret society of garment cutters, the Knights became more openly militant after the great railroad strike of 1877. When Grand Master Workman Terence V. Powderly assumed leadership in 1879, the Knights flourished, growing to seven hundred thousand members. Powderly ended the earlier rules of secrecy and committed the organization to seeking the eight-hour day, equal pay for equal work, and the abolition of child labor. In a letter to the Knights in 1887, Grand Master Powderly described the hardships of boys working in the mines, condemned child labor, and promoted education. "Examine for yourself," he wrote, "and you will see that child labor has not been abolished, even though the law calls for it. Amid the dust of the mill, where the human voice cannot be heard above the roar of the machinery, with eyes almost burning in their sockets, you will find hundreds, thousands, and tens of thousands of little boys and girls."[69] Well ahead of his time on the issue, Powderly argued that children under fifteen years of age should not be allowed to work. He advocated public support for parents and education for all children. "Let us adopt a means of maintaining the parents of the children upon whose labor the parents depend for support," Powderly recommended, "and place the children in the schoolhouses."[70]

During the height of their influence (1885–1889), the Knights of Labor achieved some success on the child labor issue. Ten states that previously had no child labor restrictions passed laws fixing a minimum age for employment, and six new states established maximum hours for working children during the period.[71] Louisiana, for example, enacted a law prohibiting the employment of boys under twelve and girls under fourteen in factories, fixing a ten-hour day, and setting aside time during the year for education. When the Knights discovered that little was being done to enforce the law, they petitioned the mayor of New Orleans and pressured him to take action to force compliance.[72] The Knights had a presence in every southern state except South Carolina and often lobbied, without much success, for the establishment of labor bureaus, safety regulations for mines and factories, and an end to child and convict labor.[73] Knights in Savannah and other cities made several attempts to pressure the Georgia legislature to limit the workday to ten hours for children, but no bill passed. The organization's activism on child labor suffered a setback, however, following the Haymarket Square Riots of May 1886, when the Knights of Labor were unfairly blamed for violence that killed seven police officers and injured sixty others. Repression and public scorn followed. With the fallout from the riots, combined with internal leadership conflicts and strong resistance from employer associations, by 1890 the Knights' membership had dropped to below one hundred thousand.

As the influence of the Knights of Labor waned, the American Federation of Labor (A. F. of L. or AFL) became the voice of organized labor. Led by Samuel Gompers, head of a cigar makers' union, the AFL was a collection of smaller craft unions. Less radical than their predecessor, the organization was not primarily concerned with protective labor laws. Gompers was never a committed socialist, although according to his biographer, Bernard Mandel, he came close to that position in 1894 when the country reeled from a serious depression.[74] More of a realist, Gompers had no vision to unite the entire working class under a socialist utopia. Adhering to a philosophy of "pure and simple unionism," the AFL focused on the eight-hour day, collective bargaining rights, higher wages, and better working conditions for skilled tradesman. Gompers believed that government should not do anything for labor that labor could not do itself through its trade unions. He favored, however, a role for government in protecting women and children, whose vulnerability undermined the standards for adult male workers. Gompers adamantly opposed child labor; he found it repulsive to every instinct of humanity. When a resolution on child labor was proposed at the first Federation of Organized Trades and Labor Unions convention in 1881 (which changed its name to AFL in 1886), a delegate opposed the proposal on the basis that it would violate individual rights. Gompers disagreed and shared a story about a recent experience investigating tenement cigar shops:

> I saw there on that visit scenes that sickened me. I saw little children, six and seven and eight years of age, seated in the middle of the room on the floor, in all the dirt and dust, stripping tobacco. Little pale-faced children, with a look of care upon their faces, toiling with their tiny hands from dawn till dark; aye, and late into the night, to help keep the wolf from the door. . . . Often they would be overcome with weariness and want of sleep, and fall over upon the tobacco heap. Shame upon such crimes; shame upon us if we do not raise our voices against it.[75]

The resolution, which called for the abolition by the states of child labor for those under fourteen, passed unanimously. Gompers never stopped fighting against child labor. The AFL began publishing the *American Federationist* in 1894, and in it constantly agitated against the evils and criminality of child labor. In a letter to a federation member in May 1896, Gompers commented on the "cruelty and barbarism of working young and innocent children in the mills twelve and fifteen hours."[76] Although Gompers strongly opposed the practice, during this period the AFL did not actively promote national reforms. Subsequently, advances on child labor extended to only a few geographical areas such as Chicago and New York. In the last decade of the nineteenth century, only seven states enacted their first child labor laws.

Outside of the labor movement, young social reformers also called attention to the problem of child labor. Professor Felix Adler of Columbia University gave a series of talks in 1887 on "The Children in the Factories" under the auspices of the Society of Ethical Culture. He noted how England struggled with terrible child labor exploitation but now had a law preventing the employment of children under ten years of age and restricting children under fourteen to five hours of work a day. "In the United States," he said, "the evil of child labor is growing to an alarming extent. In one New Jersey district, there were 476 children under 10 years of age in 178 factories employed from 10 to 12 hours per day."[77] Professor Adler asserted that in New York, "compulsory education laws are practically a dead letter in many sections and the attempts to enforce them ridiculous." A loophole allowed many children to escape compulsory schooling if they were employed in a "legal occupation." Although he favored a higher minimum age for child workers and more inspectors to enforce the laws, Adler believed that the chief remedy for child labor was compulsory education beyond the mandated fourteen weeks required in New York. Children, he argued, should be kept at school every day of the school year.[78] Professor Adler continued his advocacy on the child labor issue, and seventeen years later he would play an influential role in forming the National Child Labor Committee.

The following year another young, passionate social reformer, Florence Kelley Wischnewetzky, daughter of Congressman William D. Kelley of Pennsylvania, who had helped found the Republican Party in the 1850s, gave a speech at the Labor Lyceum in New York on "The Wage Slavery of Children in America." Using statistics from state labor bureaus and factory inspectors, Kelley warned that every year more and more children were leaving schools at an earlier age to work in the trades. Child labor, she argued, "drives out adult labor, forcing wages down below the living point and making the organization of labor in these branches difficult."[79] An ardent socialist during this period, Florence Kelley translated Friedrich Engels's *The Condition of the Working Class in England* at age twenty-four and spent the next forty years of her life advocating for better pay and working conditions for women and the abolition of child labor. As chief inspector for factories in Illinois in 1896, Kelley advocated a minimum age of sixteen for work, mandatory school attendance to the same age, factory inspectors and truant officers with resources to do their jobs, and ample state support for public schools.[80] More progressive than any child labor reforms advocated at the time, these recommendations would in the next few decades become standard features of child labor laws and public education policy.

As immigration increased—and with it the population density of many cities in the Northeast and Midwest, such as New York, Philadelphia, Boston, Chicago, and Cleveland—a new form of child labor, tenement home work, flourished. One analysis called tenement work the worst form of child labor because, in most cases, children were not even paid, but were merely helping mothers and fathers.[81] Often, the youngest were made to work. Used primarily by the garment and tobacco industries, tenement work was known for the "sweating system." In living rooms and kitchens of crowded tenements, mostly immigrant, nonunion workers were paid according to how many pieces they finished—and they had to work long hours to complete enough finished products to make a decent wage. Children assisted parents as soon as their hands were sufficiently developed for work. Five- or six-year-old children stripped tobacco, sewed buttons and ribbons, picked threads, and performed other tasks. Most child labor laws did not extend to tenement work, and, even when they did, inspectors had a difficult time finding the work rooms in a Kafkaesque maze of urban dwellings. In New York City alone, an estimated twenty-four thousand children under age fifteen were employed in the tightly packed tenement houses.[82]

In 1889, New York City had over thirty thousand people working in the tobacco industry with only eight thousand unionized. About six thousand of the cigar and cigarette makers were women, girls, and children.[83] Some worked in small shops while others labored in tenements. Eleven cigar manufacturing firms owned tenements that housed over 546 families. Parents with three or four children paid extra rent for the privilege of using their poorly ventilated three-room apartments to make tobacco products for an average of fourteen hours a day. Families who complained about the higher rent, low wages, and long hours were put out on the street. These kinds of tenement sweating practices increasingly drew the attention of reformers and government officials. Critics claimed that the sweatshop system destroyed home and family life and created numerous health hazards.

Throughout the 1800s, the US government did little to nothing to ameliorate child labor. The division of power in the Constitution between the national government and the States, known as federalism, consistently impacted the debate over child labor. Under the concept of dual federalism, many officials and citizens viewed factory conditions and child labor to be aspects of local or intrastate commerce and believed that the associated problems were reserved to state authority under the Tenth Amendment, which reads: "The powers not delegated to the United States by the Constitution, nor prohibited by it to the States, are reserved to the States respectively, or to the people." The federal government, it was argued, simply did not have the power to regulate child labor.

Slowly and, guardedly, however, the federal government began taking an interest in labor issues, including child labor. In 1883, the Senate Sub-Committee on Labor and Education held hearings on the relationship between capital and labor, wages and hours, and the condition of the working class.[84] Over 1.3 million words of testimony were taken from about 125 witnesses. Several union workers testified about the use of young boys and girls in department stores, as messengers, and in the tobacco industry. The committee issued a report but nothing came of the hearings. Critical of the proceedings, the *New York Times* opined that the exercise was about as useful as an "arctic exploration expedition."[85] In 1891, Congress passed a law restricting the employment of children under twelve years of age from working underground in any mine, but the law applied only to mines in the territories of the United States, and violations were just misdemeanors.[86] The prohibition was merely one provision in a federal mining statute, and it was so narrowly focused that it cannot be considered the first federal child labor law.

In 1892, Congress investigated tenement work and the sweating system. Senator George F. Hoar, a Republican from Massachusetts, introduced an "Anti-Sweating" bill in Congress. Any garment that was to be shipped in interstate commerce would have to carry a tag that indicated where it was produced. The bill was motivated out of concern that the crowded, unsanitary conditions in which garments were made would spread cholera, scarlet fever, and other diseases to people who purchased the finished coats, pants, dresses, underwear, and other clothing. Manufacturers claimed there was no evidence that their garments carried diseases and contagions. A subcommittee of the House Committee on Manufactures, led by Congressman John De Witt Warner (D-NY), conducted hearings from March through December that year and produced a three-hundred-page report on the sweating system. Committee members took testimony and visited several cities where the tenement sweating system was believed to be the worst, including Boston, Chicago, and New York.

During the investigation of the sweating system, committee member Judge E. B. Taylor questioned whether there was a remedy for the problem. Congress, he claimed, did not have the power to "interfere with a single room in Boston, or with what a person pays his hands or what he does not pay them. ... There is no need to take up themes because we could no more change the conditions in these rooms than we could change the moon."[87] The House Committee report, however, concluded that this was an area in which Congress could and should legislate. The report stated that a proper remedy was not the restriction of foreign immigrants, as some had suggested, and regardless, immigration was outside the scope of the committee. Congress could pass a law under its authority to regulate commerce between the states because the health of thousands of people who wore the garments made in the "miserable" tenement sweatshops was endangered and epidemics could spread. The conditions, the committee determined, justified the "interposition of the Federal Government."[88] Of the various remedies proposed to address the sweating system, the least objectionable was the marking or tagging of each piece of goods so that it could be traced to where it was made. This was a modest proposal that would have done little to prevent threats to public health. The committee cautiously recommended that Congress pass legislation with the least interference with business and the least exercise of federal jurisdiction.[89] Although no federal legislation passed, Illinois, New York, and Massachusetts enacted state laws targeting the sweating system.[90]

Congress authorized yet another investigation in June 1898 on questions related to immigration, agriculture, labor, manufacturing, and business. This inquiry was different from previous investigations in that a bipartisan Industrial Commission was established, consisting of nine citizen experts or representatives of industry and labor appointed by the president and ten members of Congress, five from each legislative chamber. The sweeping inquiry took over two years and produced a nineteen-volume report. The section on child labor was limited because the 1900 Census figures had not been published, and the commission had to work with available statistics. The commission report noted that the number of children employed was likely to be higher in 1900 than 1890 because the 1890 Census counted boys under sixteen and girls under fifteen while the 1900 survey included both boys and girls up to sixteen years. Still, the report provides a window on the scope of child labor around the turn of the century. "Child labor is employed most extensively in textile factories," the investigators concluded.[91] An estimated one-third of the cotton mill operatives in a certain town in Georgia were under fourteen years of age. The commission also discovered:

Children are employed in considerable numbers in the manufacturing of clothing, especially in sweat shops, and also in glass factories, as well as in a variety of other employments, such as making artificial flowers, feathers, neckties, cigars, paper and wooden boxes, picture frames, furniture, boots and shoes. In Chicago, numbers of children are employed in the stock yards, in the packing of meat. In the Southern cotton mills, 12 appears to be the age at which children are ordinarily expected to begin work; but some of the mills employ children under that age, sometimes as young as 9, 8, and even 7 years. In the sweat shops of Northern cities, also, very young children are often employed.[92]

The commission identified several deleterious effects of child labor. Children were being denied a normal development, both physical and mental. They were deprived of schooling, worn out by being overworked, and were more liable to accidents than adults. Child labor, the commission concluded, contributed to unemployment among adults and depressed wages. The only objection to child labor laws it seriously considered was that employment was necessary in some cases to support a family where the breadwinner was deceased or disabled. This was true in only a small percentage of cases. "The possibility that a child labor law may work a hardship in some cases," the Industrial Commission determined, "is no valid argument against the prevention of child labor in general, for special cases can be provided for in the law itself."[93] Especially where young children are concerned, it would be better for the state to provide subsistence than sacrifice the welfare and development of the child. The report found that existing child labor laws were effective in diminishing the number of children employed and where no such laws existed, the proportion of children working had increased. Finally, the commission recommended more comprehensive and efficient child labor laws in harmony with uniform school attendance beyond the twelve weeks mandated in most states. Only Massachusetts, Connecticut, Pennsylvania, Minnesota, and New York (for children under twelve) required school attendance the entire session, and California and Nebraska expected children to attend for two-thirds of the term. As with previous inquiries, no federal child labor legislation resulted from the Industrial Commission investigation.

Child labor was not only a problem in the big cities of the East Coast or southern cotton mills. In Colorado, factory inspectors reported a significant increase in child labor from 1880 to 1890. During the decade, the population of children rose 112 percent, but the increase in child labor in mercantile and manufacturing industries had been more than 800 percent, and job classifications for children grew from twenty-five to more than seventy-five.[94] According to inspectors, the child labor laws had been "continuously disregarded" because employers and parents alike showed "an utter contempt for the laws." A special agent for the US Labor Department investigating labor strikes reported that "the conditions are worse in the Wisconsin factories than anywhere else I have been."[95] The ventilation in factories was miserable and the sanitary conditions among the very worst. He found nine hundred boys and girls, ranging in age from eleven to nineteen years, working at a beer bottling plant in Milwaukee. There was no limit to the amount of beer the child employees were allowed to drink, and the "familiarity between the sexes show[s] an abominable state of affairs."[96] He also discovered children working in the cotton mills beyond eleven hours a day, a practice that had been, at least on paper, abolished for years. The factory inspection law, he asserted, was a farce.

When enacted, all labor legislation, and child labor laws in particular, had to go through three enforcement stages.[97] First, there was a "pre-enforcement stage" (roughly 1840s–1870s) in which it was assumed that the mere declaration of rights for child workers and specification of employer responsibilities was sufficient to address the problem. In this stage, no government labor agencies existed, and parents or guardians had to initiate enforcement through lawsuits in the courts or local officials had to prosecute violators.[98] The "enforcement stage" came next. During this period (1870s–1910s) government agencies were established, usually state labor bureaus, to enforce the requirements of the laws. Factory inspectors were empowered to enter establishments, check records, search for violations, and take appropriate action. Finally, during the "administrative stage" (1910s–present) the functions of labor bureaus were more broadly defined, and administrators worked with employers and labor groups in developing regulations to carry out legislative intent. In fact, administrative rulemaking, through which government agencies formulate rules without having to go back to the legislature, is one of the innovations of the Progressive Period. All three stages had no rigid historical boundaries, and they often occurred simultaneously across various states and even within the same state.[99]

Most factory inspections for child labor were conducted by a state labor bureau. In 1869, Massachusetts created the first Bureau of Labor; Pennsylvania followed in 1872 and Ohio in 1877. By 1890, twenty-one states had established such an administrative agency.[100] Of those states, only eight provided for factory inspectors.[101] Massachusetts was a pioneer here as well, establishing in 1879 an inspection force of three individuals responsible for enforcing child labor, safety, and women's maximum-hours laws. The organization, funding, and personnel of these labor agencies varied widely. Most labor bureaus did not have enough factory inspectors. With thousands of factories within a state, many were visited only once a year or not at all. Also, there were no uniform administrative procedures at the time. Most of the laws establishing the bureaus failed to give inspectors real enforcement powers. They could investigate and write reports, but factory owners often refused to answer questions or provided false information and no law compelled them to cooperate. Consequently, the quality of the reports on child labor ranged from thorough and accurate to incomplete and unreliable. Still, the reports are often the sole source of information on the scope and conditions of child labor in the last decades of the century.

One of the more effective agencies in the 1890s was the Illinois Bureau of Labor Statistics, established in 1879. Under Illinois law, children under fourteen years of age were prohibited from employment in a manufacturing establishment, factory, or workshop. The law provided for a chief inspector, assistant inspector, and ten deputy inspectors and required that an annual report be submitted to the governor. Any establishment employing children had to keep a register with the name, birthplace, age, and residence of every person employed. Affidavits made by a parent or guardian attesting to this information had to be kept on file. Certificates issued by school administrators had to confirm that a child met the minimal requirements for education. Inspectors had the power to enter an establishment, demand to see the affidavits for child workers, and dismiss any young laborer without valid documentation. If children appeared too small or weak to perform the jobs, a certificate from a doctor had to be produced attesting that they were physically capable of doing the work. In 1892, Florence Kelley was appointed the first chief inspector, and under her leadership the office produced comprehensive reports on child labor in Illinois. Ohio, the first state west of the Appalachians to pass factory legislation, had a rather progressive law compared to other states. It allowed inspectors to visit any establishment employing more than ten workers, where many laws limited inspections to factories employing women and children. Instead of just giving inspectors authority to remove children who were underage, the Ohio law empowered inspectors to remove a child working in a place "where its life or limb is endangered, or its health is likely to be injured, or its morals may be depraved by such employment."[102]

As public administrators with similar job responsibilities, state labor bureau officials and inspectors formed professional networks to share information and develop common procedures. From the start, there was a question of advocacy versus nonpartisan administration. Rather than just collect statistics, many state labor bureaus became advocates for workers, especially on child labor issues. At the first National Convention of Factory Inspectors in 1887, delegates took a strong stand against child labor and unanimously passed the following resolution: "*Resolved*, That it is the sense of this convention, that laws should be enacted, in every State in the Union, prohibiting the employment of minors under fourteen in every workshop, factory, or mercantile establishment, as we consider it a self-evident proposition that such employment pauperizes the parents, and enforces illiteracy upon the child, two conditions of society incompatible with republican institutions, and the freedom and welfare of man."[103] At the second meeting of the International Association of Factory Inspectors, the chief inspector from Ohio commented on child labor and compulsory attendance laws: "It is true that ample provision is made for securing to every child," he said, "at least an elementary education, but the state is still derelict if it fails to compel those in whose behalf such provision is made to take full advantage of it. . . . Laws do not enforce themselves. There must be an active, energetic and vigilant executive force behind them, fully armed with the power to put them into effect."[104] In many reports, state inspectors noted the flaws in current child labor and compulsory school laws and recommended improvements.

In the 1890s, a new organization of women, the Consumers' League, engaged in a different type of advocacy on behalf of working women and children. Aroused by the immorality of insufficient wages for saleswomen, excessive hours, poor ventilation in shops, and child labor, league members sought to make those practices unprofitable by boycotting certain retail establishments. In other words, the purchasing power of consumers would be used against employers who violated the conditions of a "fair house."[105] The standards of a fair house included equal pay for equal work, wages paid by the week instead of monthly, a ten-hour workday, and no children under fourteen years of age employed.[106] Although the activities of the Consumers' League were local, with several state organizations and chapters in Boston, Chicago, New York, and Philadelphia, a National Consumers' League formed at the end of the decade, and the organization played an important role in the fight over child labor in the 1900s.

Another organization joining the battle on child labor issues, the National Association of Manufacturers (NAM), formed on January 25, 1895, and represented the interests of factory owners and the large business community more generally. The country was still experiencing a deep recession from the Crash of 1893, and NAM advocated tariffs and the creation of a federal Department of Commerce and Industry. It also took a strong vocal stance against organized labor and criticized child labor reforms. In subsequent years, the longtime general counsel for NAM, James Emery, testified against federal child labor laws, authored pamphlets attacking regulations, and strongly opposed the 1924 child labor amendment.

By 1899, a patchwork quilt of state laws applied to child labor. Because factory conditions and child labor were considered by many to be a state responsibility, attempts to enact national regulation to bring about uniform standards and enforcement had failed. Twenty-eight states had some variation of child labor laws while others had no protective legislation. Of this number, nine set the minimum age for employment at fourteen years. Most state laws fixed maximum hours at ten per day and allowed children to work six days a week. Many of the laws in place were limited in scope, covering only children working in "manufacturing and mechanical" establishments or "factories and workshops." Mines were usually a separate category, and nearly all the major mining states regulated child labor. During the 1890s, the status of children working in mercantile establishments, retail stores, and the service industry drew increased attention from reformers. Although conditions were not as dangerous or unhealthy, children worked long hours in stores, especially during the holidays. By the end of the century, half the states had extended various child labor regulations to stores and shops. Only three states covered child labor in such occupations as messenger, telegraph and telephone service, printing offices, and laundries.[107] Connecticut was an exception to the generally weak regulatory regime because the state's child labor law had some teeth. The law applied to the employment of all children, rather than just those in factories and mills, and it eliminated the word "knowingly" with regard to the employer's use of child labor. The omission shifted the burden onto employers to determine whether children had met the legal requirements for employment.

Southern states had done little compared to the child labor laws of the North. By the turn of the century, the region was experiencing a manufacturing boom with textile mills leading the way. In 1880, there were 667,000 cotton spindles in the South; by 1900, there were 7 million.[108] In the "New South," as the region's boosters and modernizers termed it, labor unions were weak or nonexistent, and poverty compelled white sharecropper families to seek employment in the mills. The 1900 Census, which only counted children ten to fifteen years old, revealed a 271 percent surge in child labor in South Carolina, a 144 percent increase in Alabama, and a 119 percent increase in North Carolina.[109] In the cotton industry, nearly 30 percent of Alabama workers were children, and in North Carolina, over 7,600 children under fourteen were employed in 261 mills. In other cotton-producing states, the rate of child employment exceeded 25 percent.

The region was ripe for reform, but such reforms lagged. Alabama had passed a child labor law in 1887, but it was repealed in 1895 after a lobbying effort by northern investors who wanted to take advantage of cheap labor and expand cotton mill operations in the state. Georgia attempted to pass a law in 1897 prohibiting employment of children under thirteen years in any manufacturing establishment, laundry, or sweatshop, but it exempted orphans and employment in sawmills, gristmills, and cotton mills. Even that weak law was defeated by an overwhelming margin when opponents alleged, without evidence, that it was backed by New England manufacturers who did not like competition from southern mills.[110] Other efforts to pass protective child labor legislation in Alabama, North Carolina, and South Carolina failed.

Although more than half the states had laws restricting child labor by the end of the century, a huge gap often existed between the law on the books and the law in action. To be sure, some progress had been made in restricting child labor, especially in states like Connecticut, Massachusetts, and New York, which had regulated the practice for decades, and various state reports indicate a decline in the percentages of children employed.[111] But legal loopholes and a shortage of factory inspectors prevented effective enforcement of most laws. It was generally recognized that the laws were not working as intended. Numerous reports from state labor bureaus and observations by social reformers often characterized both child labor laws and school attendance requirements as "a farce," "dead letter," or "inoperative."

In many states, for example, the only proof of age required was an affidavit or certificate from a parent that a child had reached the legal minimum age for employment.[112] Parents often lied about their children's age and there was little that officials could do. Corrupt notaries aided in the crime by completing certificate forms for 25 cents, twice the rate for regular documents. There was even a black market through which families and children exchanged certificates (that lacked photos) by trying to match the physical descriptions on the forms with various children. One factory report noted that children "studiously misrepresent their age" if younger than fixed by law.[113] Inspectors would find boys who on paper were fourteen years old, but when investigated further, admitted to being much younger. Another inspector found that parents had erased the original birth dates of children in family Bibles in order to write in dates that made their kids legally eligible for work. One underage girl who testified before the Reinhard Committee in New York, which was established to investigate female and child labor within the city, admitted that she was not fifteen and that she had obtained a certificate of age after paying a lawyer 25 cents. To remedy the age verification problem, social reformers argued for the establishment of a birth registry in every state.

The widespread use of children in mines, factories, and mills did not peak until the first decade of the twentieth century so the exploitation of children for their labor remained an issue on the public agenda. More citizens were becoming aware of the problem. Existing laws, however, were not always enforced, and they often failed to cover child workers in the street trades, service industry, performing arts, and agriculture. Social reformers continued to push for higher, uniform standards, better compliance, expanded compulsory education, and more funding for public schools. There was still much work to be done on both child labor and school attendance, particularly in southern states that lagged behind the industrial northeast. New organizations emerged to advocate for child labor reforms, including state child labor committees and the most important national organization—the National Child Labor Committee.

Divided, We Fall

THE BEVERIDGE-PARSONS BILL

Reformers had achieved some success in state legislatures and courts in the late 1800s, but by 1900, only twenty-eight states had laws protecting children working in manufacturing and only ten more had any legislation prohibiting child labor in mining. The four leading textile states—Alabama, North Carolina, South Carolina, and Georgia—had no child labor laws.[1] An estimated twenty-five thousand children under sixteen, many illiterate, worked in the mills, with some starting at eight years of age.[2] In many southern states, the absence of compulsory school attendance laws exacerbated the problem. In the first few years of the new century, a big push by school officials, reform advocates, and the General Federation of Women's Clubs led to major improvements in compulsory education. By 1905, all but eleven states had passed laws requiring school attendance for the entire session. Seven of the states required education up to sixteen years while the others compelled attendance up to fourteen years. Of the eleven states without any compulsory school attendance laws, all but one was in the South.[3]

Even in those northern states with child labor laws on the books, most laws were limited to factory work, full of loopholes, and not strictly enforced. Only nine states had a minimum age requirement as high as fourteen years. Omissions and exemptions in southern states and the lack of effective enforcement of many state laws spurred efforts to pass national legislation to curb child labor. Financial motives certainly played a part, too. Northern textile manufacturers, for example, complained that weak child labor standards in southern states created competitive advantages for southern mill owners that could only be addressed by uniform federal regulation.

Initially, reformers and organized labor agreed that national legislation was unnecessary. When the National Child Labor Committee (NCLC) formed in 1904, it expressly rejected the goal of a federal child labor law. The largest national labor union, the American Federation of Labor, also staunchly opposed child labor—but it favored state legislative remedies. Concerned about maintaining states' rights within the federal system, many activists preferred to seek tougher state child labor laws. During the Progressive Era, however, which began in the 1890s and continued until roughly 1920, public attitudes shifted in favor of using federal power to limit the excesses of industrial capitalism and reform corrupt public institutions. Disappointed with the pace and effectiveness of state reforms, the NCLC changed its original position and endorsed national legislation. By 1906, a federal child labor bill seemed to have popular support, but party politics, sectional differences, divisions within interest groups, and constitutional arguments created roadblocks that ultimately could not be navigated. This chapter describes the growing reform spirit in the early 1900s and the political and legal battle over the first child labor legislation introduced in Congress: the unsuccessful Beveridge-Parsons bill.

The struggle over child labor intensified with the birth of the National Child Labor Committee on April 15, 1904. A number of child labor committees had been established in several states and cities by the early 1900s, but their reform efforts focused on local problems. Headquartered in New York City, the NCLC quickly became the leading national advocate for child labor reform. The new organization formed at the urging of Edgar Gardner Murphy, a former Episcopal priest from Montgomery, Alabama. Murphy was largely responsible for educating the South about its child labor problem.[4] Shocked by the findings of an American Federation of Labor investigation into southern cotton mills, Murphy and other reformers organized the Alabama Child Labor Committee (ACLC) in 1901, the first child labor committee in the United States. The ACLC, whose motto became "First agitate then legislate," brought attention to the evils of child labor by printing pamphlets, publishing editorials, and pressuring state legislators. Murphy even took his camera into the textile mills to photograph children at work, a tactic that would be used effectively by Lewis Hine and the NCLC years later.

Passionate about the causes of child labor and education, and perhaps not wanting his religious affiliation to detract from his advocacy, Murphy resigned from the priesthood. As secretary of the Southern Education Board, headquartered in New York City, he became acquainted with Dr. Felix Adler, professor of political and social ethics at Columbia University, head of the Ethical Culture Society, and central figure on the New York Child Labor Committee.[5] Murphy, Adler, and other reformers became increasingly convinced that a national organization was needed to lobby for child labor restrictions. Murphy, Adler, and Florence Kelley provided the leadership for the establishment of the National Child Labor Committee.

Edgar Gardner Murphy did not view child labor exploitation as arising from the greed of a few individuals. Rather, it was a systemic problem connected with the rise of industrial capitalism that society was slow to address. Murphy loved the South, and, like most white citizens from the region, he was sensitive to northern criticisms of southern practices and culture. Although he held southern mill owners who engaged in the worst forms of child labor exploitation accountable, much of Murphy's attention focused on northern owners of mills located in the South who opposed child labor regulations.[6] Murphy favored legislative action within the states, rather than federal control. He believed that industrial conditions varied greatly between states and localities and that federal legislation would be "inadequate if not unfortunate."[7] Still, he recognized the need for a national organization to coordinate state reform efforts.[8] Authoring many of its publications, Murphy played an influential role in the early years of the NCLC.

A board of trustees, chaired by Dr. Felix Adler and consisting of members who lived close enough to New York City to attend meetings, managed the organization between the annual conferences of the general membership. Three salaried officers played a prominent role in advancing the NCLC's agenda. The first executive secretary was Dr. Samuel McCune Lindsay, professor of sociology at the University of Pennsylvania. Owen R. Lovejoy, minister of the First Congregational Church of Mount Vernon, New York, served as assistant secretary in charge of the committee's work in the North. In the South, where the committee faced its biggest challenges, Alexander J. McKelway was appointed to coordinate efforts. Born in Pennsylvania but raised in Virginia, McKelway considered himself a southerner. Ordained a Presbyterian minister in 1891, he moved to North Carolina and served as a minister and newspaper editor in Charlotte where he became involved in the child labor movement.[9] Unlike Edgar Gardner Murphy, McKelway did not oppose federal child labor legislation.[10]

Within months the National Child Labor Committee counted among its members presidents, senators, cardinals, bishops, professors, editors, and many prominent social workers and philanthropists from all political parties, faiths, and regions of the country. Although never numbering more than fifteen thousand members, the NCLC quickly developed a reputation for effective advocacy. In a preliminary report, the committee identified between two and three million child laborers in the United States, representing almost 20 percent of children between the ages of ten and fifteen years.[11] The actual number working was thought to be even higher because the only statistics showing the number and scope of "the evil" had to be gleaned from employers themselves, who tended to underreport out of fear of prosecution.

Influenced by the views of Edgar Gardner Murphy, the NCLC specifically "disavowed" federal legislation, preferring instead to lobby for better state child labor laws and enforcement. The organization developed a model child labor law in 1904 based on the best features of the Massachusetts, New York, and Illinois laws. The model law specified a minimum age of fourteen years for factory employment and sixteen years in mining; a maximum workday of eight hours for children fourteen to sixteen; the prohibition of night work from 7:00 p.m. to 6:00 a.m.; and documentary evidence of age for employment. No state law met all five of these standards at the time.[12]

At its first general meeting on April 15, 1904, Felix Adler declared that the NCLC's humanitarian goals were to be "a great moral force for the welfare of children . . . and to combat the danger in which childhood is placed by greed and rapacity."[13] The committee identified a long list of objectives, including:

> (1) investigate and report the facts on child labor; (2) raise the standard of public opinion and parental responsibility with respect to the employment of children; (3) lobby for suitable legislation to protect children; (4) work to provide elementary education and physical development for children sufficient for the demands of citizenship and adult labor; (5) aid in enforcing child labor laws; and (6) supplement the work of State or local committees.[14]

It was an ambitious reform agenda.

Like other philanthropic movements of the Progressive Era, the NCLC used the methods of social science to gather facts on child labor and educate the public and elected officials. Over the next few years, the NCLC investigated and published reports on all aspects of child labor, including the scope and conditions of exploitation in glass factories, southern cotton mills, Pennsylvania and West Virginia coal mines, textile factories, and other settings.[15] As part of its education agenda, the organization distributed tens of thousands of information leaflets, and, after 1908, schools and churches throughout the country observed Child Labor Day to bring awareness to the problem. In 1912, the organization began publishing the *Child Labor Bulletin*, later renamed *The American Child*, to inform members and the public about all aspects of the child labor issue.

Persuaded by the NCLC studies and other accounts, national periodicals began to report and editorialize on the problem of child labor. Dozens of articles appeared in prominent publications such as *McClure's*, the *Independent*, the *Arena*, and the *Outlook*. A series of articles written by Elizabeth Van Vorst for the *Saturday Evening Post* exposed much of middle-class America to the conditions of child labor and generated support for reform.[16] Readers of the *Woman's Home Companion* launched a crusade in 1906 against the employment of children under sixteen years of age. In the spirit of muckraking journalism, Edwin Markham published a series of articles for the *Cosmopolitan* beginning in September 1906 entitled "The Hoe-Man in the Making," which created a stir because of its strong indictment of child labor. Markham asked:

> Does the enumeration bring any significance to our minds when we say that an army of one million seven hundred thousand children are at work in our "land of the free"? This was the figure in 1900; now there are many thousands more. And many of them working their long ten or fourteen hours by day or by night, with only a miserable dime for a wage! Can the heart take in the enormity?[17]

The series generated so much interest from readers that the magazine formed the Child Labor Federation with the slogan "Child Labor Must Go."[18] Samuel M. Lindsay of the NCLC welcomed the new ally and the wider publicity it would bring to the facts regarding the employment of children. However, he cautioned the group not to exaggerate the evils of the practice because the facts of child labor spoke for themselves.

Although smaller in membership, the National Consumers' League (NCL) often worked with the National Child Labor Committee on child labor issues. Founded in 1899 by Jane Addams (a famous Progressive-Era reformer) and Josephine Lowell, the NCL used the buying power of consumers to press for better working conditions and fair wages, especially for women and children. The organization's first general secretary, Florence Kelley, also served on the board of the NCLC. For thirty years she worked tirelessly to expose child labor and promote fair labor practices. By 1906, sixty factories had received the Consumers' League label, which was awarded to establishments that worked no more than ten hours a day, did not use tenement or sweatshop labor, and complied with child labor laws.[19] Under the "White Label" program, NCL members inspected stores, and those meeting the organization's standards for fair labor practices received a White Label designation. The NCL then encouraged consumers to shop only at stores that earned the label. According to Kelley, "To live means to buy, to buy means to have power, to have power means to have responsibility." In 1902, the NCL began listing states on a map based on their child labor and compulsory education laws, shading from white for the strongest laws into a gray or black hue for the weakest protections.[20]

There appeared to be growing popular support throughout the country for child labor reform. Sensitive to public sentiment, President Theodore Roosevelt proposed to study the problem. On December 6, 1904, in his fourth annual message to Congress, he asked legislators to authorize an investigation by the Bureau of Labor into labor issues, one that would pay special attention to the conditions of child labor and child labor legislation in the several states. He said:

> Such an investigation must necessarily take into account many of the problems with which this question of child labor is connected. These problems can be actually met, in most cases, only by the States themselves; but the lack of proper legislation in one State in such a matter as child labor often renders it excessively difficult to establish protective restriction upon the work in another State having the same industries, so that the worst tends to drag down the better. For this reason, it would be well for the Nation at least to endeavor to secure comprehensive information as to the conditions of labor of children in the different States. Such investigation and publication by the National Government would tend toward the securing of approximately uniform legislation of the proper character among the several States.[21]

The NCLC welcomed the president's proposal. The organization held its second annual meeting in Washington, DC, on December 8, 1905. Committee members discussed the growing evil of child labor in southern cotton mills, child labor in glass factories, possible legislative remedies, and the urgent need for a federal bureau to investigate and report on all questions pertaining to the welfare of children. Several NCLC officers met with President Roosevelt at the White House, and he expressed a "keen interest" and "sincere sympathy" in the work of the committee. He voiced support for the establishment of a national Children's Bureau and mentioned that a bill was being drawn up in Congress for such an agency as well as a model child labor statute for the District of Columbia.[22] It would take seven years, however, for the Children's Bureau to become a reality.

Congress was not ready to act on the president's proposal for a national investigation on labor issues, and Roosevelt repeated his request the following year. Some lawmakers believed that the Census Bureau could handle the investigation but Roosevelt contended that it was not the proper agency for the project. He did not want a collection of empty statistics. He sought an investigator who was empirically rigorous yet understanding of labor issues. He explained: "I want to have some man who is cool-headed, but who has a genuine knowledge and sympathy with . . . the needs of labor, so that the investigation may, if possible, bear practical fruit."[23] There was little support in Congress, however, for that kind of investigation, and no action was taken by the end of the first session.

By 1906, the public was clamoring for change, and events unfolded rapidly. In February, Upton Sinclair's muckraking novel, *The Jungle*, disgusted readers with its description of unsanitary conditions in Chicago's meatpacking plants. Alarmed by *The Jungle* and other reports of rancid meat sold for public consumption, Roosevelt appointed his commissioner of labor Charles Neill and sociologist James Reynolds to investigate the conditions in the meatpacking industry. The Neill-Reynolds report confirmed the allegations in Sinclair's novel. In fact, the investigators found the conditions much worse than described in the book. The report was so damaging that Roosevelt decided not to submit it to Congress out of fear of impacting the domestic economy. Instead, he threatened to release the report to coerce the industry to reform. When some House members who supported the industry balked at proposed regulations, the Neill-Reynolds report was made public. The resulting public outrage prompted Congress to act.

Also that year, John Spargo's *The Bitter Cry of the Children* examined how the poor lived and survived. Spargo entered the coal mines of West Virginia and Pennsylvania, where children as young as six typically worked ten hours a day. He described how the children working in mines and mills were underfed, ill-clothed, uneducated, and exposed to physical danger and disease. He showed how the lack of food and proper nutrition during infancy was linked to poverty and arrested mental and physical development. A socialist, Spargo used his findings to advocate for child labor reforms, school attendance laws, and better health care for poor pregnant women.

According to historian John Braeman, President Roosevelt watched with growing concern the multiple signs of class tension and public unrest. In a letter to Secretary of War William Howard Taft, he remarked: "The dull, purblind folly of the very rich men; their greed and arrogance . . . and the corruption in business and politics have tended to produce a very unhealthy condition of excitement and irritation in the popular mind."[24] Congress reacted to the calls for reform by passing three major pieces of legislation in two days in late June: the Hepburn Act, which gave the Interstate Commerce Commission the power to set railroad rates and expanded the jurisdiction of the regulatory commission; the Pure Food and Drug Act, also known as the Wiley Act, which prevented the manufacture, sale, or transportation of adulterated or misbranded or poisonous or deleterious foods, drugs, medicines, and liquors; and the Meat Inspection Act, which initiated federal regulation of the meatpacking industry. All three laws marked a significant expansion of federal power, critics noted, at the expense of state authority and property rights. Reformers hoped to add to the list a national child labor law.

A new leader emerged during this time to champion the cause of federal child labor reform. Republican Albert J. Beveridge had been first elected to the US Senate from Indiana in 1899. A successful lawyer and effective speaker, the freshman senator began his political career as a traditional Republican who supported tariffs, defended honestly earned wealth, and encouraged American expansion abroad. During his 1906 reelection campaign, Senator Beveridge spoke on a variety of issues, including proposed Meat Inspection Act amendments, tariff reforms, direct primaries, and tougher antitrust regulations. When he also suggested that the time was ripe for the federal government to enact legislation restricting the practice of child labor, audiences enthusiastically responded to his proposal, and Beveridge made child labor reform a central issue of his campaign. He claimed that a federal law was needed to safeguard the nation. "We can not [*sic*]," he declared, "permit any man or corporation to stunt the bodies, minds, and souls of American children. We can not [*sic*] thus wreck the future of the American Republic."[25] Passionately committed to the issue of child labor, Beveridge became the leading advocate for national reform in Congress.

Several motives influenced the senator's views. Progressive on many issues of the day, Beveridge's instincts were conservative. From his experience as a youth plowing fields, working for railroads, and laboring in lumber mills, and his own research on the issue, he came to abhor the practices of child labor. Child labor, he believed, stunted the physical and intellectual growth of children, which in turn produced future generations of degenerates that threatened the health of the nation. An ardent American imperialist before and after the Spanish-American War, Senator Beveridge's stance on child labor was influenced by a concern for the strength of the so-called American race. He noted how child labor undermined British attempts to recruit physically fit men for the Boer War.[26] He also believed that a childhood spent in the mills and factories created "an ever increasing army of haters of society at large."[27] This army, he feared, fueled the rise of anarchism and socialism. An ambitious man with presidential aspirations, Beveridge also wanted to capitalize on the popularity of the issue and hoped that the Republican Party would take the lead on reform and earn the credit before Democrats embraced the cause.[28] Following his reelection, he prepared a bill and tried to line up support.

Beveridge obviously sought the endorsement of the National Child Labor Committee for his bill. But the bill intensely divided the young organization. On November 23, 1906, Beveridge explained his bill before a special meeting of its board of trustees and asked for the committee's support. After an "animated discussion," the board decided to take no action until December 6 but to send a copy to all of the corporate members of the committee and ask for a vote on what action the NCLC should take on the legislation.[29] Edgar Gardner Murphy was not at the November 23 meeting, but he strongly opposed the proposal. Francis G. Caffey, another trustee, wrote to him and expressed that he shared Murphy's position on the Beveridge bill. Among other objections, Caffey worried that the bill might embarrass allies working for state legislation and create enemies of those opposed on principle to the expansion of federal power. Caffey also believed that Felix Adler objected to the extension of federal authority contained in the bill, but he offered no evidence.[30] Adler, in fact, voted to support the Beveridge bill.

President Roosevelt, meanwhile, was determined to get Congress to authorize an investigation into labor practices when it reconvened. For Senator Beveridge, an investigation was unnecessary. In a correspondence with Roosevelt, Beveridge asserted that the time for investigation, even one sympathetic to the cause, was over; now was the time for action on child labor. Beveridge claimed that the people were already well informed on the issue and far ahead of government officials. He sent the president a first draft of his child labor bill and reported that it enjoyed widespread support. He also noted that he had prepared a "direct bill" as a substitute, patterned after the meat inspection and pure food bills, but for tactical reasons he preferred his indirect bill.[31] Beveridge hoped that Roosevelt would favorably mention his bill, which had yet to be introduced, in the president's upcoming State of the Union address in three weeks.

President Roosevelt, however, deeply disappointed the senator. The president not only failed to mention the Beveridge bill, but also emphasized the need to address the problem of child labor at the state level. Indeed, in his message, the president repeated his call for a thorough investigation of the conditions of child labor and the labor of women. "The horrors incident to the employment of young children in factories or at work anywhere are a blot to our civilization," he declared. "It is true that each State must ultimately settle the question in its own way; but a thorough investigation of the matter, with the results published broadcast, would greatly help toward arousing the public conscience and securing unity of State action in the matter."[32] The only area for immediate action on the issue, the president recommended, was a "drastic" and comprehensive child labor law for the District of Columbia and the territories. Beveridge felt that a law for the district was a meaningless distraction. The nation's capital had no cotton mills, mines, or glass factories, and any law would have limited impact. A child labor law for the district, Beveridge believed, was a symbolic sop to the public conscience.

On December 5, 1906, the Hoosier senator introduced the first federal legislation on child labor in the Senate, and the next day Representative Herbert Parsons (R-NY) introduced a similar measure in the House to prohibit employment of children in factories and mines. The language of the Beveridge bill prohibited common carriers (railroads and steamboats) from transporting the products of factories and mines unless the business owners could produce a certificate stating that no child under fourteen years of age was employed at the establishment. Federal district attorneys were responsible for prosecuting violations. Republican senator Henry Cabot Lodge of Massachusetts also introduced a bill to prohibit the employment of children in the manufacture or production of goods intended for interstate commerce. A few days later, the Senate considered a bill, also sponsored by Lodge, which had passed the House the previous session, to prohibit child labor in the District of Columbia. The various child labor bills were referred to the appropriate committees, where they languished for the remainder of the session.

During the legislative debate over the bills, only one member of Congress, Republican senator Nathan Scott of West Virginia, spoke approvingly of child labor. He thus opposed both the Beveridge bill and legislation restricting child labor in the District of Columbia. A glass factory owner himself, Senator Scott stated that some boys had to make their own living before they were sixteen years old or had to support an elderly mother. The senator criticized Edwin Markham's description of child workers in glass factories. Whereas Markham saw children with emaciated forms, eyes protruding from sockets due to being overworked, and blistered bodies from the furnaces, Senator Scott suggested this was all made-up magazine stuff. If someone had visited his glass factory, he insisted, they would have discovered active, energetic boys, singing songs and ready to play catch and hide and seek. "People may talk about the morals of the boys and girls under sixteen being ruined by labor. What possible legislation could be passed that would lead to more direct immorality on the part of girls and boys than being compelled by this law to remain idle?"[33] He mentioned that as president of the Central Glass Works of Wheeling, he had educated four boys at night school and one went on to manage the factory. Today's glasshouse boy, he claimed, becomes the glass manufacturer of tomorrow. Instead of protecting children, Senator Scott believed that the bill would "do to the children the greatest injustice the Senate could inflict." Most members of Congress, however, either opposed child labor in principle while rejecting national remedies or refused to make public their personal views on the practice, perhaps to avoid the pressure of interest groups.

Senator Henry Cabot Lodge objected to the argument that it would be a hardship to compel children to go to school because some of them needed to support their families and themselves by working. If that were a true and sound argument, he suggested, "there ought to be no child labor law on any statute book, and we should leave children unrestrained to earn their living and go without education." Using Massachusetts as his model, Senator Lodge argued that the sound way to treat the question was to ban children from factories and mines at any time of the day until they have reached fourteen years of age. After they had received an education, he reasoned, they can seek employment.

Confident that his bill was constitutional, Senator Beveridge argued that if social reform was in the national interest, the broad language of the Constitution gave Congress the power to enact legislation. "The American people," he said, "were not made for the constitution; the constitution was made for the American people. It is our servant; we are not its servants."[34] The Meat Inspection Act, authored by Beveridge and signed by President

Roosevelt over the summer, was his model. The law prohibited uninspected meats from shipment in interstate or foreign commerce. And it gave the US Department of Agriculture authority to inspect livestock before and after slaughter and processing for consumer sale. Beveridge patterned his child labor bill after the Meat Inspection Act with one major difference: it contained no provision for factory and mill inspection of products made with child labor. In his letter to President Roosevelt in late November, Beveridge acknowledged possible constitutional objections to inspections (hence his "indirect bill" alternative) and predicted that Congress would not support such a sweeping measure. Factory and mining interests in both the North and South, he feared, would combine to defeat any child labor legislation with on-the-spot inspections, and might even try to repeal the Meat Inspection Act. Still, Beveridge was certain that Congress had the authority under the Commerce Clause to enact his child labor measure.

A day after the child labor bills were introduced, the NCLC board met to consider them. A heated discussion ensued, with Robert W. De Forest leading the dissenters to the Beveridge-Parsons bill. De Forest came from a distinguished New York family. A wealthy corporate lawyer who turned philanthropist, he was involved in numerous charitable organizations. He was president of the Charity Organization Society of New York, president of the Russell Sage Foundation, trustee of the Metropolitan Museum of Art, and former chair of the New York State Tenement House Commission.[35] De Forest noted the lack of inspection and predicted that every carrier would easily obtain a certificate and ship child-made products. He doubted whether the bill was constitutional and worried about the committee's work in the South if it supported any kind of "Force Bill." Many southerners, even some reformers, would not accept "coercive" federal legislation on child labor.

Though he made some valid points, De Forest was unable to convince a majority of the NCLC board. Even before Beveridge pressed the issue with his bill, many members had become discouraged by the progress of state child labor regulations, especially on enforcement. The board of trustees voted to endorse the Beveridge bill in the belief "that it will establish a National standard to correct the evils of child labor in their important National aspects . . . and will tend to establish equality of economic competition without minimizing state responsibility."[36] Samuel M. Lindsay explained the board's reasoning in a letter to Mr. George F. Peabody, a member concerned about the vote:

The States seem to be impotent to enforce their child labor legislation. This is true both North and South, of all the States, with very few exceptions. The reason for this impotency is largely attributable to the opposition of manufacturers who fear inter-State competition, and in part is due to the poverty of the States in supplying the necessary machinery, such as factory inspection, to carry out legislation of this kind. The Federal government, on the contrary, can establish a national uniform standard which equalizes competitive conditions, and the Federal Department of Justice has ample resources in backing up . . . and prosecuting any reports of violations.[37]

Although the Beveridge bill would increase federal power, Lindsay was confident that it would also stimulate action and enforcement by the individual states. To reassure Mr. Peabody, Lindsay noted that the vote on the Beveridge-Parsons bill was only a small portion of the committee's work and that a dozen state campaigns were ongoing.

The following week, Beveridge was the keynote speaker at the annual conference of the National Child Labor Committee in Cincinnati, Ohio. He gave a rousing defense of his bill.[38] Before he spoke, Felix Adler, chairman of the NCLC, gave a talk urging federal action on the issue of child labor. At the conclusion of the speech, Adler asked the audience whether "we shall leave the matter in the hands of the States, or shall we call in the aid of the nation?" Someone promptly shouted, "The nation," and the audience erupted with vigorous applause.[39] Jane Addams of Hull House, who followed Adler, also spoke about the need for national action. The audience seemed primed for Beveridge and the discussion of his bill. He identified the three main objections to the bill: (1) Congress was moving too fast regarding the expansion of federal power to control an evil; (2) the evils of child labor were greatly exaggerated, with one congressman calling it "a storm blown up by some of those reformers"; and (3) that it is good for kids to work.[40] Beveridge easily dismissed these arguments and suggested that "many of the worst enemies of reform" were those who publicly favored reform but stubbornly opposed any effective means to address the child labor problem. Following his speech, the four thousand receptive members in attendance adopted a proposal, based on the endorsement of the trustees, formally supporting the bill.

On December 20, 1906, Adler and Lindsay met with President Roosevelt and Charles Neill, the commissioner on labor, to obtain the president's views on the Beveridge-Parsons bill. Roosevelt commented that "he considered the bill an excellent one, and that he would give it his hearty support."[41] According to press reports, someone in the delegation remarked that undue centralization was to be avoided, and, when possible, what could be safely left to the states should remain at their level. Sometimes, however, the person noted, the interests of the nation require action by the federal government, rather than be restricted by abstract theories, and child labor was one such issue. President Roosevelt amicably agreed with the statement. For various reasons, however, including opposition from labor groups and some reformers, the president's support for the Beveridge-Parsons bill declined over the coming months, and at no point did he actively lobby for the measure.[42]

Not everyone was enthusiastic about the National Child Labor Committee's support for the Beveridge-Parsons bill. To the shock and disappointment of many on the board, Edgar Gardner Murphy, the man primarily responsible for creating the committee, resigned in protest on January 4, 1907. Upset that the committee reversed its original policy against federal legislation, Murphy complained that the board had strayed "from a compact which I regard as inviolable."[43] Lindsay tried to persuade Murphy to reconsider his action without success. Murphy's health was ailing and as a southerner, he favored states' rights on the issue of child labor. He was concerned about federal influence in the South, but he also believed that legislation would not work without the support of southern citizens.[44] Breaking with northern reformers who were unwilling to wait for southerners to change their hearts and minds on child labor, Murphy became an influential opponent of the Beveridge bill, writing essays and editorials against federal legislation on the issue. As quoted in the *New York Times*, he wrote in the *New York Evening Post* on March 9, 1907: "It is to the States alone that we may look for that system of laws, mutually reinforcing one another, which can at length provide us with a protection direct in its operation, applicable to all the child workers, accompanied by adequate enforcement, and completed by educational provisions which make it constructive as well as negative in its operation."[45] Murphy even convinced President Roosevelt to delay his support for the Beveridge bill. Roosevelt's annual message of December 3, 1906, did not even mention the senator's bill. In a letter to Murphy, President Roosevelt admitted that he was conflicted on the issue but that "his present inclination [was] not to advocate immediate action."[46] Roosevelt suggested, however, that if federal bills failed, and the states did not do their duty, such a measure as the Beveridge bill would be necessary.

Even as he worked against the federal bill, Murphy assisted the Alabama Child Labor Committee in lobbying for stronger child labor legislation. As noted earlier, Murphy was instrumental in getting Alabama to pass a child labor law in 1903. It was a weak law, however. It set a minimum age of twelve for work in factories and mills, but exemptions for orphans and children with widowed mothers or disabled fathers permitted children to work when ten years old. No child under thirteen years could be employed at night work, and none under twelve could work more than sixty-six hours a week. The law contained no provisions for enforcement or inspections, however, and was easily circumvented. Murphy secured a compromise with opponents, and the Alabama legislature passed the Child Labor Act of 1907. The new law set the age limit for factory and mill work at twelve, with no exceptions, and night work was prohibited for children under sixteen years old. A provision allowed for inspections of cotton mills and factories, but prosecutions were difficult because an employer had to "knowingly violate" the law.[47]

Senator Beveridge faced another hurdle in his campaign for a national child labor law—organized labor did not rally to support his bill. Like the NCLC, the American Federation of Labor (AFL) conducted a lively debate on the bill at its convention in November 1906. Here a resolution to support national child labor legislation was proposed, but AFL leadership, headed by Samuel Gompers, was noncommittal. Gompers detested child labor, but AFL officials favored trade union action and collective bargaining under state law to improve labor conditions. A national child labor law might set a dangerous precedent for federal meddling in labor issues.[48] The convention eventually passed an amended resolution calling for "the enactment of a law in the several states prohibiting the employment of children under sixteen years of age."[49] It was the same state-centered child labor reform strategy that the leading labor organization had been advocating for decades with mixed results.

Organized labor's stance on national child labor legislation did not change much the following year. Some union leaders backed the Beveridge-Parsons bill, but the AFL officially took no position. Samuel Gompers told attendees at the 1907 convention that Congress seemed divided on the issue, and he recommended that the federation reaffirm its support for state action to address child labor. Without the AFL's support, Senator Beveridge faced an uphill battle to get his bill passed. Somewhat disingenuously, he tried to win over President Roosevelt by claiming that organized labor was overwhelmingly, even "militantly for it."[50] Roosevelt responded by noting that he had recently met with Samuel Gompers and twenty labor leaders and that when he asked about the bill, "not a single one of them would admit that he favored it."[51] While some agreed with the senator's purpose, they worried whether his bill would be feasible and effective.

Convinced of the popularity and constitutionality of his bill, Senator Beveridge soon learned that he had underestimated the level of opposition in Congress. In the House of Representatives, the Republican leadership referred the Beveridge-Parsons bill to the Judiciary Committee for a ruling on its constitutionality. In February 1907, the committee issued a unanimous report criticizing the bill as a violation of powers reserved to the states under the Tenth Amendment.[52] "We look in vain over the list of enumerated powers," the report argued, "for jurisdiction and authority of Congress over the subject of woman [sic] and child labor. . . . The jurisdiction and authority over the subject of woman and child labor certainly falls under the police power of the States, and not under the commercial power of Congress."[53] In response, Beveridge attacked the committee as a self-appointed "junior supreme court," and he dismissed the report as "absurd."[54]

Beveridge also faced strong opposition in the Senate. The Senate leadership consisted of old-guard "stand-pat" Republicans who preferred to rest on the accomplishments of the 59th Congress (1905–1907) and return to a traditional Republican agenda.[55] Beveridge sought to push the Republican Party in a progressive direction, but the old guard was wary of extending federal power over child labor. By January 1907, the Beveridge bill was stalled in the Committee on Labor and Education. When Republican senator John Spooner of Wisconsin introduced a resolution asking the Senate Judiciary Committee to consider the constitutionality of the child labor bill, Beveridge decided not to wait for another unfavorable report. In order to bypass the Labor and Education Committee and force a yes or no vote on the record, Senator Beveridge offered his proposal as an amendment to a bill to regulate child labor in Washington, DC.

In support of his measure, the senator spoke passionately on the floor of the Senate chamber for three separate days in late January about the evils of "child slavery" and the constitutionality of his bill. Child labor, he said, was "as brutal and horrible in its inhumanity as anything the pen of Dickens ever painted."[56] He traced the history of the child labor problem in Great Britain, described the practice's debilitating impact on the population, and compared the British experience in the early 1800s to America in 1907. Beveridge emphasized that child labor was not just a matter of states' rights. Rather, it was a national problem that required a uniform federal law. "Not only . . . is there inequality of business opportunities," he argued, "but by

that inequality the ruin of citizens in any one State, the murder of the innocents in any one Commonwealth, affects the entire Republic as much as it
affects the State."[57]

The Indiana senator's tone was angry and dramatic. Some senators
mocked Beveridge's earnestness and smiled when he began reading descriptions of child labor exploitation. "Does the Senate find that amusing?" asked
Beveridge. "If so, I shall present some examples from other States that perhaps will amuse the Senate still more." For hours on end, Beveridge quoted
from Spargo's *The Bitter Cry of the Children* and read vivid descriptions, supported by NCLC affidavits, of the terrible inhumanity of child labor in
the United States.[58] He described children of ten and twelve working with
bleeding hands in the breakers of the mines and children under twelve working more than twelve hours a day. He spoke of shop managers who poured
cold water on child workers to keep them awake after they had been standing on their feet for ten hours. Beveridge warned that every year child labor
created "at least 200,000 'Hooligans,' boys and girls, who are broken in body
and stunted in mind and soul, and who *know* it, and who are living engines
of hatred toward society."[59] He did not blame the child workers for their attitudes. When the packed galleries responded to the senator's speech with
repeated applause, the presiding officer had to gavel for silence. "Of course,
these are not our children. They are the children of somebody else that are
working twelve hours at night." "If they were our children," Beveridge asserted, "we would forget lunch and not sit up at nights contriving arguments
to show that the Constitution won't let us rescue them."[60]

Impressed by Beveridge's thoroughness and the authenticity of his evidence, the smiling ceased and the Senate listened attentively to his pre-
sentation, with some interjecting supportive comments. For the first time,
child labor received serious consideration by national representatives. Most
lawyers in Congress, however, and many outside the institution, still believed that the bill was unconstitutional. Requiring every manufacturer and
mill owner to include a certificate with shipment imposed an unreasonable
burden on commerce. Moreover, the concept of dual federalism was strong
at that time. Under this theory, the Constitution embodies a strict division
of powers between the national government and the states, with very little
overlap. National authority is based on enumerated powers limited by the
Tenth Amendment, which reserves powers to the States and the people.
Congress does not have an enumerated power in Article 1 to legislate on
child labor. The only areas where it has direct control (according to this
theory) are the District of Columbia and the territories.

Nonetheless, Beveridge was confident that he had found a way around the dual federalism problem. While acknowledging that Congress could not pass a law directly affecting mines, factories, and mills, he maintained that legislative authority could be exercised under the Commerce Clause. The congressional power to regulate and even prohibit the shipment of foreign goods was unlimited, and the power of Congress over interstate commerce, which was contained in the same clause as the power over foreign commerce, was therefore, also unlimited.[61] That power extended to prohibiting objects in interstate commerce, including products made with child labor. The Constitution, Beveridge asserted, "was not written to shackle human progress, but to give human progress free play."[62] Federal regulation of child labor fulfilled the broad goals of the Constitution's Preamble to promote the general welfare and ensure domestic tranquility.

Beveridge's three-day speech failed to move most of his Senate colleagues, including many in his own party. Senate Majority Leader Nelson Aldrich of Rhode Island, John C. Spooner of Wisconsin, who was widely considered the Senate's constitutional authority, Charles Fulton of Oregon, and Philander Knox of Pennsylvania led the Republican opposition to the bill. Meanwhile, southern Democrats, even the more progressive-minded, were wedded to the dogma of states' rights and viewed child labor as a local problem best left to the states. Senator Benjamin Tillman of South Carolina opposed child labor but believed "that the good sense and the love of humanity in any State, where it is pointed to properly, will redress this wrong or cure the evil, or kill it, if the facts are ever presented to the people."[63]

Senators Tillman and Fulton questioned Beveridge on the scope of congressional authority implicit in his bill. Tillman mentioned that children aged six years and older picked cotton in the fall. Would Beveridge, he asked, stop the cotton crop from entering in interstate commerce because children were used to gather the cotton? When Beveridge replied that his bill would not prohibit cotton from being shipped, Tillman retorted that the bill did not differentiate between the kinds of labor and thus that he worried about its breadth. Beveridge suggested that the South Carolina senator had not read his bill, and Tillman admitted that he had not. Beveridge explained he had no problem with children working on a farm and that his bill only attacked child labor in factories, mills, and sweatshops. Suggesting that the principle is the same, Senator Fulton wondered whether, if child-made products from a factory could be excluded from interstate commerce, could not farm products as well? Beveridge's response probably raised some eyebrows in the Senate chamber. "Certainly we can, as a matter of *power*; but we will never as a matter of *policy*. The possible abuse of power is no argument against its existence."[64] Senator Fulton persisted, asking Beveridge directly if Congress had the authority to prohibit cotton from being shipped in interstate commerce if it was picked by children. "Yes," Beveridge responded, "or a redheaded girl."[65] Law professor Logan E. Sawyer, III, contends that Beveridge's defense of his position is a shining example of the effect of constitutionalism on Progressive-Era legislative politics.[66] Beveridge knew where the line of questioning was going. Fulton and others, he surmised, were hoping that his bill was unconstitutional because they did not want to deal with the question of legislating an eight-hour workday. Beveridge himself did not support such a measure, but he accepted the "parade of horribles" in order to bring a logical consistency to his argument on congressional power under the Commerce Clause.[67]

Beveridge relied heavily on the case of *Champion v. Ames* (1903), popularly known as the Lottery Case, in defending the constitutionality of his bill. While ubiquitous today, in the early twentieth century lotteries were widely considered a moral evil that caused numerous social problems. In a 5–4 decision, the Supreme Court upheld Congress's power to prohibit interstate shipment of lottery tickets for the purpose of guarding the people of the United States against the widespread pestilence of lotteries. The regulation of lottery tickets in interstate commerce was beyond the power of the states. Writing for the majority, Justice John Harlan argued, "We should hesitate long before adjudging that an evil of such appalling character, carried on through interstate commerce, cannot be met and crushed by the only power competent to that end."[68] Although the majority opinion did not identify the limits of Congress's power to address noneconomic evils, Beveridge believed that the precedent could be applied to the regulation of child labor.

His Senate colleagues, though, remained unconvinced. Because *Champion v. Ames* was closely divided, they cautioned not to read too much into the decision. According to Senator Philander Knox, who had served as Roosevelt's attorney general and was a sharp lawyer, Congress could only prohibit the interstate shipment of articles that harmed commerce or that were themselves intrinsically dangerous. Senators Spooner and Fulton distinguished the Lottery Case by arguing that Congress can only ban items "that are deleterious to the people to whom they are shipped."[69] They questioned whether Beveridge understood that the Lottery Case and other precedents have this common element. Beveridge responded by saying that the nature of a product has nothing to do with the power of Congress. There are no such restrictions on Congress's power over foreign commerce or with the

Indian tribes, and the same can be said for interstate commerce. Besides, Beveridge provided examples where Congress prohibited products in interstate commerce not inherently dangerous to the recipients.

Several newspapers lined up in support of the Beveridge bill, including the *Boston Herald*, the *Rochester Democrat and Chronicle*, the *Kansas City Journal*, the *Washington Times*, and the *Chicago Record-Herald*. The editors of the Chicago paper wrote: "The day that marks the passage of a Federal child-labor law will mark one of the greatest steps forward in civilization and progress, and in enlightened self-protection as well, that this country has ever taken."[70] The *Milwaukee Sentinel* emphasized the limitations of state laws. "There is evidently no uniformity of State conscience in the matter, or at least the temptation to tolerate or connive at the abuse may be stronger in one State than in another," said the paper. "In some localities, it seems that philanthropic agitators may preach and protest until the crack of doom without effecting what has been achieved in other States."[71]

Many newspapers took the other side. After the second day of Beveridge's speech, the *New York Times* published an editorial strongly criticizing the proposed law. It noted that the bill would cover only about half of working children not employed on farms. While acknowledging that child labor was cruel and evil and a threat to the republic, the editors asserted it was not worth making "further breaches in the Constitution, and new and large transfers of power to the Federal government, for the attainment of a result so deplorably imperfect."[72] The *New York Tribune* expressed similar reservations. "Congress has no direct constitutional authority over this question of child labor," the paper stated. "The several States have it. They can strike at the evil directly, honestly, and without resort to a subterfuge."[73] The *New York Sun* went further in defending child labor, claiming that it was "likely enough that many of these child laborers will grow up into capitalists and become 'too rich' like their present oppressors." Many senators agreed with these arguments. Lawmakers tabled the amendment for the remainder of the session.

The Indiana senator answered his critics with a nine-page memo, which he shared with President Roosevelt, defending the constitutionality of his bill and repeating many arguments that he made on the Senate floor. Citing *Gibbons v. Ogden* (1824) and several other Supreme Court precedents, Beveridge argued that congressional power over interstate commerce was as broad and absolute as its power to regulate foreign commerce. Further, when the Constitution was drafted, the word "regulate" encompassed the power to prohibit any articles from interstate commerce.[74] Beveridge identified at least seventeen federal laws prohibiting various items from interstate commerce, including bans on nitroglycerin, dairy or food products that are falsely labeled, cattle without a certificate, obscene books, certain insects, and other articles.[75] Most conclusive of all, a 1905 law prohibited the interstate transportation of gold and silver goods with the initials "U.S.A." on them. Those gold and silver articles themselves, like products made with child labor, injured or deceived nobody. Beveridge claimed that *Champion v. Ames* answered every question and was decisive.[76] To those who made "slippery slope" arguments—if child-made goods can be prohibited in interstate commerce, Congress can prohibit absolutely anything—Beveridge cited several precedents, including the Lottery Case: "The possible abuse of a power is not an argument against its existence."[77] It is all a question of policy, he explained. The power exists to regulate child labor; if it is abused, "the remedy is in the hands of the people at the ballot-box."

Aware of the long struggle against child labor in Great Britain and realizing that his cause could take years, Senator Beveridge persisted in his efforts. He maintained a robust correspondence with President Roosevelt, constantly urging the president to support his legislation. But the president equivocated. He had doubts regarding the constitutionality of the bill and some of the facts on child labor. Roosevelt shared with Beveridge a paper presented at the National Civic Federation meeting by an unknown labor leader who criticized the Beveridge bill and denied the scope of the child labor problem. The author accused the senator of using "socialistic and other radical writers" deceptively to prove that there were two million "child wage slaves" under fourteen, working in factories, mills, and mines. The "socialist" charge would be used against child labor reformers for the next thirty years by manufacturers, mill owners, and other groups opposed to regulations. The author estimated that only eighty-five thousand children under fourteen years were working in establishments covered by the Beveridge bill. And he or she asserted that since the 1900 Census figures, advanced child labor legislation in the states greatly reduced the number of children working in factories, mills, and mines. The writer concluded that the enormous evils of child labor portrayed by the senator existed "only in the minds of misinformed, but well-intentioned, radical advocates of national child labor legislation."[78] Senator Beveridge characterized the paper as "absurd, inaccurate, almost untruthful, and altogether worthless."[79] The figures and descriptions in his Senate speech, he insisted, were accurate and supported by statements given under oath and by people who actually witnessed the infamies that he described.

Undaunted by the setbacks, Beveridge planned to reintroduce his bill at the next session of Congress. Both President Roosevelt and the NCLC begged him not to use the same strategy of attaching his bill to child labor legislation for the District of Columbia. Roosevelt felt that the tactic contributed to the defeat of the DC bill in the previous session. Beveridge intended to repeat the same strategy, but he eventually backed down. He was confident that at the very least he could obtain a Senate vote on the measure. His hand was strengthened by growing popular support. The NCLC reported that his speech in the Senate had attracted nationwide attention to the child labor campaign and even spurred interest in tougher state legislation. Resolutions of support were received from General Federation of Women's Clubs, state teacher associations, and other civic organizations. In October 1907, bishops at the Protestant Episcopal Convention adopted a strong resolution condemning the evil of child labor. It stated: "We call upon employers and parents to exercise their influence to better legislation and better enforcement of the laws, to the end that the exploitation of the labor of children shall become impossible in this Christian country."[80] Alexander J. McKelway aided the effort by publishing an essay on why the southern states should favor a national law.[81] Even William Jennings Bryan, a populist Democrat and three-time unsuccessful candidate for president, backed the legislation, although Beveridge believed that Bryan was attempting to co-opt the issue for Democrats.[82]

Despite the publicity and endorsements, Beveridge was unable to advance his bill. For reformers, the legislative process was painfully slow. By early 1908, it was clear that the Beveridge bill was dead. Some NCLC Trustees, led by Robert W. De Forest, wanted to rescind the committee's endorsement of the bill, but others felt that was unreasonable. Senator Beveridge pleaded with the committee not to abandon him in his fight for federal legislation. NCLC members, however, voted 18 to 10 to withdraw the committee's endorsement of the Beveridge bill. Many board members questioned the effectiveness of the bill and preferred to campaign for reform in state legislatures. In an attempt to recapture some unity on the board and out of respect for the senator and his efforts, a revised resolution was unanimously adopted that the NCLC would take no action on further federal legislation with no mention of the Beveridge bill. The trustees were encouraged that Congress had authorized an investigation into child labor, and, according to Owen R. Lovejoy, the committee's new secretary, the prudent path was to wait for the results.[83] Samuel M. Lindsay was upset with the vote and angry at the reactionaries within his organization, but he told Beveridge that "it was the best we could do."[84] Florence Kelley, too, was embarrassed and incensed with the vote. "Whatever its faults," she wrote her son, "the bill embodies the first attempt to deal justly with *all* the children and all the employers. And rescinding an endorsement of a federal bill, by a so-called national body, is the most serious injury which can be inflicted on a pending bill."[85] Meanwhile, the NCLC concentrated its efforts on improving state laws, an agenda which no opponent of child labor could find objectionable.

With the bill buried, Beveridge could accomplish nothing more. He blamed the legislative defeat on the coordinated efforts of southern cotton mills, the silk and glass factories of New Jersey and West Virginia, New England mill owners, and railroads that carried the products of child labor.[86] It was to be the last serious attempt to enact a federal child labor law for almost a decade. During the interim years, legislation comparable to the Beveridge-Parsons bill was introduced in each Congress. At first, the bills never made it out of committee. In subsequent sessions, a bill passed out of committee in one chamber but would be voted down. A child labor law never came close to being enacted.

After the failure of the Beveridge bills, President Theodore Roosevelt reiterated his call for a national investigation into child labor, claiming that "the horrors incident to the employment of young children in factories or at work anywhere are a blot on our civilization."[87] Congress responded, and Roosevelt signed the bill authorizing the investigation on January 31, 1907. Even that lone victory on child labor did not come easy. Manufacturers and mill owners subsequently tried to kill the initial $150,000 appropriation for the investigation. When unable to choke funding, opponents next tried to have the Census Bureau conduct the investigation, which would have produced a purely statistical report with little public appeal. Public opinion, however, was strongly in favor of the study, and it was finally assigned to the Department of Commerce and Labor. The result was a nineteen-volume publication, issued between 1910 and 1913, on the industrial, social, moral, educational, and physical conditions of working women and children.[88] Ironically, the massive publication was generally inaccessible to average citizens, but the comprehensive findings demonstrated the need for federal legislation.

Having finally secured his investigation, President Roosevelt continued to push for a child labor law for the District of Columbia and the territories. In a special message to Congress on March 25, 1908, Roosevelt called for child labor to be prohibited throughout the nation. At the very least, he said, "a model child-labor bill should be passed for the District of Columbia" because it was "unfortunate" that in the one place where Congress had sole control over legislation, no law existed "to protect children by forbidding or regulating their labor."[89] Two months later, the House unanimously passed a child labor law for the District of Columbia and the Senate followed. The law prohibited children under fourteen from employment in factories, workshops, stores, or anywhere within the district. Any child under sixteen had to have an age and schooling certificate and could not work before 6:00 a.m. or after 7:00 p.m. or for more than eight hours. Though better than nothing, the new law was criticized for exempting pages of the Senate and the children of dependent parents.[90]

For the remainder of his term, President Roosevelt continued his call for the establishment of a national children's bureau. Since 1905, bills to create such an agency had been introduced in successive congressional sessions without advancing. In 1909, an amusing episode occurred in the Senate chamber when Senator Winthrop Crane, former governor of Massachusetts, introduced a bill providing for the establishment of a "bureau of children." The senator was teased over the awkward language. One of his colleagues joked that Crane was coming to the assistance of the stork. "The stork brings the babies," the distinguished senator quipped, "and Crane provides for their subsequent care."[91] It was a rare moment of levity in a typically contentious debate over child labor. Crane's bill did not pass that year.

Initial federal efforts on child labor faltered for several reasons. The US Constitution does not give Congress the enumerated power to regulate hours and working conditions for labor within the states, and, unlike the states, Congress has no general police power to address social evils. States may pass laws to promote the public health, safety, morals, and welfare. Unique constitutional arguments had to be made to defend federal power over child labor. Since the late 1800s, Congress had often approximated the police powers by using its control over the postal service, taxing authority, and especially its power to regulate commerce between the states to address social harms such as lotteries, sexual trafficking, impure foods, explosives, and other items. Senator Beveridge argued that Congress could legislate on child labor indirectly under the power to regulate interstate commerce. But traditional or old-guard Republicans controlled the leadership, and many of his colleagues were not swayed by the constitutional arguments. Many in government and the media clung to the concept of dual federalism and believed that the federal government simply had no authority to regulate child labor. Others worried about the potential unlimited nature of congressional power under the Commerce Clause. Business leaders pushed back against reforms, and some conservatives may just have preferred limited government intervention in the market. More important, the lack of unified support for federal regulation from the NCLC, the most prominent organization advocating child labor reforms, did not help matters. And with the American Federation of Labor and President Roosevelt on the fence, Beveridge lacked core support to give him leverage in Congress for his bill. Finally, there was a sense among some politicians and citizens that the problem of child labor was being effectively addressed by the states and thus that federal regulation was unnecessary. The public was aroused on the issue but not enough to place widespread pressure on Congress to act.

Beveridge lost his legislative battle, but his pioneering efforts were not in vain. He compelled Congress to seriously consider the problem of child labor, educated millions on the harsh realities of the practice, and developed constitutional arguments in defense of national legislation. When the NCLC renewed its focus on state laws and a southern campaign, Beveridge maintained that the problem could only be addressed effectively with a national law. "It is the sheerest folly," he insisted, "to waste the efforts of thousands of people who favor ending this twentieth century child slavery by dissipating them along the lines of state and local action instead of concentrating them upon national action."[92]

Senator Beveridge failed in his bid for reelection in 1910 and served out his term until March 3, 1911. Some blamed the loss on his progressivism, but Beveridge believed that it was because the Republican Party was not progressive enough. He broke with the Republican Party in 1912 to nominate Theodore Roosevelt as presidential candidate for the Progressive Party. Beveridge was an unsuccessful Progressive candidate for governor in 1912, and he attempted two more abortive campaigns to return to the Senate. He never again held public office. Beveridge turned his attention to research and writing and published a four-volume biography of Chief Justice John Marshall that won a Pulitzer Prize. He was working on a multivolume biography of Abraham Lincoln when he passed away. Though unfinished, the Lincoln biography is highly acclaimed among historians.

With Senator Beveridge out of office, other members of Congress emerged to champion the cause of child labor reform. The NCLC would, yet again, reverse its policy on federal child labor legislation, and there would be more support for national reform from organized labor. Despite the following years being the peak of the Progressive Era, it would take nearly a decade for Congress to enact a federal child labor law. This time, progressive Democrats and a Democratic president, Woodrow Wilson, were the forces behind the legislative effort.

Regulating Child Labor as Interstate Commerce

THE KEATING-OWEN ACT AND

HAMMER v. DAGENHART

Although federal legislation made little progress during the first decade of the twentieth century, a growing societal consensus on the evils of child labor, thanks in part to the lobbying efforts of the National Child Labor Committee, National Consumers' League, General Federation of Women's Clubs, and other groups, pushed states to enact more laws restricting child labor in factories and mines. From 1902 to 1909, forty-three states passed significant child labor legislation, either new laws, including many southern states, or strengthening existing statutes. The laws varied widely, however, in their stringency and enforcement. While a fourteen-year age minimum for factories was standard in northern states, opposition from southern textile mill owners prevented serious consideration of the age minimum until 1909. Exemptions for work outside school hours, during vacation, and for children of dependent parents seriously weakened the fourteen-year minimum.

These child labor laws were passed under a state's broad police powers to protect the health, safety, morals, and welfare of its citizens.[1] The concept of state police powers can be confusing because the phrase is not found in the Constitution, and it has little in common with modern notions of a local police force. State police powers are protected by the Tenth Amendment to the Constitution, which reads, "The powers not delegated to the United States by the Constitution, nor prohibited by it to the states, are reserved to the States respectively, or to the people." In *Lawton v. Steele* (1889), the Supreme Court stated that the police power "is universally conceded to include everything essential to the public safety, health, and morals, and to justify the destruction or abatement . . . of whatever may be regarded as a public nuisance."[2] Regulating child labor, it was argued, was good for the public welfare. Among the many legal challenges to child labor restrictions, businesses claimed that the laws fell outside the police powers of a state or violated substantive due process and a "liberty of contract" under the Fourteenth Amendment.

Originally ratified during Reconstruction to protect the rights of freed slaves, the Fourteenth Amendment's Due Process Clause declares that a state cannot deny any person "life, liberty, or property without due process of law." A similarly worded provision is found in the Fifth Amendment, which applies to the national government. Prior to the adoption of the Fourteenth Amendment in 1868, judges interpreted the due process guarantees in the Fifth Amendment as procedural limitations on government power. Procedural due process meant that people were "entitled" to fair and orderly proceedings, especially in criminal cases, where a citizen's life or liberty is at stake. Under procedural due process, government can deny citizens life, liberty, or property only when it provides fair and proper procedures.

After the adoption of the Fourteenth Amendment, lawyers representing business interests opposed to growing state regulation during the Industrial Revolution began to emphasize substantive due process arguments. Substantive due process focuses on the *reasonableness* of legislation. If a court determined that a state regulation of property rights was unreasonable, arbitrary, or "class legislation" that discriminated between citizens, the court could declare a violation of the Fourteenth Amendment. Substantive due process arguments were heavily influenced by an 1868 legal treatise entitled *Constitutional Limitations*, by Thomas Cooley. Cooley emphasized limits on legislative authority in order to protect personal liberty and private property.

State supreme courts were initially more receptive to substantive due process arguments, but the US Supreme Court gradually accepted the doctrine. Most scholars trace the origin of substantive due process in Supreme Court jurisprudence to Justice Stephen Field's dissenting opinion in the *Slaughterhouse Cases* (1873), in which he argued that the Fourteenth Amendment protected "the right to pursue lawful employment in a lawful manner, without other restraint than such as equally affects all persons." In a separate dissenting opinion in the same case, Justice Joseph Bradley wrote, "I hold that the liberty of pursuit—the right to follow any of the ordinary callings of life—is one of the privileges of a citizen of the United States."[3] In subsequent cases, a doctrine of substantive due process emerged that used the notion of a "liberty of contract" to challenge laws governing the relationship between employer and employee, especially in the arenas of minimum wage, maximum hours, workmen's compensation, unionization, and child labor.

The battle between liberty of contract doctrine and protective labor legislation had been brewing for years, but it came to a head in *Lochner v. New York* (1905), which is widely viewed as one of the most controversial substantive due process cases. In *Lochner*, the US Supreme Court invalidated a provision of the 1895 New York Bakeshop Act, a law passed unanimously by the legislature. This act contained provisions that addressed sanitation in bakeries and biscuit factories to ensure "unadulterated bread," but the only controversial section was the one that limited the number of hours that someone could work in a "biscuit, bread or cake bakery" to ten hours a day or sixty hours a week.[4] At the time, many tenement bakers worked seventy to one hundred hours a week.[5] Before the Supreme Court, New York justified the law by arguing that the police powers gave the state the right to regulate working conditions and to protect workers and consumers from sickness. Joseph Lochner, owner of a tenement bakery, argued that employees and employers have a right to agree on wages and hours and that state regulation of such terms violates the Fourteenth Amendment.

A majority of the justices agreed with Lochner, concluding that the law violated his liberty of contract because it lacked a reasonable relation to public health, safety, or welfare. Justice Rufus Peckham wrote: "We think the limit of the police power has been reached and passed in this case. There is, in our judgment, no reasonable foundation for holding this to be necessary or appropriate as a health law to safeguard the public health or the health of the individuals who are following the trade of a baker."[6] Wholesome bread, the Court claimed, does not depend on bakers' working hours. Justice John Harlan dissented, joined by Chief Justice Edward Douglas White and Justice William R. Day. Justice Harlan believed that the law was a valid health measure. The regulation, he said, "applies only to work in bakery and confectionery establishments, in which, as all know, the air constantly breathed by workmen is not as pure and healthful as that to be found in some other establishments or out of doors."[7] Harlan suggested that the majority had substituted its judgment of the efficacy of the law for that of the legislature. In a famous dissenting opinion, Justice Oliver Wendell Holmes urged deference to the legislature, and argued that the case was "decided upon an economic theory which a large part of the country does not entertain" and that "the Fourteenth Amendment does not enact Mr. Herbert Spencer's *Social Statics.*"[8]

As a consequence of the *Lochner* precedent and other cases, the liberty of contract doctrine potentially limited a state's authority to enact child labor laws if the courts determined that the laws were an *unreasonable* exercise of the police power. The liberty of contract doctrine was criticized then and now because it essentially placed courts in the role of assessing whether a statute was reasonable and therefore, necessary, to solve a social problem.[9] Because that determination is primarily a policy decision best left to a legislature, courts were vulnerable to charges of judicial activism. In fact, the *Lochner* decision spawned the term "Lochnerism" to describe conservative judicial activism in defense of business interests. The extent to which Lochnerism characterized federal court jurisprudence during this period has been a matter of academic debate for years.[10]

Both state and federal courts sustained most child labor laws, however, acknowledging a state interest in the welfare of children. In a California case, *In re Spencer* (1906), the state court upheld the child labor law by declaring: "The legislature may undoubtedly forbid the employment of children under the age of fourteen years at any regular occupation if the interests of the children and the general welfare of society will thereby be secured and promoted."[11] Likewise, the state supreme court of Oregon affirmed a 1905 child labor law prohibiting children under sixteen from working before 7:00 a.m. or after 6:00 p.m., or for longer than ten hours a day or more than six days a week. In upholding the law, the court rejected the liberty of contract doctrine of *Lochner* and applied the concept of *parens patriae*, or state as parent: "They [children] are wards of the state and subject to its control. As to them, the state stands in the position of *parens patriae*, and may exercise unlimited supervision and control over their contracts, occupation, and conduct, and the liberty and right of those who assume to deal with them. This is a power which inheres in the government for its own preservation."[12] Other decisions recognized the same governmental interest in the welfare of children. *Inland Steel Co. v. Yedinak* (1909) involved an underage, injured boy employed at a steel plant in violation of Indiana state law. The company tried to avoid liability by claiming that the boy's own youthful negligence caused the injury. In rejecting that argument, the state court wrote: "The employment of children of tender years in mills and factories not only endangers their lives and limbs, but hinders and dwarfs their growth and development physically, mentally and morally. The State is vitally interested in its own preservation, and, looking to that end, must safeguard and protect the lives, persons, health and morals of its future citizens."[13] In addition to California, Oregon, and Indiana, child labor laws were upheld in Louisiana, Minnesota, New Jersey, and New York.[14] The NCLC and other reformers were effective in convincing legislatures and courts that states had an obligation to protect children under their broad police powers.

As the nation headed into the second decade of the twentieth century, all the states had child labor laws. The problem was that the laws were not uniform and in some states enforcement was lax. Laws were on the books, but factory inspections were sometimes prohibited and often there were no financial or administrative resources for enforcement. Even in New York, a state with progressive child labor laws, there were difficulties securing compliance in mill or factory towns. John Williams, the state commissioner of labor, testified before the legislature that canning communities were hostile to child labor laws. A previous state commissioner ruled in 1905 that the laws did not apply to canneries because the work performed was agricultural labor. Williams, however, reversed that position several years later and had his inspectors enforce the law. When cannery owners were prosecuted for violating child labor restrictions, the courts were hostile to the government's case or juries refused to convict.[15]

Since the failure of the Beveridge-Parsons bill, the gap between the most progressive state child labor laws and the most regressive became more pronounced. A national fourteen-year minimum age had been achieved in most northern states, but many southern states lagged and the objective of reformers was to expand that minimum nationally. Any state that enacted tough child labor laws placed its businesses at a competitive disadvantage with respect to states with weak laws. For example, northern textile mills complained of unfair competition from southern cotton manufacturers that used child labor extensively.

The Bureau of Labor investigated the cotton textile industry in 1909 and reported to Congress the following year. When the investigation began, only five southern states prohibited the employment of children under twelve while Mississippi had no child labor law. Georgia and South Carolina exempted orphans or children with dependent parents. By the time the report was shared with Congress, Virginia had raised its age limit to fourteen, North Carolina increased its minimum age to thirteen, and Mississippi had passed a child labor law. Investigators, however, found that the age-limit laws "were openly and freely violated in every state visited."[16] Employers, parents, and mill communities had no incentive to restrict child labor because everyone had a financial stake in the practice. Widespread poverty in the South and the absence of public welfare for dependent children exacerbated the problem. Children worked because they and their families had no other means of survival. No state could solve this conundrum on its own.

The National Child Labor Committee, meanwhile, continued its campaign for tougher state laws. In 1908, the NCLC hired Lewis Hine, a former teacher and photographer, to serve as staff photographer and researcher. For over a decade, Hine traveled the country and used his outdated box camera to take several thousand photos of children in all kinds of industries, including coal mines, textile mills, canneries, meatpacking plants, and factories. He also photographed children working outside as cotton pickers, shoe shine boys, messengers, and newsboys. Hine often had to trick his way into establishments because factory managers would not have agreed to let the public see the conditions of the child workers. He posed as a fire inspector, an insurance salesman, or an industrial photographer who sought pictures of factory buildings and machinery.[17] Sometimes, managers hid the children or told Hine that they were just visiting their parents at work. He carefully documented each photo and sometimes interviewed the children. Although the NCLC admitted that the pictures may not have been representative of practices throughout the country, they were an important visual record that the evils of child labor persisted even during the Progressive Era. Hine's photographs became an effective propaganda tool to stir the public conscience in favor of national child labor reform.

In 1910, twenty-five state and local child labor committees, representing twenty-two states, worked with the NCLC in abolishing child labor. They faced a significant challenge, as the use of child labor was at its apex. The 1900 US Census revealed that there were 1,750,178, or 18.2 percent of children ten to fifteen years old, employed. In 1910, there were 1,990,225, or 18.4 percent of the age group, employed in the United States. The 1910 census figures represent the peak of child labor in America. As before, the census underreported the actual number of employed children because there were many kids under ten working in mills, shops, and factories. There were at least two million working children at the end of the first decade of the twentieth century.

After six years of lobbying by Alexander J. McKelway of the NCLC and other groups, Congress established the Children's Bureau on April 9, 1912, and the new office began its work in August. Lillian D. Wald, head of the

Nurses' Settlement of New York, and Florence Kelley first conceived of the idea of a federal bureau devoted to the study of child welfare issues.[18] A bill for the establishment of the bureau was introduced in Congress in the winter of 1905–1906. Although the bill had the backing of President Theodore Roosevelt and members of his administration, it failed in successive sessions until it was passed in the Sixty-Second Congress and signed by President William Howard Taft. Paradoxically, some child welfare advocates opposed the creation of the Children's Bureau. Elbridge T. Gerry, founder and counsel for the New York Society for the Prevention of Cruelty to Children (NYSPCC), an organization that had supported child labor laws for decades, condemned the new federal agency. Along the old fault lines of states' rights, Gerry argued that a federal bureau was a dangerous invasion of state police powers, and the bureau would simply furnish useless sinecures. John D. Lindsay, president of the NYSPCC, asserted that "the Federal government has nothing to do, directly or indirectly, with State legislation on the subject of child welfare."[19] Their opposition did not prevent the establishment of the bureau, but it further illustrates how groups allied on child labor reform sometimes disagreed on strategy.

President Taft waited for a recommendation from the NCLC for a candidate to head the Children's Bureau. When Jane Addams, Lillian Wald, and Samuel M. Lindsay refused the post, the committee decided on Julia Lathrop.[20] The daughter of a US congressman, Lathrop worked under Jane Addams at Hull House in Chicago where she served on the Illinois Board of Charities. She inspected county institutions for the sick, the homeless, and the insane. She also was a leader in the juvenile court movement and helped to found the Chicago School of Civics and Philanthropy. Lathrop's name was submitted to the president, and he appointed her the first head of the bureau. In fact, she became the first female bureau chief in US history. The Children's Bureau lacked rulemaking power to promulgate regulations, but it became an important clearinghouse for research and statistics on child welfare and labor, and under Lathrop's direction promoted a reform agenda.[21] In the coming years, the bureau worked closely with the NCLC and other groups in advocating for child labor laws and a national Child Labor Amendment.

The first research monograph published by the new Children's Bureau dealt with an issue critical to the success of child labor laws—birth registration. For decades, the inability to accurately determine the age of a child undermined the minimum age requirements for working children. Parental affidavits of age were suspect because many parents lied about the birth date of their children. In 1911, only eight states had a birth registration system that the federal Census Bureau considered acceptable, and even those statistics were not completely reliable.[22] One-third of the states had no birth registration system in 1913. The United States was far behind European countries on this issue, mainly because compulsory military service in Europe required birth information. Establishing a uniform system of birth registration was yet another dimension to effective administration of child labor laws.[23] Birth registration would make it difficult for employers and parents to circumvent the law. Registering births had other public health benefits, and it aided in school admissions and personal identity for all legal transactions.

In the presidential election of 1912, conservative and progressive Republicans split between incumbent President William Howard Taft and Theodore Roosevelt, who ran on the Progressive or Bull Moose ticket. Both the Republican and Progressive Parties called for a federal child labor law in 1912. Roosevelt's views on child labor had evolved, and he now firmly supported federal legislation. In a speech laying out the principles of the Progressive Party, Roosevelt stated that the "premature employment of children is abnormal and should be prohibited."[24] He believed that tenement work was a serious menace to health, education, and childhood, and should therefore be completely prohibited. The rift between the Republicans, however, allowed Democrat Woodrow Wilson to win the presidency. Despite the loss, Teddy Roosevelt continued his involvement in national politics after the election. In a campaign speech in Kansas City, Missouri, Roosevelt called for immediate laws to regulate child labor. "Progressives want a national law to put a stop to child labor, and we are going to have it," he declared.[25] "The Republicans and Democrats say it is against the constitution to pass such a law," he said, "but in the day when the constitution was written there was no child labor."

Before taking office in 1913, president-elect Wilson held a "secret meeting" in Hoboken, New Jersey, with social welfare advocates, including Florence Kelley, Alexander J. McKelway, Josephine Goldmark, Lillian Wald, and Owen R. Lovejoy. Much of the agenda was revealed to reporters following the gathering. Unlike a similar meeting held with Roosevelt, who let the reformers write the plank of the Bull Moose Party, Wilson did not agree with the social reformers on all issues, particularly on the need for national child labor legislation. In his book, *Constitutional Government in the United States*, published years earlier, Wilson argued against federal child labor laws: "If the power to regulate commerce between the States can be stretched to include the regulation of labor in mills and factories, it can be made to embrace every particular of the industrial organization of the country. The only limitation Congress would observe should the Supreme Court assent to such obviously absurd extravagances of interpretation would be the limitation of opinion and circumstances."[26]

Wilson's political views had softened somewhat since publication of his book, but he still favored state action on child labor. While he expressed sympathy for the cause, Wilson warned reformers that national efforts through the Children's Bureau should be confined to the collection and co-ordination of data on child labor. Regulation, he told them, must be left to the states. Wilson admitted that his position was based on the states' rights doctrine of the Democratic Party.[27] In a statement to conference partici-pants, Wilson said: "My own party in some of its elements represents a very strong States' rights feeling. It is very plain that you would have to go fur-ther than most interpretations of the Constitution would allow if you were to give to the Government general control over child labor throughout the country."[28] The new president acknowledged that every subject discussed engaged his interest and enthusiasm, but his enthusiasm was "in proportion generally to the practicability of a scheme."

Wilson may have been unconvinced about the constitutionality of federal child labor legislation, but the Supreme Court helped remove any doubts in a decision announced one month after his meeting with the social wel-fare reformers. On February 24, 1913, the Court in *Hoke v. United States* unanimously upheld the Mann Act, known as the White Slave Act. The law made it a federal crime for "any person to knowingly transport or cause to be transported, or aid or assist in obtaining transportation for, or in transport-ing, in interstate or foreign commerce . . . any woman or girl for the purpose of prostitution or debauchery, or for any other immoral purpose."[29] The law responded to a perceived national problem of women being induced or forced to become prostitutes. The broad language of the statute, which ex-tended beyond commercial vice, was the most sweeping use to date of the federal police power to protect the nation's health, morals, and welfare.[30]

Justice Joseph McKenna's opinion for the Court was just as broad in its interpretation of the Commerce Clause as the language of the Mann Act. He affirmed that the power of Congress over interstate and foreign com-merce was direct: "There is no word of limitation in it, and its broad and uni-versal scope has been so often declared as to make repetition unnecessary." Justice McKenna suggested that Congress can look beyond the inherent danger of a product: "Motives executed by actions may make it the concern of government to exert its powers. . . . It may be that Congress could not prohibit the manufacture of the article in a state. It may be that Congress could not prohibit in all of its conditions its sale within a state. But Congress may prohibit its transportation between states, and by that means defeat the motive and evils of its manufacturer."[31]

Congressional authority over interstate commerce, the Court noted, had been upheld in a number of areas, including lottery tickets, obscene literature, diseased cattle, and impure food and drugs. It did not matter that women were not articles of merchandise, for the substance of congressional power was the same. McKenna concluded: "The principle established by the cases is the simple one . . . that Congress has power over transportation 'among the several states;' that the power is complete in itself, and that Congress, as an incident to it, may adopt not only [the] means necessary but convenient to its exercise, and the means may have the quality of police regulations."[32] The opinion seemed to vindicate former senator Beveridge's views of congressional power under the Commerce Clause. Reformers recognized the significance and implications of the ruling for a federal child labor law.

Another Supreme Court decision in early December placed state child labor laws on solid constitutional ground. In *Sturges and Burn Manufacturing Co. v. Beauchamp* (1913), the Court unanimously rejected a Fourteenth Amendment due process challenge to an Illinois law prohibiting the employment of children under the age of sixteen in various hazardous occupations. Beauchamp, who was under sixteen, had been injured while working a punch press stamping metal, and he sued to collect damages (financial compensation for his loss). The company claimed that the law was a deprivation of liberty of contract or property without due process of law. The Court held that the state "was entitled to prohibit the employment of persons of tender years in dangerous occupations" and the legislation "was reasonably related to that purpose."[33] The *Sturges* decision is often cited by contemporary revisionist constitutional scholars to demonstrate that the "liberty of contract" doctrine used in *Lochner v. New York* (1905) was not uniformly applied to defend the economic rights of business.[34] Using a rational basis standard, the Court found that state child labor laws were a reasonable exercise of police powers. The *Sturges* decision, however, was to be the only victory for child labor reform in the Supreme Court for almost thirty years.

Ten years after the formation of the National Child Labor Committee, the organization touted its achievements in controlling the abuses of child labor. In his report as general secretary, Owen R. Lovejoy noted that when the committee was formed in 1904, only thirteen states set a fourteen-year age limit for work in factories. A decade later, three dozen states required a fourteen-year age minimum for factory employment.[35] In 1904, only one state provided for an eight-hour day for child workers under sixteen years; after ten years, eighteen states provided for an eight-hour day. When the committee formed, only five states prohibited night work for children under sixteen years; in 1914, thirty-four states had such restrictions. And finally, thirty-six states provided for factory inspections in 1914 compared to just thirteen a decade earlier.[36] Clearly, progress had been made, but there was also a sense that much more work remained. "It was hoped in 1904," wrote Lovejoy, "that child labor could be abolished in ten years. We have been disillusioned. More has been done than seemed possible within the period but the field is immensely larger than was supposed."[37] Looking back on the first ten years, Samuel M. Lindsay identified some of the challenges confronting the NCLC: securing effective enforcement in states with high and low standards; the magnitude of the child labor problem; resistance from forces defending child labor because of profit motives, parental selfishness, and indifference; and the inadequacy of educational opportunities for children.[38]

Variations in state child labor laws, uneven enforcement, and strong opposition from southern politicians and mill owners prompted the NCLC to shift its strategy on child labor legislation. The states were moving too slowly with reforms. In states that considered new or tougher child labor restrictions, threats by factory and mill owners to move their plants to states with lower standards often resulted in a quick death for protective legislation. By 1914, only nine states had met the five requirements of the model child labor law developed a decade earlier.[39] In a speech before the International Child Welfare League, a frustrated Florence Kelley complained that all the money and work used to protect the child through state legislation had "resulted in so little of consequence that those who have given their time and money to that work might just as well have spent the time reading French novels."[40] Some states, Kelley claimed, had passed "sham-laws" that purported to protect children but in reality allowed children to work at "any age under the guise of apprenticeship." Reformers believed that now was the time to act. Using the model law as a foundation, the NCLC drafted a federal child labor bill on January 6, 1914, and worked to secure its passage. With Edgar Gardner Murphy deceased, the NCLC officers and trustees were nearly unanimous in their desire for a national child labor law.

In December 1912 and later in 1914, two progressives in Congress— Representative Ira C. Copley (R-IL) and Senator Miles Poindexter

(R-WA)—introduced the Copley-Poindexter bill. The bill was the most radical child labor legislation ever introduced in Congress. The legislation defined "anti-social child labor" as the employment of a child under fourteen in any mill, factory, cannery, workshop, manufacturing, or mechanical establishment, or of a child under sixteen in any mine or quarry, or in any other dangerous, injurious, or immoral occupation, and prohibited the shipment in interstate commerce of the products of such labor.[41] The broad listing of job categories, including threats to physical safety and morals, guaranteed that the law would cover most forms of child labor. Another senator, William S. Kenyon (R-IA), introduced a child labor bill for several sessions that was nearly identical to the Beveridge-Parsons bill.

While these bills were pending, two Democrats—Representative A. Mitchell Palmer, a third-term congressman from Pennsylvania who would later serve as President Wilson's attorney general, and Senator Robert L. Owen of Oklahoma—introduced the NCLC-backed child labor bill in Congress. This legislation was different from previous bills. Instead of focusing on the common carriers of products made with child labor, the Palmer-Owen bill prohibited a *producer* of goods made with child labor from placing them in interstate commerce. Specifically, the bill prohibited products of mines and quarries where children under sixteen were employed, products of any mill, factory, cannery, or workshop in which children under fourteen were employed, or in establishments where children between fourteen and sixteen worked more than eight hours a day, or between 7:00 p.m. and 7:00 a.m. The standards in the bill were essentially the five requirements of the original model child labor law. Violators faced penalties more severe than found in most state laws—a fine of $100 to $1,000, imprisonment of one month to a year, or both fine and imprisonment.

In a thirty-two-page brief in support of the legislation, the NCLC argued that the bill represented the "most effective and direct method" of ending the child labor problem. After ten years of lobbying for tougher child labor laws at the state level, the NCLC had concluded that it was "difficult if not impossible to secure uniform and effective laws in the different states."[42] At the time, forty states, the District of Columbia, and Puerto Rico prohibited child labor under fourteen years in mills and factories. The brief responded to all the possible objections of the Palmer-Owen bill, including the constitutionality of federal legislation. Recent cases where the Supreme Court had upheld state and federal regulation, including labor conditions, were cited. The NCLC recognized that the most controversial part of the bill was the eight-hour restriction. Only eighteen states had an eight-hour day for children. Many mill owners in the South and glass factories in the North worked their child employees well beyond eight hours a day. An article in the *Charlotte Observer*, a paper that supported the cotton mills, claimed: "Not a cotton mill in the South could ship its goods out of the state in which they are made if this bill were a law."[43]

When NCLC leaders Adler, Lovejoy, and McKelway asked to meet with President Wilson in February 1914 to discuss the Palmer-Owen bill, the president reiterated his position from the Hoboken conference. Regardless of the *Hoke* decision, he believed the law was unconstitutional and if enacted, would open the door to unlimited federal power. He promised, however, to "give the matter very careful consideration" and say nothing to impede the issue.[44] True to his word, President Wilson made no public comments on the child labor issue as the bill was being debated in the House.

A host of national and state organizations backed the legislation: the National Child Labor Committee and state affiliates, the American Federation of Labor, the Federal Council of Churches of Christ in America, the Farmers' Educational and Co-operative Union of America, the American Medical Association, and the International Child Welfare League.[45] All three major political party platforms, Democratic, Republican, and Progressive, also endorsed the bill.

The bill eventually passed the House of Representatives on February 15, 1915, by an overwhelming vote of 233–43. The measure was blocked in the Senate, however, by Lee Overman, a conservative Democrat from North Carolina. Business groups also spoke against the bill. Although it is not clear if he was invited to give testimony on the issue, David Clark, editor of the *Southern Textile Bulletin*, demanded to be heard. Over the next twenty-five years, Clark provided one of the leading voices of opposition to federal child labor legislation and a constitutional amendment. He viewed child labor reform as a serious threat to the textile industry. In his *Bulletin*, he expressed his contempt for the "long-haired men and short-haired women" from the North who presumed to tell mill owners how to run their businesses.[46] Clark took issue with testimony by Owen R. Lovejoy and NCLC pictures that showed emaciated children too weak to stand in southern cotton mills. "But I am willing to wager," he boasted, "that the children in the mill district, boy for boy, can lick any other class of boys in America."[47] He claimed that every statement from the NCLC exaggerated conditions and told only half-truths. Finally, he said, "the fact that a boy of 13 years works in North Carolina can in no way injure citizens of New York and Massachusetts, and, plainly speaking, it is none of their business."[48] With only a few days left in the session, the bill's supporters needed unanimous consent to move the measure to the floor for a vote. When Senator Overman objected, the bill died when Congress adjourned on March 14, 1915.[49]

The Palmer-Owen bill was reintroduced on December 6, 1915, as the Keating-Owen bill. Representative Palmer had vacated his seat to campaign, unsuccessfully, for the Senate. Representative Edward Keating, a progressive Democrat from Colorado, cosponsored the bill with Senator Owen. Representative Keating's bill, H.R. 8234, provided that:

> No producer, manufacturer, or dealer shall ship or deliver for shipment in interstate or foreign commerce, any article or commodity the product of any mine or quarry situated in the United States, in which within thirty days prior to the time of the removal of such product therefrom children under the age of sixteen years have been employed or permitted to work, or any article or commodity the product of any mill, cannery, workshop, factory, or manufacturing establishment, situated in the United States, in which within thirty days prior to the removal of such product therefrom children under the age of fourteen years have been employed or permitted to work, or children between the ages of fourteen years and sixteen years have been employed or permitted to work more than eight hours in any day, or more than six days in any week, or after the hour of seven o'clock postmeridian, or before the hour of six o'clock antemeridian.[50]

Other provisions dealt with enforcement and penalties. Keating called his bill "a very conservative measure."[51] Many states had already enacted the age and hour restrictions contained in the bill, with some having tougher standards and others weaker. Ohio, for example, adopted a higher standard in 1913 by prohibiting males under fifteen and females under sixteen from being employed or forced to work in any factory, mill, workshop, or other establishments.[52] Years earlier, the American Bar Association recommended a uniform child labor law with a fourteen-year age limit for factories and canneries, an eight-hour day for children under sixteen, the prohibition of night work for children under sixteen, together with a sixteen-year age limit for employment in mines. Nineteen states had a sixteen-year age limit for work in mines or quarries, and all but three states—New Mexico, North Carolina, and Wyoming—set a fourteen-year age limit for work in factories, canneries, and mills. A number of states with a fourteen-year limit in factories exempted canneries or allowed children to plead poverty for an exemption to work. Nineteen states and the District of Columbia already had laws providing for an eight-hour day for children under sixteen. Congress recessed before action could be taken on the bill.

After Representative Keating reintroduced his bill in January 1916, the House Labor Committee conducted a study on child labor, cotton mills, and interstate commerce. Hearings were held over three days, from January 10 to 12, and the committee issued its report on January 17, 1916. The report described child labor as "a national evil" that required federal regulation.[53] While acknowledging that many laws should vary according to local conditions, child labor was an exception because the protection of children was essential to civilization itself. "The evidence is overwhelming," the report stated, "that unregulated child labor does not promote a healthy citizenship; that it tends to the deterioration of the race physically; to the dwarfing of children mentally through the denial of a full opportunity for education; and to criminality, since the statistics of our juvenile courts show that the largest percentage of juvenile delinquents are children who are put to work too soon."[54] The report concluded that the standards of ages and hours established in H.R. 8234 were "just and reasonable" and that "Congress should deny the instrumentalities of commerce to enterprises which seek to disregard them to the detriment of the public welfare." It was a far cry from the House report ten years earlier that denounced the constitutionality of the Beveridge-Parsons bill.

In testimony before the House Committee on Labor, Governor William W. Kitchin of North Carolina, representing the Southern Cotton Manufacturers, remarked that "no one could contend that a piece of cloth manufactured by the labor of little children was not pure, not good, and not sound, and therefore that it could not be considered an outlaw of commerce."[55] Many in the room noticed that Alexander J. McKelway, secretary of the National Child Labor Committee, in a sign of disagreement, shook his head at the governor. As a pastor in a community with cotton mills, McKelway had witnessed the debilitating effects of labor on children for many years. He recalled his first appearance before the North Carolina legislature in support of child labor restrictions as a representative of the NCLC. He told the story of a twelve-year-old boy who had worked in the mills for six years, twelve hours a day, and had been robbed of his childhood, education, and physical development. When he came before the Labor Committee, McKelway responded to the governor's comment with indignation: "Can you not forgive me, with the experience I have had, if I do not regard that piece of cloth manufactured by those little hands as pure and good and sound, but as impure, as bad, and unsound, in itself—as in a sense stained by the blood of little children?"[56]

The Senate Committee on Interstate Commerce issued a report on the child labor bill on April 19. Investigating the issue of unfair competition, the committee described the problem from a state and consumer perspective: "So long as there is a single state which, for selfish or other reasons, fails to enact effective child labor legislation, it is beyond the power of every other state to protect effectively its own producers and manufacturers of that state, or to protect its consumers against unwittingly patronizing those who exploit the childhood of the country."[57] In a statement for the committee, McKelway of the NCLC argued that consumers should be protected from unknowingly aiding those who profit from child labor. "No microscope will tell whether a piece of cotton has been manufactured by adult labor or by child labor," he explained.[58] McKelway demanded that the federal government protect consumers from partnership with the exploiters of child labor.

While most congressmen agreed that child labor was an evil that needed to be regulated and restricted, sectional differences, as they would for the next twenty-five years on the issue of federal child labor legislation, influenced the debate over the scope of the problem and proper remedy. The chief opposition to the Keating-Owen Child Labor Bill came from several Democratic senators and representatives from southern states. Senator Thomas Hardwick of Georgia viewed the bill as a product of the commercial rivalry between North and South. He condemned the law as an attempt to equalize labor conditions to the detriment of the South's emerging industry.[59] The control of child labor abuses, he contended, was entirely within the power of the states and not in the federal government. Hardwick believed that the Democratic Party was making a serious mistake in advocating such legislation. "I not only regret it," he said of the party's position, "but I am ashamed of it."[60] Representative Edwin Yates Webb from North Carolina specifically blamed New England states. The demand for a uniform child labor law, he asserted, was simply a pretext for New England interests "to foist upon the mills of the South the same labor laws and troubles that they experienced in New England and thereby lessen competition with them."[61] Senator Ellison DuRant "Cotton Ed" Smith of South Carolina, a segregationist who fought most Progressive economic legislation and who was the strongest opponent of the Child Labor Bill, threatened to filibuster the entire legislative program of the session after President Wilson met with several intransigent Democratic senators and urged immediate action on the bill.[62]

The only other speaker against the bill who was not connected in some way to the southern textile mills was James Emery, corporation counsel for the National Association of Manufacturers (NAM). Emery acknowledged that NAM had at no time been opposed to the regulation of child labor, but he argued against the bill anyway on the grounds of states' rights and the right of an individual to local self-government. He claimed that because few people under sixteen were employed in the four thousand manufacturing establishments represented by the association, his members would be "little affected by the bill."[63] Still, Emery argued, there wasn't a manufacturer or citizen who would not be seriously affected by the principle of control contemplated by the bill. Emery explained that the regulation of child labor, like many issues within the police power of the states, is a subject requiring knowledge of many different local conditions. It is a problem, he believed, that cannot be solved by a uniform national law. Emery viewed the bill as a "regulation of production under the guise of regulating commerce."[64] Production falls within intrastate commerce, not interstate, Emery contended, and it is a matter that should be left to the states.

Republican senator William Borah of Idaho vigorously defended the constitutionality of the measure. Taking his cue from former Senator Beveridge, Borah argued that the power of Congress was "so complete and so wide that it could apply the interstate principle to any moral question that it might see fit to control."[65] Democratic senator Paul Husting of Wisconsin brushed aside the constitutional objections to the Child Labor Bill. "The opposition to the bill," he suggested, "was hiding behind the Constitution in order to avoid doing something that humanity demanded."[66] Representative Keating called this position "constitutionitis"— a disease that develops in a member of Congress when some good cause is before the legislature and he or she has not the nerve to openly oppose it.[67] Republican senator John D. Works of California believed the bill was unconstitutional, but stated that he would vote for it so that the Supreme Court could determine the question once and for all. He recalled his years as a child laborer and admitted that he had never recovered from the hard work he did as a boy. He remembered sleeping in a dark room and how he would suddenly be awakened from a deep sleep at 4:00 a.m., "often with his muscles so stiff that he could not walk without pain."[68]

World War I, which by 1916 had been devastating Europe and parts of the globe for almost three years, was in the background as Congress debated child labor. Representative Keating even suggested that his bill, which would take children out of industry at an early age, was an important first step in national preparation for war. He cited an editorial in a New York newspaper, which reported that of the 168,000 who attempted to enlist in the army, only about 40,000 could pass the physical test.[69] Keating implied that the prevalence of child labor stunted the nation's physical and mental development. Senator Beveridge had made a similar argument a decade earlier regarding Great Britain and the Boer War. Whether a valid argument or not, the US Senate formally declared war on Germany on April 4, 1917, with the House following two days later, and the country and its military were not well prepared for hostilities.

President Wilson's July decision to intervene in the congressional debate, several months before the election, was an abrupt shift in his position of public silence on national child labor legislation. The House of Representatives had passed the bill on February 2 by a wide margin. Several Democratic senators, however, blocked action on the legislation. After Wilson visited the Capitol on July 18, the southern Democratic senators yielded and the Senate approved the bill on August 8, 1916. What prompted President Wilson to declare his support for the Child Labor Bill and pressure the wayward Democrats to allow a vote? The press debated whether it was party politics or the interests of humanity. Wilson's biographer, Arthur Link, argued that his motivations were purely political.[70] Facing reelection, Wilson needed progressive and labor support. Other scholars argue that Wilson's position evolved between 1913, when he refused to publicly support federal child labor legislation at the Hoboken conference, and 1916, when he publicly supported the Keating-Owen Act. During the Progressive period, public opinion and demands shifted in favor of national legislation to curb the excesses of industrial capitalism. Wilson's political thought was flexible enough to acknowledge the changes and modify his position. Recent scholarship suggests that Wilson was influenced by the constitutional arguments of the NCLC, at least to allow the courts to decide on the constitutionality issue, and that his decision to support a federal child labor law was a product of both "political need and principled decision-making."[71] Regardless of the president's motives, the press noted that his decision to intervene had broad support across the country. The *New Orleans Times-Picayune* described any further delay in passing the measure as "absurd" because "in only three States is the measure seriously opposed—the two Carolinas and Georgia, with some little opposition in Mississippi."[72]

Because of differences between the House and Senate versions, a conference committee worked out a compromise. Congress passed the Keating-Owen Act on September 1, 1916, with the law becoming operative one year later. The final vote in the House was 337 to 46 in favor and the Senate voted 52 to 12 in favor. Where the Republicans had failed a decade earlier, a Democratic Congress and president had enacted progressive legislation on child labor. A milestone had been reached in the House—only 45 out of 150 representatives of southern states voted against the bill.[73] Ten southern Democratic senators and two Republicans from Pennsylvania, a state with one of the highest rates of child labor, voted against the measure. Although he had voted against the Keating-Owen bill because he believed it was a dangerous encroachment on states' rights, Senator Tillman of South Carolina expressed disgust at the attitudes of some of the mill owners. "The quibbling and selfishness of the cotton-mill owners," he admitted, almost drove him to vote for the bill. Tillman was shocked to witness "men in South Carolina—rich, intelligent, well-educated men—who were willing to swell their dividends at the expense of little children."[74]

Although he deserved some credit for his late lobbying efforts on behalf of the bill, the president acknowledged the many years that social reformers had worked toward the goal of national legislation. President Wilson remarked: "I want to say that with real emotion I sign this bill because I know how long the struggle has been to secure legislation of this sort and what it is going to mean to the health and to the vigor of the country, and also to the happiness of those whom it affects."[75] Albert J. Beveridge was long gone from the Senate chamber, but his contribution was recognized. President Wilson gave the pen that he used to sign the law to the chief lobbyist for the NCLC, who presented it to Beveridge in recognition of his early campaign for child labor reform and constitutional arguments made in defense of federal legislation.

In an attempt to regulate child labor indirectly under Article 1, Section 10 authority to regulate commerce between the states, the Keating-Owen Act prohibited producers and manufacturers from shipping in interstate commerce any product, in which thirty days prior to the removal of such product, was made by children under fourteen, or merchandise that had been made in factories, mills, canneries, or manufacturing establishments where children between fourteen and sixteen had been permitted to work more than eight hours a day, six days a week, or at night. The secretary of labor was authorized to enter and inspect any establishment defined by the statute to determine violations of the law. Enforcement of the law was delegated to the Child Labor Division of the Children's Bureau, headed by Grace Abbott. A fine of $200 was imposed for each violation prior to a first offense and not more than $1,000 for subsequent violations, or imprisonment for not more than three months.

Some in the media doubted whether the act would be effective or constitutional. The *Philadelphia Inquirer* suggested the law does the right thing in the wrong way. The restriction on child labor, it noted, was the "kind of reform which every State ought to look after on its own account."[76] The *New York Globe* identified two significant hurdles that had to be jumped. The expansion of federal power under the Commerce Clause was, the paper claimed, "a matter of grave doubt." The editors also pointed to a potential implementation flaw. A factory might keep its child labor products for more than thirty days, then sell them to a buyer within the state who could then ship them in interstate commerce. Others, however, were certain that the law was a valid exercise of congressional power. The *St. Louis Republic*, for example, declared that the law "will stand the acid test of the courts."[77] That litmus test was soon to come.

The Keating-Owen Act was in force for nine months and being effectively implemented before the Supreme Court declared it unconstitutional. The Children's Bureau worked cooperatively with state commissioners and factory inspectors to enforce the law. During the nine-month period, 689 establishments were inspected in twenty-four states and the District of Columbia, and 28 mines were inspected in four states. The Children's Bureau found violations of the law in 293 of the 689 mills, factories, and other establishments, where 385 children under fourteen years of age were employed. Close to one thousand children were discovered working more than eight hours a day.[78] The bureau also reported an increase in children attending school.

Roland H. Dagenhart, who worked in a cotton mill in Charlotte, North Carolina, with his two sons, ages thirteen and fifteen, challenged the Keating-Owen Act with the support of the Executive Committee of Southern Cotton Manufacturers. Under state law, both of Dagenhart's sons were permitted to work as much as eleven hours a day. Court records indicate that Roland Dagenhart was a "man of small means" whose family needed the compensation from the work of the two boys.[79] Under the Keating-Owen Act, however, the older boy was limited to working only eight hours, and his younger brother could not work at all. William C. Hammer, US attorney for the western district of North Carolina, charged the Fidelity Manufacturing Company with violations of the Keating-Owen Act. In an unwritten opinion, US District Court judge James E. Boyd ruled the law unconstitutional because Congress cannot indirectly regulate "the internal conditions of labor."[80] Like many southerners, Boyd, a former private in the Confederate army who carried General Robert E. Lee's surrender to General Ulysses S. Grant, was a strong supporter of states' rights. Despite the ruling, government officials remained optimistic that the Supreme Court would affirm the law. Representative Keating said that the adverse decision "was not unexpected," and he was confident the law would be upheld "when Justice Brandeis and his associates get hold of Judge Boyd's economic deterministic decision."[81]

In defense of the child labor law, the US government argued that the statute fell within congressional authority to regulate interstate and foreign commerce. The Commerce Clause, it claimed, played a vital part in the history of the Constitution and nation because it addressed one of the worst evils of the government under the Articles of Confederation—conflicting commercial regulations of the various states. Citing *Gibbons v. Ogden*, the government's brief asserted that the power conferred on Congress was plenary and embraced all the power the states previously held. Regulation of the products moving in interstate commerce had been upheld by the Court in several areas. In an attempt to distinguish *United States v. E. C. Knight Co.*, where the Court struck down the application of the Sherman Anti-Trust Act to sugar refining, the government noted that the child labor law does not apply to manufacturing which stays within one state. Any manufacturer may employ children as long as the products of that labor remain within a state. Only when a manufacturer transports goods made by children to another state does the law take force.

Congress, the government argued, has the power to prevent the evil of child labor that attends such commerce.[82] Child labor, "once regarded as harmless or beneficial, had come to be regarded as immoral and injurious."[83] The government stated that a change in public opinion regarding child labor had occurred, just like the social value of lottery tickets. Admittedly, the transformation of child labor from a righteous social benefit to an unrighteous social evil took decades. The government reviewed the long history of child labor regulation, starting with the first child labor law enacted by Connecticut in 1813 and continuing through the Industrial Revolution.[84] Working around machinery, night work, and excessive hours all had a deleterious effect on a child's physical development and well-being by stunting growth and decreasing resistance to disease. States, the government acknowledged, had criminal statutes against child labor, but they were not uniform and many did not meet the due standard necessary for the protection of children. As the conviction grew that child labor was socially undesirable, it came to be viewed as an unfair discrimination in interstate commerce.

Lawyers for Dagenhart argued that Congress did not have the power under the Commerce Clause to regulate child labor. Congress, they claimed, was attempting to regulate labor conditions *prior* to transportation, rather than the actual transportation of products across state lines. Moreover, any consequences of child labor involved local conditions, and the regulation of intrastate commerce was reserved to the states under the Tenth Amendment. Congress, they contended, had no authority in this area.

In *Hammer v. Dagenhart*, decided June 3, 1918, Justice William Rufus Day, joined by Chief Justice Edward Douglas White and Justices Mahlon Pitney, Willis Van Devanter, and James Clark McReynolds, wrote that Congress lacked the authority to regulate commerce of goods manufactured by children and, therefore, the Keating-Owen Act was unconstitutional. Justice Day distinguished previous cases where the Court upheld federal attempts to control lotteries, impure food and drugs, prostitution, and intoxicating liquors by arguing that the manufacture of cotton was not a moral evil. In *Champion v. Ames*, the Court held that Congress can pass a law keeping the channels of commerce free from the flow of lottery tickets. In *Hippolite Egg Company v. United States*, the Court upheld the Pure Food and Drug Act, which prohibited the introduction in interstate commerce of impure foods and drugs, in this case adulterated eggs containing boric acid. In *Hoke v. United States*, the Court sustained the constitutionality of the Mann Act, known as the White Slave Traffic Act, where the transportation of women in interstate commerce for purposes of prostitution, debauchery, or any other immoral purpose was prohibited. And in *Clark Distilling Co. v. Western Maryland Railway Co.*, the power of Congress over the interstate transportation of intoxicating liquors was affirmed. In each of these areas, the Court noted, the use of interstate transportation was necessary to accomplish harmful results. The regulation of interstate commerce was required to prohibit the intended evil. According to Day, that "element is wanting in the present case" because "the goods shipped, are of themselves, harmless."[85] The key to distinguishing the precedents was a focus on the character of the goods.

Moreover, it was argued, the regulation of child labor within states is purely a state authority. Production of goods precedes interstate commerce and is a matter for local regulation. There is no power vested in Congress, Justice Day claimed, to force the states to exercise their police powers to prevent unfair competition. He used the Tenth Amendment to support his argument, although he misquoted the provision with regard to powers delegated to Congress. Under the Tenth Amendment, he argued, the powers "not expressly delegated to the National Government are reserved" to the states and to the people.[86] Justice Day's interpretation was historically inaccurate because James Madison and others rejected a motion to insert the word "expressly" in the language of the amendment.[87] Justice Day warned that to allow Congress such authority would end "all freedom of commerce" and eliminate the power of the states over local matters and thus "our system of government [would] be practically destroyed."[88] The majority reasoning was based on the same concept of dual federalism that over a decade earlier had helped defeat the Beveridge bill. Having decided the case on Commerce Clause and Tenth Amendment grounds, Justice Day did not consider the due process question.

Reading his dissent from the bench, Justice Oliver Wendell Holmes, joined by Justices Joseph McKenna, Louis Brandeis, and John H. Clarke, argued that the Keating-Owen Act was clearly within Congress's constitutional power. The law did not preempt state authority to regulate child labor within a state. Congress can regulate commerce that crosses state lines even though it may have an indirect effect upon the activities of the states. "It does not matter," he said, "whether the supposed evil precedes or follows the transportation."[89] Justice Holmes viewed child labor as a proper subject for congressional regulation:

> The notion that prohibition is any less prohibition when applied to things now thought evil I do not understand. But if there is any matter upon which civilized countries have agreed—far more unanimously than they have with regard to intoxicants and some other matters over which this country is now emotionally aroused—it is the evil of premature and excessive child labor. I should have thought that, if we were to introduce our own moral conceptions where in my opinion they do not belong, this was preeminently a case for upholding the exercise of all its powers by the United States.[90]

Justice Holmes did not believe that the Tenth Amendment restricted congressional power over interstate commerce. In previous cases, the effect upon state policy of an exercise of delegated power was held to be immaterial. "The act does not meddle with anything belonging to the States," he argued. They can regulate their internal affairs and commerce as they desire, but when "they seek to send their products across the state line, they are no longer within their rights."[91] Holmes concluded that the "public policy of the United States is shaped with a view to the benefit of the nation as a whole," and Congress may enforce its policy by all means at its command.

Ironically, President Woodrow Wilson, who strongly supported the

Keating-Owen Act, contributed to its demise. Wilson had appointed Brandeis and Clarke, but he also nominated his attorney general, James Clark McReynolds, to the Supreme Court in August 1914. At the time, Secretary of the Interior Franklin K. Lane was the frontrunner for the vacancy. Lane's political views were liberal, and if he had been appointed by President Wilson, he probably would have provided the fifth vote in *Hammer* to uphold the Keating-Owen Act and child labor reform would have a different historical narrative. The president, however, had lost his patience with McReynolds, whose personal prejudices and poor relationship with Congress caused tensions within the Wilson cabinet. The president promoted McReynolds to the Supreme Court unaware that he would become one of the staunchest economic conservatives on the Court for decades.

Conservatives and various media applauded the decision as a victory for states' rights and limited federal power. The *New York Times* reported that the Court's decision "caused the utmost surprise" and disappointed those who worked for nearly fifteen years to pass federal child labor legislation.[92] But in a separate editorial, the *Times*, consistent with its opposition to federal child labor legislation, supported the *Hammer v. Dagenhart* decision. It noted that when there are forty-eight varieties of temperance and state child labor laws, there is such a "wide variance of opinion that it would not be right for intolerant opinion on those subjects to impose its will upon others equally entitled to their opinions." The paper asserted that "there is a national danger in forcing Federal regulation upon States in advance of public opinion in each of them."[93] The *Chicago Tribune* also agreed with Justice Day's reasoning in the case. There is a clear difference, the editors noted, between shipping lottery tickets, circulars, and other gambling materials into another state and prohibiting products made with child labor. Lottery material may corrupt the morals of citizens in the state of destination, but buying cotton products made with child labor, the editors asserted, does not have the same corrupting influence.

Other publications voiced their disapproval of the opinion. An editorial in *Life* magazine dripped with sarcasm in its criticism of the decision:

> Heretofore, the little ones have tremblingly gone to work in the early morning, not knowing at what moment their jobs might be taken from them by means of a restraining injunction; but that fear need worry them no longer. From now on the little tots may rise at daybreak, openly and fearlessly carry their tiny lunch-boxes to the mill with them, and, during the noon-hour ponder on the realization that it is their

legal privilege to spend their tender and immature years in pursuit of the ultimate misery that inevitably follows in the wake of abused childhood.[94]

The scathing critique depicted a Court completely out of touch with the problem of child labor.

Many leading law journals published criticisms of the majority opinion in *Hammer*. Writing in the *Harvard Law Review*, Thurlow M. Gordon pointed out that the majority opinion ignored precedents under the Sherman Anti-Trust Act that allowed Congress to prohibit the transportation across state lines of trust-made goods. Like the cotton products made with child labor, trust-made goods are not inherently evil, yet the Court validated the Anti-Trust Act. Gordon argued that if "in the distribution of powers between state and nation a large part of the power to regulate commerce has been lost, a weakness in the federal system hitherto unsuspected is developed."[95] Whether or not a commodity works an evil is largely a matter of opinion, and Congress concluded that interstate shipment of goods made with child labor was an evil. Finally, Gordon argued that contrary to Justice Day's description, "the products of child labor are not harmless and there is a definite evil in their very transportation across state lines."[96] The movement of child-made goods harms the lives of young citizens in the state of production and tends to lower the standards of child labor protection in states of destination. Tougher state child labor laws were often defeated with the protest that the "unfair competition" of other states would be ruinous for local business. The Child Labor Law simply tried to level the playing field.

In the *California Law Review*, William Carey Jones criticized Justice Day's reading of precedents involving congressional power under the Commerce Clause. Jones argued that the plenary nature of the power delegated to the federal government had been emphasized numerous times since the founding. Justice McKenna wrote in *Hoke v. United States* about the commerce power: "The power is direct; there is no word of limitation in it and its broad and universal scope has been so often declared as to make repetition unnecessary, and besides, it has had so much illustration by cases that it would seem as if there could be no instance of its exercise that does not find an admitted example."[97] Jones also argued that it is wrong to conclude that Congress can only look to the protection of the receiving or consuming state. As Justice Holmes emphasized, the national welfare is protected by such regulation. Finally, Jones suggested that the Court should have granted more deference to Congress before striking down a law by a one-vote majority.

Reformers and liberals denounced the opinion in *Hammer v. Dagenhart*, and some responded with attacks on the Court's power of judicial review. Senator Robert Owen, cosponsor of the invalidated law, introduced legislation a week after the decision that proposed to take away the authority of any court, including the Supreme Court, to hear questions involving the child labor law. Under the Exceptions Clause, Congress does have the power to narrow the appellate jurisdiction of the federal courts, but it has rarely been exercised.[98] The *New York Times* characterized Owen's proposal as an attempt to abolish the Supreme Court and argued that federal child labor regulation was not so imperative that the framework of our government had to be destroyed to achieve it.[99] Father John A. Ryan, a leader in liberal Catholic social thought and supporter of child labor reform, also believed that Owen's attack was extreme and unnecessary.[100] A month later, Senator Owen advocated the right of recall of Supreme Court justices to prevent them from legislating from the bench.[101] His proposals, however, did not gain much support.

Following the *Hammer* decision, Representative Keating and Senator William S. Kenyon (R-IA) announced that they would seek a new law or an amendment to the Constitution to regulate child labor.[102] Keating suggested that Congress might tax goods from factories that employed children. The idea of using the taxing power had support among many in the legislature, and Congress soon debated the issue.

Taxing Profits of Companies Using Child Labor

BAILEY v. DREXEL FURNITURE COMPANY

The immediate impact of the *Hammer v. Dagenhart* decision did not fall evenly across America. Child workers in states with standards comparable or higher to federal law noticed little change, provided that state laws were enforced. States with child labor standards lower than those contained in the Keating-Owen Act, however, saw the swift restoration of long hours for children under sixteen, an increase in the number of working children, and a significant rise in the violation of state laws. For example, when the Keating-Owen Act was in force from September 1, 1917, through June 3, 1918, inspectors for the Children's Bureau visited forty-nine factories in one state and found only ninety-five children under fourteen at work. After the law was declared invalid, inspectors discovered that forty-seven out of fifty-three factories visited were violating state law by employing children under twelve.[1] Similar violations were found in canneries and other industries. In one state where the minimum age for employment in canneries was fourteen, inspectors discovered 721 children under that age in 205 different canneries, including over 50 who were not even ten years old.[2] It was as if the *Hammer* decision had given employers a green light to openly violate child labor laws during wartime.

A year before the United States entered World War I, child labor increased in response to labor needs from industries filling contracts for belligerent nations. After the declaration of war on April 6, 1917, the problem became more acute. Some children were drawn to industrial work by patriotic appeals or what the Children's Bureau described as "misplaced patriotism." Employers wanted to keep production costs low, but a labor shortage also contributed to the wartime increase in child employment, and high wages enticed thousands of children away from their school desks and into the factories. In some establishments, children were earning $15 a week, more than double the pay before the war.[3] According to the Children's Bureau, Massachusetts, North Carolina, Washington, and other states reported significant increases in applications for work certificates, some for children twelve and thirteen years old who sought poverty permits. In Washington, for example, applications for work permits increased 295 percent over the previous two years. Reform groups and concerned communities responded to the spate of wartime child employment with stay-in-school and back-to-school campaigns during the celebration of the Children's Year, a program created by the Children's Bureau to highlight child welfare issues. Forty-five states, the District of Columbia, and Hawaii participated in encouraging children to remain in school or return to school after the war. In some agricultural communities, few laws reached boys under sixteen working long hours on commercial farms. During the summer of 1918, various states and towns celebrated a "Patriotic Play Week" by giving child workers a chance to rest and play. Such programs, however, provided little relief.[4]

In a letter to the National Child Labor Committee, President Woodrow Wilson expressed his concern for protecting children from industrial employment, and he applauded the committee's vigilance on the issue. "As the labor situation created by the war develops," Wilson wrote, "I am more interested than ever, if that were possible, in throwing all the safeguards possible around the labor of women and children in order that no intolerable or injurious burden may be placed upon them."[5] Wilson told the committee that its efforts on behalf of children were "contributing to the efficiency and economy of production, as well as to the preservation of life and health." During the war, the NCLC urged supporters to oppose any attempts to weaken compulsory school attendance laws or cut funds for public education. Members also were told to fight any attempts to break down state child labor laws by giving children special permits to work or exempting industries from laws limiting work hours. Finally, friends of child labor protections were encouraged to support local and national agencies including recreation centers, health boards, settlement houses, and juvenile protective associations.

Recognizing the seriousness in the spike in child labor, the War Labor Policies Board, chaired by Felix Frankfurter, a Harvard-trained lawyer who had an established reputation as a social reformer, announced on July 12, 1918, that as a national policy, contractors doing work for any government departments should not directly or indirectly employ child labor contrary to provisions contained in the Keating-Owen Act, which had just been declared unconstitutional. The policy was inserted in provisions of all federal government contracts by mid-September, and the secretary of labor was given responsibility for enforcement. Most industries complied with the child labor restrictions, although some simply ignored the policy or refused government contracts.[6] The NCLC noted that the board ruling was widely accepted by manufacturers except for one sector. The American Cotton Manufacturers' Association (ACMA) protested the ruling on the basis that the board was "exceeding its power of jurisdiction in arbitrarily fixing labor standards which Congress itself is unable to do."[7] The ACMA took special exception to the eight-hour limitation on work hours for children. By adopting the provisions of the Keating-Owen Act, at least temporarily for the duration of the war, child labor could be restricted. Granted, the policy applied only to companies doing business with the federal government, but it did have the force of a national regulation and it symbolized the government's disapproval of industries that used child labor.

Meanwhile, multiple bills introduced in Congress that summer approached the child labor problem from different angles. Senator Kenyon submitted a bill on June 19 that would deny use of the mails to persons or establishments who employed child laborers in violation of national standards. Upon certification by inspectors from the Department of Labor that an offense occurred, postal authorities were to return all mail addressed to the offending company.[8] Senator Atlee Pomerene, a pro-Wilson Democrat from Ohio, introduced two bills in late June. The first one stripped products made by child labor of their interstate character so that state laws banning their sale would not violate the power of Congress to regulate commerce between the states. Based on the principle of the Webb-Kenyon law, which restricted interstate shipments of intoxicating liquors by subjecting them to state laws of destination, the Pomerene bill required states to pass legislation prohibiting articles made with child labor from being sold within the state. Not all states were likely to pass such laws, and enforcing the restrictions would be complicated. The second bill imposed a tax on articles made with child labor. Other proposals involved having the federal railroad administration refuse the use of railroad facilities under government control to employers of child labor, and there were several constitutional amendments introduced to overturn *Hammer v. Dagenhart* by giving Congress an enumerated power to regulate child labor.

A few days after the *Hammer* decision, the NCLC Board of Trustees met in emergency session and formed a special committee "to outline a course of action in connection with Federal legislation."[9] The coordinating committee consisted of two trustees, William Draper Lewis and Charles P. Neill, who had been influential in drafting the Keating-Owen Act; Dr. Samuel McCune Lindsay; and V. Everit Macy, a longtime board member. The special committee first contacted representatives of the Children's Bureau, National Consumers' League, and American Federation of Labor, in addition to friendly members of Congress—Senators Kenyon and Pomerene and Representative Keating. All of the key players and organizations responsible for the first child labor law were part of the alliance seeking new legislation. Two goals were quickly agreed upon: the need to find some immediate federal protection for all those children who were no longer covered by Keating-Owen and drafting a more permanent alternative.

Representative Keating himself introduced a bill in the House on August 15, 1918, that placed the same restrictions as to age and working hours as were contained in the Keating-Owen law. A key difference was that references to interstate shipment of goods were replaced with a direct ban on child labor, based on state child labor laws. The new bill was justified under broad congressional war powers to conserve "the manpower of the nation and thereby more effectually providing for the national security and defense."[10] If enacted, the Keating bill would be effective for the duration of the war and six months thereafter. It had the support of President Wilson, the National Child Labor Committee, and the American Federation of Labor. The NCLC stated: "The country does not need the children in the mines, factories, and shops. They are more valuable to the Nation in school. We can win the war without sacrificing the present and future interest of our children."[11] The House Committee on Labor favorably reported the bill on November 6 by a 5 to 3 vote. The three no votes, representing southern districts, doubted whether Congress had the power to pass such a bill. World War I officially ended, however, on November 11, 1918, so the child labor restrictions of the War Policies Board were in place for only a few months, and Congress did not vote on the new Keating bill.

In the months following the *Hammer* decision, opponents of child labor searched for a new strategy. At the urging of the secretary of labor, the chief of the Children's Bureau, Julia Lathrop, called a conference to discuss options for more permanent child labor legislation. On August 21, 1918, representatives from the American Federation of Labor, National Child Labor Committee, Women's Trade Union League, National Consumers' League, and various government officials who were responsible for enforcing the Keating-Owen Act met to draft a new child labor bill. The committee had decided early on not to seek a constitutional amendment but to find some path under the enumerated powers of Congress and Supreme Court precedents. The Kenyon postal bill was promptly rejected because there were too many questions over using the postal service as a federal police power and implementation would be difficult.[12] Several of the pending tax bills were also found unsatisfactory. After numerous meetings and discussions, the group coalesced around a plan to levy an excise tax upon the products of any mill, cannery, workshop, factory, or manufacturing establishment in which children under the age of fourteen were employed, or children between fourteen and sixteen years had worked more than eight hours in any day, or more than six days a week.[13] President Wilson approved the proposed legislation, and it was submitted to Senator Pomerene with the recommendation that it be attached to a pending revenue bill.

Senators Pomerene, Irvine Lenroot of Wisconsin, and William Kenyon of Iowa jointly revised the bill, without first consulting or notifying the National Child Labor Committee or the Children's Bureau, and asked that it be referred to the Finance Committee and attached to an $8 billion revenue bill. The senators made two major changes. They imposed an excise tax upon the net income of an establishment using child labor in violation of the state provisions rather than on products, and responsibility for enforcement was given to the commissioner of internal revenue, instead of the Labor Department. The minimum age and hour restrictions remained the same as the draft prepared by the reformers. But it was the second revision that troubled child labor groups. They preferred to place enforcement of the tax measure in the hands of the Child Labor Division of the Children's Bureau, which had managed the implementation of the Keating-Owen Act. Reformers worried about giving responsibility for enforcement to a potentially unfriendly or disinterested agency in the Internal Revenue Bureau.[14] However, the three senators explained their strategy. If enforcement were placed with the Department of Labor, the Supreme Court might view the law as just another child labor regulation disguised as a revenue measure. Assigning responsibility for implementation with the commissioner of internal revenue strengthened the argument that the bill was a legitimate use of congressional taxing authority to generate revenue. After receiving assurance from the senators that the Treasury Department would seek the assistance of the Child Labor Division to administer the law, Owen R. Lovejoy lined up endorsements for the Pomerene amendment.

Several examples of congressional taxing power and Supreme Court precedents seemed to furnish constitutional authority for Congress to impose the tax. In *McCray v. United States* (1904), the Supreme Court upheld a 1902 amendment to the Oleomargarine Act of 1886.[15] Oleomargarine was developed in the 1870s as a cheap substitute for butter. The margarine, naturally white in color, was dyed a buttery yellow to make it more appealing to consumers. Dairy farmers recognized the threat to their industry and successfully lobbied the states and eventually Congress to impose a tax on oleomargarine.[16] When *McCray* was argued before the Court, government lawyers admitted that the law was designed to drive oleomargarine out of the market, and there was no justification as a health measure because colored oleomargarine is no more dangerous than uncolored oleomargarine.[17] Although the tax placed a significant burden on the manufacture of oleomargarine, the Court held that it had no power to inquire into the purpose or effect of the law, even if the result was regulation or prohibition of practices constitutionally left to state regulation. Congress acted under its taxing authority, and the Court assumed that the purpose of the law was to raise revenue. Any prohibitive or regulatory effects of the tax were merely incidental to that purpose.[18] Supporters of the Pomerene amendment firmly believed that this doctrine of "judicial impotence" could not survive if the Court struck down their tax measure.

Another prohibitive excise tax used to defend the child labor tax was imposed on poisonous phosphorus matches. In 1910, the Bureau of Labor published a study by Irene Osgood and John Andrews of the American Association for Labor Legislation on phosphorus necrosis, known among workers as "phossy jaw," a terribly disfiguring, sometimes fatal disease of the teeth and jawbone suffered by employees in the white phosphorus match industry. The disease was so horrendously visible that President Taft mentioned it in his 1910 State of the Union address. Shocked by the study, Congress passed the Match Act (Esch-Hughes Act) in 1912, which placed such a high tax on phosphorus matches that it almost destroyed the industry until a safer alternative was found. Although the Supreme Court did not rule on the constitutionality of the law, the Match Tax was a clear example of Congress imposing a regulatory tax with no intention to raise revenue.

In another tax case, *Veazie Bank v. Fenno* (1869), the Court ruled that a high congressional tax on state bank notes being used as money, which destroyed their circulation, was constitutional.[19] The decision was based on two arguments: (1) the power to tax is subject to no limitation which the courts will enforce and that only the electorate and ballot box constrain the congressional power; and (2) the tax was appropriate to aid legislation aimed at securing a sound national currency. Because the *Veazie* decision was based not only on the power to tax, but also on congressional power to regulate currency, it had less application to the child labor tax. Congress also imposed a federal tax on narcotic drugs, such as opium and cocoa leaves, and provided for an elaborate regulatory regime for the sale and use of narcotics in the Harrison Narcotics Tax Act of 1914. The Supreme Court reviewed the law while Congress debated the Pomerene amendment. A closely divided Supreme Court upheld the tax in *United States v. Doremus* (1919). Justice Day affirmed the tax measure and national regulatory scheme over substances that states were not adequately controlling. Day attempted to find a nuanced position between broad congressional taxing powers and the doctrine that purely intrastate matters were beyond congressional control. He reaffirmed the doctrine of judicial impotence: "The fact that other motives may impel the exercise of the federal taxing power does not authorize the courts to inquire into that subject. If the legislation enacted has some reasonable relation to the exercise of taxing authority conferred by the Constitution, it cannot be invalidated because of the supposed motives which induced it."[20] The decision was not announced until after Congress had passed the child labor tax, but it helped remove any doubts about the constitutionality of the Pomerene amendment. Reformers and many government officials were confident that if Congress could tax oleomargarine, phosphorous matches, state bank notes, and narcotic drugs, to the point of prohibiting such items from interstate commerce, profits on products made with child labor could be taxed as well.

The Senate Finance Committee favorably reported the child labor tax amendment as part of the revenue bill on December 10, 1918. Eight days later, the Senate adopted the amendment by a vote of 50–12, nearly the same margin (52–12) as the Keating-Owen bill two years earlier. Political alignments on the issue of federal child labor legislation showed little variation. Seven of the twelve "no" votes on the Pomerene amendment had also voted against the Keating-Owen Act. The vote comparisons illustrate broad, continuing support for taking federal action against child labor as opposed to leaving the matter to the states. Conservative Democrats from seven states represented all of the no votes. Eight of the no votes on the child labor tax were cast by senators from the four leading textile states—Alabama,

Georgia, North Carolina, and South Carolina. Other southern Democrats, however, voted for the measure. Senators Thomas W. Hardwick of Georgia and Lee Overman of North Carolina led the fight against the bill.

The outcome of the Pomerene child labor tax was never in doubt, as the measure had strong backing in both chambers. Opponents of the amendment questioned its constitutionality and alleged that its primary purpose was not to raise revenue but to respond to the adverse decision in *Hammer v. Dagenhart*. Their strategy was to "load" the *Congressional Record* with statements raising doubts about legislative intent, with an eye toward the Supreme Court.[21] Because the theory of judicial impotence announced in *McCray* was strong, the justices would need some rationale to circumvent the precedent. Suggesting that the child labor tax was an attempt to undermine the Court's power of judicial review over the Constitution was a shrewd strategy. The southerners who lined up against the Pomerene amendment knew that the Court would likely review the congressional debate surrounding the bill, and they attempted to make the justices' jobs easier.

Senator Hardwick, an ardent states' rights advocate, acknowledged that there were similarities between a tax on oleomargarine, upheld in the *McCray* case, and the child labor tax. What distinguished them, however, was that Congress was prevented from exercising the taxing power in a way that destroyed the right of states to regulate their own domestic and internal affairs, as the Supreme Court ruled in *Hammer v. Dagenhart*. Senator Hardwick attempted to shift the debate from the use of federal power to eliminate the evil of child labor to the constitutional obligation of Congress to respect Supreme Court precedent. He asked senators how, in good conscience, they could vote for a bill containing "the exact language of an outlawed proposition under the guise and pretext of raising revenue for the Government?" Senator Hardwick could not bring himself to participate in what he described as the "crime of violating the fundamental right involved under our form of government . . . that each state in this Republic has the right and the power, absolute and exclusive, to control for itself and according to its own will the conditions and terms of child employment or women employment or any other and all other domestic and internal affairs and concerns within that state."[22] For most senators, including Senator Frank B. Kellogg (R-MN), lawyer and former president of the American Bar Association, their conscience was not bothered. "It rests on the conscience of every Senator," Kellogg said, "whether he believes this proposed law is a legitimate exercise of legislative power, and whether it will accomplish the object he has in mind." The senator continued: "I, for one, believe I would not have a great deal of difficulty in satisfying my conscience on that score. . . . I believe that Congress and the states should throw around the child every protection they can to insure a strong and vigorous manhood. I do not consider this to be an invasion of the Constitution."[23]

Friends of the Pomerene amendment emphasized the *McCray* precedent and other examples of congressional taxing power. The tax was necessary, they argued, because the states failed to effectively address the problem of child labor. When Senator Pomerene spoke on the measure, he compared the oleomargarine tax to the child labor tax:

I am not able to distinguish between the tax on the profits derived from child labor and the tax on the profits derived from the manufacture of oleomargarine. It is a tax on profits. The tax on oleomargarine to a certain extent discourages the manufacture of oleomargarine, but that did not make it unconstitutional. The tax upon those men who employ child labor is but a tax upon one of the instrumentalities by which they coin their profits. Is there any legal distinction between the two? If so, I am not able to see it. I feel very confident that in view of the long line of decisions sustaining the taxing power in similar legislation, the court, when it comes to review this amendment, will sustain it.[24]

Senator Joseph France, a Maryland Republican, focused on the problem of illiteracy, which was clearly associated with child labor, especially as it related to preparedness for war. "We found when we made a census," the senator stated, "to see what available man power we had for carrying on this war, that among those of military age there were 700,000 who could neither read nor write, who were unprepared to understand the simplest written orders presented to them by a commanding officer."[25] Senator France asked if the federal government must stand around helpless while certain of the states may be allowing an illiteracy rate of nearly 20 percent to exist. Although it would take more than the child labor tax to significantly reduce illiteracy, the senator favored federal action to keep kids in school.

Unlike others who spoke in favor of the amendment, who were Progressive Democrats or Republicans, Senator Henry Cabot Lodge of Massachusetts was the leader of the conservative, northeastern wing of the Republican Party. He had been concerned about child labor for many years. "It is a great evil," the senator said. "The States have had ample and abundant opportunity to deal with it themselves. Most of the States have; some have not. I think it is something that ought to be ended." Senator Lodge took a utilitarian approach to the problem: "The amount of revenue to be raised by this measure may be little or nothing. The main purpose is to put a stop to what seems to be a very great evil, and one that ought to be in some way put a stop to. If we are unable to reach it constitutionally in any other way, than I am willing to reach it by the taxing power, which the Courts have held can be used constitutionally for such a purpose. I see no other way to do it."[26]

Senator Lodge defended the tax but acknowledged that it was an extreme method to address the evil of child labor. It was justified, however, because the police power of the states had failed to regulate it as it should be regulated. "I wish the states were more alive to their own rights and duties under the Constitution than they have proved themselves to be. But when they leave us after years with a very great evil like this, as I believe it to be, in existence, I think there is no choice left for Congress."[27] If Congress could not reach child labor constitutionally under the Commerce Clause, Senator Lodge was willing to use the taxing power to address the problem. He believed that there was a stronger constitutional and jurisprudential foundation for the child labor tax than there was for the oleomargarine legislation. Considering that the harm to the public health from oleomargarine was nonexistent compared to the damage to children and society caused by child labor, he probably had a point.

Senator Overman responded to Senator Lodge by challenging the purpose of the tax. Convinced that the goal of the provision was to nullify a decision of the Supreme Court, namely *Hammer v. Dagenhart*, Overman asked Senator Simmons, chairman of the Finance Committee, if the amendment was inserted for the purpose of raising revenue. Simmons replied that there was no estimate made on the amount of revenue the amendment might generate. In a testy exchange, Senator Overman claimed that Senator Lodge had stated that the tax was inserted to nullify the decision of the Supreme Court. Senator Lodge denied that he questioned the Court's decision. He explained that his goal was to "reach the same object[ive] in a constitutional way." Senator Overman asked if that wouldn't effectively overturn the decision. Lodge retorted that it "would nullify the practical effect of the decision, but not its legal validity." Paraphrasing Senator Lodge, the Tarheel senator insinuated that the Pomerene amendment was introduced to, "in effect," nullify a decision of the Supreme Court. Senator Ellison D. Smith of South Carolina suggested that Senator Lodge was unaware that every manufacturing state had recently passed progressive legislation on its own initiative, and that federal legislation was unnecessary. Lodge responded: "If the State has made adequate laws of course it will be in no wise affected by this legislation; it will interfere in no way with their industries or their economic policies; but if the evil does exist anywhere then this law will, in my judgment, be highly beneficial."[28]

The House of Representatives had passed its version of the bill before the war had ended, and there were numerous differences between the Senate and House versions. When the revenue bill went to a conference committee, reformers expected some hostility to the child labor provisions, but no significant opposition developed. In late December, Claude Kitchin of North Carolina, the House majority leader, publicly assured Keating and other progressives that conferees would accept the child labor amendment, as that was the "overwhelming sentiment" of the House. For opponents, the stage had already been set with the Senate floor debates. They lost the battle in the Senate but were pinning their hopes on litigation and a Supreme Court victory overturning the child labor tax. The only deliberation in the House of Representatives on the Pomerene amendment was a brief verbal scuffle on February 8, 1919, when the conference committee report was up for a vote. Representatives William Venable and Benjamin G. Humphreys, II, of Mississippi lashed out against the amendment, making the familiar claims that it violated states' rights and would destroy our system of constitutional government. "We all agree that it is an outrageous wrong to abuse the child in a factory," Venable said, but the Pomerene rider was "not an exercise of the taxing power in good faith" but "a subterfuge to exercise police powers that were never granted to the Federal government."[29] Representative Venable even managed to connect the tax to the Bolshevik Revolution in Russia and rising fear of socialism. He warned that if the states lose control over local affairs under the guise of taxation, "you can completely socialize the entire Government in a year."

In an hour-long exchange, supporters of the amendment frequently interrupted the two Mississippi representatives with questions, and Representative Warren Gard of Ohio briefly rebutted their arguments. "The public policy of the United States is shaped with a view to the benefit of the nation as a whole," Gard quoted from Justice Holmes's dissent in *Hammer v. Dagenhart*. He appealed to his House colleagues to vote their conscience: "We face not a question of unconstitutionality, but we face . . . the question of voting as our conscience demands. As we face the world, we are to vote now not on the question of what the Supreme Court will say, because the Congress has the right to enact this legislation, but we vote as our conscience dictates, and my conscience dictates that I vote for the salvation of American childhood."

In a last-ditch attempt to derail the measure, Venable moved to recommit the full report to the conference committee with instructions to the House managers to disagree on the child labor amendment. The motion was voted down 171 to 15. The final House vote on the conference report and Pomerene amendment was 312–11, an overwhelming margin. Shortly after returning from the Paris peace conference, President Wilson signed the Revenue Act of 1919, which at the time was described as "the greatest revenue bill in the history of nations," on February 24, 1919.[30] Title XII, Tax on Employment of Child Labor, commonly called the Child Labor Tax Law, was scheduled to take effect on April 25, 1919. Under the law, companies employing children under fourteen years of age would be assessed an excise tax of 10 percent on their annual profits. The law defined "child labor" as the use of minors "under the age of sixteen in any mine or quarry, and under the age of fourteen in any mill, cannery, workshop, factory, or manufacturing establishment." Additionally, the definition applied to the use of children in these age ranges for more than eight hours a day or six days a week, or during certain evening hours.

Most media reports favored the tax and suggested that its validity was not in doubt. The *New York World* editorialized that the "method of dealing with wrong otherwise invincible has been established in the case of State bank notes and imitation butter. As to its application to child labor we can see no objection except that the proposed Federal tax is too small."[31] The paper argued that 10 percent "on the value of the products of enslaved childhood is not enough to emancipate the youth of the South or to curb the greed of its employers."[32] In New Orleans, the *Times-Picayune* wrote that "there is a strong demand for a Federal child-labor law that will stand the test of the court," and the *Philadelphia Public Ledger* believed that the Senate's indirect method of dealing with the problem was "at least morally defensible." The editors called the tax "an attempt to whip the devil around the stump," and they acknowledged that Congress was using a revenue bill as a vehicle for social legislation. "Yet it is quite possible," the paper said, "that there is no constitutional obstacle to the use of the taxing power to discriminate against profits to which public sentiment as a whole is antagonistic."[33] The *El Paso Times* quoted Chief Justice John Marshall's famous dictum "the power to tax is the power to destroy" and then firmly advocated destruction because "it has been conclusively proved that a common result of child labor is unemployment and poverty later in life, with discontent and rebellion as their natural consequences."[34]

Although passage of the Child Labor Tax Law was secured without much resistance, problems arose during implementation. When appropriations for the three branches of the federal government were being debated, Senator Henry Cabot Lodge introduced an amendment to provide $184,000 to the secretary of labor to make inspections and perform other duties in assisting the commissioner of internal revenue with enforcement of the child labor sections of the revenue bill. Senator Hardwick objected to the appropriation on the grounds that the bill had not yet been signed. He was overruled by the chair, however, and the funds were provided to enforce the child labor tax. The appropriation bill had to go through a conference committee to work out differences between the House and Senate versions. At that point, the text of the Lodge amendment had been changed to effectively exclude the secretary of labor from participating in the implementation of the law. Under the revision, the commissioner of internal revenue had to ask for help from the Labor Department. No one knew if, or when, the commissioner would seek that assistance.[35]

The Children's Bureau held a four-day conference in Washington, DC, from May 5 to 8, 1919, on child welfare standards. Various children's health, education, economic, and employment issues were discussed at the meeting. The conference produced a set of minimum standards for child employment, which provide insight into the prevailing views of health officials, social workers, educators, government administrators, and reformers on child labor in a post–World War I period. The standards called for a minimum age of sixteen for employment in any occupation, except that children between fourteen and sixteen could be employed in agriculture and domestic service during vacation periods. A minimum age of eighteen was required for employment in or about mines and quarries, and a minimum of twenty-one years was established for night messenger service.[36] All children were required to attend school for at least nine months each year, between the ages of seven and eighteen years. If children fourteen to sixteen years of age had completed eighth grade and were legally employed, they must attend continuation schools eight hours a week. No minor was to be employed for more than eight hours a day, and night work for minors was prohibited between 6:00 p.m. and 7:00 a.m. Minors were to be paid at a rate not less than the minimum essential for the "necessary cost of proper living."[37] Other standards specified detailed rules for obtaining employment certificates, enforcing compulsory school attendance laws, and factory inspections.

As part of a "Children's Code," which was not a collection of laws under a statutory code but a condition of laws necessary for effective child-welfare policies, like a more holistic approach, conference attendees recognized the problem of dependency by linking the welfare of adults to successful child labor reform. The conference recommended mother's pensions and unemployment insurance to keep children in school and out of child labor but still provide for the economic security of the family. No state at the time met all of these standards. For example, most states set the minimum age for employment in factories and mills at fourteen years or over for boys and girls.[38] Laws in thirty-one states and the District of Columbia established an eight-hour day for child workers in at least one industry. Only eleven states required school attendance through the eighth grade. Nineteen states and the District of Columbia had no educational requirements for employment; they only demanded that a child could read or write before starting work. Although there was much variation among states in meeting the standards, they provided a uniform model for effective child labor laws. If every state enacted the standards, federal legislation or a constitutional amendment might be unnecessary.

Despite the limitations and potential problems with enforcement, most employers believed that the child labor tax would be held constitutional. To avoid the 10 percent tax on profits, many establishments stopped using child laborers. According to internal revenue agents, the biggest decrease was in southern cotton mill districts where over 85 percent of the mills no longer employed children.[39] Other declines in child labor were reported in the mining and canning industries. Reformers recognized that states would still need to do more, such as strengthen school attendance requirements and provide mothers' pensions or assistance laws, but they were encouraged by the early success of the law. In a speech before the NCLC's Fourteenth Annual Conference on Child Labor, Senator Irvine Lenroot expressed confidence that the Pomerene amendment was not open to any constitutional objection: "I have no hesitation in saying that the Supreme Court will uphold the validity of this legislation. It cannot do otherwise without squarely overruling a very large number of decisions from the beginning of the republic to the present day."[40]

Lawsuits, however, threatened to undermine the gains made by the law in reducing child labor in the cotton mills. Before the ink was dry on the law, David Clark and the southern textile manufacturers were preparing a test case to challenge its constitutionality. Clark had realized early on during the congressional debate that the Pomerene tax had wide support in Congress, so a decision was reached not to expend much time or resources trying to defeat the bill. With the *Hammer* victory under their belts, Clark and his associates looked forward to a litigation strategy. Many of the constitutional arguments had been presented during the Senate debate, and the majority opinion in *Hammer v. Dagenhart* provided other points. Clark lined up the same legal team that argued the first case, and every resource would be deployed against the new law. The first part of the plan, loading the *Congressional Record*, was already in place. Clark and the Executive Committee of Southern Cotton Manufacturers had to decide on the form of litigation and specific arguments. Clark wanted a decision as soon as possible, even before the law went into effect, which could raise standing and other jurisdictional issues.

Although the litigation strategy paralleled the one used in *Hammer*, the obstacles to a court victory were more substantial. Only a few avenues existed to challenge a revenue law. To wait for normal litigation to run its course violated Clark's priority for a quick decision. The Pomerene tax, however, would not be collected until the end of the year when companies announced their profit margins so some other basis for the lawsuit had to be devised. Like *Hammer v. Dagenhart*, Clark and his cohorts decided to use an equity proceeding to seek an injunction blocking enforcement of the law. It was a risky course, but one that might bring quick results if they could overcome jurisdictional issues. The odds were improved, however, by filing the case in the same judicial district as the *Hammer* litigation, in other words, before Judge James E. Boyd, who favored states' rights and laissez-faire principles.[41]

Events at the state level early that year influenced the court proceedings. The Cotton Manufacturers' Association of North Carolina had decided to endorse a fourteen-year minimum age for employment in factories and mills. In March 1919, shortly after Congress enacted the Pomerene tax, the North Carolina legislature passed a child labor bill with the fourteen-year minimum, without opposition and within a few weeks. Numerous previous laws had always been defeated by the mill interests. North Carolina, the last southern state to impose child labor restrictions for factory work, had now joined the rest of the Union. The legislation prompted David Clark to boast that child labor was now abolished in the South, thanks to the cotton mill owners. But there was a critical difference between the child labor laws of North Carolina and other mill states and federal standards—the North Carolina law failed to restrict the workday to eight hours for children between fourteen and sixteen years of age. This disparity became the central issue for the test case.

In April, Clark assembled three possible test cases and presented them to counsel for the Executive Committee. They decided on a case involving a mill operative named Eugene T. Johnston and his fifteen-year-old son John. Both worked at the Atherton Mills in Charlotte, North Carolina. Just as the Dagenhart family and Fidelity Manufacturing served as a legal vehicle for the Executive Committee, Eugene and John Johnston and Atherton Mills now became the parties of record. It was a collusive suit with both parties seeking the same outcome: defeat of the child labor tax. Generally, federal courts do not decide collusive lawsuits because they fail the "case and controversy" requirement of Article III, but at times it is difficult to discern collusiveness. Because the federal government was not involved in the case in any capacity, counsel for the Executive Committee and Atherton Mills basically worked as one group that directed the litigation. The facts of the case developed along the same lines as the *Hammer* litigation. On April 12, managers at Atherton Mills posted notices on company property informing employees that because of the provisions of the federal child labor tax, all operatives under sixteen years of age would be discharged on April 25, the date the law became effective.

David Clark's litigation plan for the Executive Committee soon produced results. The child labor tax was first attacked in a decision by Judge Boyd, the same federal judge who declared the Keating-Owen Act unconstitutional, when on May 1, 1919, he enjoined the Atherton Mills of Charlotte, North Carolina, from restricting the hours or dismissing John W. Johnston, a boy between fourteen and sixteen years of age in their employ. The injunction had force only within Judge Boyd's western district of North Carolina; in the rest of the country, the law was being enforced. The *Atherton* case was argued on appeal to the Supreme Court in December 1919, but no decision was handed down. After the death of Chief Justice Edward White on May 19, 1921, the case was sent back for rehearing, and it would not be decided by the Supreme Court until a year later.

Meanwhile, a second case emerged from the Tarheel State. Vivian Spinning Mills of Cherrydale, North Carolina, asked for an injunction restraining J. W. Bailey, collector of internal revenue, from enforcing the act. The Vivian Spinning Mills faced $2,098.06 in taxes for employing children in violation of the law. On August 22, 1921, Judge Boyd again struck down the Child Labor Tax Law.[42] He noted that the only difference between the two laws, the Keating-Owen Act and child labor tax, was the substitution of the tax for the prohibition of transportation of child-made goods. He examined the motives of Congress in enacting the law and concluded that the tax was not intended to raise revenue but to impose a penalty for child-made goods.

The judge argued that regulation of labor was one of the powers retained by the States under the Tenth Amendment and not delegated to the federal government.

Government lawyers argued that the courts had no jurisdiction to hear the case because of a provision in the Revised Statutes: "No suit for the purpose of restraining the assessment or collection of any tax shall be maintained in any court." Judge Boyd, however, asserted that the provision would leave the courts powerless to review whether any tax is legal or illegal, allowing Congress to overcome any constitutional barriers. The judge dismissed the argument as based upon unsound reasoning and an unintelligent interpretation of the powers reserved to the states under the Tenth Amendment. He called the child labor tax a "usurpation of authority and a violation of the sovereign rights of the State."[43] Delving into policy analysis, Judge Boyd pointed out that the North Carolina child labor law contained similar standards to the federal law. The state child labor law, he asserted, was "undoubtedly, the more capable of prompt execution than the act of Congress" and the costs would "not be a drain upon the Federal treasury."[44] Because he began with the premise that the regulation of labor was purely a state responsibility, Judge Boyd concluded that the United States could not invade that power either directly or indirectly, as the 10 percent tax attempted to accomplish. The judge issued an order permanently restraining the federal government from collecting the revenue.

Samuel Gompers and the American Federation of Labor Executive Council vigorously protested the decision and demanded an immediate appeal of Judge Boyd's ruling. Frustrated with the federal courts continually striking down federal child labor laws, the labor group warned that the time would soon come when the American people would deny the courts the power to declare acts of Congress unconstitutional. The Executive Council could not understand how the federal courts could uphold a tax that distinguished poisonous matches from nonpoisonous ones and artificially colored oleomargarine from natural dairy products, with the effect of eliminating those harmful products from the market, but strike down a tax that classified products made with child labor. In a press statement, the Executive Council of the AFL declared: "We are told by Judge Boyd that such humane action and classification by Congress interferes with State [*sic*] rights. If ever a classification and differentiation in taxation is justified it certainly is in the case of protecting the life and health of innocent children."[45]

Not everyone was upset with Judge Boyd's decision. Winston Adams, secretary of the American Cotton Manufacturers' Association, issued a press statement explaining the position of the cotton mill owners: "The manufacturers are contesting this law as a matter of principle rather than merely the working of young people. The manufacturers claim that if this law is held constitutional, the precedent has been established whereby the federal government can make and enforce any regulation covering conditions of employment, wages, hours, and other kindred matters."[46] David Clark's legal strategy was proceeding as planned.

Several months after his decision in *George v. Bailey*, Judge Boyd issued an opinion in *Drexel Furniture Company v. Bailey*, another case challenging the Child Labor Tax Law.[47] In September 1921, the Drexel Furniture Company was found in violation of the law and was required to pay over $6,300 in taxes. During 1919, the company had employed children under the age of fourteen. The company paid the taxes under protest and filed a lawsuit challenging congressional power to tax the profits of child labor. Drexel Furniture claimed that regulation of child labor in the states was an exclusively state function under the federal Constitution and within the reserved powers of the Tenth Amendment.

At this point, outside of Judge Boyd's district, the child labor tax had been in force for two and half years, and opponents were anxious to obtain a definitive judicial decision overturning the measure. After a slow start, the Bureau of Internal Revenue was effectively administering the inspection system and imposing taxes. Businesses were assessed a total of $130,000 in taxes in 1921, although only $24,233 in penalties were received.[48] Despite the early criticisms of the bureau, the National Child Labor Committee was satisfied with the enforcement of the law. The big question mark was whether Chief Justice Taft would support the principle of a regulatory tax that generated little revenue.

In *Drexel Furniture*, Judge Boyd noted that the constitutionality of the law had been decided in the previous case, which was based heavily on *Hammer v. Dagenhart*. He elaborated that the great principle established in *Hammer* was that the preservation of the states and their sovereign powers over local matters is as important to the design of the Constitution as the preservation of the Union itself. If it was acknowledged that Congress had the power to legislate on child labor within the states, it would not only seriously affect but also destroy the form of government the Constitution was intended to create and protect. The purpose of the act, he noted, appeared on its face and was disclosed by its scope and effect. Rather than raise revenue, the tax act was designed "solely to prohibit the employment of child labor."[49] The law would eliminate the subject of taxation. According to Judge Boyd, the Child Labor Tax Law was a bald attempt to regulate a purely internal affair of the states. The decision was appealed to the US Supreme Court.

In a brief that quoted Shakespeare, cited a paper on the French Revolution, and included a Q&A section that resembled a primary textbook, US solicitor general James M. Beck defended the law on the basis that it is a mere excise tax levied by the Congress of the United States under its broad power of taxation conferred by Article 1, Section 8, of the federal Constitution.[50] Beck, a conservative Republican, had been appointed solicitor general by President Warren G. Harding in 1921. Government lawyers relied heavily on the *McCray* case, where the Court upheld the oleomargarine tax, arguing that the precedent forecloses every question arising in *Drexel Furniture*. The statute challenged in *McCray* imposed an excise tax of one-fourth of a cent per pound on oleomargarine when not artificially colored and ten cents per pound when dyed yellow. The power to tax is not limited to the raising of revenue. Beck argued that no one then or now believed the act was designed to generate revenue because the tax was so onerous that it was practically a prohibition of the article.[51] The act was a federal police regulation that encroached upon powers reserved to the states, yet it was upheld. In *McCray*, Beck noted, opponents claimed that the tax was an arbitrary discrimination against oleomargarine and a violation of equality and due process under the Constitution. The Court carefully considered these claims and rejected all of them. Because the same arguments were being made by Drexel Furniture, the Court should apply the *McCray* precedent and overrule them as well.

Congressional motives, the solicitor general argued, are immaterial. The Court must presume that the tax is designed to generate revenue, and not question the motives or intent of Congress in levying taxes. Beck cited several decisions upholding the taxing power of Congress. For a tax to be constitutional, it must be geographically uniform and not imposed on exports, and the child labor tax met those requirements. The courts have no authority to examine the reasonableness of the classifications made in selecting the subjects for taxation. Beck asserted that a valid exercise of the taxing power should not be overturned by the Court because of some incidental effect on some power reserved to the states. The government argued that the tax in no way interferes with the ability of the states to regulate or prohibit child labor. Finally, the solicitor general distinguished *Hammer v. Dagenhart*, because the tax on the profits of child labor does not depend on whether the items will or will not move in interstate commerce. The tax was identical in principle to the oleomargarine tax and should be affirmed.

Where the government claimed that *Hammer* does not apply to the child labor tax, lawyers for Drexel Furniture urged the Court to follow the precedent. The respondents made several arguments. First, the child labor tax regulates child labor, a subject over which the Supreme Court forcefully declared in *Hammer* the federal government plays no role. The Court found the Keating-Owen Act invalid for two reasons: "It not only transcends the authority delegated to Congress over commerce, but also exerts a power as to a purely local matter to which the Federal authority does not extend."[52] Lawyers for the furniture company also argued that the tax law, although forming part of a revenue bill, is not really a tax statute but an attempt to regulate a subject reserved for the states. The classification of products made with child labor is arbitrary and based outside congressional power to levy taxes. Rather than a tax designed to raise revenue, the law imposes a penalty on those who violate the terms. "The necessary effect of this Federal statute," the brief argued, "is to destroy the exclusive power of the State of North Carolina and other States to regulate child labor within their borders in such a manner as they deem best."[53]

Drexel Furniture denied the government's argument that the congressional taxing power is only limited by two provisions in the Constitution. The brief cited Chief Justice John Marshall's famous opinion in *McCulloch v. Maryland* on congressional power: "Let the end be legitimate, let it be within the scope of the Constitution, and by all means which are appropriate, which are *plainly adopted* to that end, which are not prohibited, but consistent with the letter and *spirit of the Constitution*, are constitutional."[54] Questioning the validity of the child labor tax is not inquiring into the motives of Congress, but reviewing the necessary and obvious effects of the law. To support this argument, the brief quoted the majority opinion in *Hammer*: "In our view the *necessary effect* of this act is . . . to regulate the hours of labor of children in factories and mines within the States, a purely State authority."[55] Drexel Furniture argued that the Child Labor Tax Law attempted the same result.

In *Bailey v. Drexel Furniture Company* (1922), the Supreme Court overturned the Child Labor Tax Law on the basis that it intruded on the jurisdiction of the states to adopt and enforce child labor codes. The principles of dual federalism clearly animated the Court's opinion. Chief Justice Howard Taft stated that it was the "high duty and function" of the Court to review a law dealing with a subject not entrusted to Congress but left by the Constitution to the control of the States:

> We can not avoid the duty even though it requires us to refuse to give effect to legislation designed to promote the highest good. The good sought in unconstitutional legislation is an insidious feature because it leads citizens and legislators of good purpose to promote it without thought of the serious breach it will make in the ark of our covenant or the harm which will come from breaking down recognized standards.[56]

Without overruling *McCray* or the other tax precedents, the chief justice drew a jurisprudential line in the sand and concluded that Congress had gone too far. "Out of proper respect for the acts of a coordinate branch of the Government, this court has gone far to sustain taxing acts as such," he stated, "even though there has been ground for suspecting from the weight of the tax it was intended to destroy its subject." He found the child labor tax, however, to be dangerously different:

> But in the act before us, the presumption of validity cannot prevail, because the proof of the contrary is found on the very face of its provisions. Grant the validity of this law, and all that Congress would need do, hereafter, in seeking to take over to its control any one of the great number of subjects of public interest . . . would be to enact a detailed measure of complete regulation of the subject and enforce it by a so-called tax upon departures from it. To give such magic to the word "tax" would be to break down all constitutional limitation of the powers of Congress and completely wipe out the sovereignty of the States.[57]

Chief Justice Taft argued that the tax law did much more than simply impose an "incidental restraint" on business: it exerted a "prohibitory and regulatory effect" in a realm over which Congress had no jurisdiction. The chief justice refused to distinguish *Hammer v. Dagenhart*, and in fact used the precedent to analyze the tax case.

> So here the so-called tax is a penalty to coerce people of a state to act as Congress wishes them to act in respect of a matter completely the business of the state government under the federal Constitution. This case requires, as did the *Dagenhart* case, the application of the principle announced by Chief Justice Marshall in *McCulloch v. Maryland*, in a

much-quoted passage: "Should Congress, in the execution of its powers, adopt measures which are prohibited by the Constitution; or should Congress, under the pretext of executing its powers, pass laws for the accomplishment of objects not intrusted to the government; it would become the painful duty of this tribunal, should a case requiring such a decision come before it, to say that such an act was not the law of the land."[58]

Taft feared that upholding the child labor tax would destroy state sovereignty and devastate "all constitutional limitation of the powers of Congress" by allowing it to disguise future regulatory legislation in the cloak of taxes. Associate Justice John Clarke, a Wilson appointee, was the lone dissenter, but he did not write an opinion. Justices Oliver Wendell Holmes and Louis Brandeis, who dissented in *Dagenhart*, joined the majority.

On the same day when the opinion in *Bailey* was announced, the Supreme Court decided *Atherton Mills v. Johnston* on procedural grounds. The Court noted that the record raised doubt whether "on its face this is a real case within the meaning of the Constitution upon which the judgment of this court upon the validity of an act of Congress under the Constitution can be invoked."[59] Moreover, almost three years had passed since Judge Boyd had rendered a decision in the case. John Johnston was now beyond the age limit defined by the law. The Court said that the "lapse of time since the case was heard and decided in the District Court brought the minor, whose employment was the subject-matter of the suit, to an age which is not within the ages affected by the act. The act, even if valid, cannot affect him further." The case was declared moot and dismissed.

Progressives and reformers were stunned by the reactionary *Bailey* decision, an outcome so contrary to the reform spirit of the period. The presence of Justice Holmes in the *Bailey* majority, who authored the strong dissenting opinion in *Hammer v. Dagenhart*, and Justice Brandeis, who personally opposed child labor and defended progressive labor legislation in *Muller v. Oregon* (1908), and who also dissented in *Hammer*, requires an explanation. Former constitutional law professor Alexander Bickel provided one, at least for Justice Brandeis, in his analysis of the *Atherton Mills* case and its relation to *Bailey*. In the first chapter of his first book, *The Unpublished Opinions of Mr. Justice Brandeis*, Bickel examined an unpublished opinion or "Memorandum" in *Atherton Mills v. Johnston*, dated January 26, 1920, and concluded that Brandeis recognized the *Atherton* case as a collusive lawsuit that should be dismissed.[60] Bickel also found a separate handwritten draft of the opinion, which contained the following passage, later omitted from the unpublished printed version: "I agree that the decree entered below by the District Court [declaring the Child Labor Tax Law unconstitutional] must be reversed with directions to dismiss the bill; but in my opinion the dismissal should be for want of jurisdiction. If I believed that this Court had jurisdiction to pass in this proceeding upon the constitutionality of [the Child Labor Tax Law], I should have no difficulty in holding the act valid."

From these materials, Bickel concluded that Brandeis believed the child labor tax was constitutional and that a majority of the justices had, at least tentatively, agreed to affirm the constitutionality of the law. Brandeis's preference for self-restraint and concern over jurisdictional issues, however, trumped his belief that the law was valid. Bickel suggested that the memorandum influenced the internal political discussion of the case and may have caused the decision to be postponed for two years. After hearing oral arguments in *Atherton* in 1919, the Court was divided, and just six days before his death, Chief Justice Edward D. White wrote several of his colleagues on March 13, 1921, and urged that the case be reargued on the question of jurisdiction. With the appointment of William Howard Taft as chief justice and other personnel changes, the political dynamics shifted, and the Court invalidated the Child Labor Tax Law in *Bailey* in 1922.

Subsequent scholarship paints a more complex picture of the strategic interaction among the justices in *Atherton* and Justice Brandeis's motivations.[61] Elizabeth Brandeis Raushenbush, who had closely followed the Court and child labor issues during her father's tenure on the bench, doubted that the Court was close to upholding the child labor tax, and Brandeis's two law clerks at the time, Dean Acheson and William G. Rice, could not corroborate Bickel's claims.[62] Other scholars have critiqued the argument.[63] Brandeis himself was conflicted on the issue. He clearly opposed child labor, but his well-known stance against concentrated power and "bigness" perhaps pushed him to favor state action on child labor. A letter to his friend Norman Hapgood, just two weeks after the *Bailey* decision, attempted to defend his vote: "State Rights succumbed to the Rights of Nations. State Duties were ignored and state functions atrophied. The extremes of concentration are proving its failure to the common man. . . . The new Progressivism requires local development—quality not quantity."[64] Brandeis may have been trying to justify the decision in response to widespread criticism or he may have sincerely believed that the opinion would instigate a renaissance of state progressivism. The states, however, had been dealing with the issue of child labor for decades, and southern states showed almost no inclination to enact the progressive reforms that Brandeis favored. Other problems are apparent in attempting to explain the justice's motivations. Brandeis's preference for judicial restraint and local initiatives does not explain why he dissented in *Hammer* or silently concurred in *Bailey*.

As for Justice Holmes, his presence in the *Bailey* majority is even more perplexing. Various analyses attribute his vote in *Bailey* to his constitutional jurisprudence and influence of Chief Justice Taft. Constitutional scholar Alpheus Mason noted that Taft had "an unusual capacity" for keeping his colleagues together in pursuit of unanimity. Mason writes:

> During the early years of Taft's Chief Justiceship, it was not unusual for the justices to write on the back of circulated slip opinions: "I shall acquiesce in silence unless someone else dissents"; or, "I do not agree, but shall submit." For the sake of harmony staunch individualists such as Holmes, Brandeis, and Stone, though disagreeing, would sometimes go along with the majority. It seems probable that such considerations help in accounting for the unanimity achieved in the reactionary Child Labor Tax decision.[65]

Historian Stephen B. Wood posits that Holmes may have joined the majority when it became apparent that Justice Clarke was the only other dissenter and that two justices would not present an effective opposition. Wood also critiques Alexander Bickel's suggestion that Holmes was reluctant to dissent after he had expressed his views on a subject, and that he may have decided that it was better to join his brethren because nothing more "consequential could be added to the *Hammer* dissent." That explanation, however, is unconvincing because both Holmes and Brandeis often dissented more than once on an issue. Wood suggests that constitutional philosophy and Taft's leadership skills are responsible for Holmes's vote in *Bailey*. Holmes may have concluded that the child labor tax went too far as a regulatory measure. Although he wrote a strong dissent in *Hammer*, the opinion was not based on his support for social reform but on his views on constitutional government. Unlike Brandeis, Holmes was not a social reformer, and he expressed little interest in taking up social causes at that point in his career. Holmes also was impressed with Taft's performance as chief justice and his amiable personality.[66] These explanations provide some insight, but questions remain about why Holmes would vote to undermine a position that he had so forcefully argued in *Hammer v. Dagenhart*.

In the aftermath of *Bailey v. Drexel Furniture Company*, the disappointment and anger of many people opposed to child labor was palpable. Samuel Gompers denounced the *Bailey* decision as yet another example of the Court's class bias: "The Supreme Court deals with childhood exactly as it would deal with pig iron. . . . It observes all the technicalities, weighing the lives of our little ones as so much inert material," he wrote. Gompers could not understand why the Court failed to follow the precedent of the oleomargarine case. "Perhaps there is some legal technicality which makes proper and constitutional a tax on colored oleomargarine to keep it off the market, but improper and unconstitutional a tax on child labor to keep child labor products off the market." The courts, he suggested, "were unable to comprehend and deal properly with human problems according to modern concepts."[67] With the decisions in *Hammer* and *Bailey*, Gompers argued that it was now up to unions to prohibit child labor, and organized labor demanded a constitutional amendment to eliminate child labor.

The National Child Labor Committee voiced similar views on the possible need to amend the Constitution. "The decision of the Supreme Court raises important questions regarding the ability of the people of America to express their will in legislation under the Constitution as it stands," said Owen R. Lovejoy, general secretary of the NCLC. "Twice the people of the United States have legislated against this nation-wide and nation-weakening evil of child labor and now that they have lost their second law in the courts, as they did the first one, on the issue of constitutionality, they must seriously consider the advisability of changing the Constitution."[68] The immediate concern of the NCLC Board of Trustees was to find ways to help the estimated five hundred thousand children who lost the protection of the Child Labor Tax Law, by turning to state child labor reforms. Trustees also had to decide whether to seek another federal law or launch a campaign for a constitutional amendment.

In *Outlook*, a popular periodical, a critical editorial suggested that the *Bailey* decision had backed the states and the federal government into a constitutional corner and the analysis accurately captured the dilemma faced by reformers.[69] Playing a mental game, the editors asked readers to suppose that South Carolina had an enlightened child labor law. The result of the law is that the cost of labor in its factories is higher than neighboring states, such as Georgia, and it faces an economic disadvantage. If South Carolina were a sovereign nation, it could protect itself by imposing a tariff against unfair competition from Georgia. But any student of history knows that the Constitution took away the power of the states to regulate interstate and foreign commerce because of the problems experienced under the Articles of Confederation. Under the articles, states were essentially sovereign entities, and they passed protectionist trade policies that led to economic balkanization within the country. Under the Constitution, states do not have that power. South Carolina then asks the federal government to prohibit the goods of Georgia, produced with cheap child labor, from crossing state boundaries. But now the Supreme Court says that the federal government can provide no such protection. If states cannot protect themselves from unfair competition and Congress does not have the authority to provide protection, as the Supreme Court declared in both *Hammer* and *Bailey*, then enlightened states must suffer because they choose to safeguard children's rights. Child labor legislation may be reserved to the states, but they act at their industrial peril. The *Outlook* editors begged for some constitutional authority to explain how to provide a legal remedy for the wrong of child labor.

An editorial in *Barron's*, a financial magazine, compared the *Bailey* decision to the *Dred Scott* case, where Chief Justice Roger Taney ruled that slaves were not citizens and that the right to own slaves was a property right protected by states' rights. The magazine noted that the Civil War and the Thirteenth and Fourteenth Amendments abolished the states' right to slavery, and the editors predicted that the abuse of the states' rights dogma on child labor will end with another constitutional amendment.[70] As terrible as the *Bailey* decision was for the welfare of children, it was a signal for the states to take the right path. If states do not act to regulate the years of labor as well as the hours children work, the editors warned, aroused public opinion may take away any state control of child labor problems.

Prominent constitutional law scholars also criticized the *Bailey* decision. Professor Thomas Reed Powell of Columbia University Law School commented: "Where the Court made a great mistake in the child labor case was that it did not see that interstate transportation was a cause of the evil. It distinguished the oleo [margarine] case, the white slave case, by saying that in each of those instances the use of interstate commerce was necessary to the accomplishment of the harmful result."[71] But the use of interstate commerce was necessary for the result in the child labor case, Professor Powell argued, because "if the manufacturer could not have an extra-state market he would not have employed children."

Professor Edward S. Corwin of Princeton University critiqued the reasoning of the Court:

The logic of the decision of this case, overriding previous decisions, makes the Court the supervisor of the purposes for which Congress may exercise constitutional powers. It thus cancels out the third dimension, so to speak, of the sovereignty of the national government within the field of its granted powers. At one stroke, a new canon of constitutional interpretation is created and an out-of-date one revived: legislative motive becomes a test of legislative action.[72]

Professor Corwin noted that a concept of cooperative federalism between the national government and the states recognized in *Hoke v. United States* apparently had dropped out of favor with the Court. For the first time in the history of judicial review, he argued, "legislative motive is made a test of legislative action, and any effort by Congress to bring within its control matters normally falling to the states alone raises the question of valid motive."[73] Corwin concluded: "The one thing to be said for the new doctrine is that it will probably prove so unworkable in practice that it will not long survive."[74]

Like the reaction to the *Hammer* decision, some members of Congress attacked the Supreme Court's power of judicial review. Senator Robert La Follette of Wisconsin introduced an amendment that would curtail the ability of federal courts to declare laws unconstitutional and empower Congress to repass any law declared invalid by the Supreme Court. Protesting the decision at the American Federation of Labor convention in Cincinnati, Senator La Follette declared that "the actual ruler of the American people is the Supreme Court of the United States" and that nothing in the Constitution sanctioned "the power which the courts now assert."[75] Noting the ability of Congress to override a presidential veto by a two-thirds vote, the senator proposed that the legislature override a judicial veto and declare the final public policy of the country. The *New York Globe* expressed support for the amendment. "The Supreme Court, which is not a representative body, is now sovereign so far as legislation is concerned. The Constitution provided that the Executive might veto legislation, but it gave no such power to the judiciary."[76] Because the framers of our Constitution did not anticipate the development of a judicial veto, the newspaper concluded that "nothing in our system of government precludes such an amendment as has been offered by Senator La Follette." Other media outlets were not so kind to the proposal. The plan, if carried out, announced the *Brooklyn Eagle*, "would mean a complete surrender of our system of government, which protects minorities through the courts." Even the *New York Call*, a socialist newspaper, warned that if the Supreme Court was stripped of its power, it would be transferred to Congress, which is "reactionary enough; this would make it still more so."[77] An editorial in the *New York World* pointed out that the American people generally have more confidence in the Supreme Court than in their average Congress, and that for the most part, the Court has exercised the power of judicial review with "reason and moderation." La Follette's amendment garnered little support in Congress.

The defeat by the Supreme Court of the first two federal laws regulating child labor, which had been enacted by huge majorities in both chambers of Congress, was a severe blow to reform efforts. By 1922, the states had made some progress in restricting child labor, but in many respects those laws fell below the moderate standards embodied in the federal legislation overturned by the Court. In an early treatise on child labor and the Constitution, Raymond Garfield Fuller noted that laws in thirty-one states, when compared to the federal laws, were deficient with respect to the "fourteen-year age for factories, the eight-hour day, and prohibition of night work for children employed in factories."[78] Exemptions in many state laws made them fall below federal standards. In some industrial states, for example, children as young as fourteen could legally work eleven-hour days in factories.

If the American people felt strongly enough about ending child labor exploitation, they would have to seek other solutions, including a constitutional amendment. Across the country, newspapers clamored for a resolution to the problem. The Portland Maine *Press-Herald* asserted that the "exploitation of children in mills and factories must end." The *Sacramento Bee* declared that the only way the situation can be remedied is "through a constitutional amendment abolishing child labor." The *New York Evening Mail* concurred, concluding that "even Congress must be convinced by now . . . that the only adequate recourse is to an amendment to the Federal Constitution."[79] The paper recommended that new legislation be written "into the nation's statutes immediately, on whatever ground promises success. In the meantime, the machinery of amending the Constitution should be set in motion without an instant's delay." Congress was already considering such action.

5

Congress Proposes the "Children's Amendment"

With the adverse decisions in *Hammer* and *Bailey*, proponents of child labor restrictions had run out of federal legislative options. If Congress lacked the authority to pass a child labor law under the Commerce Clause or taxing power, as the Supreme Court declared, the only way to give Congress that authority, short of the Court overturning its precedents at some point, was passage of a child labor amendment to the US Constitution. Senator Medill McCormick, a Republican from Illinois who would soon introduce an amendment, argued: "Unless Congress be empowered by constitutional amendment to act, plainly matters will grow worse. We have no recourse but to amend the constitution for the sake of the children who otherwise will be driven into the mills of the country to their own injury and so to the hurt of their more fortunate and happier fellows."[1] A campaign to use Article V to alter the Constitution began in Congress just days after the *Bailey* decision.

Senator Pomerene, coauthor of the Child Labor Tax Law, acknowledged that an amendment would be "a long and tedious route."[2] A tremendous effort and significant resources were needed by proamendment forces to secure passage and ratification. Instead of making specific legal arguments before nine justices about congressional authority under the Commerce Clause or taxing powers and winning over at least five of them, reformers would have to convince a two-thirds supermajority in Congress to propose such an amendment and obtain ratification in three-fourths of the state legislatures or in ratifying conventions. As the framers envisioned, it is difficult, but not impossible, to alter the Constitution. Over eleven thousand amendments have been proposed in Congress since the founding, but only twenty-seven have survived the proposal and ratification stages to become part of the Constitution. The process requires a substantial consensus among elected officials and citizens on the need to alter the governing charter, and it is as much political as it is constitutional. Even though reformers embarked on this campaign in a time when constitutional amendments were a viable option to overturning Supreme Court precedents, as the Sixteenth and Nineteenth Amendments demonstrated, there were still many roadblocks to ratification.[3]

The subsequent political struggle over the proposed child labor amendment is a fascinating story in itself, but the ratification battle during the 1920s also sheds light on the demise of the Progressive reform movement. Reformers, acting individually or in nascent interest groups, made gains in the late 1800s and early twentieth century in pressuring states to enact both child labor restrictions and compulsory school attendance laws. Building on this success, Progressives continued the fight for tougher state legislation and successfully lobbied Congress to pass two federal laws. The Supreme Court decisions in *Hammer* and *Bailey*, however, brought an abrupt end to a twenty-year campaign to enact federal legislation. By the time a constitutional amendment was considered, the Progressive coalition of organized labor, middle-class social reformers, western and southern farmers, and left-wing intellectuals and radicals was disintegrating.

The fracturing of the Progressive coalition presented challenges for supporters of the amendment, but reformers succeeded in getting a measure through Congress. After two years of congressional hearings and debates, a Child Labor Amendment passed by large majorities in Congress in 1924. That turned out to be the easy part. Congress did not place a time limit on ratification, and there were two distinct periods in the struggle over the amendment: in 1924–1925, when the proposal was first sent to the states, and during the Great Depression, from 1933 to 1940. This chapter covers the first phase of the ratification process, including the congressional debates over the text of the amendment, the strategies of major interest groups on both sides, and key battles in Massachusetts and New York to secure ratification.

Over the roughly fifteen-year ratification campaign, the proposed twentieth amendment was endorsed by the national platforms of the Republican and Democratic Parties, and it had the backing of presidents from both parties, including Warren Harding, Calvin Coolidge, and Franklin D. Roosevelt. Others who supported the amendment included Republican senators Henry Cabot Lodge and Robert La Follette. During the early ratification struggle, Secretary of Commerce Herbert Hoover, who headed the American Child Health Association, endorsed the amendment. Although Hoover believed that an eighteen-year age restriction was too high, he still favored the amendment to eliminate a condition that was "more deplorable than war" and "poisoning the springs of the nation at their source."[4] After serving as president from 1929 to 1933, Hoover joined FDR in urging ratification during the Depression. Public opinion polls in the 1930s, which for the first time were based on scientific survey methods, also indicated that most citizens favored the amendment.[5]

Despite such broad political support at the national level, the child labor amendment never became part of the Constitution. It is one of six amendments in US history that passed Congress but failed to be ratified. Why did the amendment ultimately fail to win the necessary state votes for ratification? The answer is complex because several factors influenced the ratification campaign. As this chapter will detail, the broad language of the amendment generated much opposition, but fundamental political and economic forces worked against the amendment as well.

Some historians link the failure of the amendment to the times. Under this view, the Progressive movement exhausted itself as the interests and agendas of the two prominent groups within the coalition, organized labor and farmers, diverged and sometimes clashed. Also, in the aftermath of the Great War, American culture was more conservative and suspicious of concentrated political power. The successful child labor reforms achieved at the state level early in the century ran into a roadblock at the federal level, first in the Supreme Court, and then in the states during the ratification campaign. Legal scholar Julie Novkov argues, however, that the time period only partially explains the defeat of federal reforms. She contends that legal interpretation and political pressure were important factors in the battle over child labor laws. Groups like the NCLC and NCL successfully "historicized" the plight of the child worker by convincing legislators and judges that the state and child had a special relationship.[6] The state had a duty to protect children from economic exploitation that went beyond sentimental reasons. A self-interested state must safeguard future citizens in order to maintain a strong polity. The concept of *parens patriae*, or the state as parent, embodies this relationship.

Support for an amendment among national party officials and reform groups turned out to be deeper than among the general public, especially during the critical years of 1924–1925. Granted, popular opinion was influenced by the alarmist rhetoric of the antiamendment forces. A well-financed and organized coalition of opposition groups, including manufacturers, textile mill owners, farm groups, and Catholic Church leaders in several states, was able to "frame" the issue to their advantage by appealing to a populace weary of increasing federal power following World War I.[7] These groups successfully recast the paternalistic relationship between state and child with an image of unbridled government threatening parental authority and family values.

Sectional tensions also played a role in the ultimate defeat of the amendment, as they had since the first federal law was introduced in Congress. Westerners emphasized a rugged individualism and work ethic rather than a paternalistic state where federal agents replaced the authority of parents. But unlike the South, nearly all western states ultimately ratified the amendment. In fact, California and Arizona were the second and third states to affirm the measure. There was stronger opposition in the South. Southern politicians favored states' rights and warned of Yankee intervention into southern culture. Antiamendment forces emphasized the threat to southern values from northern agitators. Of the twenty-eight states that ultimately ratified the amendment, only one—Arkansas—was from the South. Kentucky also did not ratify, but it was a border state during the Civil War.

Constitutional scholar David Kyvig and others have also argued that the demise of the amendment must be viewed within the context of constitutional politics during the first few decades of the twentieth century. Between 1913 and 1933, the Constitution was amended six times, more than any other period since the founding and ratification of the Bill of Rights.[8] There was amendment fatigue, especially following ratification of the Eighteenth and Nineteenth Amendments. Prohibition and women's suffrage disrupted cultural traditions, and some citizens believed there was too much social change. Moreover, opponents of the child labor amendment often highlighted the national government's problems with enforcing prohibition and argued that federal bureaucrats were incapable of effective administration. Those arguments resonated with many citizens.

The economy was a factor as well. With a robust market and laissez-faire economic philosophy dominant in the 1920s, there was little appetite for expanding federal regulation of business. The ideology of laissez-faire capitalism emphasized individualism and hard work for self-advancement, a rejection of social welfare legislation, and limited government intervention in the market, especially at the federal level. These arguments were supported by appeals to states' rights and local control over labor conditions. During this period, the Supreme Court's "liberty of contract" doctrine, which limited congressional and state power over the economy, reached its jurisprudential peak with the decision in *Adkins v. Children's Hospital* (1923). In *Adkins*, the Court ruled that a minimum wage law for women and children in Washington, DC, designed to prevent conditions detrimental to their health and morals, violated the Fifth Amendment's Due Process Clause. The decision in *Adkins* reinforced the precedents in *Hammer* and *Bailey* and signaled that during the 1920s, the Court would not be receptive to national regulation of labor.

Amendment foes also argued that the worst forms of child labor exploitation had been ameliorated, and that more federal bureaucratic control was unnecessary and dangerous. Some statistical data buttressed this position. For the first time, the 1920 Census indicated a drastic reduction in the number of child laborers.[9] The number of child workers had declined from almost two million in 1910, to just 1,060,858 in 1920. What caused such a significant decrease over the decade? Amendment opponents viewed the drop in employed children as proof that state laws were effective. Miriam Keeler of the NCLC, however, suggested that the federal law in force that was ultimately struck down by the Court in *Bailey* was responsible for the drop. The biggest decline was found in manufacturing and mechanical industries, where the fourteen-year age limit federal law resulted in a 71 percent decline in child workers. In mines, where the age limit was sixteen years, the number below the age limit fell 60 percent. The law did not cover children in agricultural labor.

These statistics suggested that during the few years that the Child Labor Tax Law was enforced, it was successful in reducing the number of child workers. Though these numbers were encouraging, Grace Abbott and others noted that only thirteen states met the standards set under both federal laws struck down by the Court. Studies conducted by the Children's Bureau found that shortly after the laws were invalidated, children were employed in violation of the federal standards in the legislation. The bureau also noted that between 1920 and 1924, child labor increased in thirty-four industrial cities, including New York.[10] Moreover, Census statistics and applications for work permits only reflected those children legally employed, omitting entirely those illegally working. For example, the 1,060,858 figure did not include children under ten, or children doing seasonal work or industrial homework. Reformers were convinced that child labor exploitation was still a serious problem, and they felt that the constitutional issues with the child labor tax law identified in *Bailey* could be overcome by passing a constitutional amendment that gave Congress clear authority to enact federal legislation.

On May 17, 1922, Representative Roy G. Fitzgerald, a Republican lawyer and World War I veteran from Dayton representing Ohio's Third District, introduced a resolution for an amendment that would empower Congress to regulate the employment of children under eighteen. The proposed amendment read: "The Congress shall have the power to regulate throughout the United States the employment of persons under 18 years of age." Republican senator Hiram Johnson of California, who was Theodore Roosevelt's running mate for the Progressive Party in 1912, introduced a similar resolution in the Senate two days later. Claiming that the amendment was needed to protect children, Senator Johnson asserted that the national government must "slightly invade state [*sic*] rights" when the welfare of children was at stake. "Ordinarily I would not wish to invade the prerogatives of the states," Johnson said, "but if the welfare of little children requires it, I would not for an instant hesitate."[11]

According to press reports, Johnson's proposed amendment precipitated a sectional fight between northern and eastern senators and those from southern and western states over constitutional principles similar to slavery, states' rights, and secession. Senator Lee Overman (D-NC) "bitterly condemned" the proposal as a "clear attempt to wipe out state lines."[12] Other senators warned that the amendment would create a "paternalistic super-structure of a federal government." Johnson's amendment, it was argued, would give Congress the authority to enact antilynching laws and usurp state police powers. Although public pressure to respond to the *Bailey* decision was growing, the battle lines were drawn, and Congress adjourned without acting on the amendment.

That summer, reformers mobilized in support of an amendment. Samuel Gompers, longtime president of the American Federation of Labor, invited various national civic, religious, and labor groups to the AFL headquarters in Washington, DC. Gompers had opposed child labor for decades, viewing the capitalist exploitation of children as a threat to workingmen and "a crime against civilization" that was "repulsive to every instinct in humanity."[13] Joining Gompers at the June 1 meeting were Florence Kelley, general secretary of the National Consumers' League; Reverend E. O. Watson, executive secretary of the Federal Council of Churches of Christ in America;

Matilda Lindsay of the National Women's Trade Union League; US representative Walter Chandler, Progressive Republican from New York; and Father John A. Ryan of Catholic University and the National Catholic Welfare Council.[14] The meeting resulted in the establishment of the Permanent Conference for the Abolition of Child Labor, with Samuel Gompers as the chair. Members of the new organization committed themselves to abolishing for-profit child labor throughout the United States, its possessions, and territories, by constitutional amendment.

While the meeting was taking place, Gompers and several reformers, including Owen R. Lovejoy and Florence Kelley, testified before the House Judiciary Committee on the need for federal legislation restricting child labor. Gompers told the committee that forty states had child labor laws that were more or less effective, but eight states still had no substantial legislation. Although hesitant to attack the Supreme Court, Gompers questioned how the high court could uphold a tax on matches made with phosphorus, which ate away at the bones of any man, woman, or child producing them, but strike down a tax on the profits of goods made with child labor. He noted that Congress protected dairy farmers by imposing a tax on oleomargarine, and the Supreme Court ruled the tax was constitutional. Gompers wanted any federal action that effectively abolished child labor, whether a federal law or constitutional amendment. He presented a novel bill drafted by James F. Lasson, a government lawyer, based on the Thirteenth Amendment, which prohibits slavery and involuntary servitude except as punishment for conviction of a crime. In a brief supporting the amendment, child labor was described as an evil "species of involuntary servitude" where children are in some manner compelled to perform their grinding tasks.[15] The proposed amendment made any contract entered into by a child under fourteen years of age void on the basis that it was involuntary servitude.[16] Members of the Judiciary Committee appeared to be either reluctant to advance a new child labor law or hostile to protective legislation. They warned that an amendment could take years and suggested that it might be more effective to seek laws in the eight states without child labor legislation through a campaign of propaganda and public pressure. The recommendation and probing questions irked Gompers. "If the attitude of the committee is a guide to Congressional sentiment," he remarked, "we have a fight on our hands, strange and mid-Victorian as that may seem."[17]

During his testimony, Owen R. Lovejoy, representing the NCLC, did not support any specific legislation, but he told the committee that his organization favored any federal action necessary to correct the abuse of child labor, which cannot be addressed at the local level. He admitted that the two previous federal laws were limited in that they applied to only 15 percent of child workers. He recommended a broader law to cover children in the street trades, tenement sweating industries, domestic services, and agricultural activities.[18] When it was her turn to speak, Florence Kelley of the NCL told the committee that she had no intention to deliver an oration. That month, she remarked, would be her fortieth year studying and working on child labor issues. She favored a federal child labor law because her organization witnessed the "continual failure of the States . . . to give to the children anything approaching uniform advantages in the different parts of the country."[19] When asked by Representative Ira G. Hersey (R-ME) what remedy for the evil of child labor would she recommend, Mrs. Kelley retorted that she "looked forward to a Federal amendment authorizing Congress to legislate." Following their testimony, the reformers met to discuss their options. Within a year, the Permanent Conference included representatives from twenty-five national organizations. The group prepared a draft amendment and led the lobbying efforts in Congress for its adoption.

Advocating for an amendment presented new challenges for opponents of child labor. To be successful, reformers would have to convince elected federal and state officials and many citizens that the decisions in *Hammer* and *Bailey* were wrong, that state laws were insufficient in solving the problem, that Congress needed to have the power to regulate child labor spelled out in the Constitution, and that once ratified, Congress would not abuse the power by legislating in areas beyond the commercial exploitation of children. Even some longtime activists on the issue of child labor were uncertain if all this was possible within the prevailing political climate.

On June 9, 1922, the National Child Labor Committee held its seventy-third meeting of the Board of Trustees. The organization polled the trustees and Advisory Committee members on the proposed amendment to the Constitution. Among the trustees, the vote was thirteen in favor and six opposed. With the Advisory Committee members added, the vote was thirty-one in favor of the amendment, fourteen opposed, and over a dozen absent or with no vote recorded. Several members wanted to link the labor of children and women under a broad federal authority to regulate workplace conditions. Jane Addams of Hull House favored an amendment "permitting industrial legislation over all interstate commerce."[20] Another trustee, Professor Samuel M. Lindsay of Columbia University, wanted a broad amendment that would give Congress the power to regulate all labor and industrial problems, but he acknowledged that it wouldn't be politically feasible to propose such an amendment.[21] Still, Lindsay supported the child labor amendment. Other "yes" votes believed that a state strategy was ineffective, and that there was no alternative to an amendment.

Those in the minority, however, made several compelling arguments that were prescient in their assessment of public sentiment. Many of the "no" votes preferred to intensify public education programs at the state level and secure more rigorous state legislation. With the recently ratified Eighteenth (1919) and Nineteenth Amendments (1920), and the fight over the Sheppard-Towner Act, which provided federal funds to prevent maternal and infant mortality, several noted that the public mood was not favorable toward more centralization of power in the federal government. Julia Lathrop, first head of the federal Children's Bureau, commented that she was "astonished to find the popular distaste for governmental activity" in her region and suspected that the attitudes were widespread.[22] She favored a strong effort to raise standards in the states providing the least protection to child workers. Others felt that the state of public opinion would make a national campaign difficult and expensive. One trustee, Colonel Francis G. Caffey, former lieutenant colonel in the Spanish-American War and US attorney for the southern district of New York, voted "no" on the amendment because he believed that something could be done under the treaty-making power of the federal government. His idea, however, was not pursued.

The meeting ended with the NCLC adopting a motion to support an amendment dealing exclusively with the labor of children. A consensus of the committee favored an amendment drafted by Dr. William Draper Lewis, a Progressive Republican and the first full-time dean of the University of Pennsylvania Law School, and George W. Alger, a Republican lawyer from New York. The draft amendment contained the following language: "Congress shall have the power to regulate or forbid the employment of minors at an age, or under conditions deemed injurious to their health and morals. Such power shall be concurrent and not exclusive and the exercise thereof by Congress shall not prevent any state from adopting other or further regulations, not inconsistent therewith."[23] The phrase "concurrent power" would give Congress the authority to regulate "employment" of children while still leaving room for the states to legislate on child labor.

Felix Frankfurter, now a Harvard law professor and future Supreme Court justice who supported the work of the NCLC, disagreed that an amendment was necessary. He recommended a "deeper statesmanship" that would awaken the conscience of the community on the need to eliminate child labor. He also believed that the slow pace of state reforms was not necessarily a measure of future progress. Frankfurter suggested that a new political tool—the women's vote—could be used to achieve more effective laws. "Why should not the League of Women Voters in every state," he asked, "make it the order of the day to put a wise child labor law upon the statute books of every State?"[24] Although many women and women's groups were leaders of the child labor reform movement, Frankfurter overestimated the impact women's suffrage would have on the issue. The introduction of millions of female voters into the electorate did not significantly shift the debate in favor of child labor reform. Women were perhaps more sympathetic to child labor concerns, but like men, they could be influenced by political rhetoric, and they were about as diverse as men in their support or opposition to child labor restrictions.

Several days after the NCLC meeting, the American Federation of Labor held its annual convention. Senator La Follette, who was the keynote speaker at the "child labor protest session," was greeted with raucous cheers and applause. In his speech, which was repeatedly interrupted with shouts of approval, La Follette condemned the *Bailey* decision and attacked the Taft Court as a judicial oligarchy.[25] He believed that it was futile to talk about an amendment to correct the Court's objections to the Child Labor Tax law. Rather, he proposed a much broader amendment that would prohibit lower federal court judges from declaring a law enacted by Congress void and would allow Congress to veto a Supreme Court decision declaring a federal law unconstitutional by simply repassing the law. "Federal judges," the senator declared, "must be made responsive to the popular will."[26] Organized labor backed the proposal, but it languished in Congress. Senator La Follette persisted, making the issue part of his campaign platform in his attempt to revive the Progressive Party as a presidential candidate in 1924, but he was unable to put together a broad coalition of farmers and urban workers.

President Warren G. Harding had voiced his support for an amendment to regulate child labor in a June 6 letter to Representative John Jacob Rogers (R-MA) and promised to express his views on the issue more completely in an address to Congress later that year. In his second annual message to Congress on December 8, 1922, Harding urged the legislature to submit a child labor amendment to the states. He observed that twice Congress had attempted to correct the evils incident to child employment, but the Supreme Court placed the problem outside the proper domain of federal regulation. An amendment was needed to clearly give Congress that authority. Acknowledging two schools of thought on amending the Constitution, one that believes that every alteration weakens the document and another that welcomes amendments for every issue, the president said we should amend "to meet the demands of the people when sanctioned by deliberate public opinion."[27] He believed that child labor was such an issue where change was needed.

Several New York newspapers strongly endorsed the amendment. The *New York Post* opined that the adoption of an amendment might help rescue children by prompting backward states to strengthen their laws. "The only way to stop the exploitation of boys and girls in states that refuse to give them this protection," the editors wrote, "is by an amendment of the Federal Constitution."[28] The *New York Globe* recommended that the amendment be "promptly disposed of both by the Senate and House and sent to the states for ratification in order that the ancient evil of exploiting children may be definitely ended in America." The *New York Tribune* suggested that Congress give the children of America an early Christmas gift by quickly approving the amendment and sending it to the states. "Amending the Constitution," the paper said, "is never a slight task; but the sentiment of the country is overwhelmingly in favor of such a step."[29] The *Tribune's* assessment of public opinion, however, may have been too optimistic.

In an essay for *The American Child*, Owen R. Lovejoy echoed the *Tribune's* appraisal of public opinion with a caveat. "The overwhelming sentiment of the country," he wrote, "is probably in favor of a Constitutional Amendment which will make it possible for Congress to deal efficiently with our problem of child labor."[30] Lovejoy acknowledged that there were many earnest and sincere reformers who held a contrary opinion on the campaign for an amendment. He admitted that some of his best friends and trustees of the NCLC "doubted the wisdom of invading that sacred territory of the Constitution." He noted the amendment fatigue following the recent battles over the Eighteenth and Nineteenth Amendments. Lovejoy expected a difficult fight for ratification. One of the chief objections against the amendment would be the fear of increasing the concentration of power in the federal government. He explained that amendment supporters do not favor centralization of government; many preferred to see an increase in local responsibility. Those who desired an amendment were not seeking to transfer state authority to the federal government. All that they sought was to remove the restrictions on congressional power that the Supreme Court had imposed in *Hammer* and *Bailey*. Even the Supreme Court, Lovejoy argued, supported their cause because the justices "indicated a feeling that child labor was a disgrace and a menace to our public health and that a way should be found by which it could be controlled."[31]

Congress reconvened in late fall 1922, and the Senate acted first. A subcommittee of the Judiciary Committee held hearings in early January 1923 on five variously worded resolutions for a child labor amendment. Samuel Gompers and a host of witnesses from the Permanent Conference for the Abolition of Child Labor testified in support of an amendment introduced by Medill McCormick of Illinois in the Senate and Israel Moore Foster in the House. Witnesses included Grace Abbott, chief of the Children's Bureau, and Julia Lathrop, Florence Kelley, and Owen R. Lovejoy of the National Child Labor Committee. Others endorsing an amendment were Emily Newell Blair, vice chair of the Democratic National Committee; Harriet Taylor Upton, vice chair of the Republican National Committee; John Jay O'Connor, representative of the National League of Women Voters; and Selma Borchardt of the American Federation of Teachers. All of the witnesses supported the language of the amendment.

On January 18, amendment opponents were given an opportunity to present testimony. The few adversaries who testified offered restrained criticisms. For example, Everett P. Wheeler, chairman of the American Constitutional League of New York, expressed concerns about the impact of an amendment on federalism and state authority, and David Clark, the ultraconservative editor of the *Southern Textile Bulletin* and the voice of southern textile manufacturers, introduced several administrators from North and South Carolina to rebut arguments that southern states were not effectively enforcing child labor laws.[32] Their testimony suggested that an amendment was an unnecessary violation of states' rights.

The McCormick-Foster resolution, while giving Congress the power to restrict or prohibit the labor of persons under eighteen years of age, reserved power to the several states "to limit or prohibit such labor in any way which does not lessen any limitation of such labor or the extent of any prohibition thereof by Congress." Implicit in this text is the concept of federal preemption. Congress and the states may share power to regulate child labor, but if state laws conflict with federal law, national law takes precedence under the Supremacy Clause of Article VI. On February 19, 1923, the Judiciary Committee reported favorably on an alternative amendment that was submitted at the last minute by Owen R. Lovejoy and the NCLC's legal advisor William Draper Lewis. The amendment would grant Congress power "concurrent with the several States, to limit or prohibit the labor of persons under the age of 18 years." Opponents declared they would fight the measure in the full Senate. Congress adjourned, however, before final action could be taken on the resolution.

While members of the Permanent Conference were happy with the favorable committee report, the late changes suggested by Lovejoy and the NCLC created divisions within the coalition. The debate pitted Owen Lovejoy on one side against Grace Abbott and Florence Kelley, each camp with their supporters. Abbott blamed the failure to produce a final bill on the confusion created by the last-minute proposal by the NCLC. In its defense, the NCLC did not want any language in the amendment that might be interpreted as restricting the power of the states to regulate or prohibit child labor, particularly if the states wanted to exceed federal standards. Abbott and Kelley distrusted Lovejoy's judgment and believed the NCLC language would lead to legal disputes between the states and federal government that could undermine the effectiveness of the law. In his study of the ratification process, David Kyvig describes Kelley as inflexible and impatient, viewing any attempt at compromise as a sellout to the opposition.[33] She doubted whether the concurrent power language would help with ratification. The political differences within the Permanent Conference threatened to transfer any influence reform leaders had over the content of the amendment to members of Congress who sought to further their careers by sponsoring the amendment. Many who were working to advance the amendment were frustrated and disappointed with the slow progress in Congress.

In early November, Edward P. Costigan, a member of the US Tariff Commission (and future Democratic senator from Colorado), warned Grace Abbott that friends of the amendment needed to speak clearly and firmly with one voice. If supporters are "wavering and uncertain" about the content of the amendment, the politicians would fill the void with their own agendas.[34] Costigan urged Abbott to keep the coalition together. A series of meetings and informal exchanges occurred over the next month. The Women's Joint Congressional Committee and the Permanent Conference for the Abolition of Child Labor agreed on the form of an amendment by December, but the NCLC was not on board. Grace Abbott enlisted the help of Republican senator George Pepper of Pennsylvania in finding a compromise that would not weaken the amendment while securing its passage. Senator Pepper was a former law professor at the University of Pennsylvania and a member of the commission on constitutional revision in Pennsylvania from 1920 to 1921. Ultimately, the differences were resolved, and by the time Congress reconvened, a general consensus existed on the language of an amendment.

An interview published in *Labor* in late November only reinforced the need for an amendment. Five years after the *Hammer v. Dagenhart* case, reporter Lowell Mellett of the Scripps-Howard Newspaper Service attempted to track down the Dagenhart boys to see how they were doing following their Supreme Court victory. Although he was unable to locate John Dagenhart, Mellett found his brother Reuben in Charlotte, North Carolina. Describing the Dagenhart children as "ungrateful sons," Mellett recorded the following account of his meeting with Reuben:

> I found him at his home in Charlotte. He is about the size of an office boy—weighs 105 pounds, he told me. But he is a married man with a child. He is 20 years old.
>
> "What benefit," I asked him, "did you get out of the suit which you won in the United States Supreme Court?"
>
> "You mean the suit the Fidelity Manufacturing Company won? [The Dagenharts worked for the Fidelity Manufacturing Company.] I don't see that I got any benefit. I guess I'd been a lot better off if they hadn't won it.
>
> "Look at me! A hundred and five pounds, a grown man, and no education. I may be mistaken, but I think the years I've put in the cotton mills have stunted my growth. They kept me from getting any schooling. I had to stop school after the third grade and now I need the education that I didn't get."
>
> "How was your growth stunted?"
>
> "I don't know—the dust and the lint, maybe. But from 12 years old on, I was working 12 hours a day—from 6 in the morning till 7 at night, with time out for meals. And sometimes I worked nights besides. Lifting a hundred pounds and I only weighed 65 pounds myself."
>
> "Just what did you and John get out of that suit, then?" he was asked.
>
> "Why, we got some automobile rides when them big lawyers from the North was down here. Oh, yes, and they bought each of us a coca-cola! That's all we got out of it."
>
> "What did you tell the judge when you were in court?"
>
> "Oh, John and me never was in court! Just Paw was there. John and me was just little kids in short pants. I guess we wouldn't have looked like much in court. We were working in the mill while the case was going on. But Paw went up to Washington."
>
> Reuben hasn't been to school but his mind has not been idle.
>
> "It would have been a good thing for all the kids in this state if that law they passed had been kept. Of course, they do better now than they used to. You don't see so many babies working in the factories, but you see a lot of them that ought to be going to school."

"What about John? Is he satisfied with the way things turned out?"

"I don't know. Prob'ly not. He's not much bigger than me and he has flat feet."

"How about your father?"

"Oh, he's satisfied, I guess. But I know one thing. I ain't going to let them put my kid sister in the mill, like he's thinking of doing! She's only 15 and she's crippled and I bet I stop that!"[35]

While Congress debated a Child Labor Amendment, the print media solidly backed the idea. If the newspapers reflected the voice of the people, the amendment had the broad support of many citizens. The NCLC had been tracking editorials on the amendment for months. Although the organization admitted that the statistics were incomplete because not every newspaper was represented, the committee reported that 125 newspapers definitely supported the amendment, 5 did not have strong objections, and only 9 were fundamentally opposed to the measure.[36] The committee speculated that the favorable editorials were influenced by several events, including a Children's Bureau announcement that child labor had increased following the *Bailey* decision, interstate complications resulting from a sweatshop controversy between New York and New Jersey, and Census figures indicating that at least one million children between ten and fifteen were employed.

When President Harding died of heart failure on August 2, 1923, reformers lamented the loss of a powerful ally. They were not disappointed for long, however. President Calvin Coolidge shared his predecessor's view on the need to amend the Constitution. In his first annual message to Congress on December 6, Coolidge supported a constitutional amendment to give Congress the authority to limit child labor. "For purposes of national uniformity," he declared, "we ought to provide, by constitutional amendment and appropriate legislation, for a limitation of child labor."[37] Congress quickly obliged the new president. By the time the 68th Congress reconvened in early December, fourteen resolutions for a child labor amendment were introduced in the House and four in the Senate.[38] Support coalesced around a new measure introduced early in the session by Congressman Foster of Ohio and Senator Samuel Shortridge of California. From February 7 to March 8, 1924, the House held hearings on various changes to the amendment. At this point, opposition voices became more resolute and alarmist with their arguments.

On February 29, 1924, several groups opposed to the Child Labor Amendment testified before the House Judiciary Committee. Represented were the Moderation League, which had formed to oppose the Volstead Act and prohibition; the Constitutional League of Maryland, which had been created to fight the Nineteenth Amendment and the Sheppard-Towner Maternity Act; the Anti-Suffragists; and the Manufacturers' Association of Pennsylvania. All the speakers seemed opposed to any government regulation in general and specifically federal regulation. Members of the NCLC were present to hear the testimony, and they sarcastically reported on the comments of the various witnesses. One speaker claimed that compulsory school attendance laws were an invasion of the sacred rights of parents over their children. A second claimed that because he had worked on his father's farm when he was a little child and was not injured, child labor laws were unnecessary. Another warned that the amendment would result in "a change from an indissoluble union of indestructible States to a group of French departments regulated by bureaucrats from Washington."[39]

In early March, representatives from the American Farm Bureau Federation (AFBF) testified against the amendment in a House committee hearing. Gray Silver, legislative representative for the AFBF, reported that the proposal "does not find a favorable response among the farmers," and he believed that the amendment was "unnecessary, especially as it might apply to families on the farms." He argued: "The farmers will be among the first to resent the activities of the Federal bureau if it tried to take the place of the parents by telling the children what duties they should or should not perform and what kind of work they should do."[40] In his study of the NCLC and child labor, Walter I. Trattner notes that the testimony marked the first time members of a farm organization appeared before Congress to oppose the child labor amendment.[41] The fracturing of the interest groups that were part of the Progressive coalition was now evident.

Several state Granges joined the American Farm Bureau in combating the amendment, and the national Grange, with delegates from only three states dissenting, voted to oppose the amendment at its annual convention that year. "The prohibition on child labor," the Grange stated in a resolution, would be "dangerous to the best interests of the communities of the nation and to the welfare of children themselves." The proposed amendment, the Grange added, "would tend toward centralized, costly, bureaucratic control."[42] An editorial in *The Farm Journal* expressed contempt for reformers backing the amendment: "There is a kind of mush-headed opinion abroad in the land that seems to consider work an evil, and hard work a device of Satan. The danger of the Child Labor Amendment is that the enforcing of the laws which would infallibly follow the amendment would be in the hands of some of these soft-brained child-cranks."[43]

Not all agricultural publications opposed the amendment. *Farm and Fireside*, *Successful Farming*, and *The Southern Agriculturalist* published editorials endorsing the measure. E. T. Meredith, secretary of agriculture in the Wilson administration, wrote in *Successful Farming*: "But when a southern cotton mill uses children it competes unfairly with a cotton mill in another state where child labor is forbidden. It is an interstate interest. When the children of a certain state are allowed to pick coal at the mines, it is unfair competition with coal production in states where this is prohibited. It is an interstate affair."[44] Meredith also emphasized the cooperative nature of our federal system. "It is the business of other states to see that the children of all the states have a chance to get a common school education at least." George Martin, editor of *Farm and Fireside*, tried to allay the fears of rural communities. "The proposed Child Labor Amendment to the Constitution is not intended to meddle in the affairs of farm families. . . . The Amendment is to protect children who are now at the mercy of greedy mill owners and the unscrupulous bosses of the great industrial centers."[45]

During congressional debate over the amendment, Grace Abbott, chief of the federal Children's Bureau, testified before the Senate Judiciary Committee. According to her biographer, Abbott's expertise on the issue of child labor was "unsurpassed," and she was influential in drafting the amendment and providing congressional testimony. Her experience in administering the first federal child labor law allowed her to clarify misconceptions and provide convincing answers. She stayed in regular contact with leaders of reform groups and consulted famous lawyers of the day, including Ernst Freund, Felix Frankfurter, Edward P. Costigan, and Roscoe Pound.[46] During the congressional hearings on the amendment, some committee members were condescending, but others acknowledged her expertise. Senator LeBaron Colt remarked, "Miss Abbott, you are a master on this whole subject."[47] From her administrative experience and consultations with legal scholars, Abbott developed strong convictions about the appropriate language of a child labor amendment.

Abbott's agency supported the amendment, but she expressed doubt about the word "employment" in the original draft. As she explained to the committee, "children often work with their parents and are not on payroll, and are not held to be employed, and we feel that it is a dangerous word to use, as far as the protection of children is concerned."[48] Abbott urged that the word "employment" be changed to "labor," and Congress subsequently made the revision. Critics of the amendment, however, would later seize upon the substitution by arguing that the amendment was no longer restricted to paid employment, but it would give Congress the power to regulate chores done by children in the home and on the farm. Although highly improbable, the argument confirmed the fears of citizens concerned about the scope of federal power, and it became an effective rhetorical weapon in the campaign against ratification.

After the hearings, the "Children's Amendment," as it was called by supporters, was offered by Congressman Israel Moore Foster (R-OH) on April 26, 1924, in the form of House Joint Resolution No. 184. In its report on H.J. Res. 184, the Judiciary Committee noted that it had received twenty-three resolutions proposing to amend the Constitution to regulate and prohibit child labor. Almost one hundred members spoke either for or against the amendment. No one, however, championed child labor itself. The principal objection was a fear that too much power was being transferred from the states to the federal government. Opponents were unable to derail support for the measure, however. The amendment passed the House with bipartisan approval by a vote of 297 to 69 on April 26, 1924. Although there was support throughout the country, of the 69 votes against the bill, 37 were from five southern states: Texas, Alabama, Virginia, Georgia, and North Carolina.[49]

The Senate debated the issue for another month. Senator James Wadsworth (R-NY) led the foes of the amendment. He and his wife, Alice Hay, were the country's most vocal anti–women's suffrage couple, with Alice serving as president of the National Association Opposed to Woman Suffrage, an organization largely bankrolled by the wealthy couple from the Genesee Valley. Wadsworth also was the state's most visible "wet" in the debate over prohibition. With the ratification of the Eighteenth (prohibition) and Nineteenth (women's suffrage) Amendments, and the proposed Twentieth Amendment, Wadsworth sensed that the America of the founders was disappearing. He believed that the Constitution existed to limit government power and protect individual rights.

Eventually, over 120 pages of testimony, speeches, and other evidence, including the full text of both the *Hammer* and *Bailey* decisions, became part of the *Congressional Record*. By an overwhelming majority, the Senate voted down a proposal to use state ratifying conventions under Article V and rejected a time limit on ratification.[50] Both of those votes impacted the ratification battle in the years to come. Attempts to limit the scope of the amendment by setting the age at sixteen years, exempting farm labor, or by specifying that the power applied only to commercial employment of children in mills, factories, and mines were also turned back. Opponents could not defeat or narrow the measure. At 10:00 p.m. on June 2, 1924, the Senate voted 61 to 23 in favor of the amendment, five more than the required two-thirds majority. The proposed constitutional amendment was submitted to the state legislatures for ratification pursuant to Article V of the Constitution. With forty-eight states in the Union, thirty-six were needed for ratification. The text of the amendment read:

Section 1. The Congress shall have power to limit, regulate, and prohibit the labor of persons under eighteen years of age.

Section 2. The power of the several States is unimpaired by this article except that the operation of State laws shall be suspended to the extent necessary to give effect to legislation enacted by the Congress.

While Section 1 of the amendment gave Congress the authority to set national standards regarding child labor, Section 2 acknowledged state powers to enact child labor laws unless they conflict with national legislation, and it allowed the states to enact higher standards than those set by federal law. The language of the approved amendment mirrored the one jointly drafted by the NCLC and the Permanent Conference, with some modifications requested by the Senate Judiciary Committee.[51] Two senators considered as authorities on the Constitution—George Wharton Pepper of Pennsylvania, a Republican and a Protestant, and Thomas J. Walsh of Montana, a Democrat and a Catholic—were primarily responsible for the final language. Each word was carefully considered. Because the amendment was to be a general grant of power to Congress to enact child labor legislation, the language had to be broad and inclusive. Congress would determine the specific occupational, age, and wage restrictions in response to changing social circumstances.

The proposed amendment gave Congress the power to regulate labor up to eighteen years rather than the usual sixteen-year limitation found in many laws. That age limit allowed Congress to regulate and prohibit, if necessary, the labor of sixteen- and seventeen-year-olds in mines and other hazardous occupations.[52] Florence Kelley had pushed for the eighteen-year age limit and the elimination of "concurrent power" language. As Grace Abbott suggested, the word "labor" was substituted for "employment" to prevent evasions from compliance in situations where children were simply "helping" their parents in canneries or doing industrial homework. Finally, the word "child" was eliminated from the Child Labor Amendment to avoid confusion because the courts had defined the term differently in several precedents.

Supporters were convinced that the final language of the amendment was practical and necessary for effective federal legislation. Based on decades of experience, they knew how opponents used legal loopholes to weaken and elude child labor restrictions. Reformers never intended for Congress to regulate all labor of workers less than eighteen years. The various groups in the Permanent Conference never imagined that Congress would use the authority granted in the amendment for anything other than the economic exploitation of children for their labor. Regardless of their intentions, the text of the amendment became a flashpoint for opponents.

The only state delegations to vote against the amendment in both the House and Senate were Alabama, Florida, Georgia, Louisiana, Maryland, North Carolina, and South Carolina. After observing the debate in Congress, Wiley H. Swift, director of legislation and investigation for the NCLC, predicted a hard fight in the state legislatures for ratification and commented that "the old prejudice against Federal control will . . . be one of the chief stumbling blocks" in the path of placing control over child labor in the national government.[53] Although proponents recognized that there would be a battle over ratification, they were optimistic about the chances for success. Florence Kelley expected swift ratification. The size of the congressional majorities in favor of the amendment and perceived support in midwestern states were encouraging signs. A vote in favor of ratification in Arkansas at the end of June, just weeks after the amendment had been sent to the states, also raised hopes among reformers. Moreover, all three major political parties—Republican, Democratic, and Progressive—and their respective presidential candidates backed the amendment.

In fact, the campaign for ratification started off well. In addition to Arkansas, two other states, Arizona and California, ratified by January 1925. Wisconsin joined the list the following month. Believing that their cause was just and that the child labor amendment was the solution to a national problem, supporters of the amendment felt that most opposition would collapse once the inflammatory rhetoric and misrepresentations were corrected by reasoned arguments. Suddenly, however, the ratification campaign faced a series of defeats in the states and growing public opposition nationwide. Friends of the amendment seemed blindsided by the campaign opposed to ratification, and they were slow to respond. More than three months passed before the groups supporting the amendment met to discuss strategy.[54]

Debate over the amendment in the states was fervent and acrimonious. A study of the propaganda over the amendment identified more than seventy-five organized groups involved in the campaign to defeat or ratify the amendment in the twelve years (1924–1936) that it had been a prominent issue.[55] The National Child Labor Committee served as a clearinghouse for all groups in favor of the amendment. Proponents included the American Association of University Women, the National Federation of Teachers, Camp Fire Girls, American Legion, the Young Women's Christian Association, and the Northern Baptist Convention.

There was less coordination among opposition interests, but they were unified by the common goal of defeating the measure. The National Association of Manufacturers (NAM), under the direction of David Clark and James A. Emery, corporate counsel for NAM, led the opposition. Some organizations were created solely to defeat the amendment while others were strongly opposed to any kind of federal social or welfare legislation. NAM was joined by the National Farm Bureau Federation, the Grange, and various farm journals. Other groups included those who had fought against the Eighteenth and Nineteenth Amendments, such as the National Association Opposed to Woman Suffrage, renamed the Woman Patriots, and the American Constitutional League. The Nebraska and Missouri Synod of the Lutheran Church, the Chamber of Commerce of New York, and the Catholic Diocese of Boston were all vocal critics.

Opponents often dubbed the proposal the "So-called Child Labor Amendment" or referred to it as the "Disingenuous Amendment" to suggest a hidden agenda of socialism and federal encroachment on states' rights, parental authority, and liberty. Others said that the amendment would replace the authority of parents with federal authority and that it would threaten parochial schools. Some compared the proposed amendment to the problems of regulating alcohol under Prohibition and warned that the federal government could not effectively enforce child labor restrictions. Reflecting the hyperbole used by the antiamendment groups, one committee in New England, organized by A. Lawrence Lowell, president of Harvard University, called itself the Citizens' Committee to Save Our Homes and Children. Another group, the Sentinels of the Republic, was formed in 1922 by Louis A. Coolidge, treasurer of the United Shoe Manufacturing Company, and financed mostly by business and industry. Organized around the broad agenda of opposition to any social or labor reforms and concentration of federal power, the Sentinels focused most of their efforts on defeating the child labor amendment and other reforms as "the surest means of safeguarding our institutions from the assaults of communism."[56]

In an age before television and the Internet, the battle over the amendment was waged in the print media, public forums, and radio. Both sides printed pamphlets, leaflets, and other literature for public distribution. Newspapers and magazines were flooded with editorials, photographs, cartoons, and paid ads. Proponents of the amendment wrote supportive essays for national periodicals such as the *Nation, Collier's, Good Housekeeping, Literary Digest,* and the *Saturday Evening Post.* Radio talks, at a cost of $5 per minute, were mostly used by opponents of the measure. Those against the amendment also wrote scathing editorials in trade journals such as the *Southern Textile Bulletin* and *Manufacturers' Record.* Prominent politicians and reformers gave speeches at association and community meetings, schools, and churches.[57] Representatives from both sides also testified before national and state legislative committees.

Any hope of support in the South quickly faded when in June 1924, the Louisiana House rejected the amendment by a near unanimous vote, and on July 2, both legislative chambers in Georgia voted nearly unanimously against the amendment. The Georgia House of Representatives voted 170 to 3 to reject the amendment, and the Senate voted 34 to 0 the following day. When Representative Viola Napier of Bibb, one of only two women in the Georgia House, urged support for the amendment, she was greeted with a chorus of "Nays." Representative James McCorsey denounced the amendment as the work of a bunch of "long-haired agitatists [*sic*]" in Washington. "We weren't born under the same regime and don't drink out of the same bottle," he said. "We don't want them interfering with our affairs."[58] Apparently, those views were shared by many in the chamber. Georgia legislators expressed their disapproval in a sharply worded resolution. The proposed amendment, it was claimed, would "destroy parental authority and responsibility throughout America" and encourage a "rebellion of childhood" that threatened civilization.[59] Moreover, the amendment would give Congress "parental authority" and "destroy local self-government . . . eviscerate the states . . . and give Congress the power to destroy agriculture and manufacturing at will."[60] In rather perverse logic, the resolution concluded that the amendment was "really intended to enslave the children of this republic."

At a meeting of the NCLC trustees on September 16, 1924, Secretary Lovejoy reported that opposition to the amendment was "widespread" and coming from cotton, beet, and onion growers, state Granges, and particularly the National Association of Manufacturers, which had published a strongly worded pamphlet against the amendment.[61] In a sign of just how badly things were going for the reformers, Representative Foster, the sponsor of the Child Labor Amendment in the House, was defeated in the Republican primary. In a letter to her friend and mentor, Jane Addams, Florence Kelley blamed the loss on the National Association of Manufacturers' "lavish" financial support of Foster's opponent, Thomas A. Jenkins, and suggested that Foster's electoral "slaughter" was intended as a warning to all legislators who might support the amendment.[62] Another blow to amendment supporters came several months later when Samuel Gompers, the nation's most influential labor leader and longtime advocate for child labor reform, died on December 13, 1924, in San Antonio, Texas.

Advocates for the Child Labor Amendment complained of an intense and unfair propaganda campaign to defeat the measure. The *New Republic*, which supported the amendment, described the situation in the summer of 1924: "The friends of the amendment were totally unprepared to combat the flood of distorted propaganda which let loose upon them. They had been accustomed to argue their case before reasonable and attentive human beings. They suddenly found themselves compelled to discuss a matter of public policy with a monstrous jazz band."[63]

There certainly was no shortage of outrageous and self-serving criticisms of the amendment. For example, one dissenter writing in the *Manufacturers' Record* claimed that if adopted, the "amendment would be the greatest thing ever done in America in behalf of the activities of Hell. It would make millions of young people under 18 years of age idlers in brain and body, and thus make them the devil's best workshop."[64] Personal attacks on proamendment women, such as Jane Addams, Florence Kelley, and Julia Lathrop, implied that they were spinsters and lesbians who loved children in the abstract but who hated to be around real kids. Opponents often noted the "childlessness of the child savers," and they emphasized class differences between middle-class reformers and working-class families. Pennsylvanian Edward J. Maginnis wrote an open letter that was widely distributed by antiamendment forces: "One class of citizens composed principally of cultured men and women of small or no families at all, living in comfort, albeit with good intentions, are attempting to force legislation on the industrial class, composed mostly of humble, stalwart men and women of large families."[65]

One slippery-slope argument drew a connection between the amendment and federal regulation of all aspects of education, public and parochial. The Catholic weekly, *America*, made the link explicit but only by piling inference upon inference. The argument began by saying that if the goal was to keep children from gainful employment, the most obvious way to accomplish that objective would be to make kids go to school, so under the amendment, school attendance can be required by federal law. "But if the federal government can send children to school, it can define what constitutes a satisfactory school. It can prescribe the studies for children and training of teachers, and erect or subsidize schools to give the required training."[66] Such reasoning fueled Catholic sentiment against the amendment. Catholics had long felt that public schools were too Protestant, and they rejected threats to their system of separate parochial schools. Moreover, churchgoers generally followed the lead of the Church hierarchy. When prominent cardinals warned that the amendment threatened parental rights, Catholic education, and the moral authority of the Church, many parishioners accepted the arguments.[67]

There were, however, a number of honest, if not reasonable, arguments made against the amendment that resonated with many citizens in the political climate of the 1920s. Since World War I, people were concerned about the growth of the federal government and its ability to successfully administer programs. Six criticisms, first identified by Walter I. Trattner in his study of the NCLC, were commonly circulated by various antiamendment groups throughout the campaign:

(1) The amendment was unnecessary because state regulations were effective in eliminating the worst forms of child labor exploitation. According to the 1920 Census, the number of employed children was in decline compared to a decade earlier. Almost one million fewer children were working in 1920. As previously mentioned, however, reformers had an explanation for this decline, but the interpretation of the statistics did not convince everyone.

(2) The text of the amendment was too broad. Opponents attacked the use of the word "labor" as opposed to "employment" and argued that the eighteen-year-old age limit was too high. Previous child labor laws had set a sixteen-year-old limit for most employment. Although Grace Abbott had valid reasons for preferring the word "labor" in the text of the amendment, the term gave opponents a huge opening to attack the measure. Advocates for the amendment countered that the word "labor" would be used in the ordinary sense. If interpretative conflicts emerged, they noted, the Supreme Court in the past held that "all laws should receive a sensible construction," and on two occasions interpreted labor to mean paid manual work.[68] Those arrayed against the amendment were not swayed by such arguments.

(3) Based on the concept of dual federalism, the amendment undermined

national-state relations within the constitutional system. Federal regulation of child labor threatened states' rights and local control of economic conditions and undermined policy responsibilities reserved to the states and local governments. Labor conditions varied in each state, and it would be ineffective to impose uniform, national regulations. These arguments were used to challenge the earliest federal child labor proposals, and they were effective against the amendment. As Florence Kelley predicted, amendment opponents were not mollified by the language of Section 2, asserting that the provision did nothing to protect state authority because federal power is supreme under the Supremacy Clause of Article VI. State laws, opponents argued, would be preempted by any federal regulations.

(4) The amendment would substantially increase the federal bureaucracy, and "an army" of federal agents would invade businesses and homes to enforce the law. An editorial in the *Manufacturers' News* reflected this position: "Office holding parasites want to prohibit work by all minors under 18. Why? So they can put to work several thousand inspectors to see that the youth of the land are properly idle. Too much sociology. Too much bureaucracy. Too many payrollers. Too many drones in the hive."[69] Antiamendment essays claimed that there were already over six hundred thousand federal employees in DC and in the field, and that we do not need to add to that number. This critique also alluded to federal incompetence in administering prohibition laws and warned that the same thing would happen with child labor regulations.

(5) Parental control over children would be replaced by federal bureaucrats. Opponents of child labor regulations asserted that reform advocates wanted to substitute parental authority with the dictates of federal regulators. The homes as "castles" metaphor was used to suggest a fundamental invasion of privacy by federal bureaucrats. Antiamendment groups presented an image of ruddy-cheeked, happy children doing wholesome labor on the farm or in the home out of respect for, and in obedience to, their parents.[70] This ideal relationship between parents and children was threatened by the amendment. Those in favor of the amendment, however, argued against the absolute rights of parents to control their children's lives. Implicit in this argument was an image of lazy, ignorant, and selfish parents who used their kids for economic gain while injuring their health and denying them an education.[71]

(6) Finally, the amendment was alleged to be a communist plot designed to subvert American institutions. This line of attack drew upon fears from the Red Scare of 1919–1920, a nationalistic response to the Bolshevik Revolution in Russia. Although those fears had largely abated by the mid-1920s, concerns over foreign influence in American culture still resonated with many citizens. The measure was endorsed by the American Socialist and Communist Parties, but the broad bipartisan support for the amendment among Democrats, Republicans, and Progressives was ignored. Opponents frequently argued that the amendment was "Russian in origin" and instigated by "Socialists, Communists, and Bolshevists."[72] Senator Hubert D. Stephens (D-MS) described the proamendment campaign as a "socialistic movement" that was part of a "hellish scheme laid in foreign countries to destroy our government." "Many of the propagandists of the measure," Senator Stephens asserted, were "communists and socialists."[73] It probably did not help matters when Victor L. Berger of Wisconsin, the only avowed socialist in Congress, declared, "It is a socialist amendment, and that is why I am for it," when the amendment was under consideration in the House in April. Florence Kelley was singled out because of her past association with the Socialist Party. David Clark regularly referred to his enemies as "un-American," and he flooded rural newspapers with sinister descriptions of their associational guilt. For example, Owen R. Lovejoy of the NCLC was an "active socialist and close friend of Eugene Debs," while Grace Abbott "hailed from that 'hotbed of socialism'—Hull House in Chicago." Some radicals and socialists, however, actually opposed the amendment, believing that it would improve wages for adult workers and undermine the class struggle toward socialism.

Many farm journals labeled the amendment the "Loafer Law" because opponents believed it would prevent farmers from having their sons and daughters do chores on the family farm until eighteen years of age. Florence Kelley was "horrified" to see letters in every issue of *Rural New Yorker* threatening that if the amendment were ratified, "no farm boy will be able to drive the cows to pasture, or pick berries on his father's New Hampshire hillside, until after his eighteenth birthday."[74] David Clark of NAM and the *Southern Textile Bulletin* effectively targeted farm journals and associations with antiamendment literature. The amendment, it was argued, would not significantly impact manufacturers; rather, it was aimed at children on farms and the effect would be "to make a criminal of the farmer who allows his son to milk a cow."[75] NAM claimed that under the measure, "The mother would have no right to teach her daughter to do any housework whatsoever, whether it be the sweeping of floors or the washing of dishes."[76]

In July 1924, Clark secretly organized the Farmers' States' Rights League (FSRL) of North Carolina, which disseminated antiamendment propaganda in papers throughout the Midwest. Although appearing to be a grass-roots farm group, David Clark funded and managed the league and wrote and disseminated all the organization's literature. Initially, Clark denied any involvement with the organization. Even after it was revealed in early 1925 that the supposedly agrarian group was a tool of the southern cotton mill interests, the damage had been done, and the disclosure had little impact in stemming the tide of opposition against the amendment.[77] Eventually, Clark admitted his complete control of the FSRL and boasted that from June 1924 to February 1925, he had single-handedly pursued a "campaign of enlightenment" by distributing over 250,000 pieces of literature and advertising against the amendment.[78]

Voters in Massachusetts dealt a significant blow to the ratification campaign in a November 4 advisory referendum when they overwhelmingly rejected the amendment. The vote was 697,563 against the amendment to 241,461 in favor.[79] No legislative district in the state voted in favor of the amendment. Voters were clearly interested in the issue. Of the seven propositions on the ballot, the child labor issue received the highest number of votes, 939,024, a total almost equal to the number of votes for governor. The vote followed two months of intense campaigning by various groups against the amendment, described by one observer as "distinguished by misrepresentation, ignorance, and deceit."[80]

The defeat of the amendment in Massachusetts was surprising and definitive in many ways. Historically, the state had enlightened child labor laws, was the home of several reform groups, and was often in the vanguard of protective legislation. Massachusetts was already feeling the pains of unfair competition, as some of its textile mills moved to southern states to take advantage of their lax labor regulations. The state legislature, known as the General Court, had adopted a resolution in February 1924, urging Congress to propose a child labor amendment. Also, Massachusetts senators Henry Cabot Lodge and David I. Walsh, the state's first Irish-Catholic senator, supported the amendment, as did several members of the House delegation and former congressman James M. Curley, mayor of Boston and candidate for governor in 1924. It appeared that the child labor amendment would receive swift ratification.

The amendment, however, became mired in the rush of the last days of the legislative session, and representatives hesitated to approve the proposal without adequate debate. A few days before adjournment, legislators discovered a decision made by the General Court in 1920 requiring the legislature to submit a proposed amendment to the federal constitution to the voters before the General Court voted on ratification. Instead of voting on the amendment in the waning hours of the session, the legislature called for a referendum in November. The months-long delay allowed opposition forces time to organize and launch an effective campaign against the amendment.

NAM and the Sentinels of the Republic led much of the opposition, with grassroots support from the Citizens' Committee to Protect Our Homes and Children, a group organized by A. Lawrence Lowell, president of Harvard University. Lowell represented earlier upper-class Protestant reformers who had become concerned about the growth of federal power. The Citizens' Committee distributed literature throughout the state warning that the amendment gave Congress "undisputed power for all time to control and prohibit the labor of every person up to eighteen years of age, in the home, on the farm, and in the school. . . . It would enable Congress, through Federal agents, thus to interfere in the discipline of every household, and take from parents the right and duty to educate and guide their children."[81] Louis A. Coolidge of the Sentinels expressed similar arguments in a radio address entitled "The Child Labor Amendment: An Appeal to the Christian Men and Women of Massachusetts." In his address, he warned of the impact of the amendment on families:

> We want to cultivate the family with its domestic ties. We need the benediction of home-loving Christian mothers. We need to stimulate in youth a feeling of responsibility, of thrift, of industry. . . . If there is any chance that this [child labor] amendment might be used to blight the children of America, you do not want it ratified. . . . Can you afford to gamble with your children's happiness at stake? Can you afford to risk contamination of the Massachusetts home?[82]

The Roman Catholic Church played a central role in the Massachusetts ratification battle. Prominent members of the Church hierarchy and

Catholic lay leaders clashed over the amendment. Monsignor John A. Ryan, a Catholic progressive reformer, professor of economics at Catholic University, NCLC board member, and director of the Social Action Department of the National Catholic Welfare Conference, had been a longtime opponent of child labor. In 1919, Father Ryan authored what was called the Bishops' Program for Social Reconstruction. Based on Pope Leo XIII's encyclical *Rerum novarum* ("Of New Things"), the Bishops' Program "explicitly advocated legislation to regulate child labor, establish minimum wages, and provide national health insurance."[83] Monsignor Ryan had encouraged the National Council of Catholic Women to support the child labor amendment, and his office issued two newsletters endorsing the amendment two months before the Massachusetts referendum.[84]

Monsignor Ryan's efforts in defense of the amendment infuriated the conservative archbishop of Boston, Cardinal William Henry O'Connell, a powerful member of the Church hierarchy in America. Cardinal O'Connell's opposition to the amendment was influential and ultimately fatal to the ratification campaign in Massachusetts. Like many members in the Church hierarchy, he felt that the government should not intervene in an area properly reserved to the family and parental authority under the moral guidance of the Church.

During the 1920s, much of the Catholic Church hierarchy was socially conservative. Anti-Catholic sentiment was widespread during the decade. The resurgence of the Ku Klux Klan, with its virulent anti-Catholic rhetoric and cross burnings, alarmed Church leaders. In 1922, Oregon voters passed an initiative requiring children to attend public schools. The Compulsory Education Act was designed to eliminate parochial schools, including Catholic schools. Other states were considering such laws. In 1925, the US Supreme Court overturned the law in *Pierce v. Society of Sisters*, but there was a feeling that the Church was threatened by various cultural forces. Many cardinals and bishops viewed the Child Labor Amendment as an attack on the moral authority of the Church and a potential danger to Catholic schools.

One month before the vote, Cardinal O'Connell sent a pastoral letter to every priest in Boston's large Catholic archdiocese, ordering them to read a statement from the pulpit for three successive weeks condemning the amendment. Parishioners were encouraged to vote against the amendment because the measure would allow Congress to send "swarms of paid Governmental workers throughout the country, seeing that parents are complying with the bureau's ideas of bringing up their children, supervising their education as well as their hours of work and interfering in the sacred rights of parents over their children."[85] The archdiocesan newspaper, *The Boston Pilot*, also published a series of articles warning that the amendment would "commit this country forever to the communistic system of the nationalization of her children." The attacks prompted both Senator Walsh and James Curley to reverse their earlier endorsements. Senator Walsh fell silent on the issue while Curley became a vociferous opponent of the measure.

The opposition of the Catholic Church to the amendment proved decisive. With the vote margin nearly 3 to 1 against the amendment, supporters had either badly misjudged public sentiment on the issue of child labor, or they were outcampaigned by opposition forces, or both. Dr. Felix Adler, cofounder of the NCLC and chair for seventeen years, blamed the loss on a "total eclipse of the public" and a "lunatic shade spread across the solar disc of reason."[86] In late December, the NCLC published a pamphlet arguing that the alarmist campaign in Massachusetts was organized by those with a financial stake in the perpetuation of child labor. They called the results a "panic vote, cast by a public deceived and alarmed by a deliberately planned propaganda of fear, whose authors kept themselves in the background."[87] The campaign against the amendment in Massachusetts may have been all of that, but it was effective. Regardless of the motivations and tactics of antiratification groups, Massachusetts lawmakers decided to follow the results of the advisory referendum. In February 1925, almost one year after urging Congress to send a child labor amendment to the states, the legislature overwhelmingly voted against ratification. The amendment was dead in Massachusetts; it was a demoralizing defeat for the reformers.

By January 1925, only three states had ratified the amendment—Arkansas, Arizona, and California.[88] Wisconsin joined them in February, but the momentum was clearly against the amendment. Six states had voted down the amendment, often by wide margins: Georgia, Kansas, North Carolina, South Carolina, Oklahoma, and Texas. Anxious for a victory, supporters of the amendment looked to New York to turn the tide.

New York was a key state in the ratification battle. With its large population and diverse economy, a vote to ratify the amendment in the Empire State could change the momentum in favor of ratification. Home to the NCLC, New York had some of the most progressive child labor laws, and its standards equaled or exceeded those of the two federal child labor laws that were invalidated by the Supreme Court. The political environment appeared favorable for ratification. Every member of the state's congressional delegation, with the exception of eight who were absent, and Republican senator James W. Wadsworth, had voted in favor of the amendment. But the campaign for ratification was not going to be easy. The same organizations that had worked to defeat the amendment in Massachusetts—NAM, the Sentinels, the American Farm Bureau Federation, and the Citizens' Committee to Protect Our Homes and Children—geared up for another fight.

Amendment supporters desperately wanted to avoid another referendum because they knew that they lacked the resources to compete with NAM and the other groups. Reformers assumed that Governor Alfred E. Smith, a longtime opponent of child labor with an outstanding record on social legislation, would back the amendment. But they were wrong. Rumors surfaced that although Governor Smith supported the amendment, he favored a referendum to gauge popular opinion. When Florence Kelley and other reformers met with Governor Smith, the stories were substantiated. The governor included a call for a referendum in his annual message to the legislature on January 7, 1925. In a letter to an amendment ally, Florence Kelley expressed her bitterness by commenting that Smith's reversal was a "staggering blow" and complained that "Governor Smith has gone over to the enemy."[89] Kelley believed that Governor Smith, the country's most prominent Roman Catholic politician, had been "turned" by New York City's Cardinal Patrick Hayes. As in Massachusetts, most of the Church hierarchy was against the amendment, and reformers expected that many of the same arguments made in Massachusetts would be directed at Catholic New Yorkers.

In response to the governor's call for a referendum, politicians in Albany seemed ready to set a date for a referendum vote. Aware that they did not have the resources to match opponents in a referendum campaign, and fearful of another Massachusetts debacle, amendment representatives met with Governor Smith in February and negotiated a "gentleman's agreement" that the measure should be tabled for the legislative session and that no vote by the legislature or the people should be taken.[90] In March 1925, however, the New York State Senate passed the Fearon Bill, which called for a fall referendum. The New York Committee for the Ratification of the Child Labor Amendment denounced the vote, claiming that senators were evading the issue and failing their duty to represent the people. The ratification committee looked to Governor Smith to carry out his part of the gentleman's agreement. Apparently, the governor obliged because after a five-hour conference, the assembly announced that it would neither vote on the amendment nor the referendum bill. Consideration of the amendment was suspended, and the measure was dead. Over the next decade, bills to ratify the amendment were introduced in every legislative session, but they never made it out of committee. New York, then, never formally voted on the Child Labor Amendment during the initial campaign for ratification, but it revisited the issue a decade later.

As early as March 1925, the NCLC was already raising the white flag of surrender on the amendment. In a memo to Owen R. Lovejoy, Dr. Samuel M. Lindsay, chair of the NCLC Ratification Committee in Washington, DC, acknowledged the "popular tide" against the amendment and admitted that for "at least two years, and probably four years," there was no possibility of ratification.[91] He recommended a renewed push to strengthen state legislation and swift opposition to any proposed state referendum on the amendment. Lindsay remained confident that once the people truly understood the meaning of the amendment, it would obtain ratification.

In an effort to improve the morale of amendment supporters, Florence Kelley and Grace Abbott offered hope that some states might one day reverse their vote. Although this event would actually happen a decade later, at the time it provided little comfort to those who had worked so long and passionately for the cause of child labor. Indeed, after eight years, only six state legislatures had ratified the amendment. During this period, the amendment was rejected in one or both houses in thirty-two states and by 1932 was largely thought to be defeated.

Historians have argued that the collapse of the ratification campaign in 1924–1925 revealed that the general public had a far deeper distrust of the federal government and its ability for social reform than supporters of the amendment recognized. The defeat of the amendment also illustrates the collapse of the Progressive coalition of the early twentieth century. The diverse groups within the coalition that helped reelect Woodrow Wilson in 1916—urban workers, western and southern farmers, middle-class reformers, and intellectuals—were by the 1920s unable to agree on common policy objectives and strategies.[92]

With support from powerful industry groups, the antiratification campaign had a substantial financial advantage over reform advocates. To a certain extent, however, the success of their alarmist rhetoric about the amendment is unusual. The purpose of the amendment was not a new or radical idea. Two federal laws concerning child labor had been enacted, and both were limited to curbing the commercial exploitation of children. Although the Supreme Court found constitutional flaws with both statutes, Congress showed no inclination to regulate anything beyond the employment of children in factories, mills, mines, and other industries. Amendment supporters were frustrated that the American Farm Bureau Federation and other rural farm organizations came out so strongly against the measure. There was nothing in the first two federal laws on child labor that suggested Congress was interested in regulating whether farm kids could milk the cows or help with chores. In fact, both federal laws exempted the labor of children on farms. Unlike the first two federal laws, however, the amendment contained broad language, and that gave opponents an opening for all kinds of criticisms. For example, nothing indicated that the federal government desired to regulate Catholic schools or mandate military training, but the vast power granted to Congress in the text of the amendment created the *possibility* of such restrictions. With communism firmly entrenched in the Soviet Union and fascism on the rise in Europe, fear of concentrated political power was substantial.

Progress on child labor also may have diluted support for the amendment. *Recent Social Trends* reported that while in 1890 almost one in five ten- to fifteen-year-olds was employed, by 1930 that number had dropped to one in twenty. One could argue that reform groups were a victim of their own success. State laws were not uniform, but gains had been made. Most of the worst forms of child labor exploitation in mines and factories had been significantly reduced. The biggest problems remaining involved children in agriculture and various service industries.

The stock market crash in October 1929 led to the worst economic crisis in the nation's history. When unemployment increased during the early years of the Great Depression, many child laborers were discharged from work. In 1932, however, manufacturers increased employment of children because it was simply cheaper than paying adult wages. Child labor in the mills and sweatshops became commonplace again. Though the child labor amendment was believed to be dead, public opinion on the relationship between government and the economy shifted, and the 1932 election results breathed new life into the amendment.

However, one of the most dedicated and passionate advocates for child welfare and the Child Labor Amendment would not take part in the renewed campaign to secure ratification. Florence Kelley passed away on February 7, 1932. She was seventy-two years old. Two decades later, Supreme Court justice Felix Frankfurter honored the social reformer, writing that Kelley had "dedicated her life to the well-being of others. . . . She was an inextinguishable flame. [She] had probably the largest single share in shaping the social history of the United States in the first thirty years of this century."[93] Although Kelley was unable to witness the final victory over oppressive child labor, her tireless efforts for child labor reform would ultimately be vindicated during the New Deal period. Taking the baton from Kelley was Frances Perkins, secretary of labor under Franklin D. Roosevelt from 1933 to 1945. Perkins "felt deeply responsible to Kelley's legacy," and as labor secretary, she worked to promote the Child Labor Amendment and federal labor legislation.[94] In 1934 Perkins came out strongly in favor of the amendment and responded to every criticism made by opponents.[95] In subsequent speeches, regardless of the forum or assigned topic, she incorporated her support for the amendment.[96] In many ways, Secretary Perkins became the conscience of the Roosevelt administration on child labor reform and fair labor standards throughout the 1930s.

The Great Depression and
the Renewed Fight over the
Child Labor Amendment

As employment conditions worsened during the height of the Depression, support for the Child Labor Amendment increased. Organized labor believed that children should not compete with adults for scarce job opportunities, and public attitudes about the need for federal regulation of the economy became more favorable. Prospects for the amendment greatly improved in November 1932 with the election of Democratic president Franklin D. Roosevelt, huge Democratic majorities in Congress, and new state legislators. In the depths of the Great Depression, public opinion had suddenly shifted in favor of government efforts to regulate the economy. These developments triggered what can be described as the "second round" in the fight over the amendment. Between 1933 and 1939, more states ratified the Child Labor Amendment, new federal legislation restricting child labor was enacted, and several Supreme Court decisions affected the regulatory power of Congress and the states, with one opinion settling two important questions concerning the ratification of the 1924 amendment.

At the urging of the Children's Bureau, reformers met in Washington in early 1933 to discuss strategy. Supporters of the amendment, who may have been disillusioned by the early amendment battles, seemed to misjudge the significance of the 1932 elections. Most were against concentrating efforts on ratification of the amendment, and even though many believed that national legislation was essential, a consensus opposed pushing for a new federal law. The group concluded that maybe the best option was to abandon the effort to amend the Constitution and press for a sixteen-year minimum age for employment in all the states.

The NCLC Board of Trustees met on January 30, 1933, to discuss a path forward. In a report to the Board of Trustees, Professor Noel T. Dowling, Columbia University School of Law, stated that the sentiment of those meeting at the Washington conference was against focusing on the amendment, and even a federal law regulating child labor seemed remote. Although the prospects for federal action were dim, there were signs of hope for national legislation. Professor Dowling promised to meet with Senator Hugo Black, who had drafted an early version of what would become the Fair Labor Standards Act. Although it is not clear where he received the information, Senator Black reportedly said that the "Supreme Court had indicated that it might reverse its opinion on the child labor law."[1]

When Franklin D. Roosevelt took office in 1933, his New Deal programs harnessed the power of the federal government to increase employment, stabilize financial markets, regulate various industries, and promote economic growth. During the first three years of the Roosevelt administration, Congress passed landmark legislation creating new federal regulatory agencies in all sectors of the economy and significantly expanding the welfare state.[2] Complex and hastily crafted, many of these laws faced constitutional challenges and Supreme Court review. State governments as well responded to the Depression by enacting labor laws and mortgage moratoriums to help farmers and urban families keep their homes.[3]

In this flurry of government activity at the federal and state level, the moribund Child Labor Amendment was revived. Between February and July, nine state legislatures ratified the amendment.[4] Five more states approved the amendment in special sessions held in December. Of the fourteen states ratifying in 1933, all but two had previously rejected the amendment. Among the fourteen to ratify that year were important industrial states such as Pennsylvania, New Jersey, Illinois, Ohio, Michigan, and West Virginia. Pennsylvania was significant because it was the largest child-employing state in the Union. The Child Labor Amendment now had half the number of states needed for ratification. There were also gains on the legislative front. Eleven states considered bills fixing sixteen years as the minimum age for employment in industry, and two states enacted such laws. Many state legislatures were inactive in 1934, but in the eleven states that considered the amendment, the measure was either rejected or not advanced for a vote.[5]

Reformers hoped that in 1935, the amendment would finally receive the thirty-six state votes needed to become part of the Constitution.

Growing support for the amendment and state child labor laws followed a spike in child employment. During the first few years of the Depression, adult unemployment was high and many children were released from their jobs. A countertrend developed in 1932, however, when employers, anxious to maintain profit margins, took advantage of cheap child labor rather than pay their parents adult wages.[6] In some households, children as young as thirteen or fourteen went off to work while parents spent idle days at home. It was a deplorable situation, but families often had no choice.

A children's strike in western Pennsylvania in spring 1933 called attention to this form of child labor exploitation. About 200 boys and girls, ranging in age from fourteen to twenty, went on strike against a shirt factory in Northampton when they were told—with three weeks' back pay due—that there would be no payroll. In Allentown, 150 boys and girls, joined by Cornelia Bryce Gifford Pinchot, the governor's wife, struck against another shirt factory.[7] A third strike was called in, fittingly, Uniontown, when 250 female shirt-workers had their wages cut to below 50 cents a day.[8] An estimated forty sweatshops operated in the region, employing over three thousand boys and girls, about one-fourth under age sixteen. An NCLC researcher found children working for the paltry sum of $1 to $2 a week or less. A fourteen-year-old girl lost four weeks' pay when her employer left town in the middle of the night. Others suffered the same fate. Another fourteen-year-old girl named Mary earned only $1 a week as a trimmer. With her father unemployed for three years, she and her brother were the sole breadwinners for a family of six. Despite their grievances, many of the strikers soon returned to their machines. Some feared the presence of police, who were called to protect the companies, a few strikers were pressured to return by their parents, and others may have been influenced by rumors that unemployment benefits would be cut off from the families of strikers.[9]

When the NCLC Board of Trustees met in May 1933, Grace Abbott "doubted the wisdom" of pushing for any federal legislation modeled on the same congressional Commerce Clause or taxing powers that had been declared unconstitutional.[10] She and other members favored a more vigorous campaign to ratify the Child Labor Amendment. There was also discussion of the National Industrial Recovery Act (NIRA) pending before Congress. If enacted, the NIRA would give President Roosevelt "full authority to control or eliminate child labor."[11] With that kind of executive power, a constitutional amendment might be unnecessary. For now, the battle over child labor would be waged on two fronts. The trustees voted to refocus efforts on the amendment and present provisions to the Roosevelt administration to eliminate child labor under the NIRA before the enactment of the bill.

President Roosevelt signed the National Industrial Recovery Act on June 16, 1933. It was the last measure enacted during the first one hundred days of the New Deal. The law directed companies to write industry-wide "codes of fair competition" that established standards on prices and wages, set production quotas, and imposed restrictions on other business practices, including a sixteen-year minimum age for employment.[12] Committees representing business, labor, and the public were responsible for writing the codes and submitting them to the president for approval. If a business sector did not develop codes, the president was authorized to draft codes himself using legislative authority delegated by Congress. As an incentive for self-regulation, industries that worked under the codes would be exempt from antitrust prosecution. There were numerous patriotic appeals to the public, and companies participating in the National Recovery Administration (NRA) program were awarded the Blue Eagle, a poster that was often prominently displayed in storefronts and on packages. Favored by workers, any business not displaying the symbol might be boycotted. Viewed as "emergency" legislation, the codes were temporary, only remaining in effect during the economic crisis, which by law was two years, unless the president declared an end to the emergency earlier. The National Recovery Administration (NRA) was created separately by executive order to implement the program, and President Roosevelt appointed General Hugh S. Johnson as head of the agency for industrial recovery.

Recognizing that child labor would be an important part of the NRA discussion, the NCLC seized on the opportunity to help draft the codes. In July, the committee submitted to the NRA a statement of general principles recommending a sixteen-year age minimum for employment in every industry code, and for industries where unemployment was acute or where the dangers make adult workers advisable, an eighteen-year age limit was specified. The principles also suggested that the limit be set at eighteen years in the coal, steel, logging, and dry goods codes.[13] Finally, the committee recommended strict regulations for the number, wages, and length of apprenticeships.

Over five hundred codes of fair practice were established in various industries, with the first code adopted in July by the cotton textile industry. At the historic opening meeting on June 27 in the auditorium of the Commerce Department, over eight hundred people watched as management, labor, and consumer leaders negotiated codes of fair competition, with General Johnson presiding over the hearings. Representatives of the NCLC and Children's Bureau were on hand to push for child labor regulations. The initial proposal from the textile manufacturers included a forty-hour work week and a minimum weekly wage of $11 for the North and $10 for the South. William Green, president of the American Federation of Labor, pushed for a thirty-hour workweek, although thirty-two hours was acceptable, and a minimum weekly wage above $14. Because the draft code contained no minimum age for employment and there was no mention of child labor, the NCLC protested the omission and urged other groups and individuals to contact General Johnson to ask for a child labor ban. The media responded with strong editorials in favor of the committee's position. On the second day of hearings, the cotton industry offered to the NRA a voluntary plan for the abolition of child labor. When T. M. Marchant, president of the American Cotton Manufacturers' Association, read the statement in the auditorium, several hundred spectators erupted in cheers.[14]

Negotiations continued for about a week until the final code was announced on July 9. The textile code contained a provision favored by the NCLC that banned the employment of children under sixteen in cotton textile mills.[15] The mill owners, however, did not agree to this position out of goodwill for children. Desperate to curb overproduction, representatives of the textile industry were prepared, in exchange for restricting mills to two forty-hour weekly shifts, to accept the elimination of child labor and a $13 minimum weekly wage ($12 in the South).[16] The Code of Fair Competition for the textile industry became effective on July 17. In his study of the NCLC, Walter I. Trattner noted that this was a major achievement for reformers, not only because "the mills had traditionally been a stronghold of child labor, but also as the first one adopted this code set a standard for other industries."[17]

Two weeks later, President Roosevelt issued a blanket code effective until December 31. The executive order specified a sixteen-year minimum working age, except for nonmanufacturing or nonmining industries where fourteen- to sixteen-year-old children could work three hours a day between 7:00 a.m. and 7:00 p.m., when school was not in session. Although the codes were temporary, with the stroke of a pen President Roosevelt accomplished what the NCLC, NCL, and other reform groups had been working toward for decades. Even an editorial in a British newspaper acknowledged that the codes did more in one day than "England had been able to do in . . . eighty-five years of effort."[18]

Although the codes did little to improve the economy, they had an immediate impact on child labor, as the employment of children in nonagricultural occupations reached an all-time low.[19] Prior to the codes, only four states set sixteen years as the minimum for factory work. Now a sixteen-year minimum became the national norm for nonhazardous manufacturing jobs and an eighteen-year minimum for hazardous occupations. In just the six months between July and December 1933, an estimated one hundred thousand child workers under age sixteen were removed from industries covered by the codes. Between thirty thousand and fifty thousand others were removed from hazardous occupations, such as mining, logging, and sawmill operations.[20] Among that number were 20,625 working in the textile industry, with half that number in cotton mills.

The standard for child labor established by the textile industry code seemed to enjoy wide support and generated little opposition. Basically, the age and wage standards were in everyone's interest. They reduced the fear that manufacturers might be at a competitive disadvantage in sectors that used child labor, and organized labor favored them because adult workers would not have to compete with children for jobs, which depressed wages. Some parents might be upset if a child is the only employed member of a family, but much higher-paying jobs would now be available for adult workers. By the time the blanket code expired in December 1933, 119 separate industry codes had been promulgated and approved. Only two of these codes contained exemptions for employing children under age sixteen: the motion picture industry and legitimate theater were permitted to employ children of any age, subject to state laws, and fourteen- to sixteen-year-olds could work in retail three hours a day or one eight-hour day a week from 7:00 a.m. to 7:00 p.m. when not required to be in school.

One industry group, however, refused to accept the child labor standards. While the press celebrated the child labor provisions in other industries, newspaper and periodical publishers contested any restrictions on their estimated five hundred thousand child workers. When the American Newspaper Publishers' Association (ANPA) proposed the first draft of their code in August, it contained no age or hour restrictions. Any minor boy or girl, regardless of age, could sell or deliver newspapers at any hour of the day or night, as long as it did not interfere with school attendance. The ANPA claimed that the sole interest of its members was the welfare of the boy carriers rather than financial gain. Among other subjects, the ANPA demanded a freedom of the press provision and publishers wanted to exempt their "professional" employees from the codes, but the child labor section was one of the most contentious issues in the code negotiations.

At a hearing for the proposed code, the NCLC requested a sixteen-year minimum for boys who sold or delivered newspapers at night, with the employment of girls in the evening prohibited, and a fourteen/sixteen-year age minimum for boys and girls selling or delivering during the day between 7:00 a.m. and 7:00.p.m. Newspaper representatives strongly objected to the recommendations. In defense of the practice, H. W. Stodghill, president and circulation manager of the *Louisville Courier-Journal* and chairman of the newspaper boy welfare committee of the International Circulation Managers' Association, questioned whether newsboys were engaged in child labor or simply playing.[21] He described newsboys as merchants "engaged in healthful outdoor work while learning the fundamentals of citizenship and receiving a training that had contributed directly to their success."[22] Stodghill's group urged modifications to the child labor sections of the code to increase the age limits and prevent the employment of girls. Other industry groups, however, including the International and Daily Press Association, representing 250 Midwest newspapers, and the Southern Newspaper Publishers Association, supported the code.

When the final newspaper code was promulgated in February 1934, it contained the weakest child labor provisions of any of the industry codes. The code established a fourteen-year minimum age for street vendors in cities over fifty thousand population, a twelve-year minimum in cities with fifty thousand or fewer people, and a twelve-year limit for carriers, with an exemption for ten-year-old boys already employed in smaller municipalities of fifty thousand or less. Young carriers were permitted to begin work at 5:00 a.m., and night work was prohibited only to those carriers under sixteen who sold newspapers.[23] President Roosevelt signed the code "conditionally" on February 17, but he was not satisfied with the newspaper carrier provisions and he asked government officials to prepare a study within sixty days.[24] With the help of the Children's Bureau, a revised code was worked out and announced by the Code Authority more than a year later in May 1935. By then, the entire NIRA was being challenged in a case pending before the Supreme Court.

President Roosevelt took pride in the success of the codes. When he signed the textile industry code, the president cited the prohibition of the employment of children under sixteen years of age as one of the "many significant circumstances" resulting from the process. "Child labor in this industry is hereby abolished," he declared. He remarked that "after years of fruitless effort and discussion, this ancient atrocity went out in a day, because this law permits employers to do by agreement that which none of them could do separately and live in competition."[25] Commenting on the subject again in a radio address, President Roosevelt stated that the abolition of child labor in the textile code and other industry codes "made him personally happier than anything with which he has been connected since he came to Washington."[26]

In fact, the success of the codes significantly slowed the momentum to ratify the Child Labor Amendment in 1934–1935. Some people began arguing that the amendment was no longer necessary. The NCLC warned that the codes were a temporary, emergency measure, and that it was dangerous to develop an attitude of "complacent optimism" regarding the regulations.[27] In his annual message to Congress on January 3, 1934, President Roosevelt celebrated the progress made under the National Industrial Recovery Act and, perhaps prematurely, reiterated his earlier claim that "child labor is abolished."[28] Labor Secretary Perkins fretted that the president "had really bollixed things up."[29] Opponents used the declaration to argue against the amendment, and that may explain why no state legislature meeting in 1934 approved the measure. Reformers hoped that in 1935, they would regain the momentum for ratification.

Meanwhile, opponents of the Child Labor Amendment remained resolute and drew upon many of the arguments that had been used effectively against the amendment a decade earlier. At the annual meeting of the American Bar Association in August 1933, President Clarence E. Martin urged the group to oppose the amendment. Calling it the "broadest grant of power ever attempted to be given to the National Government," Martin argued that there was no reason for the amendment. As did many opponents of the measure, he worried that the power could not only be used to "prevent children under eighteen from laboring" but also it would give Congress the power to "nationalize education" and "be the basis for required military training."[30] Although well intentioned, President Martin warned that the amendment was a "communistic effort to nationalize children, making them responsible primarily to the government, instead of their parents."[31]

The American Bar Association at this time was a conservative organization composed of mostly white, male corporate lawyers, and many members no doubt shared Martin's views of the amendment. The association adopted a resolution to actively oppose the Child Labor Amendment. In part, the resolution stated that the cure for the evil of child labor "must be sought through state legislation," and the group urged the states to adopt the Uniform Child Labor Act. A special committee appointed by the ABA to oppose ratification issued a report in 1934, making the novel argument that the amendment was already dead and therefore could not be ratified. William D. Guthrie, chair of the special committee, cited for support the Supreme Court precedent of *Dillon v. Goss* (1921). Among other issues, the *Dillon* case involved a challenge to the seven-year time limit placed on ratification of the Eighteenth Amendment. Finding that the seven-year limit was reasonable, Justice Van Devanter commented that nothing in Article V suggested that an amendment "once proposed is to be open to ratification for all time, or that ratification in some states may be separated from that in others by many years and yet be effective."[32] The Court concluded that a fair inference from Article V is that the ratification must be "within some reasonable time" after the proposal, and Congress had the authority to determine the proper time frame. The rationale of Guthrie and the ABA lawyers was that ten years had been enough time for ratification. Moreover, their report asserted that once a state had rejected a proposed amendment, a legislature could not "validly annul, withdraw, or revoke its prior rejection."[33] Ultimately, the Supreme Court would decide these issues.

An influential new foe of the amendment emerged during this period. When the amendment was debated in 1924–1925, most newspapers supported the proposal. There were exceptions. During the 1924 referendum fight over the amendment in Massachusetts, NCLC leaders complained that newspapers would not publish editorials in response to antiamendment letters and rejected requests for paid ad space.[34] Now many newspapers, magazine publishers, and their trade associations became staunch opponents. By late 1933, at least seventy publications that had earlier supported the amendment switched their position, including the *New York Herald Tribune*, *New York Sun*, and *St. Louis Post-Dispatch*.[35] The defection of the *New York Herald Tribune* is noteworthy. Senator Medill McCormick, a substantial stockholder in the *Tribune*, had introduced the Child Labor Amendment in the form adopted by the House in 1924. By 1936, the *Tribune* described the amendment as a "bogus" amendment and a "fraudulent conspiracy to socialize the youth of America."[36] Not stopping there, the editors called for the entire removal of the New Deal regime from power.

The NCLC attributed the rise of newspaper opposition to the organization's attempts to secure meaningful provisions for the newspaper codes under the NRA. In what the NCLC described as distortions of their positions, the major newspaper trade associations portrayed both the codes and the amendment as attempts to prevent all children under eighteen from selling or delivering newspapers.[37] Not every newspaper, however, jumped ship on the amendment issue. *Editor and Publisher*, a trade journal for newspapers, still favored the amendment. Scripps-Howard publications also continued to write strong editorials in support of the measure. On April 5, 1935, the *New York World-Telegram* wrote an editorial criticizing the ANPA's position on the amendment. A successful campaign against the amendment, the paper suggested, would not compensate for the loss in "public confidence should the impression prevail that publishers used their journalistic strength to preserve an advantage to themselves at the expense of the youth of the nation."[38] Even William Allen White, prominent editor of the *Emporia Gazette*, urged newspapers to stop the fight against the amendment. "It is discrediting the newspaper profession," he warned, "and weakening our just position in other matters."[39]

Missouri became the center of opposition to the Child Labor Amendment in 1933–1934. The state had rejected the amendment in 1925, but it was now under reconsideration. A newly created group, the National Committee for the Protection of Child, Family, School and Church, joined the fight against the amendment in January 1934. Based in St. Louis, Missouri, the organization was formed by Sterling E. Edmunds, a St. Louis attorney who served on the executive committee of the Sentinels of the Republic. Funded by business interests, the committee drew support from the Catholic Church hierarchy. Archbishop John J. Glennon of St. Louis strongly opposed the amendment, and although he was not a member of the National Committee, the executive committee included the archdiocesan director of Catholic Charities, the director of the Central Bureau of the Catholic Central Verein, and other prominent Catholics.[40] There were some Catholic leaders in St. Louis and Kansas City, however, who supported the amendment.

The National Committee focused on defeating the amendment in Missouri and every state where it was up for a vote. The group resurrected the alarmist rhetoric used against the amendment in the 1920s. For example, the organization claimed that the amendment would lead to the "nationalization of the entire population under 18 years of age, compulsory military training in the schools, and federal 'snoopers' descending on every home and preventing young Henry from milking cows and his sister Jane from washing dishes."[41] The arguments proved effective once again. While the Missouri House approved the amendment, the motion to reconsider was killed in the Senate Constitutional Amendment Committee in December. The full Senate could have acted, but by 1935 there was no movement toward a vote. Fearful of the consequences of another legislative defeat, supporters of the amendment decided not to press the issue. Missouri failed to join the list of states ratifying the Child Labor Amendment.

Proamendment forces, however, had friends in high places. President Roosevelt and his cabinet members, including Secretary of Labor Frances Perkins, supported ratification, and the battle over the amendment intensified. In a letter to Courtenay Dinwiddie, the general secretary of the National Child Labor Committee, on November 8, 1934, President Roosevelt urged ratification of the Child Labor amendment as a way to solidify the gains made under the National Recovery Act in curbing child labor. The president wrote:

One of the accomplishments under the National Recovery Act which has given me the greatest gratification is the outlawing of child labor. It shows how simply a long desired reform, which no individual or State could accomplish alone, may be brought about when people work together. It is my desire that the advances attained through the NRA be made permanent. In the child labor field the obvious method of maintaining the present gains is through ratification of the Child Labor Amendment. I hope this may be achieved.[42]

President Roosevelt understood that the Supreme Court could be a stumbling block for his New Deal programs. Although the 1932 elections gave Democrats control of the White House and Congress, the political composition of the US Supreme Court did not change. During this period, the Court was led by Charles Evans Hughes, a former governor of New York and unsuccessful nominee for president, who served as chief justice of the United States from 1930 to 1941. The Hughes Court was closely divided between liberal and conservative justices, with Chief Justice Hughes and Justice Owen Roberts somewhere in the middle. Three justices constituted the liberal bloc: Louis Brandeis, Harlan Fisk Stone, and Benjamin Cardozo (who replaced Oliver Wendell Holmes in 1932). The conservative bloc of the Hughes Court consisted of Willis Van Devanter, James McReynolds, Pierce Butler, and George Sutherland. Sutherland and Van Devanter were Republicans, while McReynolds and Butler were Democrats. These four justices shared an unquestioned faith in rugged individualism, limited government, and free markets. Federal judge Learned Hand called the four conservatives "the mastiffs" based on their eagerness to bite into and overturn the New Deal's major initiatives. The media occasionally dubbed them the "Four Horsemen of the Apocalypse," or the "Four Horsemen of Re-action," because their strident warnings about the evils of government in-tervention seemed to prophesize the imminent demise of capitalism and republican government. Given their backgrounds and voting records, these four justices were not likely to support federal child labor legislation.

In 1934, with encouragement from the Roosevelt administration and by the recent votes in nine states to ratify the amendment, New York and six other states moved to reconsider the Child Labor Amendment. Taking their cue from the president, reformers argued that the amendment was necessary to make permanent the gains established under the NRA codes. Like the de-bate ten years earlier, the Child Labor Campaign Committee of New York charged that opponents of the amendment had circulated "gross exaggera-tions and wholly misleading statements" in an organized effort to defeat the amendment.[43] The committee produced a list of over one hundred promi-nent New Yorkers who supported the measure, headed by the President and Mrs. Roosevelt, Secretary of Labor Frances Perkins, Senator Robert F. Wagner, Senator Royal Copeland, Governor Herbert H. Lehman, and Mayor Fiorello LaGuardia.

However, a statewide group called the New York State Committee Op-posing Ratification organized in April 1934 and distributed a forty-three-page brochure against the amendment. Distinguished members included Elihu Root, former American Bar Association president who served as sec-retary of war under President McKinley and secretary of state under Teddy Roosevelt, and Dr. Nicholas Murray Butler, president of Columbia Uni-versity for forty-two years, Nobel Peace Prize recipient, and close friend of Benito Mussolini. William D. Guthrie, past chairman of the American Bar Association Committee and head of the ABA Committee Opposing Rati-fication, served as vice chair of the New York Committee. Another promi-nent member was former governor Alfred E. Smith, who had now become an outspoken foe of the amendment and FDR's New Deal. In a series of edi-torials for *The New Outlook*, Smith wrote that the child labor amendment "was badly drawn; that it was extraordinarily like the Eighteenth Amend-ment and had all its vices and potentialities for trouble . . . that it could not be enforced; that it was unreasonable, and that it would lead inevitably to all sorts of attempts at Federal usurpation and extension of authority over fields and activities to which the amendment was never meant by its more sensible authors to apply."[44] The former governor advocated a substitute amendment that lowered the age to sixteen years and established a regulatory regime that prohibited the "transportation or importation into any State, Territory, or possession, articles manufactured by persons" under that age limit. The NCLC derided the former governor's substitute amendment, calling it "unenforceable" and a proposal that "cannot be considered seriously" by anyone who desired to eliminate child labor.[45] In contrast, the committee noted that Henry A. Wallace, secretary of agriculture, "heartily" endorsed the original amendment.

Governor Lehman continued his strong support for the amendment by recommending ratification in a message to the legislature in early January 1935. Lehman had succeeded Franklin D. Roosevelt as governor in 1933, and he established a record of progressive programs, modeled after FDR's New Deal, in response to the Great Depression. Resolutions were soon introduced in both chambers and referred to the Judiciary Committee. The bills were debated and reintroduced for three years, however, before final action was taken on the resolutions. George Hall of the NCLC complained that Judiciary Committee members in both chambers "were all conservative lawyers or Catholics" who fundamentally opposed the measure.[46]

On January 7, 1935, the Supreme Court dealt a blow to Roosevelt's New Deal. In *Panama Refining Company v. Ryan* (1935), the Supreme Court, by an 8–1 vote, voided the "hot oil" provision of the NIRA on the basis that it amounted to an unconstitutional delegation of legislative power to the president. Based on the separation of powers, the nondelegation doctrine suggests that Congress should refrain from delegating lawmaking power to the executive branch. On July 11, 1933, the president had issued Executive Order 6199, which prohibited interstate and foreign transport and commerce of petroleum and its products in violation of state laws. The president vested the secretary of the interior with presidential powers for the purposes of carrying out this "Petroleum Code."

In enacting the Petroleum Code, the Court ruled, the president subsumed legislative powers that Congress does not have the power to delegate. According to the decision, the lack of sufficient standards to control the discretion of the executive doomed this section of the act. "Congress," the Court argued, "left the matter to the President without standard or rule, to be dealt with as he pleased," and the failure to specify criteria allowed the president to function as a legislature rather "an executive or administrative officer."[47] It was the first time the Court had ruled that a law was an unconstitutional delegation of legislative power to the executive.

In January 1935 a new organization, the National Non-Partisan Committee for Ratification of the Federal Child Labor Amendment, joined the fight to secure ratification of the amendment. Chaired by Charles C. Burlingham, former president of the Association of the Bar of the City of New York, the Non-Partisan Committee sought to counter efforts by the American Bar Association and its committee opposing the amendment. The name of the group was also intended to blunt claims that amendment backers were socialists, communists, and radicals. Prominent lawyers, law professors, university presidents, religious leaders, journalists, and social activists served on the Non-Partisan Committee. Notables included Roscoe Pound, dean of Harvard Law School; Dr. Harold W. Dodds, president of Princeton University; Carl T. Compton, president of Massachusetts Institute of Technology; William Allen White, editor of the *Emporia Gazette*; and Monsignor John A. Ryan of Catholic University.[48] With twenty-four states considering or reconsidering the amendment in 1935, the Non-Partisan Committee hoped to help the NCLC and other groups secure the remaining sixteen states to make the amendment part of the Constitution.

While the amendment was stalled in New York in 1935, that year advocates obtained ratification in four more states—Idaho, Indiana, Utah, and Wyoming. At a conference on the Child Labor Amendment held at the Children's Bureau on April 10, organizers reported that the vote was close in two other states. The Nevada House overwhelmingly voted in favor, but the measure lost in the Senate by two votes. Even in North Carolina, the House defeated the amendment by only three votes, 52 against and 49 in favor. New York, Missouri, and Georgia were disappointing losses, but both Connecticut and New York passed state laws setting sixteen years as the age when children could leave school and enter the workforce. Conference leaders also noted that the American Farm Bureau Federation had almost completely withdrawn its opposition to the amendment (in December 1935, the AFBF formally endorsed the amendment).[49] These developments were encouraging, but they fell far short of the goal of sixteen ratifications for the year.

As President Roosevelt feared, the permanency of the labor gains under the NRA codes was seriously threatened on May 27, 1935, a day known as "Black Monday," when the Supreme Court overturned the NIRA system in *Schechter Poultry Corporation v. United States* and struck down two other New Deal efforts.[50] Sometimes called the "sick chicken" case, *Schechter* involved a constitutional challenge to NIRA codes adopted for the poultry industry and applied in New York, the country's largest chicken market. The industry suffered from graft and terrible health and sanitation conditions. The Live Poultry Code approved by the president established a maximum workweek of forty hours and a minimum hourly wage of fifty cents. Health inspections, regulations on slaughterhouses, and compulsory record keeping were also required by the code. Government regulators found the Schechter Poultry Corporation, owned by four brothers, in violation of the poultry code on several counts, including selling unsanitary poultry unfit for human consumption. The government obtained a sixty-count indictment against the brothers, and a jury found them guilty on nineteen. The Schechter brothers claimed that the NIRA system was an unconstitutional delegation of lawmaking power to the executive branch, and that Congress had no authority under the Commerce Clause to regulate intrastate commerce.

In *Schechter*, a unanimous Court concluded that the NIRA was an attempt by Congress to delegate its legislative power to private groups and to the president without any standards to limit their discretion. Reading the opinion from the bench, Chief Justice Hughes stated that such delegation was beyond the constitutional power of Congress. Justice Cardozo, one of the more liberal members of the Court, referred to the NIRA as "delegation running riot."[51] More important, the Court concluded that Congress could not regulate under its Commerce Clause powers because the Schechter firm was employed in a local trade. The "stream of commerce" rationale was held not applicable because the flow had ceased. Applying the direct-indirect test of precedents and the principles of dual federalism, Hughes argued that the company's wages and hours had no direct effect on interstate commerce. To rule otherwise, the Court warned, would be to practically subject all activities of the people and state authority over domestic matters to the power of the federal government. "The authority of the federal government," the chief justice argued, "may not be pushed to such an extreme as to destroy the distinction, which the commerce clause itself establishes, between commerce 'among the several States' and the internal concerns of a State."[52] The US Constitution, Hughes concluded, did not provide for such a centralized economic system. Because all the NIRA codes contained child labor provisions, the *Schechter* decision was the third defeat of federal child labor legislation at the hands of the Supreme Court.

The *Schechter* decision and its unanimity stunned the courtroom audience. Even the three reliable liberals on the Court voted against the New Deal. In *FDR v. The Constitution*, Burt Solomon describes a meeting between Justice Brandeis and Thomas G. "Tommy the Cork" Corcoran, a Washington lawyer and presidential advisor who was part of the "brain trust" of the New Deal, in the Court's chambers following the decision. "This is the end of this business of centralization," the justice told Corcoran, "and I want you to go back and tell the president that we're not going to let this government centralize everything. It's come to an end."[53] The absence of dissent rattled President Roosevelt, and he worried about the fate of other New Deal programs. Attorney General Homer Cummings was frustrated and angry with the Court. "If this decision stands and is not met in some way," Cummings said, "it is going to be impossible for the government to devise any system which will effectively deal with the disorganized industries of the country, or rout out, by any affirmative action, manifest evils, sweat-shop conditions, child labor, or any other unsocial or anti-social aspects of the economic system."[54]

Roosevelt did not publicly react to the *Schechter* decision for several days, but when he did comment at a press conference on May 31, he sharply criticized the opinion. The decision was an anachronism, he suggested, that took the country back "to the horse-and-buggy days of 1789." In his opinion, the Court had ruled "in effect that the Federal government was powerless to cope with the tremendous social and economic problems that came as by-products of our growth from a strip of seaboard colonies to a great industrial nation."[55] Roosevelt's condemnation of the *Schechter* opinion did not go over well with many press correspondents who viewed the Constitution as a "divine parchment," and who believed that it was bad politics or strategy to criticize the Court.[56]

Following the *Schechter* decision, the NCLC declared that the invalidation of the NRA code system meant a return to child labor. Removing the age and wage restrictions would again make it "profitable for unscrupulous employers to exploit low-paid children, and reputable employers will be forced to meet their competition."[57] Although the *Schechter* decision was a serious setback, Grace Abbott of the Children's Bureau reported that businesses did not rush to reemploy child workers. Many industry associations promised to voluntarily comply with the codes. But there were signs that child labor was on the rise. In August 1936, the Labor Department reported a 58 percent increase in the number of children going to work in factories and stores. For all of 1934, when the NRA codes were in place, in 6 states and 102 other cities, 7,000 regular employment certificates were issued, and only 1 percent were for work in factories and 4 percent in stores. In contrast, during the 7 months following *Schechter*, in those same localities, 11,000 work certificates were issued with 12 percent for factories and 17 percent for retail.[58] In North Carolina, State Department of Labor officials urged employers to voluntarily maintain the gains made under the codes, but demands for certificates in textile mills increased.[59] In New England and Pennsylvania, "fly-by-night" textile sweatshops returned. Set up in abandoned barns or factories, these establishments worked employees mercilessly for several weeks, then they would shut down and secretly move at night, often without paying the meager wages owed to the workers.[60]

The 1935–1936 Supreme Court term turned out to be just as bad for the New Deal and market regulation as the previous term. In the spring of 1936, Justice Owen Roberts, sometimes joined by Chief Justice Hughes, combined with the four conservatives in overturning several pieces of federal and state legislation. In *United States v. Butler* (1936), Roberts wrote for a majority of six in striking down the 1933 Agricultural Adjustment Act, more specifically its provision that imposed a tax on food processors in order to fund benefit payments to farmers who participated in the government's voluntary crop-reduction program. While holding that the federal government has broad taxing and spending powers to promote the general welfare, Roberts relied on the commerce versus production distinction to characterize agriculture as a local productive activity that Congress could not regulate under the Commerce Clause. In the same term, the Court dealt a further blow to economic regulation in *Morehead v. New York ex rel. Tipaldo* (1936). Justice Roberts joined the four conservatives in striking down New York's law mandating minimum wages for women and children, reasoning that the law violated the liberty of contract protected by the Due Process Clause. The decision in *Morehead*, however, would be the last victory for that doctrine.

On May 18, 1936, the Supreme Court announced another decision impacting Congress's power to regulate commerce and child labor. When the NIRA was voided in 1935, Congress passed the Bituminous Coal Conservation Act to establish a new code for the industry. The law stated that the coal industry was "affected with a public interest"—a feature that was used to justify governmental price fixing. Famously applied in *Munn v. Illinois* (1877) to the regulation of grain elevators, the common law doctrine allows government to regulate businesses whose activities impact the public interest. The goals of the Bituminous Coal Conservation Act included the promotion of interstate commerce in coal and provision of the general welfare. The statute created a commission empowered to develop regulations regarding fair competition, production, wages, hours, and labor relations. The act also levied a 15 percent tax on coal sold at the time. Ninety percent of that tax was refunded to producers who accepted the code.

Stockholders of the Carter Coal Company, including James W. Carter, sued the company to test the validity of the law. The stockholders did not want the company to agree to the code. Carter argued that coal mining was not in interstate commerce. The decision was closely divided with Justice Roberts joining the Four Horsemen for a 5–4 majority, but the outcome was the same for Roosevelt's New Deal policies as the Court invalidated several provisions of the law and rebuffed arguments concerning congressional power. The Court rejected the assertion that Congress has an inherent power, apart from the Constitution, to deal with problems that affect the nation as a whole. It also rejected the contention that Congress can pass laws to promote the general welfare, independent of its delegated powers. Probably the biggest blow for child labor regulation, however, concerned the scope of congressional power under the Commerce Clause. The majority opinion, written by Justice Sutherland, held that matters leading up to the mining of coal—such as employment, wages, hours, and working conditions—are part of production, not commerce, and are local in nature. Production, including mining, manufacturing, and farming, is a purely local activity and not part of commerce. Wages and hours do not have a direct effect on interstate commerce. Justice Sutherland extended the *Schechter* precedent to cases where interstate commerce had not yet begun.

The ruling in *Carter* was a significant addition to a set of cases involving a narrow interpretation of the federal commerce power. The decisions in *E.C. Knight*, *Hammer*, *Schechter*, and others had emphasized the principle that production and labor-management relations within a firm were not interstate commerce, but local matters. The Court emphasized that if these matters were regarded as part of interstate commerce, there would be little left of individual or state autonomy. These cases rejected the view that aspects of production were part of a continuing series of events that involved the crossing of state boundaries, or were activities having direct injurious effects that transcended state borders. Under that line of reasoning, Congress does not have the power to pass child labor laws. Within a year, the Court would turn away from its precedents that had interpreted the commerce powers narrowly, and *Carter* would be Roosevelt's last major defeat at the hands of the Four Horsemen and their allies.

In the national elections of 1936, Roosevelt was reelected in a landslide victory over his Republican opponent, Kansas governor Alf Landon, capturing 98 percent of the electoral votes (523 to 8). Democrats also won huge majorities in Congress, controlling about 80 percent of the seats in both the House and Senate. In late December, Secretary of Labor Perkins sent the president a memo explaining that "the immediate outlook for ratification of the child labor amendment is encouraging but definite impetus by you is necessary to turn the scale. A letter from you to the incoming Governors of the States that have not ratified, which will have regular sessions in 1937 would be immensely valuable."[61] The president agreed and the letter was sent to the governors on January 7, 1937:

> I AM sure that you will agree with me that one of the most encouraging developments of the past few years is the general agreement that has been reached that child labor should be permanently abolished. Outstanding gains were made under the NRA codes which have been maintained in many establishments through the voluntary cooperation of employers.
>
> However, it is clearly indicated that child labor, especially in low-paid, unstandardized type of work, is increasing. I am convinced that nation-wide minimum standards are necessary and that a way should be found promptly to crystallize in legal safeguards public opinion in behalf of the elimination of child labor.
>
> Do you not agree with me that ratification of the child-labor amendment by the remaining twelve States whose action is necessary to it in the Constitution is the obvious way to early achieve our objective? I hope that you will agree that this can be made one of the major items in the legislative program of your State this year.[62]

On January 10, former Republican president Herbert Hoover joined Roosevelt in urging ratification. "The President is right," he said. "The Child Labor Amendment should be passed now." Hoover believed that children have a right to health and a fair chance. Responding to Democratic attacks on the Court, he insisted that it was important to have "orderly constitutional change, instead of pressure on the independence of the Supreme Court."[63]

Several governors responded positively to the Roosevelt and Hoover statements. Democratic governor Fred P. Cone of Florida indicated that he would recommend ratification to the legislature. "I'm in favor of the President's entire program of humanitarian legislation," Cone said. "We ought to get these children out of the factories and other jobs."[64] Governor A. B. Chandler of Kentucky also planned to call a special session of the General Assembly to ask for ratification of the amendment. Some governors, however, rejected the president's plea or did nothing to advance resolutions. Governor-elect Gordon Browning, a Democrat, opposed ratification, asserting that Tennessee was "not ready to turn over to a Washington bureau the discrimination as to whether a farmer can have his boy help him make a crop."[65] "Our State," Governor Browning concluded, "knows how to manage its own household." In several other states the prospects for the amendment looked dim because the legislature had recently defeated ratification proposals, often by large margins.

Law professor Gerard N. Magliocca argues that Roosevelt's letter to the governors was purely strategic. Magliocca sees a link between Roosevelt's strong public support for the amendment in January and his plan to reorganize the federal judiciary, which at the time was secretly being written by Attorney General Cummings and a few Justice Department lawyers. Magliocca contends that prior to 1937, FDR "did not lift a finger" to help the Child Labor Amendment.[66] That claim is too strong, however, because FDR took actions in support of the amendment prior to 1937. For example, in March 1934, Larue Brown, legislative chair of the Massachusetts League of Women Voters, received a letter from President Roosevelt in which he clearly aligned himself with amendment advocates. He wrote: "Of course I am in favor of the Child Labor Amendment. A step in the right direction was achieved by demonstrating the simplicity of its application to industry under the N.R.A. . . . the matter hardly requires further academic discussion."[67] Also, the names of the president and Mrs. Roosevelt were on a NCLC list of supporters made public in 1934 when New York reconsidered ratification, and the president's letter to Courtenay Dinwiddie in November 1934 unambiguously urged ratification of the amendment. Granted, there is evidence that FDR believed that the thirteen-year campaign to ratify the child labor amendment would ultimately be unsuccessful. When the judicial reorganization plan was announced in February, President Roosevelt used the ratification struggle to build support for his court plan.

Emboldened by his electoral majority and frustrated with Supreme Court decisions invalidating his New Deal programs, FDR announced his plan to reorganize the federal judiciary on February 5, 1937. Publicly, the president characterized the plan as administrative relief for an overworked and understaffed judiciary. The plan featured proposals to increase the number of lower federal court positions, streamline federal jurisdiction, and make it more flexible to move judges to jurisdictions with backlogs. To many observers, even within his own party, these reforms were a smokescreen for proposals impacting the Supreme Court. The president asked Congress to authorize the creation of one new seat on the Supreme Court for every justice who had attained the age of seventy but did not retire. The maximum number of these new positions would be six, bringing the potential size of the Court to fifteen. At the time of the proposal, six sitting justices were over seventy years old. If the plan was enacted, Roosevelt could appoint six New Deal justices, who would certainly pick up the support of two of the current liberal justices for a pro–New Deal majority. Critics dubbed the proposal the "Court-packing" plan. Opposition came not only from Republicans but also some Democrats, the American Bar Association, several sitting justices, and most of the public.[68]

As the Court-packing plan was being debated in Congress, momentum had swung in favor of ratification of the Child Labor Amendment. A poll released in February by the American Institute of Public Opinion, under the direction of George Gallup, asked citizens in every state the following question: "Do you favor an amendment to the Constitution giving Congress the power to limit, regulate, and prohibit the labor of persons under 18?" The survey found that 76 percent of the respondents supported the amendment. The result was a sixteen-point increase from a similar survey conducted in May 1936. The amendment had majority support in all forty-eight states, with the lowest percentage at 53 percent in Minnesota. Idaho, Massachusetts, Nevada, and West Virginia were close behind at 55 percent in favor. The states with the highest level of support included Colorado (86 percent), New Hampshire (88 percent), New Jersey (84 percent), and Rhode Island (88 percent).[69] It was clear that the amendment had become a nonpartisan issue, with Republican voters averaging 67 percent support compared with 77 percent for Democrats. In fact, the survey results revealed significant differences between voters of the states and their state legislatures. Support for the amendment was over 80 percent in Connecticut, Louisiana, New York, and Rhode Island, but the legislatures in those states had not ratified the amendment.[70] The poll results reinforced the views of Roosevelt and many reformers that a powerful minority could effectively block an amendment that had popular support.

That theory seemed to play out in New York, where the years-long battle over the amendment continued. The *New York Times*, silent on the amendment for many years, published an editorial on January 22, 1937, supporting the Child Labor Amendment and rejecting the prison-made goods theory of regulation, discussed below, recently upheld by the Supreme Court. After Governor Lehman of New York sent a special message to the legislature asking for ratification, the Democratic Senate passed its bill 38–12 with little debate. Friends of the amendment were buoyed by the news, but Catholic opposition loomed large in the assembly. Gertrude Zimand of the National Child Labor Committee warned that "all our advice from Albany is that the opposition expressed by Catholics is the one thing that really matters."[71] Although unprepared for the swift vote in the Senate chamber, the Church hierarchy organized its forces to defeat the measure, known as the Kleinfeld resolution, in the assembly.

On February 22, 1937, President Roosevelt sent a message to Governor Lehman expressing hope for prompt ratification of the amendment in his home state.[72] But the plea seemed to have little effect. A delegation of several hundred supporters of the amendment descended on Albany for a hearing that day, but they were met by an equally large number of opponents consisting of farm group members, parochial-school students, nuns, and priests. At the hearing, Bishop Edmund F. Gibbons read letters from the seven other dioceses that had officially condemned the amendment. The bishop criticized the Senate vote, calling it "not only an outrage but mighty poor politics," and he defended the Church's position against the amendment. "We may be charged with ultra-conservatism," he asserted, "but menaces of alarming proportions to religion and morality, the family, the home, the child, the workingman, the capitalist, the businessman, and the lawfully constituted government, demand that we be conservative."[73] The speech influenced many Catholic members of the assembly because it allowed them to vote according to their religion rather than party politics. Even non-Catholic representatives facing reelection in heavily Catholic districts had to carefully consider their vote.

Catholic opposition to the amendment was extremely high throughout the state. As was done thirteen years earlier during the Massachusetts referendum, on February 28, New York's Cardinal Hayes issued a letter denouncing the amendment. The letter was read at Mass in St. Patrick's Cathedral and many other parishes. At church services, ushers distributed printed postcards calling for the defeat of the "youth control" amendment. Each card had the printed address of the local assemblyman, and their office mailboxes no doubt received many of them from concerned Catholics.

In a radio address prior to the assembly vote, Governor Lehman made a special plea to Republicans in the assembly to match the votes of Democrats for the Kleinfeld resolution. The ensuing three-hour floor debate repeated many of the well-known arguments concerning the amendment. Although conceding that perhaps not everyone who supported the amendment was a socialist or communist, opponents claimed, without evidence, that the proposal was inspired by Moscow. The grant of power to Congress, they argued, was too broad, and as the Eighteenth Amendment and Volstead Act demonstrated, Congress cannot always be trusted to be reasonable in exercising powers. Democratic assemblyman Bernard J. Moran asserted that not many children were working in the cotton mills in the South, and none were illegally employed in New York. Another antiamendment representative noted that the dictionary definition of labor included "mental exertion," which could be applied to regulate education. Some opponents read statements from the Grange and other farm groups against the amendment. Finally, the amendment, it was suggested, substituted one form of slavery for a "controlled, regimented, legal slavery."[74]

In response, those in favor of ratification argued that the amendment was simply an enabling act. The Reverend Dutton S. Peterson, a Republican from Schuyler County, stated that Congress is composed of reasonable, moderate people who can be trusted to use their power wisely. This was not a radical, hysterical proposition with origins in the Kremlin. It was a reasonable proposal from Americans concerned with the welfare of children. Even former Republican presidents Hoover and Coolidge supported the amendment, and they were certainly not leftist radicals. Finally, the Supreme Court had never interpreted the word "labor" to encompass education, so fears of the amendment leading to the regulation of all education were overblown. The Court would check any abuse of congressional power. Reverend Peterson's appeal to common sense and moderation failed to convince many opponents.

The lobbying efforts of the Catholic Church, opposition of farm groups, and the president's plan to reorganize the Supreme Court led to a disastrous defeat in the assembly on March 9, 1937, by a vote of 102–42. Governor Lehman and Democratic Party leaders had severely underestimated the number of defections. Only thirty-three Democrats voted in favor of ratification while forty-one opposed. Republican opposition was nearly unanimous, with sixty-one voting against and only nine joining the Democrats in support of the amendment. The *New York Times* reported that President Roosevelt's Court-packing plan brought about a "pronounced change in sentiment on the Republican side of the Assembly."[75] In two weeks, Republican support dropped from twenty to nine. Following the vote, the National Child Labor Committee blamed the defeat on the "Hierarchy of the Roman Catholic Church" and "powerful reactionary economic groups."[76] The committee asserted that the vote was "only the first skirmish in the battle to be waged for ratification," and it confidently predicted that the New York Assembly would reconsider its vote before adjournment.[77] But the battle was largely over. Although the amendment was reintroduced at the next legislative session, it was again rejected by a large majority. New York never ratified the Child Labor Amendment.

In an attempt to overcome some of the leading objections to the Child Labor Amendment, Republican senator Arthur Vandenberg of Michigan introduced a revised amendment to the US Senate in late March 1937. There were several key differences between Vandenberg's proposal and the original amendment. First, Vandenberg's amendment would be sent to state ratifying conventions, rather than state legislatures, ostensibly to avoid the pressure politics and propaganda of antiamendment forces. Secondly, the age limit was lowered to sixteen years, a level that had more political support. Finally, the text of the amendment omitted the word "regulate," using only language that Congress can "limit and prohibit the labor for hire" of persons under sixteen years of age.[78] Senator Vandenberg hoped that the revised language would meet the objections of Catholic Church hierarchy who feared the word "regulate." The "for hire" language also responded to those who complained that the original amendment went beyond commercial employment. Opponents could no longer argue that kids would be prevented from doing chores around the house or farm. Senator Vandenberg optimistically believed that the revised amendment could be ratified within ninety days with the full support of the Roosevelt administration.[79] The amendment, however, was referred to the Senate Judiciary Committee, which had its hands full reviewing President Roosevelt's bill to reorganize the judiciary—the aforementioned Court-packing plan. The committee eventually issued a report on June 21, 1937, recommending that the Vandenberg amendment pass but adding a section limiting the ratification process to seven years.[80] No action was taken in either chamber. The senator reintroduced his amendment in subsequent sessions of Congress without success.

Senator Borah of Idaho also offered a new Child Labor Amendment in late March. His amendment fixed an age limit of fourteen years instead of eighteen years and authorized Congress to limit, regulate, and prohibit the labor of persons fourteen years and under. A second section declared state laws to be unimpaired except to the extent necessary to implement federal legislation. Senator Borah explained that he proposed the amendment because he didn't believe that the pending amendment had any chance of ratification. Even if ratified, he believed that the Supreme Court might hold that the amendment was not ratified within a reasonable time. Finally, he was not in favor of prohibiting young men and women fifteen and older from working.[81] The fourteen-year age limit in Borah's amendment would do little to improve state laws.

Dozens of other bills directed at child labor that did not require a constitutional amendment were pending in Congress at this time. Many of these were generated in response to a Supreme Court decision validating a law that had nothing to do with child labor. The Ashurst-Sumners Act prohibited the introduction into interstate commerce of prison-made goods in violation of state laws of destination and required the labeling of such goods. The legislation was upheld by the Supreme Court on January 4, 1937, in *Kentucky Whip and Collar Co. v. Illinois Central Railroad Co.* The Court distinguished the *Hammer v. Dagenhart* precedent and compared the law to the Webb-Kenyon Act and state regulation of intoxicating liquors.[82] The Court emphasized that the evil or harm sought to be regulated by the exclusion of products from interstate commerce must exist *after* the product had arrived in the state of destination. Some congressional opponents of child labor believed that the *Kentucky Whip* decision created an opening to address the problem if a law could be fashioned along the lines of the Ashurst-Sumners Act.

On March 24, Senators Burton K. Wheeler of Montana and Edwin O. Johnson of Colorado introduced a bill that would make the products of child labor subject to the laws of the state into which they are shipped. A similar bill was sponsored by Democratic senator Bennett Champ Clark of Missouri. Reformers, however, complained that the Wheeler-Johnson bill would not solve the problem, and it would be a poor substitute for the pending Child Labor Amendment. The Wheeler-Johnson bill protected only children employed in industries that shipped goods in interstate commerce and excluded many others working for local businesses. It would also require every state to pass a law banning the sale of child-made goods within state borders. Finally, the labeling of such goods would create a nightmare from an industry perspective and an administrative headache for regulators. Courtenay Dinwiddie, general secretary of the National Child Labor Committee, commented that "the enforcement difficulties would be fantastic."[83] In testimony before the US Senate Committee on Interstate Commerce, Grace Abbott rejected the prison-goods analogy for child labor and buttressed Dinwiddie's criticism of the Wheeler-Johnson bill. She feared the economic balkanization resulting from state laws. "I object to all this state legislation," she testified, "affecting the free flow of goods. . . . If it is going to be decided, it should be decided by the federal government and not by 48 different standards. That gets us back to the days of the old Confederation, instead of in modern times."[84]

While these bills were pending, a *New York Times* editorial argued that a federal wages and hours bill should be handled separately from a child labor provision and recommended the Wheeler-Johnson bill to address child labor. Dinwiddie, however, penned a critical response to the editorial. He noted that there were two types of child labor legislation proposed in Congress—the Wheeler-Johnson method, which forbids the shipment of goods made by child labor in violation of state law, and the method used in the first federal child labor law, forbidding the shipment of goods from an establishment in which any children have been employed.[85] The latter method, Dinwiddie observed, is preferred because it is a preventive measure that does more to reduce the illegal employment of children. "The Wheeler-Johnson bill, on the other hand, is a punitive measure" that relies on prosecution after children have been exploited, and is more easily evaded and difficult to enforce.[86]

Dinwiddie and other supporters of the Child Labor Amendment viewed many of the pending bills as ineffective distractions that took the focus away from the campaign to ratify the 1924 amendment. If Congress was going the legislative route to address child labor, the NCLC and National Consumers' League preferred a bill sponsored by Senator Alben Barkley that was modeled on the Keating-Owen Act and based on congressional power under the Commerce Clause. The bill prohibited the shipment in interstate commerce of articles produced in factories where children under sixteen had been employed within sixty days of the removal of the product for shipment. A similar ban was placed on products of five hazardous industries: mines, saw mills, planing mills, foundries, and establishments manufacturing explosives.[87] The Senate Committee on Labor and Education favored this approach as did the House of Representatives, which voted down several attempts to substitute the principle of federal regulation with the weaker, state-based regulatory provisions of the Wheeler-Johnson bill.

One influential organization expressed overwhelming support for the Vandenberg amendment. The American Bar Association conducted a referendum of its members in 1937 on the various child labor amendments and legislation pending in Congress. Of the estimated 31,000 members of the association, 13,816 cast ballots. There was strong opposition among the organized bar to the 1924 Child Labor Amendment, with 2,743 votes in favor of the amendment and 10,840 votes against.[88] When given a choice between the 1924 amendment and Senator Vandenberg's proposal, most of the ABA lawyers preferred the Vandenberg amendment. Only 1,797 supported the 1924 amendment while 11,254 favored the Vandenberg amendment.[89] Asked whether Congress should enact the Wheeler-Johnson bill, the lawyers were closely divided: 6,347 voted yes and 6,907 voted no. Compared to the Gallup surveys on the 1924 Child Labor Amendment, the results of the

ABA referendum reflected a wide gap in opinion between average citizens and members of the nation's largest bar association.

Several landmark decisions by the Supreme Court in spring 1937 transformed the whole debate over government regulation of the market and held the potential for federal legislation on child labor. The change began when Justice Owen Roberts switched to the liberal bloc, and with the support of Chief Justice Hughes, the Supreme Court in *West Coast Hotel v. Parrish* and *NLRB v. Jones and Laughlin Steel Corporation* abruptly shifted its view of economic regulation. *West Coast Hotel* dealt a major blow to substantive due process. In rejecting the freedom of contract challenge to a Washington state minimum wage law, Chief Justice Hughes stressed the Constitution neither mentions liberty of contract nor recognizes "an absolute and uncontrollable liberty."[90] On the same day, known among liberals as White Monday, the High Court upheld three acts of Congress that expanded federal power, including the revised Frazier-Lemke Act. Writing for the Court in *Wright v. Vinton Branch of Mountain Trust Bank* (1937), Justice Brandeis sustained the new federal farm bankruptcy law because it limited state mortgage moratoriums to three years and gave secured creditors the opportunity to force a public sale, although the farmer could redeem the sale by paying the same amount.[91]

Two weeks later, on April 12, the Court handed the Roosevelt administration a landmark victory in five consolidated cases involving the National Labor Relations Act. In *NLRB v. Jones and Laughlin Steel Corporation*, Chief Justice Hughes argued, "Although activities may be intrastate in character when separately considered, if they have such a close and substantial relation to interstate commerce that their control is essential and appropriate to protect that commerce from burdens and obstructions, Congress cannot be denied the power to exercise that control."[92] A month later, the Court sustained the Social Security Act in *Helvering v. Davis* (1937). Collectively, these decisions represent what is called the Constitutional Revolution of 1937. In upholding Washington State's minimum wage, the National Labor Relations Act, the Social Security Act, and other New Deal programs in a span of a few months, the Court applied a new deferential stance to government regulation of economic activity. States now had significant authority to regulate intrastate commerce using their police powers, and Congress had broad powers under the Commerce Clause to regulate the market and enact social welfare programs, including child labor laws.

Dubbed the "switch in time that saved nine," Justice Owen Roberts's sudden shift toward voting with the liberal bloc effectively killed the

Court-packing plan and preserved a Supreme Court composed of nine justices. Congressman Maury Maverick (D-TX), who had sponsored the judicial reorganization plan in the House, called it "the Greatest Constitutional Somersault in History." Maverick explained how Owen Roberts, "one single human being, had amended the Constitution of the United States by nodding his head instead of shaking it. The lives of millions were changed by this nod."[93] Why did Justice Roberts switch his votes in 1937 to affirm state and federal regulation of the market? The question has generated volumes of scholarly research and contentious debate.[94] A traditional interpretation, articulated by many observers in the 1930s and historians thereafter, assumes that Roosevelt's plan to "pack" the Supreme Court with justices more receptive to the constitutionality of New Deal initiatives was the catalyst for Roberts's reversal. Traditionalists stress other external factors as well, such as public protests for economic relief and the Democrats' landslide victory in the 1936 elections. The Court, it was argued, was simply following the election returns.

Other constitutional scholars note that Roberts had voted in conference in December 1936 to sustain wage regulation in *West Coast Hotel*, two months before the Court-packing plan was made public. To be sure, it is not implausible that Roberts was influenced by the Democrats' overwhelming victory in 1936. Roosevelt administration officials also suspected that electoral politics played a role. But Roberts may have changed his mind even before the election. On October 10, 1936, weeks prior to the fall elections, the Court granted review of the *West Coast Hotel* case. Under the rule of four for granting certiorari, Roberts joined the three liberals and Chief Justice Hughes in voting to consider the case.[95] According to Burt Solomon, Roberts's action prompted one of the Four Horsemen to ask, "What is the matter with Roberts?" No one had an answer, including Roberts. He probably changed his mind on his own, for reasons known only to himself, although various explanations have been offered: Chief Justice Hughes successfully lobbied him to change his mind; he had ambitions to receive the Republican nomination for president; and he was stung by criticisms of his earlier decisions rejecting the New Deal. The truth is that we may never know for certain. Justice Roberts burned all of his personal and judicial papers. Regardless of motivations, the decisions of 1937 fundamentally altered our constitutional system and the dynamics of the child labor issue.

Following the "switch in time," there was a burst of congressional and administrative activity in Washington, DC, on the problems of minimum wages, maximum hours, and child labor. Lawyers and politicians immediately recognized the implications of the 1937 Supreme Court decisions. It was now possible that the problems of wages and child labor could be addressed without the Court-packing plan or Child Labor Amendment.[96] In a message to Congress on May 24, President Roosevelt recommended passage of legislation dealing with the problems of fair wages, maximum hours, and child labor. He declared, "A self-supporting and self-respecting democracy can plead no justification for the existence of child labor, no economic reason for chiseling workers' wages or stretching workers' hours."[97] In his remarks the president quoted extensively from Justice Oliver Wendell Holmes's dissenting opinion in *Hammer v. Dagenhart*, which argued that Congress has the power to prohibit the shipment in interstate or foreign commerce of the product of labor of children in factories. "Surely the experience of the last twenty years," Roosevelt said, "has only served to reinforce the wisdom and the rightness of his [Holmes's] views." The president reasoned that if the justices' views were right about the power to regulate labor by children, then it is equally true that Congress has the authority over decent wages and hours in those same factories.

By the late 1930s, twenty-eight states had ratified the Child Labor Amendment. All of them, except Arkansas and Kentucky, were northern, midwestern, or western states. The recent ratification votes in Kentucky and Kansas raised two constitutional issues that had been articulated by William D. Guthrie in the 1934 ABA report opposing the amendment. In that report, Guthrie had argued that the amendment was dead because too much time elapsed since proposed to the states and that states could not reverse a rejection vote under Article V procedures. Although Guthrie passed away in 1935, his arguments became the basis for legal challenges in both states.

Kentucky's vote to ratify was challenged in the state supreme court on the grounds that once the state had rejected the amendment in 1926, it could not reverse that vote, and that the second vote in favor of ratification had not taken place within a reasonable time frame after Congress had sent the proposed amendment to the states. In *Wise v. Chandler*, a mandatory injunction was sought directing the governor to notify the State Department that the certification was void because the time period for ratification had passed.[98] Similar issues were raised in the Sunflower State. Kansas rejected the amendment in 1925 and ratified it in 1937. When the Kansas legislature took up the issue for the sixth time, the Senate divided 20 to 20 on the new ratification resolution. Lieutenant Governor W. M. Lindsay broke the tie in favor of the amendment, and the Kansas House followed with a 64 to 52 vote in support of the resolution.[99] Although few people probably realized it at the time, Kansas would be the last state to ratify the Child Labor Amendment.

More than two dozen Kansas senators and several representatives sued, however, arguing that the lieutenant governor did not have the authority to break the tie. In *Coleman v. Miller*, an injunction was requested for the same reasons as in Kentucky. Both state supreme courts handed down conflicting opinions. The Court of Appeals of Kentucky agreed with Guthrie's theory on the timeliness and reversal arguments and voided the certification while the Kansas Supreme Court decided in September that the amendment was still pending and that ratification after a rejection was valid. The US Supreme Court granted review in both cases. If the Kansas Supreme Court decision was upheld, then the amendment was still alive, but if the US Supreme Court affirmed the Kentucky decision, the campaign for ratification of the Child Labor Amendment was over.

The petitioners in *Coleman v. Miller*[100] made several arguments. They asserted that the lieutenant governor was not a sitting member of the Kansas legislature and therefore was not entitled to vote on the resolution. Also, the affirmative vote to reject the amendment in 1925 cannot be reversed. Because more than one-fourth of the states had rejected the amendment, it had effectively been defeated. In *Dillon v. Goss*, the Supreme Court suggested that seven years was a reasonable time frame for ratification. The 1924 amendment, however, had not been ratified over a thirteen-year period. Even if the amendment received the necessary votes in subsequent years, almost twenty years, an entire generation, separated congressional proposal from state ratification. Quoting Charles Dickens from *A Christmas Carol*, the petitioners concluded that the proposed amendment was as "Dead as Old Marley."[101]

The respondents in *Coleman* urged the High Court to respect the decision of the Kansas Supreme Court that the vote of the lieutenant governor on a concurrent resolution was valid under the state constitution and laws. The resolution passed by the Kansas legislature in 1925, the brief contended, had no effect on the proposed amendment because the US Constitution does not give a state the power to affirmatively reject an amendment. It is simply a refusal to ratify. Moreover, one legislature, "while acting within its sovereign power, cannot take any action which will bind the hands of any succeeding Legislature."[102] In response to the argument of the petitioners that the amendment had already been defeated because more than one-fourth of the states had voted affirmatively to reject the proposal, the respondents noted that the petitioners cited no authority for that position other than an article from the American Bar Association Journal in 1934. Finally, the respondents argued that the amendment had not lost its potency because of age. Federal attempts to prevent child labor had "agitated the minds of the people for many years" prior to the proposed amendment, and the "felt need for the amendment is as strong today as when the resolution was adopted by Congress."[103] The abolition of child labor, the respondents argued, never ceased to be a matter of paramount importance during any period since 1924. Congress decided to send the proposed Child Labor Amendment to state legislatures, rather than ratifying conventions, which are less permanent, and it placed no time limit on ratification because it realized that politicians and citizens alike may need to be educated on the issue.

Both the United States and the State of Wisconsin, one of the first four states to ratify the Child Labor Amendment, filed amicus curiae briefs supporting the respondents in *Coleman v. Miller*, defending the vote of the Kansas legislature, and in defense of the petitioners in *Chandler v. Wise*,[104] who sought to overturn the state supreme court decision in Kentucky. The petitioners in *Coleman* and respondents in *Chandler* represented citizens and legislators who opposed the Child Labor Amendment.

In the amicus brief for the United States, Solicitor General Robert H. Jackson made several arguments common to the parties seeking to affirm the ratification resolution votes in both states. First, the US government argued that Article V speaks only in terms of ratification. The "concept of rejection is extra-constitutional."[105] The brief characterized a vote of rejection of a proposed amendment, or an adverse vote, or a failure to pass a resolution of ratification as one in the same—all constitutionally neutral acts. If rejection of an amendment precluded reconsideration by a legislature it would alter the "deliberative and representative" nature of the amendment process. Second, a ratification process is not invalid by reason of lapsed time when Congress has placed no time frame on ratification. Congress rejected attempts to place five-year and seven-year time limits when the amendment was debated in 1924. Thirteen years, the US government argued, is not an unreasonably long time to consider an amendment. Resolutions for ratification had been introduced in state legislatures, in some cases multiple times, on a regular basis since 1924. Federal government officials also treated the amendment as still pending, from President Roosevelt to members of Congress. Finally, the conditions giving rise to the amendment had not been ameliorated. Statistics from the Children's Bureau, the White House Conference on Child Health and Protection, and scholarly research indicated that child labor was still a problem. Moreover, there was continuing public support of the amendment to address the problem. The brief cited the advocacy record of the American Federation of Labor and other labor groups, the National Child Labor Committee, and the polls conducted by George Gallup in 1936 and 1937 as testament to the vitality of the amendment.[106]

Wisconsin's amicus brief argued that the broad language of Article V, containing the phrase "when ratified by the legislatures of three-fourths of the several states," does not preclude ratification by a subsequent legislature after a prior rejection. There are no implied limitations on state authority to ratify contained in the text of Article V.[107] To support this position, the brief cited the history of the adoption of the Fourteenth Amendment, which was ratified by North Carolina and South Carolina subsequent to earlier rejections. Also, a onetime rejection of an amendment by more than one-fourth of the states does not defeat the amendment. The only action that matters is ratification within a reasonable length of time or withholding of ratification for an unreasonable period. Finally, the brief argued that the amendment has not lost its vitality because of the lapse of time.[108] There were four separate amendments to the proposed draft of the Child Labor Amendment specifying time limitations from five to seven years, but those revisions were rejected by Congress. Congress, then, intended for the states to have the longest possible period to consider ratification. The history of federal legislation on child labor, the brief asserted, indicates that it is a contemporary issue that will not go away. The issue had been a matter of public debate for almost twenty years, and it is just as relevant in 1937 as in 1924.

The Supreme Court heard oral arguments in the consolidated cases on October 10–11, 1938, but the Court was forced to delay consideration of the cases. Justice Benjamin Cardozo passed away on July 9, 1938, and Justice Louis Brandeis announced his retirement. President Roosevelt nominated Harvard law professor Felix Frankfurter, his close friend and advisor, to succeed Justice Cardozo. The nomination was controversial because Frankfurter was Jewish, and he had defended anarchists Sacco and Vanzetti in the 1920s. Frankfurter became the first Supreme Court nominee to appear before the Senate Judiciary Committee, although he refused to answer questions, claiming that he would let his public record speak for itself. Justice Frankfurter took his seat on January 30, 1939. The president then nominated loyal New Dealer William O. Douglas to replace Justice Brandeis, and Justice Douglas was sworn in on April 17, 1939, the same day that *Coleman v. Miller* was reargued before the Court.

In *Coleman v. Miller*, the Court held (7–2) that the Child Labor Amendment was still alive and that a state that had rejected the amendment may reverse itself and vote for ratification. The justices seemed divided over whether the Court even had the authority to hear the case. Justice Frankfurter authored an opinion, joined by Justices Roberts, Black, and Douglas, that the Court lacked jurisdiction to consider the Kansas case. But they were overruled, and since the Court had accepted jurisdiction, the same group of justices held that the amendment was still open for ratification. The Court addressed three questions in the case: did the participation of the lieutenant governor, the prior rejection by the Kansas legislature then reversal, or the length of time between proposal and ratification violate Article V of the Constitution? Writing for the Court, Chief Justice Charles Evans Hughes described these questions as inherently political. He said that there was no constitutional or statutory authority for the courts to restrain state officers from certifying a ratification after a previous rejection or determine a proper length of time for ratification. Article V contains no provision on rejections and leaves a decision on the time frame for ratification to the discretion of Congress. While the petitioners contended that the Court should decide what constitutes a "reasonable time" for ratification, Chief Justice Hughes said, "We are unable to agree with that contention."[109] The Court was "equally divided" on the participation of the lieutenant governor and chose not to decide the issue.

Chief Justice Hughes dismissed the appeal in the Kentucky case on the basis that after the governor of Kentucky had forwarded the certification of ratification of the amendment to the secretary of state of the United States, there was no longer a justiciable controversy for a judicial determination. The two remaining members of the Four Horsemen, Justices McReynolds and Butler, dissented, arguing that the Kentucky Appellate Court's decision should be affirmed. Justice Butler wrote that a more than "reasonable" time had passed between the proposal by Congress and its adoption by the Kansas legislature. He argued that since the Court ruled in *Dillon v. Goss* that seven years for ratification was reasonable, it should not now claim to lack the power to decide whether thirteen years between proposal and ratification in Kansas was reasonable.

The 1924 Child Labor Amendment was still alive. In a 1939 report on the status of child labor, Courtenay Dinwiddie believed it was possible to secure eight more states to make the amendment part of the Constitution. Alabama and Delaware were still in session, and in 1940, seven states that had not ratified were to meet in regular sessions.[110] But there would be no more ratification votes. After the Constitutional Revolution of 1937, no state approved the amendment. Five states—Alabama, Mississippi, Nebraska, New York, and Rhode Island—took no formal action on the amendment. Alaska and Hawaii, admitted to the Union in 1959, also have not voted on the amendment. Because Congress set no time limit, the Child Labor Amendment is still, technically, pending ratification. Currently, twenty-eight states have ratified the amendment, but that falls short of the three-fourths or thirty-eight now needed for ratification. Ultimately, the amendment was not necessary because in 1941, the Supreme Court upheld the fourth federal child labor law, the Fair Labor Standards Act, thus achieving by legislation what could not be obtained by constitutional amendment.

7

The Fair Labor Standards Act and Final Victory in *United States v. Darby Lumber*

In 1933, President Roosevelt asked Frances Perkins to be his labor secretary. Perkins responded that she would accept only if she could advocate a wages and hours bill and to abolish abuses of child labor. According to a Department of Labor history, when Roosevelt enthusiastically agreed to the terms, Perkins asked him, "Have you considered that to launch such a program . . . might be considered unconstitutional?" The president retorted, "Well, we can work out something when the time comes."[1] Perkins joined the administration, becoming the first female in a presidential cabinet. As the NRA codes were being challenged in the courts, Secretary Perkins asked lawyers at the Labor Department to draft two wage-hour and child labor bills. She informed Roosevelt that she had the bills "locked in the lower left-hand of my desk against an emergency."

Following his unsuccessful attempt to pack the Supreme Court with justices supportive of his New Deal policies and after the "switch in time" in 1937 where the Court upheld state and federal regulation of wages, hours, and workplace conditions, President Roosevelt asked Frances Perkins what she had done with "that nice unconstitutional bill you had tucked away?" The bill that Perkins had locked away, which was the second bill in her desk, was a general fair labor standards act. Anticipating Supreme Court review, Labor Department lawyers based the bill on several constitutional principles, hoping that if one or two were rejected by the Court, the law would still stand. Perkins sent the bill to the president. White House lawyers Thomas G. Corcoran and Benjamin V. Cohen spent months revising the bill and adding more provisions. At that point, it is unclear whether their various drafts included child labor restrictions. A late change at the urging of Grace Abbott, chief of the Children's Bureau, was a clause prohibiting goods produced with the labor of children under sixteen in industries engaged in or affecting interstate commerce. "You are hoping that you have found a way around the Supreme Court," Abbott pleaded. "If you have, why not give the children the benefit by attaching a child labor clause to this bill?"[2] Believing that a child labor provision would increase support for the legislation, Roosevelt readily agreed.[3]

On May 24, 1937, the president sent the bill to Congress. In his remarks to legislators, he urged support for fair labor standards: "A self-supporting and self-respecting democracy can plead no justification for the existence of child labor, no economic reason for chiseling workers' wages or stretching workers' hours." He continued, "All but the hopelessly reactionary will agree that to conserve our primary resources of man power [*sic*], Government must have some control over maximum hours, minimum wages, the evil of child labor, and the exploitation of unorganized labor."[4] Multiple bills on labor conditions were introduced on the same day as the president's message to Congress.

The first bill under consideration was the administration plan, known as the Black-Connery bill, in honor of Senator Hugo Black of Alabama and Representative William Connery of Massachusetts, both of whom had worked tirelessly for years on wage and hour legislation.[5] Black chaired the Senate Labor Committee, and Connery held a similar post in the House. Senator Black had been persuaded by the president to drop his plan for a thirty-hour workweek, which he had sponsored as early as 1932, in favor of the administration plan that would eventually become the Fair Labor Standards Act (FLSA), popularly called the wages and hours bill. The road to the FLSA, however, was long and winding. Thirteen months and one day expired before the bill reached President Roosevelt's desk, and it was amended so many times during legislative negotiations that few features of the original bill remained intact.[6] An observer described it as one of the "most bitterly fought pieces of legislation" ever enacted by Congress.[7]

A Joint Hearing of the Senate Committee on Education and Labor, chaired by Senator Black, and House Committee on Labor, chaired by Representative Connery, held hearings for over a month on the Black-

Connery bill. When Congressman Connery died on June 15, leadership in the House on the bill passed to Representative Mary T. Norton of New Jersey, and Senator Black became the bill's most vocal advocate in the Senate and Congress overall. The original bill provided for the creation of a five-member regulatory agency called the Fair Labor Standards Board to enforce the provisions of the law. The measure relied upon the power of Congress to regulate commerce between the states. It banned the movement of goods produced under substandard labor conditions from entering interstate commerce. Flexibility was the hallmark of the bill. Unlike the NRA, it did not regulate fair trade practices and marketing methods nor did it specify work hours or a fixed minimum wage for all industries.[8] Congress would give the proposed board the authority to fix minimum "fair" wages and a maximum "reasonable" workweek of not less than thirty and not more than forty hours. Child labor under the age of sixteen was prohibited, and the chief of the Children's Bureau was authorized to bar the labor of those under eighteen in any occupation that was thought to be "particularly hazardous" or detrimental to their health or well-being.

Assistant Attorney General Robert H. Jackson, who within a few years would serve as US attorney general, US solicitor general, associate justice of the US Supreme Court, and lead US prosecutor at the Nuremburg war crimes trials following World War II, testified on the constitutional foundations of the bill. Jackson stated that the proposed bill, except to the child labor case of *Hammer v. Dagenhart*, was "backed by long established precedents defining Federal power to regulate interstate commerce." He cited the *Shreveport Rate Cases, NLRB v. Jones and Laughlin Steel Corporation*, and the *Kentucky Whip and Collar* case as supporting a broad authority of Congress to regulate unfair competition within a state, competition in interstate commerce, the movement of goods across state lines in violation of national policy, products moved in interstate commerce in violation of state laws, and labor conditions that lead to conflicts that obstruct or burden interstate commerce.[9] The only exception was the child labor decision in *Hammer v. Dagenhart*, which, Jackson noted, affected only a portion of the bill. The assistant attorney general asserted that "the doctrine of the majority in the *Child Labor case* belongs to the same dark era of legal thought as the decision holding that the minimum-wage law was unconstitutional (referring to *Adkins v. Children's Hospital*, 1923). . . . We should give the courts a chance to remove this blemish from our judicial history."[10] Aware of the Supreme Court's sudden change in doctrine since 1937, Jackson concluded: "We may reasonably entertain the hope that *Hammer v. Dagenhart* will be laid to a tardy and unmourned repose beside the lifeless remains of *Adkins v. Children's Hospital*."[11]

Industry leaders were divided on the bill. The northern textile industry favored the legislation and opposed regional differentials in wage scales. Northern mill owners preferred a national scale as a means of protecting themselves against competition from southern mills with lower wages. Liberal-minded employers also spoke in favor of the bill. Robert Johnson, president of Johnson and Johnson, urged that the bill be approved out of self-interest and social awareness. He acknowledged that business succeeds when workers have adequate wages to purchase products, and to enact the bill would be "a great thing for business and a great thing for millions of American employees."[12] Jay C. Hormel, owner of the Hormel meatpacking company, also backed adequate wage and hour legislation. He believed that stable worker income and employment were good for his business. Another business leader, R. C. Kuldell, head of the Hughes Tool Company in Texas, an oil well machinery and equipment firm with four thousand employees, told the Joint Committee that he was "fully in accord" with the purposes of the bill. Kuldell remarked, "If the Labor Standards Board administered the law as a doctor and not a policeman, it can be assured of the whole-hearted cooperation of industrial employers."[13]

Powerful business groups, however, appeared before the Joint Committee against the bill. The US Chamber of Commerce, the National Association of Manufacturers, the National Publishers Association, the National Association of Wood Manufacturers, and most southern manufacturers opposed the bill, either on principle or because they demanded regional differentials in wages. George H. Davis, president of the Chamber of Commerce of the United States, worried about uncertainty in future labor costs if the bill passed. James A. Emery, general counsel of the National Association of Manufacturers and a veteran of the campaign against the Child Labor Amendment, argued that "the bill used an unconstitutional view of the commerce power, and was also an invalid delegation of power."[14] Southern mill owners and manufacturers demanded lower wage scales for the South because compared to the North, the cost of living was alleged to be lower in the South, employees were less skilled, and freight costs were higher.[15] Other business leaders assailed the Black-Connery bill as "a bad bill badly drawn" that would take the country down a path to "tyrannical industrial dictatorship."[16] Industry representatives pointedly asked how could business "find any time left to provide jobs if we are to persist in loading upon it these everlastingly multiplying governmental mandates and delivering it to the mercies of multiplying and hampering Federal bureaucracy?"[17]

Organized labor supported the bill but disagreed over wage provisions and the authority of the Fair Labor Standards Board. William Green of the American Federation of Labor (AFL) and John L. Lewis of the Congress of Industrial Organizations (CIO) differed on various aspects of the bill. Lewis favored a thirty-five-hour workweek but suggested that the board should have the power to raise the number to forty hours or lower it to thirty hours. He was strongly opposed to giving the board discretionary power to raise wages above forty cents an hour, and he urged the abolition of Section 5.[18] His rationale for this position seemed to be a fear that minimum "fair" wages and maximum "reasonable" hours would actually become the maximum wage and minimum hours. Moreover, employers would have a powerful propaganda tool if unions decided to strike against the "fair" wages and "maximum" hours set by the board. William Green of the AFL wanted no overlapping between collective bargaining and government control over wages and hours. He even opposed letting the board raise standards reached by collective bargaining. Green favored a forty-hour workweek but would allow the board flexibility to lower it down to thirty hours. Unlike Lewis, he backed giving the board discretion to increase wages up to eighty cents an hour.[19] But both Lewis and Green "favored legislation which would limit labor standards to low-paid and essentially unorganized workers."[20] They did not want the board undermining union power by interfering in areas they wanted reserved for labor-management negotiations. When the bill was later amended to exclude work covered by collective bargaining, the two labor leaders were satisfied.

Sidney Hillman, president of the Amalgamated Clothing Workers of America and one of the earliest proponents of fair labor standards, and David Dubinsky of the International Ladies' Garment Workers' Union supported a strong bill that would give the proposed board the discretion to set fair wages and reasonable hours higher than the basic standards set by Congress.[21] Hillman explained that unlike John L. Lewis's CIO and United Mine Workers of America, which collectively bargain on a national scale, collective bargaining cannot effectively cover industries such as textiles, garments, and shoes, and the only way to raise standards uniformly is to have them established by government.

Courtenay Dinwiddie, general secretary of the National Child Labor Committee, drew upon thirty-three years of organizational experience in commenting on the child labor provisions of the bill. His organization "vigorously" supported a new federal law restricting child labor, but he also warned that such a law would not entirely solve the problem. Child labor in interstate commerce encompassed only about 25 percent of the children employed, excluding agriculture.[22] That left 75 percent of working children outside federal regulation. "The only permanent solution for this large area of exploitation," Dinwiddie argued, "is through the Federal child-labor amendment," which would give Congress the power to deal with child labor in the service trades, such as hotels, restaurants, and laundries, which are local in nature.[23]

Dinwiddie noted that unlike the maximum hours and minimum wage provisions of the Black-Connery bill, the child labor regulations could easily be implemented with the Children's Bureau working with state agencies. All that was needed were uniform national standards. Dinwiddie criticized several sections of the bill that applied the method of prohibiting prison-made goods to the interstate transportation of child-made goods. As he had argued previously, applying the prison-made theory to child-made goods would not work. It would be an administrative nightmare. Also, Dinwiddie recommended that the legislation abolish industrial home work, "one of the most vicious and persistent practices for sweating labor ever devised."[24] Finally, he urged that the law cover smaller and more scattered manufacturing establishments, such as "fly-by-night tie and shirt factories, so-called 'wild' shrimp and oyster canneries, 'grasshopper' sawmills, and small box and crate factories" that use destructive child labor practices.[25]

Larue Brown, representing the National League of Women Voters, an organization that had fought for effective child labor legislation since its formation in 1921, echoed many of the arguments made by Courtenay Dinwiddie on the child labor provisions. While supporting the age restrictions for various industries in the bill, she also "strenuously objected" to adopting the prison-goods theory of regulation, pointing out that the only way the model could be effective was if every state passed identical laws and enforced them uniformly, which was virtually impossible to accomplish.[26] Brown favored a law based on the "simple and direct" congressional power to regulate interstate commerce, and she insisted that the Children's Bureau be responsible for administering the child labor provisions in cooperation with state agencies.

When the hearings concluded, the Senate Education and Labor Committee made substantial changes to the bill that weakened the power of the proposed Fair Labor Standards Board and narrowed the child labor provisions. The board would not be permitted to fix wages above forty cents an hour or mandate a standard working week of less than forty hours. Agricultural exemptions were broadened to include farming, dairying, forestry, fishing, horticulture, and local retailing.[27] The child labor provisions excluded children in agriculture and those employed by their parents. Children under sixteen were permitted to work in jobs that would not injure their "health and well-being" nor interfere with their education as determined by the chief of the Children's Bureau. The proposed prison-goods theory of regulation was rejected. Finally, to calm the fears of some business leaders that higher wages and lower hours would lead to competition from cheap foreign imports, a provision was added that gave the Tariff Commission investigatory power to see if higher tariff rates were needed. The revised bill was unanimously reported to the Senate on July 8.

The bill arrived on the Senate floor on July 26. Senator Black's southern colleagues denounced the bill, resurrecting sectional arguments that northerners wanted to "crucify" southern industry in order to stifle competition and prevent the South from rising from the devastation of the Civil War.[28] Senator Ellison D. Smith of South Carolina declared that the spirit behind the bill was nothing more than a "vote-getting proposition," and he "bitterly condemned it as hostile to the South."[29] Many Republicans opposed the bill as well as some Democrats from outside the South. Known for his hyperbole, Republican senator Vandenberg of Michigan called the wages and hours bill "the essence of Fascism."[30] Senator William H. King (D-UT) refused to back the bill. "Wages and hours," he asserted, "are a matter for the states to decide."[31]

According to his biographer, Senator Black replied with one of the most dramatic performances of his Senate tenure. "We must face two tribunals with this law," Black said. "The first is Congress. The second is the Supreme Court."[32] He first dealt with Congress. Waving mill vouchers that showed pay scales at eight cents an hour, Black angrily chastised his colleagues. "I subscribe to the gospel that a man who is born in Alabama and who can do as much work as a man born in any state in New England is entitled to the same pay if he does the same work."[33] Black was prepared to address the constitutional issues surrounding the FLSA as well. He had served five years on the Senate Judiciary Committee honing his knowledge of constitutional law, and he had spent most of six months in the Supreme Court library studying precedents and doctrine relevant to the law.[34] With an eye to the Supreme Court, Black praised the minority opinion in the *Hammer* case for being more faithful to the "plain intent and purpose of the Commerce Clause" and for being "more consonant . . . with progress than the majority opinion."[35] He embraced a living Constitution approach rather than a static reading of the text. The Constitution, he said, "has been interpreted from time to time to meet new situations and conditions that could not have been foreseen by the writers of that great document. . . . If change is needed to cure evils growing out of old practices, change must come."[36]

After five days of debate the bill passed the Senate on July 31, 1937, by a vote of 52 to 48. Despite their strong testimony against the prison-goods theory of regulation, child labor advocates were deeply disappointed to learn that the only major change on the floor of the Senate was the substitution of the Wheeler-Johnson child labor amendment, which was based on the prison-goods formula, in place of all of the child labor provisions in the original Senate Committee bill. Reformers found the change unacceptable and worked to remove the provision.

As the legislative wrangling continued that summer, seventy-eight-year-old associate justice Willis Van Devanter (one of the Four Horsemen) announced his retirement from the Court on June 2. President Roosevelt nominated Senator Hugo Black to take his seat, although he failed to carefully vet the nominee's political background. While Senator Black guided the Black-Connery bill through the Senate, his past Ku Klux Klan affiliation embroiled the nomination in controversy. Hugo Black was eventually confirmed in mid-August by a Senate vote of 63–16, and he took his seat on October 4. With Senator Black's task in the Senate on the FLSA practically finished, the Roosevelt administration gained a potential New Deal ally on the Court.

After the Senate vote, the debate on the wages and hours bill shifted to the House of Representatives. On August 6, 1937, the House Committee on Labor issued a favorable report on the Senate bill with amendments. Among the changes, the AFL received protections for collective bargaining agreements by denying the Board jurisdiction over wages and hours in areas where collective bargaining procedures were adequate. More important, the House bill eliminated the Wheeler-Johnson child labor amendment and restored the provisions in the Senate Committee bill. All subsequent attempts to reinsert the Wheeler-Johnson amendment during House debate were unsuccessful.[37] With labor now strongly in favor of the legislation, it appeared that the amended House bill had enough votes to secure passage if it could be reported out of committee. A coalition of four Republicans and five southern conservative Democrats on the House Rules Committee, however, refused to permit the bill to be brought to the floor.[38] Congress adjourned without a House vote on fair labor standards.

In an October 12 radio address, President Roosevelt issued a call for a special session of Congress to convene on November 15, 1937, with wages and hours legislation as one of the top items on the agenda. Recently returned from a tour of western states, the president believed that he had the support of the American people. In an address to Congress in early November, Roosevelt identified a legislative agenda for the session. In addition to a farm bill to stabilize crop prices and a plan for executive branch reorganization, labor issues were a priority. The president said: "I believe that the country as a whole recognizes the need for immediate congressional action if we are to maintain wage income and the purchasing power of the nation against recessive factors in the general industrial situation. The exploitation of child labor and the undercutting of wages and the stretching of the hours of the poorest paid workers in periods of business recession have a serious effect on buying power."[39] President Roosevelt urged legislation relating to goods moving in or competing with interstate commerce for two purposes: banning child labor and ending the practice of some communities that seek new industry by maintaining low wages and excessively long hours.

When the special session convened, however, members of the Rules Committee had not changed their position and refused to issue a rule permitting House consideration of the bill. On the second day of the session, Norton, chair of the House Committee, started a petition to discharge the Rules Committee from further consideration and allowing the bill to come before the floor. Although it took a lot of negotiation, which opponents claimed involved political favors in exchange for signatures, Chairman Norton secured the 218 signatures necessary for a petition on December 2. As Democrats cheered and whistled, Representative Joseph Mansfield, a seventy-six-year-old wheelchair-bound Texas Democrat, provided the last signature.[40] It appeared that the House would now have a chance to vote on the measure. But renewed opposition from President William Green and the AFL complicated the legislative maneuvers. Labor leaders from the AFL opposed granting discretionary power to an administrative board, charging that the NLRB had favored industrial unionism and the CIO over craft unionism and the AFL.[41] Resistance from organized labor delayed and threatened to defeat the wages and hours bill.

Administration opponents in Congress were also emboldened by President Roosevelt's loss of political capital following the defeat of the

Court-packing plan. Influential senator Joe Robinson, majority leader and the administration's advocate for the Court reorganization plan in the Senate, died on July 14, and the Court plan followed him to the grave. The Senate voted to recommit the judicial reorganization bill on July 22, effectively defeating the legislation, at least the provisions regarding Supreme Court appointments.[42] Moreover, by the fall 1937, the economic recovery had collapsed. Industrial production fell by 33 percent, national income dropped by 12 percent, stock prices lost 50 percent of their value, and unemployment increased. The "Roosevelt recession" within the Depression that hit the country during the president's second term was largely due to the administration scaling back government spending and focusing on balancing the federal budget.[43] The economic situation provided more ammunition to the administration's adversaries.

In an attempt to mollify AFL concerns, the House Labor Committee offered a new bill that replaced the Fair Labor Standards Board with a single administrator within the Department of Labor appointed by the president. Mr. Green, however, was not satisfied with the draft legislation. He wrote to House members that "if a Board is dangerous . . . certainly the Administrator is even more dangerous and should be rejected."[44] Congressmen John Dockweiler (D-CA) and Glenn Griswold (D-IN) then offered an AFL substitute bill. The bill provided for a strict forty-cents-an-hour and forty-hours-a-week standard for workers in nonunionized plants with no regional or industrial differentials and enforcement by the attorney general. The bill was defeated 162–131.[45] On December 13 the House by a vote of 258–113 discharged the Rules Committee from further consideration, and it appeared the bill had enough support. President Green of the AFL, however, now aggressively lobbied against the bill, and more than sixty amendments were offered over the next five days.[46] Finally, shortly before the Christmas recess, the House unexpectedly voted 216–198 to send the bill back to the Labor Committee.[47] When the final tally was announced by Speaker William Bankhead, a fervent cry of "Thank God" erupted from the Democratic side before a burst of applause and shouting filled the House chamber.

In her memoir of President Roosevelt, Frances Perkins wrote: "This was the first time that a major administration bill had been defeated on the floor of the House."[48] According to Perkins, the press characterized the vote as the "death knell of wage-hour legislation as well as a decisive blow to the President's prestige." But President Roosevelt was undeterred. In his State of the Nation address on January 3, the president reiterated his call for wages and hours legislation. "We are seeking only, of course, to end starvation wages and intolerable hours. More desirable wages are, and should continue to be, the product of collective bargaining."[49] The following day, the *New York Times* published editorial excerpts from twenty-five major newspapers throughout the country. Many of the editorials noted that the president's remarks were more conciliatory and reasonable toward business, but a majority were critical of New Deal policies in light of the economic downturn.[50]

President Roosevelt may have had a better grasp of the pulse of the average citizen than many of his critics. Several events improved the prospects for passage of fair labor standards during the regular session. The day after his address to Congress, Representative Lister Hill, an ardent Roosevelt supporter, won an Alabama election primary for Senator Black's vacated seat by an almost 2–1 margin over J. Thomas Heflin, an aging anti–New Deal former senator.[51] Heflin was backed by the so-called Big Mules of Alabama business and agriculture that strongly opposed the Black-Connery bill. Hill's decisive victory was significant because much of the opposition to the wages-hours bill came from southern congressman. In February 1938, a national poll conducted by George Gallup's Institute of Public Opinion reported that 67 percent of the population favored the wages and hours bill, with even the South showing a substantial plurality of support for higher standards.[52]

President Roosevelt privately told Secretary Perkins that he thought the wages and hours bill encountered so much opposition because of its length and complexity. Although miniscule compared to modern legislation, the president asked if the forty-page bill could be "boiled down to two pages." Perkins reminded him that the bill had been written more with an eye toward Supreme Court review rather than for the average layman. The Labor Department solicitor, Gerard Reilly, attempted but failed to meet the president's two-page goal but he did cut the bill down to ten pages. Reilly and Perkins brought the revised bill to the president in late January. He accepted the revisions and the leaner bill was submitted to Congress.

The president and Secretary Perkins geared up for the legislative battle that was sure to come. Roosevelt arm-twisted Democratic congressmen who had ridden his coattails to victory in 1936 but who then fought New Deal legislation. Secretary Perkins hired a young lawyer, Rufus Poole, a former assistant solicitor in the Interior Department, who was assigned to do nothing else but track the daily progress of the bill, identify difficulties, and forestall objections. Perkins recalled that Poole became so good at this task that he "could predict with reasonable accuracy the vote for or against any amendment."[53]

Chairman Norton appointed a subcommittee of the House Labor Committee, with Representative Robert Ramspeck as chairman, to bridge the gap between various proposals and amendments. The subcommittee produced the Ramspeck compromise, which made some modifications to the truncated bill that the president had approved. The compromise provided for a five-member wage board less powerful than under the original Black-Connery bill, but with authority to gradually impose the forty-cent minimum wage and forty-hour maximum work week.[54] Perkins believed that the compromise "contained the bare essentials the administration could support."[55]

In a case of politics creating strange bedfellows, both the American Federation of Labor and National Association of Manufacturers opposed the Ramspeck compromise. The CIO favored the bill, but a canvass of the House indicated that there were not enough votes to carry the compromise. The House Labor Committee voted down the compromise 10 to 8, but Chairman Norton offered an alternative bill based on a proposal backed by the AFL. The bill provided for a "floor" of twenty-five cents an hour and a "ceiling" of forty hours per week with the minimum wage to increase five cents a year until forty cents an hour was reached. The maximum hour workweek was to decrease two hours over two successive years until it reached forty hours. There were no regional or industry differentials. With this gradual scale, the idea of a wage board was eliminated and the secretary of labor was given investigatory and enforcement powers, including the authority to declare which industries operated in interstate commerce. The rationale behind the AFL-backed plan was to reduce or eliminate administrative discretion on wages and hours. The bill was reported favorably to the House on April 21.

As before, the Rules Committee refused to report a resolution allowing the House to consider the measure. A frustrated President Roosevelt called Representative John J. O'Conner of New York, chairman of the Rules Committee, an "obstructionist" who "pickled" New Deal programs.[56] At that point, Roosevelt felt that a little executive pressure was needed. For the sixth time in his presidency, he communicated with Congress over the need for fair labor standards through a letter sent to Norton. In his message, he did not comment on the specifics of the bill, but he emphasized the national importance of the legislation and urged the House to allow full consideration of the bill. The president hoped "that the democratic processes of legislation will continue." For this to happen, the House needed another discharge petition.

Several days after the president's message to Congress a primary election shifted the landscape of debate over the bill. Senator Claude Pepper, who campaigned in Florida to retain his seat, won a resounding victory over anti–New Dealer representative J. Mark Wilcox. An ally of President Roosevelt and leader of the left-liberal coalition in the Senate, Pepper campaigned on support for the New Deal and wages-hours bill. Wilcox had made New Deal programs his central issue, and he labeled his opponent "Roosevelt's rubber stamp."[57] The more than 2 to 1 margin of victory sent a strong message to southern congressman regarding how their constituents felt about fair labor standards. On May 6 at noon, a petition to discharge the wages and hours bill from the Rules Committee was placed on the desk of the Speaker of the House. Unlike the special session, when it took several weeks to round up the necessary signatures, 218 members signed the petition in just two hours and twenty minutes, with more "waiting in the aisles" ready to sign.[58] The bill now moved to the House floor for debate.

All but the most conservative members of the southern delegation abandoned their opposition. Labor standards in the South were the most contentious issue. Northern representatives shared "horror stories" of labor exploitation in the region. One Indiana congressman claimed that women in Georgia were working ten hours a day in canning factories for $4.50 a week, or the equivalent of nine cents an hour based on a five-day work week. Southern congressman accused their northern colleagues of "sentencing Southern industry to death," and they told the Labor Department that businesses could not survive with a twenty-five-cent minimum wage. As a concession to these southern concerns, a requirement was added that wage administrators would consider lower costs of living and higher transportation costs in the region before recommending wages above the minimum. Exemptions were also made for the fishing industry and some agricultural commodities. On May 24, 1938, the House passed the bill 314–97.

Because there were significant differences between the Senate and House versions of the bill, a conference committee had to work out a compromise. A major point of contention, as it had been throughout the whole debate on the bill, was whether to provide regional differentials for minimum wages. Ultimately, southern congressman yielded on this point, and the conferees agreed on a national minimum wage of twenty-five cents an hour with increases to forty cents over a period of seven years. Concessions were also made to critics who claimed that immediately imposing a forty-hour workweek would be devastating to business. The conference agreed to set maximum hours at forty-four with a gradual reduction to forty hours over three years.

Labor leaders appeared satisfied with the compromise language. President Green sent a telegram commenting that although the conference report did not comply fully with the agenda of the AFL, he did not oppose its passage.[59] John L. Lewis of the CIO was also on board. The House passed the conference committee report on June 13, 1938, by a vote of 291 to 89. The following day, the Senate approved the bill without a recorded vote. Congress then sent the Fair Labor Standards Act to the president.

In a "fireside chat" the night before he signed the law, FDR warned: "Do not let any calamity-howling executive with an income of $1,000 a day . . . tell you . . . that a wage of $11 a week is going to have a disastrous effect on all American industry."[60] The president explained that the FLSA's objective was the "elimination of labor conditions detrimental to the maintenance of the minimum standards of living necessary for health, efficiency, and well-being of workers." He described the law as "the most far-reaching, far-sighted program for the benefit of workers ever adopted in this or any other country."[61] After more than a year of presidential speeches, three sessions of congressional debate, ten versions of the bill, and over seventy proposed amendments, President Franklin D. Roosevelt signed the Fair Labor Standards Act on June 25, 1938.[62] "That's that," the president sighed as he put his signature to the bill.[63] And it was that in more ways than one. Not only had the long fight over wage and hours legislation come to an end, but also the FLSA was the last piece of New Deal legislation passed during the Roosevelt presidency.[64] On October 24, 1938, the minimum wage, maximum hours, and child labor provisions of the FLSA went into effect.

The FLSA was historic legislation, but the original law had its shortcomings. It was estimated that the law initially applied to industries whose combined employment was one-fifth of the labor force, or roughly 11 million workers.[65] The FLSA stipulated that all employers engaged in interstate commerce must pay their employees a minimum wage of twenty-five cents an hour and not permit them to work longer than forty hours per week without paying them time-and-a-half overtime pay. With exemptions for various business sectors, an estimated 750,000 workers benefited from the twenty-five-cent minimum wage provision, and the law reduced the hours of 1.5 million who had been working more than the forty-four-hour weekly maximum.[66]

The child labor provisions of the FLSA received far less attention from the press and public than the wage and hour provisions so it is worthwhile to examine them in detail. Like other provisions in the FLSA, the child labor sections had their limitations and exemptions. The law defined "oppressive child labor" as employment of a minor under the age of sixteen years, unless the employer is the child's parent or guardian. Even a parent or guardian, however, may not employ the child in manufacturing or mining operations. For children under sixteen years, employment in manufacturing and mining is banned in all circumstances. Children fourteen and fifteen years old employed outside those occupations were not deemed to be engaged in oppressive child labor if the chief of the Children's Bureau determines that such work does not interfere with a child's education or health and well-being.[67] If minors between the ages of sixteen and eighteen are working in industries that the chief of the Children's Bureau declares to be hazardous, that is oppressive child labor.

Under the FLSA, "no producer, manufacturer, or dealer" was permitted to send into interstate commerce "any goods produced in an establishment in the United States in or about which within thirty days prior to the removal of such goods any oppressive child labor had been employed.[68] There were several general exemptions, however, that weakened the protections of the law. Other than excluding children working for parents or guardians, the law exempted children working in agriculture "while not legally required to attend school" and children employed as actors in movies or theatrical productions. Additionally, the law did nothing to protect child laborers in occupations that do not produce goods in interstate commerce. For example, girls working as domestic servants or boys and girls employed in local service trades at laundries, hotels, restaurants, and beauty parlors were not protected by the provisions. One early analysis of the FLSA concluded that the act did not begin to deal with the general problem of child labor. An estimated 30,000 to 50,000 minors under age sixteen were withdrawn from the workforce out of 850,000 children fifteen years and under who were employed. The law only covered about 6 percent of working kids.[69]

The biggest problem was the agricultural exemption where an estimated 70 percent of all child laborers were employed. Approximately five hundred thousand to six hundred thousand children were working in agriculture either as laborers on the family farm or in commercialized agriculture. Migrant labor and children working in tobacco or cotton fields, where some of the worst exploitation existed, received little protection under the law. Agriculture was defined so broadly that children who worked in turpentine camps were not covered.[70] In a review of the law one year after enactment, Courtenay Dinwiddie noted that the child labor ban in agriculture only applies if a child works in violation of compulsory school attendance laws, but in many states "school laws expressly permit children to be absent for farm work."[71]

Given responsibility for enforcing the child labor provisions of the Fair Labor Standards Act, the Children's Bureau was able to pick up where it left off when the first federal child labor law, the Keating-Owen Act, went into effect September 1, 1917. The Keating-Owen Act was implemented for about a year before the Supreme Court struck it down. The bureau could draw upon that experience and the expertise gained in the subsequent twenty years dealing with child labor issues. The agency designated an expanded industrial division to implement the law and appointed an assistant director in charge of Child Labor Administration. The bureau hoped to work cooperatively with state agencies in order to avoid duplication of efforts. States themselves had improved their child labor and compulsory attendance laws since 1917. Many had established labor departments and special inspectors to enforce child labor laws. The administrative machinery was now in place to effectively implement the law.

Priority was given to the issuance of temporary certificates of age for all working children. Contrasted with the Wheeler-Johnson amendment, which critics claimed was punitive and only operated after a child labor law had been violated, the certificate system served as a preventive measure and protected employers who honestly attempted to comply with the law. The first child labor regulation issued by the Children's Bureau announced that the certificates of age issued by thirty-one states would have the same effect as federal certificates for a six-month period.[72] During that time federal and state officials developed a more permanent plan. Within a year, state employment certificates were accepted in forty-three states and the District of Columbia.[73] The first regulation also described the information that must be contained in a certificate, evidence of age that would be accepted, and rules governing acceptance, suspension, and revocation of certificates. Any employer of children holding a valid state or federal certificate would not be deemed as engaging in oppressive child labor.

Measuring compliance with the law was based on inspections carried out in cooperation with the wages and hours division of the Labor Department. The Children's Bureau focused on canneries, packing plants, and local industries notorious for child labor. Inspections uncovered numerous violations of the law. During the first ten months under the FLSA, "nearly 500 children under sixteen years of age had been found working illegally in establishments producing goods in interstate commerce" with some as young as eight or nine found at work.[74] When violations were found, most employers dismissed the underage worker or sought to obtain a certificate of age. Court action was necessary in only three cases, with two resulting in a permanent injunction against the shipment of goods and one ending in a criminal prosecution. Two years into implementation of the law, the Children's Bureau reported seven criminal cases and nineteen civil suits for flagrant child labor violations, none of which were contested by the employer. In assessing the impact of the law, the bureau cited "definite gains" in reducing child labor in interstate commerce, improved administration of state child labor laws, new state child labor legislation, and "greater realization on the part of the public and of employers of the value of good child labor standards."[75] Many businesses voluntarily stopped employing children.

Upon its enactment, some business groups and their supporters in Congress attempted to repeal the Fair Labor Standards Act. The Cotton Textile Institute described the legal foundations of the law as "not indigenous to America." David Clark, who was still editing the *Southern Textile Bulletin*, condemned the law as strongly as he opposed the Child Labor Amendment. He called the wages and hours law "an illegal usurpation of power by the Congress." He warned that the law marked the end of states' rights and our form of government and would lead to a dictator.[76] Perhaps too advanced in years to take up the cause himself, Clark urged a legal challenge to the act.

Efforts to repeal the law failed but the implementation of the FLSA prompted several legal challenges. In late December 1938, in what is considered the first formal test of the law, a state circuit court judge in Michigan ruled that newsboys operating under carrier contracts were not subjects covered by the law.[77] Mac Myers, a thirteen-year-old boy, had his carrier contract canceled as a result of the FLSA. Young Mac delivered papers in his home town of Ithaca, Michigan, which was miles from where the paper was published, and had them delivered to him by truck. The Children's Bureau did not intervene in the case because the solicitor of the Labor Department ruled that the boy's employment was not "in or about" the newspaper company's establishment and therefore did not fall under the child labor provisions.

Although he questioned the constitutionality of the FLSA, Judge Kelly S. Searl did not formally address that issue. Rather, his ruling established the concept of newspaper boys as "independent contractors" not protected by the act. The judge admitted that his ruling ran counter to decisions of the National Labor Relations Board. His opinion included a rambling diatribe against child labor reformers. He surmised that the FLSA was probably enacted in response to the lobbying of child welfare activists, but, if the utterly fallacious and unsound theories of these well-meaning reformers, many of whom have never brought up a child to maturity, which find expression in this act and also in the so-called Child Labor Amendment, are adopted, except as applied to child labor detrimental to the health or dangerous to life and limb . . . it will result in the filling, by the coming generations, of the reformatory institutions and prisons beyond their capacity.[78]

As a young boy, Judge Searl delivered newspapers, and he attributed his success in life to being compelled to work as a child.

A ruling by the Children's Bureau on April 12, 1939, based on an opinion by the solicitor of the Labor Department, also threatened to exclude many newspaper carriers from the protection of the FLSA. The administrative opinion held that minors under sixteen years of age would be considered under the act if their work "required them to come in or about the establishment in which the newspapers are produced."[79] Critics of the ruling pointed out that it would be easy for newspapers to deal with the "little merchant" by designating a delivery spot for the papers outside the place of business, thus making them "independent contractors" outside the law.

In March that year, representatives from eighteen different organizations met in Washington, DC, for a conference on the Child Labor Amendment. Miss Beatrice McConnell of the Children's Bureau reported on the implementation of the FLSA one year after enactment. At this time, *Coleman v. Miller* and *Chandler v. Wise* were still pending before the Supreme Court and a decision was several months away. There was a lot of uncertainty regarding the status of the amendment and what direction to take pending the outcome of the cases. Of those present, a consensus favored continued support for the amendment. If the Supreme Court ruled the amendment no longer valid, the conference should be ready to react to the Vandenberg amendment and other proposals.[80] Even with passage of the FLSA, many reformers believed that a Child Labor Amendment was still necessary. The exemptions and gaps in the law could be corrected with the power given Congress under the amendment.

The most important case challenging the FLSA was *United States v. Darby Lumber*. Fred W. Darby owned a lumber mill that manufactured and shipped products in interstate commerce. He was indicted on multiple counts for not adhering to the minimum-wage requirements of twenty-five cents per hour, working his employees more than forty-four hours a week without paying them one and a half times their normal pay, and failing to keep employment records as required by law. Darby appealed the convictions. Although the case did not involve the employment of minors, the litigation threatened the constitutionality of the FLSA and the child labor provisions.

Several other federal cases involving the FLSA had been decided or were pending at the time. In *Opp Cotton Mills, Inc. v. Administrator Wage and Hour Division*, the Fifth Circuit Court of Appeals ruled on April 2, 1940, that the FLSA was a valid exercise of congressional power under the Commerce Clause. In *United States v. Darby Lumber*, however, District Court judge William H. Barrett ignored the Fifth Circuit and six other district judges by quashing the indictments against Darby Lumber. Using the distinction between manufacturing and commerce, which had been largely discredited in *NLRB v. Jones and Laughlin Steel Corporation*, Judge Barrett struck down the FLSA as it applied to both the production of goods for interstate commerce and the prohibition of interstate shipment of articles in interstate commerce produced under substandard labor conditions. Grounding his decision in *Hammer v. Dagenhart*, Judge Barrett argued that the alleged violations involved primarily intrastate activities rather than interstate commerce. He warned that if the law were upheld, government regulation of labor could extend not only to the man who cut the timber or hauled it to the mill, but also to the man who planted and cultivated the trees.[81] Such a view of federal power, Judge Barrett believed, was dangerous. His decision was appealed.

Using *Hammer v. Dagenhart* as precedent and other pre-1937 cases that made a distinction between manufacturing and commerce, Fred Darby argued that the FLSA violated the Tenth Amendment because it was an unconstitutional attempt to regulate conditions in production of goods and commodities. Darby's lawyers distinguished *NLRB v. Jones and Laughlin Steel Corporation* by arguing that federal control over manufacture and production is justified only when the relation to interstate commerce is "close and substantial." No precedents, they claimed, allowed the national government to directly regulate production. The lumber company's failure to comply with the FLSA, they asserted, did not affect interstate commerce, constitute unfair competition, or lead to labor disputes. Additionally, the FLSA deprived Darby of liberty and due process in violation of the Fifth Amendment. The act was arbitrary and capricious because Congress did not adequately define persons subject to its penal provisions. Finally, Darby claimed that the government was wrong to seek unrestricted power beyond its enumerated powers and to legislate for the general welfare.

The US government made several constitutional and pragmatic arguments. When the Commerce Clause was drafted, the meaning of the phrase *interstate commerce* included production, manufacturing, and all aspects of commercial activity. Supreme Court decisions, from the earliest days of the Union, recognized that Congress has power to confront the economic problems of the country. The government cited Chief Justice John Marshall's opinion in *Gibbons v. Ogden*, which held that Congress has power over "that commerce which concerns more states than one," including "those internal concerns which affect the states generally."[82] The US government contended that no state alone could require standards higher than those of other states where competition exists. As had been the practice for decades, employers with weak labor standards would have an unfair advantage in interstate competition. Markets had become national rather than local and only the federal government can impose uniform wage and hour standards.

The government's brief also argued that *Hammer v. Dagenhart* was now a constitutional relic wholly inconsistent with subsequent decisions that have "repudiated or abandoned each premise upon which the opinion rests."[83] Because the FLSA is a valid exercise of congressional power under the Commerce Clause, the law does not violate the Tenth Amendment, which merely reserves to states powers that are not delegated to the United States. The origins of the Tenth Amendment confirm that its purpose was merely declaratory. Finally, the government argued that the FLSA does not violate due process and a liberty of contract under the Fifth Amendment. The Court had already upheld legislation fixing maximum hours for men and women and minimum wages for women generally and for men in some situations. Consequently, the due process clause "imposes no greater restriction upon federal legislation in the field of interstate commerce than upon state regulation regulating intrastate activities."[84]

By the 1940–1941 term, the composition of the Supreme Court had changed significantly from the Court that issued the landmark 5–4 decisions of the Constitutional Revolution of 1937. The Four Horsemen were gone, replaced by ardent New Dealers Hugo Black, Felix Frankfurter, Stanley Reed, and William O. Douglas. Through deaths and retirements, President Roosevelt's appointments reshaped the Supreme Court and its jurisprudence without his Court-packing plan. Justice McReynolds, the last of the Four Horsemen, retired from the bench on January 31, 1941. President Roosevelt did not nominate his successor, James F. Byrnes, until June 12, 1941, so McReynolds's seat was vacant when the Court decided *United States v. Darby Lumber*. Overall, the Court appeared both politically and jurisprudentially more receptive to New Deal regulatory and social welfare policies.

And that turned out to be true. In *Darby Lumber*, the Court upheld the

Fair Labor Standards Act by a vote of 8–0 using many of the arguments in Holmes's dissenting opinion in *Hammer*. Memos exchanged between Chief Justice Charles Evans Hughes and Justice Harlan Fiske Stone reveal that Hughes had his doubts about the FLSA and decided not to exercise his prerogative of authoring the opinion. "Of course, there is much that could be said with respect to the indefiniteness of the present statute, because of the failure of Congress to define the phrase 'production for commerce.' Congress gives a sweeping definition of 'production' and of 'goods' but not of production *for* commerce."[85] Hughes made several suggestions to clarify the meaning of the phrase. "Even with the best possible test," he concluded, "the statute is a highly unsatisfactory one, but as it is a borderline case I should prefer not to write."[86] Justice Stone responded by saying that the phrase "for commerce" was no more vague than provisions of the Sherman Anti-Trust Act, which had been sustained by the Court in *Nash v. United States*. Stone was worried about overelaboration, and ultimately Hughes conceded the point.[87]

Writing for the Court, Justice Stone stated that the motive and purpose of this regulation of interstate commerce are to make effective the congressional conception of public policy that interstate commerce should not be the instrument of competition in the manufacture of goods produced under substandard labor conditions. Stone based the opinion on Chief Justice Marshall's broad definitions of regulation and commerce in *Gibbons v. Ogden* (1824). Quoting the former chief justice, Justice Stone wrote that the power over interstate commerce "is complete in itself, may be exercised to its utmost extent, and acknowledges no limitations other than are prescribed in the Constitution."[88] These matters are for the legislature, "upon which the Constitution places no restrictions, and over which the courts are given no control." It was not the role of the courts to question the motives of Congress in regulating interstate commerce. Congress may regulate or prohibit any articles from commerce that are deemed injurious to public health, morals, or welfare regardless of the "exercise or nonexercise of state power."[89] Thus, regulations of commerce that do not infringe on some other constitutional prohibition are within congressional power.

Most important for the child labor provisions, the Court declared that *Hammer v. Dagenhart* is overruled. Taking his cue from Justice Holmes's "powerful and now classic" dissenting opinion in *Hammer*, Justice Stone characterized the precedent as an artifact of a bygone age. The decision was based on a distinction that congressional power was limited only to articles which intrinsically had some harmful or deleterious property. That interpretation, however, was novel when it was made and lacked any constitutional foundation. "The conclusion is inescapable," Stone argued, "that *Hammer v. Dagenhart* was a departure from the principles that have prevailed in the interpretation of the Commerce Clause both before and since the decision, and that such vitality, as a precedent, as it then had, has long since been exhausted."[90]

Following the argument made by the US government, the Court concluded that the decision is unaffected by the Tenth Amendment. Justice Stone famously wrote:

> The amendment states only a truism that all is retained which has not been surrendered. There is nothing in the history of its adoption to suggest that it was more than declaratory of the relationship between the national and state governments as it had been established by the Constitution before the amendment or that its purpose was other than to allay fears that the new national government might seek to exercise powers not granted, and that the states might not be able to exercise fully their reserved powers.[91]

The amendment gives the government the authority to resort to all means for the exercise of a granted power that are appropriate and plainly adapted to the permitted end. In his biography of Justice Stone, Alpheus T. Mason suggests that the justice had waited five years for a chance to exorcise from constitutional jurisprudence laissez-faire principles and the belief that "dual federalism" under the Tenth Amendment limited federal power.[92] The *Darby Lumber* decision was Stone's definitive statement on the issue.

Congress now had broad authority to regulate labor, wages, and working conditions under the Commerce Clause. Justice Stone explained to Professor Noel T. Dowling, a member of the NCLC Board, that the *Darby* decision was designed to "make two things clear, namely (1) that the commerce power of Congress is not restricted to intrinsically harmful commodities, and (2) that the motive of Congress in passing commerce clause laws is none of the Court's business."[93] Stone's brethren praised the opinion, and a jubilant Justice Reed commented: "It has been a long journey, but the end is here. We should have overruled *Hammer* years ago."[94]

In *Opp Cotton Mills v. Administrator*, decided on the same day as *Darby Lumber*, a unanimous Court specifically upheld the wage requirement and industry committee procedure for raising wages.[95] The constitutionality of the FLSA and its child labor provisions was firmly established. After the long struggle to regulate child labor, the final victory in *United States v. Darby Lumber* was a bit anti-climactic but still of great consequence. The decision is significant because it upheld congressional power to regulate wages and hours, erased the *Hammer v. Dagenhart* precedent, a decision that had frustrated the efforts of child labor reformers for over twenty years and affected the federal system by holding that the Tenth Amendment does not limit the delegated or implied powers of Congress under the Commerce Clause. One historian commented: "It is not too much to say that *United States v. Darby* is one of the half-dozen most important cases in the whole . . . history of American constitutional law."[96]

Most media recognized the historical and constitutional significance of the *Darby Lumber* decision. The opinion removed any constitutional obstacles to New Deal reforms. "The change that has been effected," the *Washington Post* commented, "is scarcely less significant than it would have been if accomplished through a constitutional amendment." In the Tarheel state, editors bitterly acknowledged that states' rights were as dead as "the gallant boys from North Carolina who fell on the scarred slopes of Gettysburg" and that the states "have no real rights which the Federal government is bound to respect."[97]

The National Child Labor Committee, which had lobbied for federal child labor legislation for nearly three decades, described the decision as "most gratifying."[98] The editor of the *Social Service Review*, the leading professional journal of social workers, was more critical of the Supreme Court. Describing the Court as a "sinner who finally repenteth," the editor suggested that the decision was poor compensation for the damage done to children in *Hammer v. Dagenhart*. "But what of the army of children who have come and gone from the mills and factories and lumber yards, the millions of weary days of work, and the lost vision of an education to do a proper share of the world's work? These children now living as unemployed workers should indict the Supreme Court of these United States for their stunted minds and broken lives."[99] For many who had devoted much of their lives to abolishing child labor, *Darby Lumber* was a bittersweet victory.

Unlike other civil rights and liberties issues during the twentieth-century, such as racial equality, religious freedom, or the rights of criminal defendants, the Supreme Court was not a catalyst for social change on child labor. By the time the Court validated federal power to regulate child labor, the most egregious forms of the practice had ended. Over half a century of lobbying by reformers had established a legal environment at the state and federal level that discouraged and prohibited oppressive child labor. Structural and technological changes in the economy also contributed to the decline in child workers. In some sectors of the market, machines displaced children. Finally, higher wages and welfare programs established during the New Deal provided a safety net that lessened the need for children to start work early to support themselves and their families.

Despite the progress in reducing child labor, there were still several areas ripe for reform. Gerard D. Reilly, Labor Department solicitor, said that the *Darby* decision and any subsequent legislation under the FLSA would not remove the "necessity of State ratification of the Child Labor Amendment if the labor of minors in intrastate commerce was to be protected."[100] The National Child Labor Committee noted that legislation was urgently needed to shelter four large groups of children not covered by the FLSA: children under sixteen years old working in commercialized agriculture, kids in street trades and intrastate industrial employment, and sixteen- and seventeen-year-old children laboring in hazardous jobs in intrastate industries.[101] Those battles would continue for decades.

In another victory for child labor advocates, home work was prohibited in several industries where it was most predominant. Industrial home work involved workers and their children toiling long hours at poverty wages often in unsanitary conditions that threatened not only their own health but also had the potential to spread disease to anyone who purchased the products.[102] States attempted to regulate home work, but enforcement was difficult. Under the FLSA, the administrator of the Wage and Hour Division was empowered to issue regulations to protect the minimum wage and prevent the circumvention or evasion of wage orders. The administrator convened a committee for the embroideries industry. The committee recommended a minimum wage rate of forty cents an hour. The administrator accepted the recommendation and promulgated a regulation banning all home work in the industry on the grounds that it was necessary to enforce the wage order. An estimated 40 percent of all workers engaged in the industry, or 8,500 to 12,000, performed their work at home. Several home workers and employers who used home workers sued to challenge the regulation.

In *Gemsco, Inc. v. Walling*, the Supreme Court held 7–2 that under Section 8(f) of the Fair Labor Standards Act, the administrator has the authority, if necessary to make effective a minimum wage order for the embroideries industry, to prohibit industrial home work.[103] Writing for the Court, Justice Wiley Rutledge noted that the statute itself provides the answers in two ways: by its explicit terms and the necessity to avoid self-nullification. In his findings, the administrator construed "necessary" not as helpful or convenient, but as meaning that "the prohibition is absolutely essential to achieve those purposes."[104] If the prohibition on home work did not exist, it would be impossible to secure a floor of minimum wages. Because Section 8(f) commands the administrator to include in the order "such terms and conditions" as he "finds necessary to carry out" its purposes, the administrator has the authority to prohibit industrial home work. Secretary of Labor Frances Perkins described the Court's opinion as a "major advance in the control of home work which has baffled State labor departments for over half a century."[105]

Six months after the *Darby Lumber* decision, the Japanese attack on Pearl Harbor thrust the United States into World War II. With millions of adult males going off to war, numerous jobs became available for school-age children. In the two decades prior to 1940, child labor had been steadily declining. The number of employed minors fourteen through seventeen years of age dropped from 2.5 million in 1920 to 1 million in 1940.[106] All of these gains in reducing child labor were lost during the war years. The National Education Association's Commission for the Defense of Democracy noted that work permits had increased 400 percent since 1940, creating what the commission called "a real threat to the future of this country."[107] The appeal of high wages, state compulsory attendance laws that exempted fourteen- and fifteen-year-olds if they were employed, and the gaps in child labor restrictions under the Fair Labor Standards Act all combined to produce an increase in child labor during the war years.

By 1944, almost three million boys and girls under eighteen years either quit school for work or tried to balance their studies and work obligations. Of this number, about nine hundred thousand were fourteen- to fifteen-years-old, with many working illegally. A report written by L. Metcalfe Walling, director of the Wage and Hour Division of the Department of Labor, identified 1,722 establishments employing 4,567 minors in violation of child labor laws during 1942–1943. The number was a 200 percent increase from 1941.[108] In just the first six months of 1943, 3,658 children were found working illegally in various industries. Those figures only covered businesses engaged in interstate commerce. The numbers may have been worse because Congress cut appropriations for the Children's Bureau in 1943, making inspection and enforcement of child labor laws difficult.

A disturbing consequence of the growth in employment of children was reported in New York where the total amount and the average award for workmen's compensation increased. The rise was attributed to penalty awards made in cases involving injured minors illegally employed. In 1941, the penalty accounted for one-fifth of the total amount in compensation, but that climbed to two-thirds in 1943.[109] On February 6, 1943, the *Chicago Tribune* reported that a thirteen-year-old boy died of injuries suffered when he was drawn into a dough-mixing machine at a bakery. A sixteen-year-old boy working in Connecticut was crushed to death while cleaning an elevator in a factory. He had been employed for two months from 7:00 p.m. to 7:00 a.m. in violation of child labor laws.[110] Working on a local farm because of a labor shortage, a thirteen-year-old boy lost his arm when the sleeve of his sweater became entangled in a threshing machine. Another thirteen-year-old boy working in a New Jersey butcher shop was impaled on a meat hook while the owner was absent from the store.[111] There were reports of injuries and deaths to child workers all over the country, often in occupations and situations that were illegal.

Schools that initially encouraged part-time work as a patriotic contribution soon noticed a high drop-out rate because a decent paycheck was more appealing than sitting in the classroom. Across the country, schools reported many empty seats in the classroom. In Starbuck, Washington, 20 percent of the students under sixteen left school for full-time jobs. In Oakland, California, where 15 percent of the children under sixteen quit school for employment, officials complained that child labor and school attendance laws could not be enforced. Other school districts warned that child labor laws were being ignored. In East St. Louis, high school enrollment dropped 20 percent. Often, the child workers were earning higher wages than their teachers. In Cherryvale, Kansas, a senior was earning more money than his teachers even though he was working only part-time.[112] In Gary, Indiana, high school boys were paid more money working part-time in the steel mills than their teachers. As more children left school for factory jobs or worked late hours after school, some "broke down physically under the combined strain of study and excessive work."[113] In Cleveland, Ohio, forty children in a single school fell asleep in class one morning because all of them had been setting up pins in a bowling alley the previous night.[114] Most educators agreed that the best contribution a student could make to the war effort was to stay in school until they graduated and were called into service.

A sharp increase in delinquency, particularly by girls, was reported in many areas of the country. Alarmed by reports of young girls roaming the streets and boys hanging out in taverns, First Lady Eleanor Roosevelt hosted a forum at the White House attended by over one hundred social workers, educators, and government administrators in the field of child labor. Mrs. Roosevelt blamed the increasing delinquency rates on the appeal of high wages for young workers, the lack of recreational facilities for youth, and the loss of parental supervision because fathers and mothers were preoccupied with war duties.[115] To solve the problem, Charlotte Carr, head of Chicago's Hull House, suggested "vocational counseling to steer youth into the right kind of employment." Others recommended closer cooperation between social agencies and families with children, more emphasis on "responsibility" in school curriculums, and "enlightening" the proper officials who have the resources to address the problem.

Employers and some officials in the Defense Department, however, sought to relax, if not repeal, child labor laws. Governors, anxious to demonstrate their patriotism, also backed legislation to repeal state labor laws with the support of some army and navy officials. According to Frances Perkins, "Army-Navy procurement offices were harassed by contractors who constantly complained of their inability to operate with speed and efficiency under state and federal labor laws."[116] In some situations, federal defense agencies themselves were to blame for employing children in wartime industries. A report from Somerville, Massachusetts, found navy yards and arsenals where fourteen- and fifteen-year-old boys were employed operating machines in violation of the sixteen-year-old minimum.[117]

The National Child Labor Committee, the National Education Association, the Children's Bureau, Secretary Perkins, and President Roosevelt resisted these efforts to weaken or abolish child labor protections. The issue was not so much as prohibiting all work, because children could make a contribution to the war effort, but making sure that child welfare was protected. In January 1942, the National Child Labor Committee issued a policy statement: "The chief contribution a child can make to his country in the present crisis is to remain in school and prepare himself for future work and for the future responsibilities of citizenship."[118] The NCLC Board recognized that child labor restrictions imposed in peacetime might have to be modified to meet national emergencies and wartime necessities, but the welfare of children must be safeguarded.

Facing constant pressure to relax definitions and regulations under the FLSA, the Children's Bureau established a fifty-six-member Commission on Children in Wartime "to consider urgent steps for the protection and welfare of children in emergency situations resulting from the war."[119] Chaired by Dr. Leonard W. Mayo, dean of the School of Applied Science at Western Reserve University, the commission spearheaded educational programs to inform the public and government officials about services available to support children. Toward this goal, the commission had organized the forum on delinquency held at the White House in 1943. While Allied troops invaded the beaches of Normandy in June 1944, the Commission on Children in Wartime announced specific recommendations to protect children and youth during demobilization: (1) extend health service and medical care for all mothers and children; (2) regulate child labor and plan for young workers during the demobilization period; (3) develop community recreation and leisure activities for young people to keep them out of trouble; and (4) safeguard family life in wartime and during the postwar period.[120]

Even though the Children's Bureau, the NCLC, and other organizations tried to hold the line against weakening child labor protections, many states revised their laws to allow for more young workers. Two years into the war, more than three-fourths of the states had considered modifications to their child labor laws, and in twenty-seven states changes had been made either to the statutes themselves or granting executive authority to alter or suspend the laws.[121] Most of the changes involved allowing sixteen- and seventeen-year-old minors to work longer hours. Laws allowing the employment of children in bowling alleys as pinsetters were relaxed in nine states.[122] Also, age limits were reduced from eighteen or twenty-one years to fourteen or sixteen years for girls doing messenger work and jobs in restaurants, hotels, theaters, and drug stores. Eleven states relaxed their laws to enable employment of school-aged children in agriculture by permitting alterations in the school day and calendar.

When President Roosevelt was informed of the attacks on state and federal labor laws, he agreed that the laws must be defended. "The eight-hour day," he argued, "is the most efficient productive day for the worker." He believed that three eight-hour shifts were the most effective way to maintain wartime production. The president asserted: "Protection of workers against accidents, illness, and fatigue are vital for efficiency. Children under sixteen, certainly under fourteen, are not productive workers."[123] The only concession that he made to wartime manpower needs was part-time or vacation employment of older high school students to help harvest crops or work in nonhazardous war industries. Although there were some modifications, Secretary Perkins credited the president's position with blocking efforts to repeal labor legislation and making it through the war with fundamental labor protections intact.

In January 1943, the War Manpower Commission issued a statement on the employment of minors. While acknowledging that many young people under eighteen would be needed in the workforce, it emphasized the importance of safeguarding their physical and intellectual development. The statement pointed out that in most cases, the best thing that youth under eighteen could do for the war effort was to stay in school, and when their services were needed, work during vacations or part-time. The War Manpower Commission announced a "basic National policy" consisting of ten items. These items included a declaration that existing school attendance and child labor standards should be preserved and enforced, a prohibition on either full- or part-time employment for children under fourteen years of age, and a recommendation that children fourteen or fifteen should only be employed if adult workers are unavailable and never in manufacturing or mining operations.[124] The policy also suggested that youth should not be employed during school hours except when a temporary emergency might require such activity and that the combined hours for school and work should not exceed eight a day for children under sixteen years.

Working with the War Manpower Commission and federal procurement agencies, the Children's Bureau adopted a flexible policy to meet wartime needs for labor. A few exemptions were granted to employers but none that exposed child workers to serious risk to their health. For example, fourteen- and fifteen-year-old children were permitted to work until 10:00 p.m. rather than 7:00 p.m. in fruit and vegetable packing plants, but only outside of school hours and not more than forty hours a week or eight weeks a season. Some industries were exempted from the eighteen-year minimum age in hazardous occupations. There were abuses of child labor, but those primarily happened outside the legal regime established by the FLSA and state regulations. For the most part, the experience of World War I, with its lax regulations and spike in child labor, would not be repeated. The FLSA stood as a bulwark against such exploitation, and any exemptions made during the conflict were revoked following the war.

In late 1944, the NCLC issued a fortieth anniversary booklet entitled "The Long Road." The publication reviewed the organization's forty-year struggle against child labor in America. A *New York Times* editorial commented that the strains of the war and the manpower shortage had nullified much of what had been accomplished during the "brave fight" made by the National Child Labor Committee. It was a fight that must continue, the editorial claimed, as evidenced by the "high percentage of Army draft rejections for illiteracy and physical and mental disability."[125] Although the editors probably overstated the impact of the war on the significant achievements of the NCLC on the issue of child labor, they were correct on the imperative for further progress.

With most of Europe in ruins, the United States emerged from the war as a superpower and the leading voice for democracy in global affairs. In order to meet those responsibilities from a position of strength, many people in the United States recognized the need to defend the right of children to stay in school and develop intellectually and physically. A national consensus emerged following the war that understood it was best for the nation and democratic institutions to restrict child labor. The country needed scientists, engineers, doctors, and other specialists to compete with the Soviet Union during the Cold War. To be sure, the legal struggle over child labor would continue in the postwar period. Reformers sought to eliminate exemptions and correct some of the gaps in the child labor provisions of the FLSA, and with the movement away from an industrial economy, new issues developed involving young workers.

8

Contemporary Child Labor Issues

Over the last seventy-five years, changes were made to federal child labor laws at the margins. With the worst forms of child labor ameliorated,
new challenges emerged in the postwar period. Laws and regulations were
proposed and sometimes enacted involving child actors, batboys and batgirls, young Amish workers, child models, and children working on family
farms. As the US economy moved from an industrial base with many unskilled, blue-collar jobs, to a service- and technology-based market, youth
unemployment became a major concern. In the new economy, more jobs required some kind of technical training or college education. These market
transformations prompted efforts to reform child labor laws. The Reagan
administration, for example, attempted to weaken labor protections for
fourteen- and fifteen-year-olds in the 1980s without much success, in part
because the proposals were introduced during a recession when unemployment was already high for young workers.

Immediately following World War II, reformers sought two major
changes in the child labor provisions of the Fair Labor Standards Act. First,
they wanted to directly prohibit child labor, as found in state laws, rather
than prohibit the shipment of goods, which had used child employment
within thirty days prior to shipment. Some companies tried to evade the restrictions by simply holding back shipment for more than a month. Second,

reformers wanted to prohibit the employment of children "in commerce" as well as goods produced in interstate commerce. The text of the original child labor provisions did not cover children employed as telegraph messengers or working on boats or railroads.[1] As part of the Pepper-Hook bill, the Senate enacted the changes in April 1946, but the House did not follow.

After four years of hearings Congress amended the Fair Labor Standards Act on October 19, 1949. President Harry Truman signed the legislation one week later, and the changes took effect on January 25, 1950. In addition to raising the minimum wage from forty to seventy-five cents an hour, the amendments broadened the child labor provisions to prohibit the employment of children in commerce or the production of goods in commerce. Also, the definition of "oppressive child labor" was changed to include "parental employment of a child under sixteen years of age in an occupation found by the Secretary of Labor to be hazardous for children between the ages of sixteen and eighteen."[2] The amendment closed a loophole because the original law prohibited parents from employing a child between sixteen and eighteen years in a hazardous occupation but allowed the employment if the child was fifteen and younger. The 1949 amendments also tightened the agricultural provisions. Children could be employed on farms only outside school hours in the district in which they lived. Other changes provided an exemption for newsboys and extended exemptions for performers and actors to radio and television.

There were constant attempts in the 1950s to weaken child labor laws by lowering standards and protections. Opponents continued the old argument that child labor regulations resulted in idleness and contributed to delinquency. They proposed that fourteen- and fifteen-year-olds who are "incorrigible" or bored in school should be permitted to work.[3] The National Child Labor Committee, however, responded to those claims in its fiftieth anniversary report, asserting that there was no general relationship between employment and juvenile delinquency. "Delinquency," the report stated, "is the result of the interplay of many forces, internal and external." For some youth, work was a steadying influence; for others, the wrong job might push a teen toward antisocial conduct. The report noted that almost 2 million boys and girls, fourteen to seventeen years old, worked full- or part-time during the 1954 school year, and an additional one million were employed in the summer.[4]

In the early 1960s, there was a growing concern about the lack of job opportunities for youth and the problem of delinquency. About five hundred social workers, school administrators, government officials, and others met in Washington in May 1961 for a Conference on Unemployed, Out-of-

School Youth in Urban Areas.[5] The conference report noted that for students who dropped out of high school, the unemployment rate was 17.1 percent for young workers sixteen to twenty-one years old, with a slightly higher rate for minority youth. In the past, there were usually enough unskilled positions for young job applicants with limited education, but the economy was changing and those types of jobs were becoming scarce. Some of those jobs moved overseas as corporations established manufacturing plants in countries with weak labor protections.

On February 24, 1964, Secretary of Labor W. Willard Wirtz, a liberal champion for the unemployed who served under Presidents John F. Kennedy and Lyndon B. Johnson, proposed to raise the age of compulsory school attendance to eighteen from the usual sixteen years. If the age were increased to eighteen, he claimed, 2 million teenagers would exit the job market and return to school.[6] He also advocated two years of free universal post–high school education. The proposals were designed to reduce the number of unemployed youth and provide them with the skills needed for the new service-based economy. Wirtz admitted that the ideas were not federal government policy. States controlled compulsory education laws, and they would be responsible for finding the resources for the two years of free post-secondary education. Critics worried that the schools could not handle an influx of students, and some doubted that two more years of schooling would solve the labor problem. States did not implement the proposal, but the Labor Department organized a jobs-training program to provide young workers with the skills needed for the new economy.

Over the next twenty years the literature on youth employment surged, and there were numerous proposals to create more jobs for teens. Although there was a consensus that the problem was serious, few policy analysts seemed to agree on the best course of action. Some proposals focused on job training while others emphasized college education. There were even articles published in *New Generation*, the journal of the National Committee on the Employment of Youth, advocating a new model of child labor participation and a loosening of labor laws to allow youth to enter the job market earlier to gain needed skills.[7] Minority teens faced the biggest challenges. For example, in July 1977 almost half (45.5 percent) of minority youths between sixteen and nineteen who were in the workforce were unemployed.[8] There were many young people under age fifteen employed as well, but a lack of data on their job situations and socioeconomic status prevented any meaningful analysis.

After a thirty-year period that saw no major reforms of child labor laws, the issue of working kids returned to the public agenda in the early 1980s.

The Reagan administration attempted to weaken child labor restrictions in order to create more employment opportunities for young workers, especially fourteen- and fifteen-year-olds. Proponents of the changes argued that when the child labor standards were established in 1938, fast-food restaurants, retail stores in malls, and other service-oriented establishments were not part of the market. In July 1982, Secretary of Labor Raymond Donovan introduced a plan that fundamentally altered child labor policy. The administration's proposal sought to: (1) open up more opportunities for the employment of children fourteen and fifteen years of age, (2) extend the number of hours per day and per week that children might be employed, (3) revise the standards for child workers in jobs once considered too hazardous, and (4) simplify and broaden the manner in which employers become certified by the Department of Labor to employ full-time students at a substandard minimum wage.[9]

At a hearing held by the House Labor Standards Subcommittee, William Otter, the Labor Department's wage and hour administrator, told the subcommittee that the proposed new regulations "would improve the employment opportunities of young workers without harming their health, well-being, or opportunity for schooling."[10] He read letters from parents, teens, and potential employers that urged a relaxing of regulations to allow fourteen- and fifteen-year-olds to work. Concerned about unemployment for all age groups, Otter stated that "unreasonable and artificial impediments to the employment of all age groups should be eliminated."[11]

The administration's plan for youth work, however, was roundly criticized by witnesses from labor and education groups who denounced the idea as an attempt to "create a kiddy work force" and an act of "insensitivity and stupidity."[12] Lane Kirkland, president of the AFL-CIO, called the proposal a "social outrage," and Thomas Donahue, secretary-treasurer of the labor union, testified that the proposed rules would "create a pool of cheap, part-time child labor, the beneficiaries of which would be the various industries that already have notorious records for violating and undercutting fair labor standards."[13] Laurence E. Steinberg, an assistant professor at the University of California, Irvine, and a specialist in adolescent development, testified that teens who work more than fifteen to twenty hours a week "spend less time on their studies, receive lower grades, are absent more often, and are less involved in school activities."[14] Other opponents said that teenagers who work increased hours spend less time with their families and friends and tend to use more tobacco, alcohol, and marijuana.

Jeffrey Newman, executive director of the National Child Labor Committee, acknowledged that child labor standards could use some modernization but contended that during a recession and a period of high unemployment, the proposed changes were in the "wrong context at the wrong time." He described the Reagan administration plan as a "slap in the face for the nation's working class and a pig in a poke for both business and young people."[15] He favored well-designed work and education programs, both public and private, that provided structured training and employment opportunities. Representative George Miller, a California Democrat who headed the subcommittee, scheduled a second day of hearings because no one in the Labor Department had consulted education, labor, or parent organizations in forming the proposed regulations. Miller and Senator Edward M. Kennedy (D-MA) introduced a joint resolution to stop Secretary of Labor Donovan from implementing the proposals.

Under pressure from Congress and various interest groups, the Reagan administration extended the comment period for the proposed regulations from 30 days to 180 days. Administrators received numerous letters from restaurant owners supporting the new standards, but the plan also generated intense opposition from educational groups, labor unions, and members of Congress who viewed the regulatory plan as a "scheme to enable restauranteurs to exploit school age workers."[16] Public pressure against the changes seemed to have an effect. The regulations remained under review for more than two years. Ultimately, a final rule was never issued.

Congress and the Department of Labor considered additional reforms to child labor standards through the 1980s and 1990s, but no major legislation or new regulations were enacted. In April 1986, Senator Dan Quayle, a Republican from Indiana, advocated that child labor laws be relaxed to allow fourteen- and fifteen-year-olds to work as batboys and batgirls for professional baseball teams, even when the games ran late into the evening. Senator Quayle described baseball as the "All-American Sport," and he believed that youth should not have to wait until they were sixteen to "associate with players of their hometown teams." Congress enacted legislation to study the issue.[17] After a yearlong investigation that surveyed 157 sports teams, the Labor Department concluded that "changes in permissible hours and time standards for batboy/girl work would not be detrimental to their health or well-being." Moreover, the department found "no evidence that school grades were adversely affected by such work." Despite these findings, no action was taken on the issue for years.

By the late 1980s violations of child labor laws were on the rise. The Labor Department reported that it found 22,508 children working in violation of the Fair Labor Standards Act in 1989, twice the rate of the first half of the decade and the highest number of violations since the law was enacted in 1938.[18] Officials attributed the increase to the nation's low unemployment rate, which forced some employers to turn to minors to fill menial jobs and intensified competition from foreign companies. In New York, an estimated 7,500 children worked illegally in the garment industry every day.[19] Some of them were as young as ten or eleven years old. The state labor commissioner testified before the legislature in Albany that the number of children found illegally employed had more than doubled from 1984 to 1989. Hugh Mc-Daid, director of a New York apparel industry task force, stated that some children, especially in neighborhoods with recent Latin American immigrants, did not attend school and worked long hours for wages that rarely reached the legal minimum. "This is a trap for them," McDaid said. "They sacrifice their education and literally commit themselves to a life of working in a sweatshop. They have no future."[20]

With reports indicating widespread levels of illegal child labor across the country, Secretary of Labor Elizabeth Dole promised to intensify enforcement efforts and impose stiffer penalties for violations.[21] At the time, fines amounted to just a few hundred dollars and were considered by child employers to be just another cost of doing business. But Labor officials announced plans for a fivefold increase to effectively deter those who might violate child labor laws. Moreover, repeat offenders could face additional penalties. William C. Brooks, assistant secretary for employment standards, also announced plans to establish a working group to explore tougher enforcement practices and a possible revision of job classifications deemed hazardous. Child welfare advocates welcomed the stricter enforcement regime but remained skeptical because the Labor Department was not given additional personnel or funding. Linda F. Golodner, executive director of the National Consumers' League and chairwoman of the Child Labor Advisory Committee, formed by the Labor Department, called for more resources and a focus on industries not covered by the laws.[22]

In 1993 the Clinton administration attempted to improve labor standards by cracking down on child labor law violations. The Labor Department charged Food Lion, one of the nation's fastest growing supermarket chains, with fourteen hundred violations of federal child labor laws. The allegations involved eighty-five stores in twelve states. More than twelve hundred of the alleged violations involved sixteen- and seventeen-year-old minors using meat slicers and power-driven paper balers and children working more hours than federal law allows. Vincent G. Watkins, Food Lion's vice president for projects, disputed the charges, claiming that the company was "the victim of a corporate campaign" by the United Food and Commercial Workers Union.[23] Although the supermarket chain admitted no violations, in August 1993 Food Lion agreed to pay $16.2 million in fines and back wages to settle the allegations. It was the largest settlement ever by the Labor Department with a private company.[24] Publix, another supermarket chain based in Florida and Georgia, also paid a $500,000 fine to settle claims that it violated child labor laws, and the Great Atlantic & Pacific Tea Company, better known as A&P, paid $490,000 for more than nine hundred alleged violations of child labor laws.[25] Neither company denied or admitted guilt. Commenting on the fines, Secretary of Labor Robert B. Reich said his department "will not tolerate companies that seek to gain a competitive advantage" by undermining federal labor standards.[26]

The batboy issue returned with a vengeance during the Clinton administration. Tommy McCoy was hired to be the batboy for the Savannah Cardinals, then a Class A affiliate of the St. Louis Cardinals. Tommy was a big fan of the team, and he was thrilled to work with the players. A local media outlet ran a story about Tommy's day as a batboy. A Georgia labor official read the story and noticed a problem. Tommy was only fourteen years old, and state child labor laws prohibited fourteen- and fifteen-year-olds from working past 7:00 p.m. on school nights or 9:00 p.m. during the summer. A Labor Department investigator notified the club that the boy's employment violated child labor laws. The team reluctantly dismissed Tommy and replaced him with a sixteen-year-old. The *Savannah Morning News* ran a story about the incident that generated an intense local uproar that was quickly noticed by national media. Within days, CNN, CBS, *Good Morning America*, the Associated Press, *Inside Edition*, and numerous other stations and media shows wanted to interview Tommy.[27]

Secretary of Labor Reich suddenly had a public relations nightmare on his hands. Critics claimed that "insensitive bureaucrats were trampling on the national pastime."[28] Reich did not want to provide ammunition to those who believed that the federal government was out of touch with the American people. The secretary's top deputies, however, advised that it would hurt Labor Department morale if he reversed the investigator's decision.[29] Just before Peter Jennings reported the story on the *ABC Evening News*, Secretary Reich issued a statement calling the application of child labor laws to batboys "silly" and that it was "not the intent of the law to deny young teenagers employment opportunities so long as their health and well-being are not impaired."[30] The Labor Department announced that it would not enforce any hourly violations against baseball pending a review, and Tommy was granted a waiver from state child labor laws. Secretary Reich and the Georgia labor commissioner announced that the Savannah Cardinals could rehire Tommy for batboy duties.

On May 13, 1994, the Labor Department proposed a rule "to provide an exception from the permissible hours and time standards for minors fourteen and fifteen years of age when employed as attendants in professional sports." In the public notice for the proposed reform, the department stated that a change in the existing federal hours and times standards to allow employment of fourteen- and fifteen-year-olds as batboys and batgirls or as attendants in other professional sports would not be inconsistent with FLSA's oppressive child labor provisions. Citing the 1986–1987 study conducted by the department on sports attendants in professional baseball, which concluded that such employment would not be detrimental to a child's health or well-being, the secretary believed that the findings were equally applicable to other sports.

A total of twenty-six comments were received on the regulatory proposal.[31] Eight minor-league baseball teams supported the rule change, arguing that the sports-attendant experience offers young people a chance to interact with role models in a healthy, character-building activity within a family-friendly atmosphere. The National Consumers League, Child Labor Coalition, National PTA, and a labor organization (Food & Allied Service Trades) opposed the proposed rule based on their concern that "the increased hours and late time of day would be deleterious to the young people's health, safety, and education."[32] Two groups wanted to limit the change to baseball, and the National PTA suggested a case-by-case evaluation of a student's academic and attendance record before granting an exemption. Commenters from the restaurant industry complained that it was unfair to exempt the sports industry from child labor regulations while leaving them in place for other industries. Secretary Reich considered all the comments but concluded that the exemption for fourteen- and fifteen-year-old sports attendants would not constitute oppressive child labor. Rather, the work opportunity would provide a "positive, formative experience." The final rule, with certain restrictions, was announced on April 17, 1995. Sports fans could now relax and enjoy the game.

There were two other attempts in the 1990s to modify child labor regulations. Under Hazardous Occupations Order No. 12, minors under eighteen were not allowed to load waste paper and boxes into industrial paper balers and compactors. Operating such equipment was deemed hazardous for young workers. The Department of Labor feared that child workers might place their arms into the equipment to unjam material. The National Grocers Association, however, characterized the rule as "a prime example of regulatory excess."[33] In March 1995, Representative Thomas Ewing (R-IL) introduced a bill to allow minors under eighteen years of age to operate baling/compacting machinery so long as the equipment met safety standards. Senator Larry Craig (R-ID) sponsored a similar bill in the Senate. Backed by the National Grocers Association but opposed by the Child Labor Coalition and trade unions, a more restrictive version of the bill passed and was signed into law by President Clinton on August 6, 1996. Under the law, sixteen- and seventeen-year-old workers could load materials into the equipment but not operate the machinery. Interest groups disagreed over whether the compromise legislation adequately protected young workers.[34]

Another Hazardous Occupations provision, Order No. 2, was slightly modified during the Clinton administration. The order restricted work-related operation of certain motor vehicles by persons under eighteen years of age because that was viewed as "particularly hazardous" for teen workers. The rule permitted only "occasional and incidental" employment-related driving by young employees. Representative Mike Kreidler (D-WA) introduced legislation in April 1994 that would allow child workers seventeen and under more freedom to drive as part of their jobs.[35] Although no action was taken on the bill, two Republicans, Representative Randy Tate (R-WA) and Senator Slade Gorton (R-WA), sponsored a similar bill in the 104th Congress without success. Finally, Representative Larry Combest (R-TX) introduced the Drive for Teen Employment Act in July 1997. Supported by automobile dealers, the bill was opposed by the Child Labor Coalition and NCL, who worried about the risks that young, inexperienced drivers posed to themselves and the public. A more restrictive bill passed, allowing only persons seventeen years of age to engage in limited work-related driving under strict safety conditions. President Clinton signed the law on October 31, 1998.[36] Under current regulations, employees sixteen years of age and younger may not drive a vehicle on a public road even if they have a valid state driver's license.

During the administration of George W. Bush, some groups representing homeschoolers criticized contemporary child labor laws. While recognizing the historical importance of child labor restrictions in ending exploitation in the workplace, the Home School Legal Defense Association (HSLDA) describes federal and state child labor laws as "out of date."[37] The HSLDA challenged state and federal regulations that prohibit children from working during school hours. In 2003, the Homeschool Non-Discrimination Act was introduced in Congress and reintroduced in successive years. HSLDA sought exemptions under the legislation to allow children as young as twelve to work during school hours. The bill, however, died in the 109th Congress.

Agriculture has always been an area with the weakest child labor protections. Seventeen states exempt farmwork from child labor laws, and the age, hour, overtime, and minimum wage provisions of the Fair Labor Standards Act do not apply to agriculture. For decades, reformers have targeted agricultural work but without much success. For example, during the Obama administration the Department of Labor had to withdraw a proposed rule in 2012 that attempted to protect child farmworkers under age sixteen from dangerous tasks. The Centers for Disease Control's National Institute for Occupational Safety and Health reported that agriculture is the most dangerous work open to children in the United States. Federal law allows sixteen- and seventeen-year-olds to work under hazardous conditions in agriculture, while in all other occupations the minimum age is eighteen years.[38]

The proposed rule would have expanded the Hazardous Occupations category to include limits on children under sixteen operating tractors and using ladders taller than six feet. Although the regulations would not have applied to children working on family farms, there was a political firestorm over the rule. Opponents argued that it would prevent children from learning the basics of farming. Kent Schescke, of the National Future Farmers of America Organization, was concerned about the regulation's student learner exemption. "The proposed rules would severely limit or eliminate opportunities to participate in the experiential learning aspects of our program," Schescke said. "We believe we provide safe learning environments for students that help them succeed in the industry of agriculture."[39]

Opponents of the rule preferred information campaigns and safety training over regulation. Agriculture, however, remains one of the most dangerous occupations for children under eighteen years of age. Unlike other occupations, in agriculture children can work on any farm at age twelve and at any age on a small farm. The Bureau of Labor Statistics reported that the fatality rate for young agricultural workers is 4.4 times higher than the average for workers in the same age group. Those most at risk are the children of poor migrant farmworkers. The defeat of the proposed regulation leaves the issue unsettled, at least for now. Cultural traditions are strong in rural America, and agriculture will continue to be an area targeted for reform.

Those "Truly Stupid" Child Labor Laws

Newt Gingrich, former House Speaker and political consultant, was one of nearly a dozen candidates seeking the Republican nomination for president in 2012. Speaking at Harvard's Kennedy School of Government in November 2011, Gingrich proposed a plan to allow poor children to work as janitors in schools. Attacking public schools, teachers, unions, and child labor laws in the same breath, Gingrich asserted that his plan would help students rise out of poverty. His proposal was based on a claim that parents, especially single mothers living with their children in housing projects, do not provide a role model for hard work. "It is tragic what we do in the poorest neighborhoods," he argued, "entrapping children in child [labor] laws which are truly stupid. Saying to people you shouldn't go to work before you're 14, 16 years of age fine. You're totally poor, you're in a school that's failing with a teacher that is failing."[1]

For a person with a PhD in history and college teaching experience, Gingrich demonstrated a lack of historical understanding of why we have child labor laws. Critics noted that his plan was based on false assumptions about single parents and child labor. According to Census Bureau data, more than 65 percent of mothers in single-parent households with children are employed.[2] Moreover, the Fair Labor Standards Act sets sixteen as the minimum age for most nonagricultural paid work, except in dangerous occupations, although states can pass stricter laws. The FLSA restricts the employment of fourteen- and fifteen-year-olds to hours that will not interfere with schooling and from job conditions that might injure their health. Federal law allows youth to deliver newspapers, do yard work for neighbors, babysit, and perform various chores around the home. No law prevents children from learning the value of work at an early age while still complying with educational requirements. To suggest, as Gingrich did, that nine-year-olds should be allowed to work as janitors, replacing unionized adult janitors, reflected an unawareness or carelessness about the physical demands and inherent dangers of the job. Janitorial work is more than just sweeping and mopping floors and emptying trash cans. Building maintenance requires technical expertise, and some tasks involve the use of chemical products or potentially dangerous tools.

The *Los Angeles Times* lambasted the proposal: "Child labor laws were enacted because children, who are easy to exploit, were once thrown into factory sweatshops instead of being sent to school. There is no surer way to create a permanent underclass than to fail to educate poor kids, which is why today they're not allowed to work during school hours and kids under 14 can't perform most forms of nonfarm paid labor."[3] Many other media outlets and interest groups strongly criticized the idea.[4] Given his penchant for bombast, Gingrich's comments might be dismissed as overblown campaign rhetoric, but his attack on public schools and child labor laws was within the mainstream of a Republican Party that had moved much farther to the right than during his tenure as Speaker of the House in the 1990s.

The 2010 midterm elections were historical. A Tea Party wave swept libertarian and conservative Republicans into the majority party in the US House of Representatives, and Republicans made significant gains in state legislatures and governorships. Many of the new Tea Party Republicans were strongly opposed to the Patient Protection and Affordable Care Act, dubbed "Obamacare," but their disdain for federal programs ran much deeper. Many Tea Party members were hostile to welfare programs and any government regulation of the market. Challenging a long-held societal consensus, some openly questioned the wisdom of child labor laws and argued for their repeal or reform. The attacks on child labor restrictions represented just one front of a broad-based ideological assault on the welfare state and government regulations of the economy that originated during the Progressive, New Deal, and Great Society periods.[5]

At both the federal and state level, various Republicans argued that the government should stay out of the field of child labor altogether while others simply wanted to allow kids more freedom to work, often at much cheaper wages than adults. Republican senator Mike Lee of Utah, for example, claimed in a video lecture posted to his YouTube channel that the federal government has no authority to regulate child labor. Emphasizing states' rights under the Tenth Amendment, he cited *Hammer v. Dagenhart* to support his position that child labor was an intrastate issue, ignoring the fact that the Supreme Court unanimously overturned the decision in *United States v. Darby Lumber*. "This may sound harsh," he admitted, "but it was designed to be that way. It was designed to be a little bit harsh."[6] Maine's Republican governor Paul LePage expressed a desire to lower the legal working age to twelve in his state. Although opposed to permitting twelve-year-olds to work forty hours a week, he said children that age working "eight to ten hours a week . . . is not bad."[7] Maine state representative David Burns criticized child labor regulations, saying, "We have usurped the responsibility of families to make intelligent decisions and transferred that responsibility to school officials and the state."[8] These comments were part of a widespread campaign to use the crisis of the Great Recession to roll back child labor protections.

Some of the rhetorical broadsides against child labor laws landed nowhere, but several states enacted laws weakening child labor protections. In a report for the Economic Policy Institute, a nonpartisan think tank that focuses on the needs of low- and middle-income workers, political economist Gordon Lafer noted that in 2011–2012, four states lifted restrictions on child labor.[9] Idaho was the first state to "make Gingrich's vision reality" when it permitted children as young as twelve to work up to ten hours a week doing custodial tasks in their schools. Wisconsin abolished all restrictions on the number of hours that minors—age sixteen and over—were permitted to work during the school year. Under previous regulations, sixteen- and seventeen-year-olds were prohibited from working more than twenty-six hours during the school week and more than fifty hours a week during vacations. Ignoring social science evidence that suggested increased workloads make it difficult for teens to concentrate on their studies, sixteen- and seventeen-year-old students were now allowed to work an unlimited number of hours seven days a week throughout the school year. Michigan increased, from fifteen to twenty-four, the number of hours students may work during the school week.

Maine also expanded the number of hours high school students could work each day and week during the school year. The legislature initially considered the "Enhance Access to the Workplace for Minors Act," which would have established a subminimum wage of $5.25 for anyone under twenty years of age and removed all restrictions on the number of hours that teens could work.[10] The law proved too radical even for the conservative legislature so a watered-down bill was approved. Backed by the Maine Restaurant Association, the law expanded the number of hours students can work per school day from four to six and increased total hours for the school week from twenty to twenty-four. One supporter of the legislation expressed the extreme libertarian position that child labor restrictions themselves are wrong. "Kids have parents," argued state representative Bruce Bickford. "It's not up to the government to regulate everybody's life and lifestyle. Take the government away. Let the parents take care of their kids."[11]

Similar laws were introduced in Minnesota, Missouri, Ohio, and Utah but were not passed. In February 2011, legislation (S.B. 222) introduced in Missouri by state senator Jane Cunningham (R-Chesterfield) would have eliminated nearly all state restrictions on child labor. According to the legislative summary, the bill proposed to abolish prohibitions on employment of children under fourteen, repeal the requirement that a child aged fourteen or fifteen obtain a work certificate or work permit in order to be employed, end restrictions on hours and time when a child could work during the day, and remove the authority of the state Labor Division to inspect records on child employees.[12] Senator Cunningham defended her bill by arguing that her two boys worked as minors, and they benefited from the experience. The bill, however, was widely condemned by the NCL, labor unions, and education groups across the country, and comedian Jay Leno mocked the proposal in his monologue on the *Tonight Show*.[13] Of more than one thousand bills, the editors of the *St. Louis Dispatch* described S.B. 222 as probably "the meanest of the mean bills" introduced that session.[14] By March, the bill was dead. Cunningham decided not to seek reelection in 2012.

Many of these bills were touted as instilling a "work ethic" and discipline in children—the same arguments used a century ago to defend child labor exploitation. Some studies show that learning a work ethic at an early age can teach youth punctuality, frugality, and respect for supervisors. But the attacks on child labor laws were not motivated out of genuine concern for the welfare of teenagers. Looking for a source of cheap labor, all of these measures were pushed by lobbyists for state restaurant and grocer associations, lodging and tourism associations, small business associations, and chambers of commerce. One lobbyist for the Wisconsin Grocers Association, which successfully worked to repeal child labor restrictions, rejected any comparisons to the days of Upton Sinclair. "Our members are not trying to overwork these kids or create a sweatshop," she stated. "They just want to give kids that first great opportunity you get in a grocery store."[15] Critics, however, warned against weakening protections. "It seems that conservative politicians are trying to take us back to the nineteenth century," said Justin Feldman of Public Citizen, "a time when children went to work instead of school and toiled under dangerous conditions for little pay."[16]

With states still recovering from the 2008 Great Recession, the attacks on child labor laws were surprising and controversial. From a policy perspective, critics pointed out that it made little sense to expand the labor pool when unemployment in 2011 was still above 7 percent in many states. Children should not compete with adult wage earners for scarce jobs. The weakening of child labor restrictions also sacrifices educational development for short-term financial gains. Expanded work hours make it difficult to complete homework. Students who enter the workforce and fail to earn a high school diploma are often doomed to a difficult life of low-paying jobs with little opportunity for advancement. There will always be anecdotal exceptions, but finishing high school and earning a college degree is still the best path for economic success.[17]

More recently, Republicans, mostly in red states, have continued to undermine child labor laws.[18] The proposals include the creation of a separate wage requirement lower than the federal minimum wage, creating exemptions to job categories that bring a state to the baseline guarantees of federal protection, excluding parental approval from the work permit application, weakening the already minimal protections for agricultural employment, and expanding the number of hours youth may work when school is in session. For example, Missouri enacted a law in 2013 exempting farmwork performed by children under sixteen from various child labor requirements, including the need for a work permit, work days and hours, and prohibitions on hazardous jobs. In Minnesota, a new law went into effect in August 2014 that established a youth wage of $6.50 an hour for workers under eighteen where previously there had been no separate wage category for child workers. Indiana's Republican governor and future vice president, Mike Pence, signed a state law on March 31, 2014, exempting legal entities standing in place of a parent from child labor laws and allowing hazardous work on a farm by a minor under certain circumstances. Michigan passed a law in 2014 broadening exemptions from youth employment laws for sixteen-year-olds who obtain a high school equivalency certificate.[19]

Despite the coordinated attack on child labor laws, there have been a few areas where labor laws were strengthened. New York enacted a law increasing protections for child models. Under the regulations, employers must provide nurses for young models and establish trust-like bank accounts for compensation. In addition, models are prohibited from working past midnight on school nights. Employers that violate these laws face fines starting at $1,000 for the first violation and up to $3,000 for the third. After that, they can lose the privilege to employ child models.[20] California also passed a Child Labor Protection Act in 2014 that allows for damages to be tripled when a minor has been a victim of labor law violations by employers.

That same year, the North Carolina Tobacco Growers Association issued a policy recommending that tobacco farmers not hire children under sixteen, even if they have parental permission.[21] Another group, the Council for Burley Tobacco, also issued a statement that it does not condone the hiring of anyone under the age of sixteen for work in tobacco anywhere in the world. "Burley farmers in the United States understand the dangers Burley production jobs pose to children and (believe) the incidence of children working in tobacco production is low in this country."[22] The proposed changes followed a 2013–2014 report by Human Rights Watch on the dangers of teens working on tobacco farms.[23] Children ages seven to seventeen who worked tobacco farms from sunup to sundown exhibited symptoms of nicotine poisoning, known as Green Tobacco Sickness.[24] Influenced by the report, Senator Tom Harkin (D-IA) urged tobacco companies to stop using child labor in their supply chains.

Even with an improved economy, lower unemployment, robust corporate profits, and weakening of the Tea Party movement, conservative Republicans continued their assault on child labor protections in recent years. In Wisconsin, state representative Amy Loudenbeck (R-Clinton) and state senator Chris Kapenga (R-Delafield) introduced a bill during the spring 2017 session to completely eliminate the Department of Workforce Development permit process that is required of children aged sixteen and seventeen entering the workforce. According to an analysis by the Wisconsin AFL-CIO, the proposed legislation "undermines parental rights by eliminating the requirement for moms and dads to approve their kid's work schedule and other workplace conditions."[25] The proposal contradicts the libertarian rhetoric about returning responsibility for children's employment back to parents.

Child labor was back in the news following the contentious 2016 presidential election and Donald Trump's victory. On October 31, 2016, the *Washington Post* ran a montage of twenty "haunting portraits of child laborers in 1900s America" on its website.[26] The photos were among the five thousand that Lewis Hine took during his years with the National Child Labor Committee. The images depicted children who worked in textile mills, mines, factories, and as newsboys. A brief article preceded the photo spread and explained how Hine often tricked his way into the factories and mills or approached children as they entered or exited the workplace. The author noted how the photos helped stir the nation's conscience against child labor.

More than a century after the photos were taken, not everyone was moved by the powerful images. Jeffrey Tucker, director of content for the Foundation for Economic Education, a libertarian, free-market organization, published an essay on November 3, 2016, in response to the child labor photos. In his article entitled "Let the Kids Work," Tucker admitted that the children looked scruffy, dirty, and tired, but strangely, he looked beyond the photos and projected on them an exciting life of opportunity:

> But I also think of their inner lives. They are working in the adult world, surrounded by cool bustling things and new technology. They are on the streets, in the factories, in the mines, with adults and with peers, learning and doing. They are being valued for what they do, which is to say being valued as people. They are earning money.
>
> Whatever else you want to say about this, it's an exciting life. You can talk about the dangers of coal mining or selling newspapers on the street. But let's not pretend that danger is something that every young teen wants to avoid. If you doubt it, head over [to] the stadium for the middle school football game in your local community, or have a look at the wrestling or gymnastics team's antics at the gym.[27]

Tucker compared the children in the photos to a contemporary class of thirty children in public schools, whom he claimed are all "bored out of their minds, creativity and imagination beaten out of their brains, forbidden from earning money and providing value to others, learning no skills, and knowing full well that they are supposed to do this until they are 22 years old."[28] His comments reflected a person who is completely tone-deaf on the evils of child labor exploitation and the long struggle to abolish the practice. He dismissed the role played by reformers and government regulation in helping end child labor, giving the free market all the credit. The Fair Labor Standards Act, Tucker asserted, "helped shore up the power of labor unions against cheaper wage competition." He conveniently ignored the fact that a thirteen-year-old working at a mill or factory more than twelve hours a day in the early 1900s could hardly be described as enjoying an exciting, creative, and imaginative experience. Elevating economic liberty above all other values, Tucker also condemned the coercive nature of compulsory education laws and advocated their abolishment. He urged that we give children the freedom to quit school at an early age so they can work "fantastic jobs" at Chick-fil-A or Wal-Mart, two companies known for their conservative business practices, in order to realize their human value in gainful employment and real learning.

Working within the same network of libertarian, antigovernment institutes, associations, and think tanks, Joseph Sunde of the Acton Institute, on the same day that Tucker's article came out, posted on the group's Power Blog an essay entitled "Bring Back Child Labor: Work Is a Gift Our Kids Can Handle" that repeated and endorsed many of the arguments made by Tucker. Based in Grand Rapids, Michigan, the Acton Institute promotes laissez-faire policies within a conservative Christian framework. Sunde suggested that we stop prioritizing *intellectual* work (italics in original), or what most people would call educating our children, and allow fourteen-year-olds to gain "practical" knowledge and character development by working at fast-food restaurants and grocery stores. To accomplish this goal, Sunde argued we need to eliminate child labor laws, minimum wage requirements, and other regulations. Neither Tucker nor Sunde explain where the sixteen- and seventeen-year-olds will be working if younger teens are to be taking their jobs.

These libertarian screeds against child labor laws would have stayed within a right-wing echo chamber had it not been for the nomination by Donald Trump of Betsy DeVos for secretary of education. Around the time of her confirmation hearing, opponents of the nomination discovered that she had funded the Acton Institute and served on the board of directors from 1995 to 2005.[29] With her close ties to the Acton Institute, Sunde's post on bringing back child labor created a storm of controversy and negative publicity for the nominee. Sunde quickly revised the title of his piece, eliminating the line "Bring Back Child Labor" and backpedaled on some of his arguments. He explained that he didn't support replacing education with paid labor, sending kids back into the coal mines, or ending compulsory education. Despite the incident and a host of potential conflicts of interest, Betsy DeVos was ultimately confirmed as the secretary of education when for the first time in US history, the vice president, in this case Mike Pence, voted to break a 50–50 tie in the Senate on a cabinet nomination.

For over seventy-five years, society was in general agreement that oppressive child labor undermined the intellectual and physical development of children. That social consensus is now being attacked on a variety of fronts.

Many of the child labor issues contested over a century ago are being re-hashed. Critics argue that the contemporary assaults on child labor laws are an attempt to weaken government regulation, undermine the power of unions, and produce a cheap source of labor. We are not going to see a return of children working in coal mines or textile mills because those jobs have largely disappeared even for adults. However, weakening child labor laws will result in young workers being employed in the service industries for longer hours and lower pay. Society must decide whether that development is good for our youth and the nation. With Republican gains in Congress and the states during the 2014 midterm and 2016 presidential elections, the battle over child labor and compulsory education laws is likely to continue for many years. A sober understanding of the history and reasons for child labor laws should inform any subsequent debate.

CHRONOLOGY OF EVENTS

May 1813	Connecticut enacts first law requiring schooling of working children and making employers responsible for the moral education of their young employees. As with subsequent child labor laws, it was rarely enforced.
February 16, 1832	New England Association of Farmers, Mechanics, and Other Working Men creates a committee to investigate child labor.
July 22, 1836	Union members at the National Trades' Union Convention make the first formal public proposal recommending that states establish minimum ages for factory work.
March 3, 1842	Massachusetts limits work of children under age twelve to ten hours per day; other states pass similar laws, but they are not consistently enforced.
March 27, 1848	Pennsylvania becomes the first state to set a minimum age for factory workers at twelve; in effect, the law is the first statewide ban of child labor based on age.
April 16, 1852	Massachusetts becomes the first state to limit child labor by passing a comprehensive compulsory school attendance law. The law required children between ages eight and fourteen to attend school at least three months a year.
December 28, 1869	Knights of Labor founded; responsible for introduction of labor legislation in the South in the 1880s.
November 15, 1881	Federation of Organized Trades and Labor Unions founded and calls for abolition of child labor. The organization changed its name to the American Federation of Labor (AFL) in 1886.

October 29, 1901	Indiana compulsory education law upheld in *State v. Bailey*.
April 25, 1904	National Child Labor Committee formed by Edgar Gardner Murphy.
September 11, 1906	Oregon Supreme Court upholds regulation of child labor hours in *State v. Shorey*.
December 5, 1906	Senator Albert J. Beveridge introduces first bill in Congress to prevent the industrial exploitation of children.
January 23, 1907	Legislation passed to allow secretaries of commerce and labor to investigate and report on child labor.
1908	Lewis Hine begins his ten-year project of taking over five thousand photographs of working children for the National Child Labor Committee.
April 9, 1912	US Children's Bureau established with the mandate to investigate and report on the welfare of children.
May 9, 1913	Ohio prohibits boys from working until the age of fifteen and girls until sixteen.
August 1, 1913	Alexander J. McKelway authors "Declaration of Dependence" for child labor.
September 1, 1916	Congress passes the Keating-Owen Act, the first federal child labor law. Most large businesses, except cotton manufactures in the South, support national legislation on child labor.
June 3, 1918	Supreme Court overturns the Keating-Owen Act by a 5–4 decision in *Hammer v. Dagenhart*.
February 24, 1919	Congress enacts the Revenue Act, also called the Child Labor Tax Law, using its taxing power to regulate and prohibit child labor.
April 25, 1919	Child Labor Tax Law takes effect.
May 15, 1922	In *Bailey v. Drexel Furniture Company*, the Supreme Court strikes down the Child Labor Tax Law, arguing that the law was not a valid exercise of the congressional power to lay and collect taxes.
June 19, 1922	NCLC Board of Trustees votes to support a constitutional amendment on child labor.
April 9, 1923	In *Adkins v. Children's Hospital*, the Supreme Court strikes down minimum wage for women and children in Washington, DC.

April 26, 1924	House of Representatives adopts the Child Labor Amendment with a vote of 297 yeas, 69 nays, 2 absent, and 64 not voting.
June 2, 1924	US Senate adopts the Child Labor Amendment with a vote of 61 yeas, 23 nays, and 12 not voting. The amendment is sent to the states for ratification.
June 28, 1924	Arkansas becomes first state to ratify the Child Labor Amendment.
January 8, 1925	California ratifies the Child Labor Amendment.
January 29, 1925	Arizona ratifies the Child Labor Amendment.
February 25, 1925	Wisconsin becomes fourth state to ratify the Child Labor Amendment.
February 11, 1927	Montana becomes the last state to ratify the Child Labor Amendment before the Great Depression.
April 28, 1931	Colorado becomes first state to ratify the Child Labor Amendment during the Depression.
June 16, 1933	President Roosevelt signs the National Industrial Recovery Act. The National Recovery Administration passes codes preventing persons under sixteen from working in various industries.
May 27, 1935	The Supreme Court rules that the National Industrial Recovery Act is unconstitutional.
December 11, 1935	The American Farm Bureau Federation reverses a twelve-year policy and endorses the Child Labor Amendment.
June 30, 1936	Public Contracts Act of 1936 (Walsh-Healy Public Contracts Act). The law required those receiving government contracts to have a forty-hour work-week, fair pay, and minimum age of sixteen for boys and eighteen for girls to work.
February 25, 1937	Kansas becomes twenty-eighth state to ratify the Child Labor Amendment (after initial rejection on January 30, 1925).
April 12, 1937	The Supreme Court upholds the National Labor Relations Act in *NLRB v. Jones and Laughlin Steel Corporation*.
February 1938	Majority of Americans (67 percent) favor higher wage/labor standards.

April 30, 1938	Frustrated by a lack of progress in the legislature, FDR addresses Congress on wages and hours for the sixth time since taking office.
June 25, 1938	Congress passes the Fair Labor Standards Act. FDR signs the law the same day.
June 5, 1939	The Supreme Court decides in *Coleman v. Miller* and *Chandler v. Wise* that the Child Labor Amendment was still alive and that a state that has rejected the amendment may reverse itself and vote for ratification.
June 19, 1939	Grace Abbott, chief of the Children's Bureau from 1921 to 1934, dies.
February 3, 1941	The Supreme Court upholds the Fair Labor Standards Act in *United States v. Darby Lumber*.
October 19, 1949	Congress amends FLSA, broadening child labor provisions.
July 16, 1982	Secretary of Labor Donovan proposes changes to child labor laws: (1) easier for fourteen- and fifteen-year-olds to work, (2) extend hours worked, (3) reclassify hazardous jobs, and (4) make it easier to employ people for under minimum wage.
April 21, 1986	Senator Dan Quayle proposes fourteen- and fifteen-year-olds to be batboys or batgirls for baseball teams.
August 5, 1987	Secretary of Labor Brock forms Child Labor Advisory Committee to help examine child labor issues. Child labor was often a low priority even with the committee.
April 17, 1995	Department of Labor regulations revised to allow fourteen- and fifteen-year-olds to be batboys and batgirls for professional sports teams.
August 6, 1996	Legislation passed to allow sixteen- and seventeen-year-olds to load materials into, but not operate or unload materials from, paper balers and box compactors.
October 31, 1998	President Clinton signs bill allowing seventeen-year-olds to be professional drivers.
July 25, 2001	Legislation introduced to allow Amish youth to work at a younger age, but proposal goes nowhere.

May 1, 2003	Legislation introduced to allow fourteen-year-olds to work in sawmills and woodworking facilities, aimed at Amish community.
September 23, 2003	Youth Worker Protection Act introduced, designed to prevent people under eighteen from "youth peddling."
January 23, 2004	H.R. 2673 signed by President Bush. Aimed at Amish community, the law permits fourteen- to seventeen-year-olds to work with machinery used to process wood products.
March 8, 2005	Child Modeling Exploitation Prevention Act introduced.
July 27, 2005	Children's Act for Responsible Employment introduced. Young persons under sixteen would not be able to work on farms unless owned or operated by family.
June 8, 2007	Child Labor Protection Act introduced. Bill increases civil penalties for child labor violations. Bill passes House but not the Senate.
February 15, 2011	Missouri hears S.B. 222, which proposed to eliminate state child labor laws, but the bill is not passed.
June 26, 2011	Wisconsin reverses restrictions on how much sixteen- and seventeen-year-olds can work per week and per day during school and over summer.
April 26, 2012	Labor Department withdraws a proposed rule that would have limited work that children perform on farms.

STATES RATIFYING THE PROPOSED 1924 CHILD LABOR AMENDMENT

Arkansas—June 28, 1924
California—January 8, 1925
Arizona—January 29, 1925
Wisconsin—February 25, 1925
Montana—February 11, 1927
Colorado—April 28, 1931
Oregon—January 31, 1933
Washington—February 3, 1933
North Dakota—March 4, 1933 (after State Senate rejection—January 28, 1925)
Ohio—March 22, 1933
Michigan—May 10, 1933
New Hampshire—May 17, 1933 (after rejection—March 18, 1925)
New Jersey—June 12, 1933
Illinois—June 30, 1933
Oklahoma—July 5, 1933
Iowa—December 5, 1933 (after State House rejection—March 11, 1925)
West Virginia—December 12, 1933
Minnesota—December 14, 1933 (after rejection—April 14, 1925)
Maine—December 16, 1933 (after rejection—April 10, 1925)
Pennsylvania—December 21, 1933 (after rejection—April 16, 1925)
Wyoming—January 31, 1935
Utah—February 5, 1935 (after rejection—February 4, 1925)
Idaho—February 7, 1935 (after State House rejection—February 7, 1925)
Indiana—February 8, 1935 (after State Senate rejection—February 5, 1925, and State House rejection—March 5, 1925)
Kentucky—January 13, 1937 (after rejection—March 24, 1926)
Nevada—January 29, 1937
New Mexico—February 12, 1937 (after rejection—1935)
Kansas—February 25, 1937 (after rejection—January 30, 1925)

Between 1924 and 1937, fifteen states rejected the amendment, either by a resolution or a vote in one or both chambers of the state legislature: Connecticut, Delaware, Florida, Georgia, Louisiana, Maryland, Massachusetts, Missouri, North Carolina, South Carolina, South Dakota, Tennessee, Texas, Vermont, and Virginia.

Of the forty-eight states in the Union in 1924, five have taken no action of record on the amendment: Alabama, Mississippi, Nebraska, New York, and Rhode Island. Alaska and Hawaii, which became states in 1959, also have taken no action.

Source: US Congress, House of Representatives, 69th Cong., 1st Sess., *Statement of Status of Proposed Child Labor Amendment.* Transmitted by secretary of state. February 10, 1926; James J. Kilpatrick, ed., *The Constitution of the United States and Amendments Thereto* (Virginia Commission on Constitutional Government, 1961), 67–69.

CASES CITED

Adkins v. Children's Hospital, 261 U.S. 525 (1923)
Atherton Mills v. Johnston, 259 U.S. 13 (1922)
Bailey v. Drexel Furniture Company, 259 U.S. 20 (1922)
Bryant v. Skillman Hardware Co., 76 N.J. 45 (1908)
Carter v. Carter Coal Co., 298 U.S. 238 (1936)
Champion v. Ames, 188 U.S. 321 (1903)
Chandler v. Wise, 307 U.S. 474 (1939)
Clark Distilling Co. v. Western Maryland Railway Co., 242 U.S. 311 (1917)
Coleman v. Miller, 307 U.S. 433 (1939)
Dillon v. Goss, 256 U.S. 368 (1921)
Drexel Furniture Company v. Bailey, 276 F. 452 (WD NC 1921)
Ex Parte Weber, 149 Cal. 392 (1906)
Fitzgerald v. International Flax Twine Co., 104 Minn. 138 (1908)
Gemsco, Inc. v. Walling, 324 U.S. 244 (1945)
George v. Bailey, 274 F. 639 (1921)
Gibbons v. Ogden, 22 U.S. 1 (1824)
Hammer v. Dagenhart, 247 U.S. 251 (1918)
Helvering v. Davis, 301 U.S. 619 (1937)
Hippolite Egg Company v. United States, 220 U.S. 45 (1911)
Hoke v. U.S., 227 U.S. 308 (1913)
Inland Steel Co. v. Yedinak, 172 Ind. 423 (1909)
In re Spencer, 149 Cal. 396, 86 Pac. 896 (1906)
Kentucky Whip and Collar Co. v. Illinois Central Railroad Co., 299 U.S. 334 (1937)
Lawton v. Steele, 152 U.S. 133 (1889)
Lochner v. New York, 198 U.S. 45 (1905)
McCray v. U.S., 195 U.S. 27 (1904)
McCulloch v. Maryland, 17 U.S. 316 (1819)
Morehead v. New York ex rel. Tipaldo, 298 U.S. 587 (1936)
Muller v. Oregon, 208 U.S. 412 (1908)
Munn v. Illinois, 94 U.S. 113 (1877)

Myers v. State Journal Company, 290 (Mich. Cir. Ct., 1938)

Nash v. United States, 229 U.S. 373 (1913)

National Labor Relations Board (NLRB) v. Jones and Laughlin Steel Corporation, 301 U.S. 1 (1937)

Opp Cotton Mills, Inc. v. Administrator Wage and Hour Division, 312 U.S. 126 (1940)

Panama Refining Company v. Ryan, 293 U.S. 388 (1935)

People v. Taylor, 192 N.Y. 398 (1908)

Pierce v. Society of Sisters, 268 U.S. 510 (1925)

Schechter Poultry Corporation v. U.S., 295 U.S. 495 (1935)

Shreveport Rate Cases, 234 U.S. 342 (1914)

Slaughterhouse Cases, 83 U.S. 16 Wall. 36 (1873)

State v. Rose, 51 So. 496 (La. 1910)

State v. Shorey, 48 Oregon 396 (1906)

State v. Shorey, 86 P. 881 (Ore. 1906)

Sturges and Burn Manufacturing Co. v. Beauchamp, 231 U.S. 320 (1913)

United States v. Butler, 297 U.S. 1 (1936)

United States v. Darby Lumber, 312 U.S. 100 (1941)

United States v. Doremus, 249 U.S. 86 (1919)

United States v. E. C. Knight Co., 156 U.S. (1895)

Veazie Bank v. Fenno, 8 Wall. 533 (1869)

West Coast Hotel v. Parrish, 300 U.S. 279 (1937)

Wise v. Chandler, 271 Ky. 1 (Ky. Ct. App. 1937)

Wright v. Vinton Branch of Mountain Trust Bank, 300 U.S. 440 (1937)

NOTES

Introduction

1. Library of Congress, National Child Labor Committee Collection, Lewis Hine photos, http://www.loc.gov/pictures/collection/nclc/ (accessed April 11, 2017).

2. Hugh D. Hindman, *Child Labor: An American History* (New York: M. E. Sharpe, 2002).

3. Raymond G. Fuller, *Child Labor and the Constitution* (New York: Thomas Y. Crowell, 1923), 3.

4. Edward F. Waite, "The Child Labor Amendment," *Minnesota Law Review* 9, no. 3 (1925): 179.

5. Walter I. Trattner, *Crusade for the Children: A History of the National Child Labor Committee and Child Labor Reform* (Chicago: Quadrangle Books, 1970), 9–10.

6. Code of Federal Regulations, 29 Chapter V, Subchapter B, 779.505.

7. Shelley Sallee, *The Whiteness of Child Labor Reform in the New South* (Athens: University of Georgia Press, 2004), 92–113.

8. The first major work on the subject was Fuller's treatise, *Child Labor and the Constitution*. As former director of research and publicity for the National Child Labor Committee, Fuller drew upon his experience in the movement to regulate child labor. While his work discusses two important child labor cases, *Hammer v. Dagenhart* (1918) and *Bailey v. Drexel Furniture Co.* (1922), and the need for a constitutional amendment, it misses the rest of the story. Another text, Stephen B. Wood's *Constitutional Politics in the Progressive Era: Child Labor and the Law* (Chicago: University of Chicago Press, 1968), focuses on the Progressive Period and thus ends its discussion of child labor reform in the 1920s.

Trattner's *Crusade for the Children* provides the best narrative on the struggle over federal child labor legislation and the strategic role played by the National Child Labor Committee, but as it was published nearly fifty years ago, a broader, updated work is needed. More recently, James D. Schmidt, in *Industrial Violence and the Legal Origins of Child Labor* (New York: Cambridge University Press, 2010), identifies a large shift in the cultural perception of youthful labor during the late nineteenth and early twentieth centuries. The shift was a product of competing visions of how children would fit into the increasingly dangerous nature of work in industrial America. On one side, young workers and their families sought an industrial childhood because it instilled a strong work ethic and contributed to the household income. In opposition, reformers fought to exclude children from productive life and articulated a new definition of childhood centered on schooling and recreation. The battle between these two sides played out in the courts. In cases involving industrial violence and child injuries, the courts in the Appalachian South fashioned a new definition of youthful work. Schmidt expands our understanding of class divisions over child labor and how state courts adjudicated industrial violence cases involving young workers, but he does not examine the legal struggle at the federal level or areas outside the South.

Child labor is also discussed in more general works on childhood. See Steven Mintz, *Huck's Raft: A History of American Childhood* (Cambridge, MA: Harvard University Press, 2004), 133–153. Several other texts are directed at adolescent readers. See William G. Whittaker, *Child Labor in America: History, Policy, and Legislative Issues* (Hauppauge, NY: Nova Science Publishers, 2004), and Russell Freedman, *Kids at Work: Lewis Hine and the Crusade against Child Labor* (New York: Clarion Books, 1994). The latter is primarily a collection and description of some of the five thousand photos taken by Lewis Hine in the early 1900s that document the worst period of child labor in America. These books teach young audiences about an important social and economic issue in American history, but they do not provide a comprehensive analysis of the legal and political battles involving working children.

9. Grace Abbott, *The Child and the State*, vol. 1, *Legal Status in the Family Apprenticeship and Child Labor*, sec. 3: "The Administration of Child Labor Legislation" (New York: Greenwood Press, reprinted 1968), 405.

10. John Fabian Witt, *The Accidental Republic: Crippled Workingmen, Destitute Widows, and the Remaking of American Law* (Cambridge, MA: Harvard University Press, 2006). In dealing with the problem of industrial accidents, a variety of social and legal institutions—including courts, employers, social reformers, and government officials—developed new legal remedies and laid the foundations for the administrative state.

11. "Article 13," *Christian Nation* 34, no. 2 (September 23, 1886): 2.

12. Roscoe Pound, "The Scope and Purpose of Sociological Jurisprudence," *Harvard Law Review* 25, no. 6 (April 1912): 514.

13. https://www.dol.gov/oasam/programs/history/dolorigabridge.htm (accessed December 8, 2016).

14. William R. Brock, *Investigation and Responsibility: Public Responsibility in the United States, 1865–1900* (Cambridge, UK: Cambridge University Press, 1984); David Brian Robertson, *Capital, Labor, and the State: The Battle for American Labor Markets from the Civil War to the New Deal* (Lanham, MD: Rowman and Littlefield, 2000).

15. Scholars have debated the extent to which courts can promote social change. See Michael J. Klarman, "Rethinking the Civil Rights and Civil Liberties Revolutions," *Virginia Law Review* 82, no. 1 (1996): 1–67; Gerald N. Rosenberg, *The Hollow Hope: Can Courts Bring about Social Change?* 2d ed. (Chicago: University of Chicago Press, 2008); David A. Schultz, ed., *Leveraging the Law: Using Courts to Achieve Social Change* (New York: Peter Lang, 1998). For a positive account of courts, social change, and social movements, see Jack M. Balkin, *Constitutional Redemption: Political Faith in an Unjust World* (Cambridge, MA: Harvard University Press, 2011).

16. Daniel J. Elazar, *The American Partnership* (Chicago: University of Chicago Press, 1962); Martin Grozdins, *The American System* (Chicago: Rand-McNally, 1966). Although there are other theories of federalism, dual and cooperative are the most useful tools in understanding the debate over child labor.

17. Joseph Sunde, "Work Is a Gift Our Kids Can Handle," Acton Institute Powerblog, November 3, 2016, http://blog.acton.org/archives (accessed March 25, 2017).

18. Joan Walsh, "The Right's Crusade to Repeal the 20th Century," published on March 14, 2014, http://www.alternet.org/tea-party-and-right/rights-crusade -repeal-20th-century (accessed March 25, 2017).

19. Office of Child Labor, Forced Labor, and Human Trafficking, *2015: Findings on the Worst Forms of Child Labor*, Bureau of International Labor Affairs, US Department of Labor, 2016.

Chapter 1. From Public Good to Moral Evil: State Laws and Child Labor in the 1800s

1. US Department of Labor, Bureau of Labor Statistics, *Summary of the Report on Condition of Woman and Child Wage Earners in the United States*, US Bureau of Labor Statistics Bulletin No. 175 (Washington, DC: GPO, 1916), 227.

2. Edith Abbott, "Child Labor in America before 1870," Appendix A, in *Women in Industry: A Study in American Economic History* (New York: D. Appleton, 1918).

3. Grace Abbott, *The Child and the State*, vol. 1, *Legal Status in the Family Apprenticeship and Child Labor* (New York: Greenwood Press, reprinted 1968), 271.

4. "Child Labor: Conditions and Attempted Legislation before 1840," *American Economic Association* 9, no. 3 (October 1908): 5–7.

5. George Washington, January 22, 1790, *The Diaries of George Washington, 1748–1799*, ed. John C. Fitzpatrick (Boston: Houghton Mifflin, 1925).

6. Alexander Hamilton, *Report on the Subject of Manufacturers*, Philadelphia, December 5, 1791. Section III.

7. Abbott, *The Child and the State*, 277.

8. Ibid., 81.

9. Charles B. Spahr, "Child Labor in England and the United States," *The Chautauquan: A Weekly Newsmagazine*, 30, no. 1 (October 1899): 41; Katrina Honeyman, *Child Workers in England, 1780–1820* (Aldershot, England: Ashland, 2007).

10. Carolyn Tuttle, "Child Labor during the British Industrial Revolution," August 14, 2001, *EH.Net Encyclopedia*, edited by Robert Whaples, http://eh.net/encyclopedia/child-labor-during-the-british-industrial-revolution/.

11. US Department of Labor, "Factory Inspection Legislation," 2001, https://www.dol.gov/general/aboutdol/history/mono-regsafepart02 (accessed December 12, 2016).

12. "Child-Labor in England," *American Economic Association* 5, no. 2 (March 1890): 13, 17.

13. See Jane Humphries, *Childhood and Child Labour in the British Industrial Revolution* (New York: Cambridge University Press, 2011); Peter Kirby, *Child Labour in Britain, 1750–1870* (New York: Palgrave MacMillan, 2003).

14. Massachusetts Legislative Files, 1825, *Senate, No. 8074*. Report on Returns of Children Employed in Factories. Reprinted in Abbott, *The Child and the State*, 274.

15. Ibid., 277.

16. Abbott, "Child Labor in America," 272.

17. Frances Wright, "Lecture on Existing Evils" (pamphlet, New York, 1829), 13.

18. Grace Abbott, *The Child and the State*, 280.

19. Ibid., 283.

20. Hugh D. Hindman, *Child Labor: An American History* (New York: M. E. Sharpe, 2002), 21.

21. Steven Mintz, *Huck's Raft: A History of American Childhood* (Cambridge, MA: Harvard University Press, 2004), 136–137.

22. Walter I. Trattner, *Crusade for the Children: A History of the National Child Labor Committee and Child Labor Reform in America* (Chicago: Quadrangle Books, 1970), 27.

23. For a good description of life in the Lowell mills, see Chaim M. Rosenberg, *Child Labor in America: A History* (Jefferson, NC: McFarland, 2013), 14–18; John F. Kasson, *Civilizing the Machine: Technology, and Republican Values in America, 1776–1900* (New York: Grossman, 1976).

24. Ruth Wallis Herndon and John E. Murray, eds., *Children Bound to Labor: The Pauper Apprenticeship System in Early America* (Ithaca, NY: Cornell University Press, 2009); Mintz, *Huck's Raft*, 137–139.

25. Abbott, *The Child and the State*, 223.

26. Ibid., 273.

27. "Child Labor: Conditions and Attempted Legislation before 1840," 11.

28. *Report on Conditions of Woman and Child Wage-Earners in the United States*, vol. 6, Senate Document No. 645 (Washington, DC: GPO, 1910), 52–53.

29. Raymond Garfield Fuller, *Child Labor and the Constitution* (New York: Thomas Y. Crowell, 1923), 19.

30. "Proceedings of the New England Convention of Farmers, Mechanics, and Other Working Men," *Workingman's Advocate* (October 20, 1832): 4, 10.

31. Elizabeth Sands Johnson, "Child Labor Legislation," in John R. Commons et al., *History of Labor in the United States*, 4 vols., volume 3, *Working Conditions* (New York: Macmillan, 1935), 403.

32. Abbott, *The Child and the State*, 260.

33. Ibid. See US Department of Labor, Bureau of Labor Statistics, *Summary of the Report on Conditions of Woman and Child Wage-Earners in the United States*, 246.

34. Connecticut established a maximum of ten hours for children under fourteen; New Hampshire, 1847, children under fifteen; Maine, 1848, children under sixteen; Pennsylvania, 1849, children thirteen to sixteen; Ohio, 1852, children under fourteen years old; Rhode Island in 1853 set eleven hours as the maximum workday for children twelve to fifteen.

35. Trattner, *Crusade for the Children*, 31.

36. Abbott, *The Child and the State*, 275.

37. Enrollment of young people age five to nineteen in grammar school reached 60 percent by 1870, but schooling varied by region. Enrollment was much higher in the Northeast, Midwest, and Far West than in the South. Mintz, *Huck's Raft*, 135.

38. Johnson, "Child Labor Legislation," 411.

39. *Second Annual Report of the Factory Inspectors of the State of New York*, December 1, 1887, 50.

40. "Factory Children: Their Condition in This City," *New York Times*, January 25, 1871, 5.

41. "Evils of Child Labor: Prof. Adler Calls Attention to a Menacing Danger,"

New York Times, January 10, 1887, 8; "Social Aspects of Child-Labor," *American Economic Association* 5, no. 2 (March 1890): 59; "The Children at Work," *The Catholic World: A Monthly Magazine of General Literature and Science* 43 (August 1886): 619.

42. "The Little Slaves of Capital," *New York Times*, January 29, 1871, 4.

43. "The Employment of Children in Factories," *New York Times*, October 1, 1871, 4.

44. *First Annual Report of the Factory Inspections of the State of New York*, December 1, 1886, excerpted in Abbott, *The Child and the State*, 414.

45. "Social Aspect of Child-Labor," 60.

46. *Second Annual Report of the Inspector of Factories and Workshops of the State of New Jersey*, Trenton, NJ, 1884, 14–18.

47. "The Little Slaves of Capital," *New York Times*, January 26, 1873, 4.

48. Ibid.

49. "Child Labor in the United States," *American Economic Association* 5, no. 2 (March 1890): 29.

50. Trattner, *Crusade for the Children*, 33.

51. David Glasner and Thomas F. Cooley, eds. *Business Cycles and Depressions: An Encyclopedia* (New York: Garland Publishing, 1997).

52. H. W. Brands, *American Colossus: The Triumph of Capitalism, 1865–1900* (New York: Anchor Books, 2010), 515.

53. Helen Campbell, "Child Labor and Some of Its Results," *The Chautauquan; A Weekly Magazine* 10, no. 1 (October 1889): 22.

54. Ibid., 23.

55. For an early discussion of child labor and wages, see "The Political Economy of Child Labor," *American Economic Association* 5, no. 2 (March 1890): 41.

56. Ibid., 48.

57. For an excellent description of some of the dangerous jobs, see Hindman, *Child Labor*.

58. *Second Annual Report of the Inspector of Factories and Workshops of the State of New Jersey*, 14.

59. Alzina Parsons, "Child Slavery in America: The Child, the Factory, and the State," *The Arena* 10, no. 1 (June 1894): 117, at 122. For a detailed description of the working conditions of child laborers, see Miss Clare de Graffenried, "Child-Labor," *American Economic Association* 5, no. 2 (March 1890): 71.

60. "Boys Employed in Coal Mines," *New York Times*, July 19, 1885, 3; see also Hindman, *Child Labor: An American History*, 89–120.

61. "Child Labor," *The Chautauquan: A Weekly Newsmagazine* 7, no. 10 (July 1887): 631.

62. "The Children at Work," 619.

63. From a muckraking article published by Irene Ashby, in *Public Policy*, August 9, 1902. Quoted in Rosenberg, *Child Labor in America*, 21.

64. Parsons, "Child Slavery in America," 123.

65. "Factory Children," 5.

66. Charles Loring Brace, *The Dangerous Classes of New York* (New York: Wynkoop & Hallenbeck, 1872), 353.

67. Susan J. Pearson, *The Rights of the Defenseless: Protecting Animals and Children in Gilded Age America* (Chicago: University of Chicago Press, 2011), 3.

68. The seven states with age minimums were Massachusetts, New Hampshire, New Jersey, Pennsylvania, Rhode Island, Vermont, and Wisconsin. The twelve states with maximum hours were: Connecticut, Indiana, Maine, Maryland, Massachusetts, Minnesota, Ohio, Pennsylvania, Rhode Island, South Dakota, Vermont, and Wisconsin. See William F. Ogburn, *The Progress and Uniformity of Child Labor Legislation* (New York: Columbia University Studies, 1912), vol. 48, part 2, 71.

69. "Powderly Gives Advice: Child Labor, Labor-Saving Machinery, and Education Discussed," *New York Times*, December 16, 1887, 3.

70. Ibid.

71. Johnson, "Child Labor Legislation," 404.

72. "Children's Labor in Factories," *New York Times*, January 1, 1887, 1.

73. Melton Alonza McLaurin, *The Knights of Labor in the South* (Westport, CT: Greenwood Press, 1978), 102–103.

74. Bernard Mandel, *Samuel Gompers: A Biography* (Yellow Springs, OH: Antioch Press, 1963), 65.

75. Ibid., 181.

76. Letter to L. H. McAtteer, May 8, 1896, in Stuart B. Kaufman, Peter J. Albert, and Grace Palladino, eds., *The Samuel Gompers Papers*, vol. 4, *A National Labor Movement Takes Shape, 1895–1898* (Urbana: University of Illinois Press, 1991), 167.

77. "Evils of Child Labor: Prof. Adler Calls Attention to a Menacing Danger," 8.

78. "Education the Remedy," *New York Times*, January 17, 1887, 3.

79. "Evils of Child Labor," *New York Times*, April 23, 1888, 2.

80. Frederic W. Sanders, "Hull House Maps and Papers," *Political Science Quarterly* 11, no. 2 (June 1896): 340, 342.

81. "Child Labor in the United States," 25.

82. Helen Campbell wrote a five-part series on the woman wage worker for the *New York Tribune* entitled "Prisoners of Poverty," October 1886. Her investigation of sweatshops and tenement work was published in book form the following year. See Helen Campbell, *Prisoners of Poverty: Women Wage-Workers, Their Trades, and Their Lives* (Boston: Roberts Brothers, 1887).

83. "New York Cigar Makers," *Scientific American*, February 23, 1889, 113.

84. "Opinions about Labor," *New York Times*, August 28, 1883, 3; "The Senate Committee," *New York Times*, October 14, 1883, 2.

85. "The Investigation Mania," *New York Times*, September 7, 1883, 4.

86. US Department of Commerce and Labor, Bureau of Labor, *Laws Relating to the Employment of Women and Children in the United States*, chapter 564, "Employment of Children in Mines, Enacted March 3, 1891" (Washington, DC: GPO, July 1907, 145).

87. "Sweating System Inquiry," *New York Times*, April 14, 1892, 3.

88. "Sweating-System Evils," *New York Times*, January 21, 1893, 10.

89. US House of Representatives, 52nd Cong., 2d Sess., Report of the Committee on Manufactures on the Sweating System, Report No. 2309, January 20, 1893.

90. "Factories of New York: Annual Report of State Inspector O'Leary," *New York Times*, January 18, 1897, 3.

91. US Industrial Commission, Final Report (Washington, DC: GPO, 1902), 19: 917–918.

92. Ibid., 917.

93. Ibid., 919.

94. *Third Biennial Report of the Bureau of Labor Statistics of the State of Colorado,* 1891–1892, 142–143, excerpted in Abbott, *The Child and the State,* 418.

95. "Wisconsin Children at Work: Their Condition More Serious Than in Any Other State of the Union," *New York Times,* June 17, 1895, 8.

96. Ibid.

97. Elizabeth Brandeis, "Section III: Labor Legislation," in *History of Labor in the U.S., 1896–1932,* in John R. Commons et al. (New York: Macmillan, 1932), 626.

98. James D. Schmidt, *Industrial Violence and the Legal Origins of Child Labor* (New York: Cambridge University Press, 2010).

99. Brandeis, "Section III: Labor Legislation," 626.

100. "Child Labor in the United States," 25. The following states had organized labor bureaus, with the dates of their organization: 1869, Massachusetts; 1872, Pennsylvania; 1877, Ohio; 1878, New Jersey; 1879, Illinois; 1883, New York; 1883, Michigan; 1883, Wisconsin; 1884, Iowa; 1885, Connecticut; 1879, Indiana; 1883, Missouri; 1883, California; 1884, Maryland; 1885, Kansas; 1887, Rhode Island; 1887, Maine; 1887, Colorado; 1887, Minnesota; 1887, North Carolina; 1887, Nebraska.

101. By 1890, eight states provided for factory inspectors: Massachusetts, New York, New Jersey, Ohio, Wisconsin, Connecticut, Maine, and Rhode Island. Illinois joined the list in 1892.

102. Parsons, "Child Slavery in America," 124.

103. Rufus R. Wade, *First National Convention of Factory Inspectors* (Columbus, OH: Myers Brothers, 1887), 46. Inspectors from seven states attended the convention.

104. International Association of Factory Inspectors, Second Annual Convention, 1888, 33.

105. Mary Gay Humphreys, "The Consumers' League Holds an Annual Meeting," *Harper's Bazaar,* June 21, 1890, 23, 25.

106. "It's Work for Women: The Consumers' League Holds an Annual Meeting," *New York Times,* February 13, 1896, 10.

107. The states were Illinois (1897), Minnesota (1895), and Wisconsin (1899). See Johnson, "Child Labor Legislation," 416.

108. A. J. McKelway, "Child Labor in Southern Industry," *American Academy of Political and Social Science* 25 (May 1905): 431.

109. "Child Labor," *The Independent,* August 21, 1902, 2032.

110. "Georgia for Child Labor: A Bill to Restrict It Killed Because of Its New England Backing," *New York Times,* November 10, 1897, 1.

111. The 700-page Eighth Annual Report of Factory Inspectors for New York found the number of children under sixteen employed in 1893 to have been a fraction under 34 in each 1,000 persons, as against 38 out of 1,000 in 1892, and 112 per thousand in 1887. The report concluded: "The continued reduction in the number of children employed indicates that manufacturers are becoming convinced by experience that child labor is not cheap labor, and also indicates that a greater interest is taken by parents in the education of their offspring." "Factory Report," *New York Times,* February 1, 1894, 3. A detailed historical review of Connecticut's child labor

laws also concluded that by 1900, the restrictions had been effective in reducing the employment of children in factories. "Child Labor in the United States," *American Economic Association* 8, no. 3 (August 1907): 1.

112. Johnson, "Child Labor Legislation," 405.

113. *Eighth Biennial Report of the Bureau of Labor and Industrial Statistics*, State of Wisconsin, 1897–98, 491.

Chapter 2. Divided, We Fall: The Beveridge-Parsons Bill

1. John Braeman, "Albert J. Beveridge and the First National Child Labor Law," *Indiana Magazine of History* 60, no. 1 (March 1964): 9.

2. Edgar Gardner Murphy, *Problems of the Present South* (New York: Macmillan, 1904), 142.

3. Elizabeth Sands Johnson, "Child Labor Legislation," in John R. Commons et al., *History of Labor in the United States*, 4 vols., volume 3, *Working Conditions* (New York: Macmillan, 1935), 412.

4. Murphy, *Problems of the Present South*.

5. The Southern Education Board was founded at Winston-Salem, North Carolina, in 1901 as the executive board of the Conference for Education in the South. The group collected information, reported on educational conditions in the region, and promoted public education, primarily in rural areas of the South.

6. Stephen C. Compton, "Edgar Gardner Murphy and the Child Labor Movement," *Historical Magazine of the Protestant Episcopal Church* 52, no. 2 (June 1983): 181–194, 190; Murphy, *Problems of the Present South*.

7. Murphy, *Problems of the Present South*, 129.

8. Stephen B. Wood, *Constitutional Politics in the Progressive Era: Child Labor and the Law* (Chicago: University of Chicago Press, 1968), 10.

9. Braeman, "Albert J. Beveridge and the First National Child Labor Law," 13.

10. See Alexander J. McKelway, "The Evil of Child Labor: Why the South Should Favor a National Law," *Outlook*, February 16, 1907, 360.

11. "National Effort to Solve Child Labor Problem," *New York Times*, November 27, 1904, SM8.

12. Johnson, "Child Labor Legislation," 409.

13. Minutes of the first general meeting of the National Child Labor Committee, April 15, 1904, National Child Labor Committee Papers, Manuscript Division, Library of Congress, Washington, DC.

14. "Evils of Child Labor," *New York Observer and Chronicle*, 83, no. 9 (March 2, 1905): 280.

15. Alexander J. McKelway, "Child Labor in the Southern Cotton Mills," *Annals of the American Academy* (March 1906): 1–11, and "The Child Labor Problem: A Study in Degeneracy," *Annals of the American Academy of Political and Social Science* (May 1906): 135–147; Owen R. Lovejoy, "Child Labor in the Glass Industry," *Annals of the American Academy of Political and Social Science* (March 1906): 42–53, and "Child Labor in the Coal Mines," *Annals of the American Academy of Political and Social Science* (March 1906): 35–41.

16. Elizabeth Van Vorst, "The Cry of the Children," lead article of series, *Sat-*

urday Evening Post, March 10, 1906, 1–3, 28–29. Van Vorst and her sister worked undercover as factory operatives, and the articles detailed the conditions in Alabama mills. The articles were developed into a book, Elizabeth Van Vorst, *The Cry of the Children: A Study of Child-Labor* (New York: Moffat, Yard, 1908).

17. "A Plea for Reform in Child-Labor Laws," *Literary Digest*, October 20, 1906, 537.

18. "*The Cosmopolitan*'s Readers Agree That This Disgrace Must Go," *The Cosmopolitan*, November 1906, 109.

19. "Child Labor and the Consumers' League," *Friends' Intelligencer*, February 24, 1906, 124.

20. Florence Kelley, "Wanted: A New Standard Child Labor Bill," *Child Labor Bulletin* 7 (May 1917): 32.

21. Theodore Roosevelt, "Fourth Annual Message to Congress," December 6, 1904, *The American Presidency Project*, Gerhard Peters and John T. Woolley. http://www.presidency.ucsb.edu/ws/?pid=29545 (accessed March 26, 2017).

22. Samuel McCune Lindsay, "The National Child Labor Meetings," *Federation Bulletin* (February 1906): 221–222.

23. Theodore Roosevelt to Edgar D. Crumpacker, May 12, 1906, quoted in Braeman, "Albert J. Beveridge and the First National Child Labor Law," 16.

24. Theodore Roosevelt to William Howard Taft, March 15, 1906, *The Letters of Theodore Roosevelt*, ed. Elting E. Morrison et al., 8 vols. (Cambridge, MA: Harvard University Press 1951–1954), 5: 183; John Braeman, "Albert J. Beveridge and the First National Child Labor Law," 1.

25. Braeman, "Albert J. Beveridge and the First National Child Labor Law," 17.

26. The British inspector-general reported that 40–60 percent of the recruits were unfit for military duty. Senator Beveridge asserted that the physical inferiority of recruits resulted from labor in factories and mines, often at an early age. His remarks were prescient. Prior to World War II, thousands of potential American recruits were deemed too illiterate or physically unfit for wartime service.

27. Beveridge to John C. Shaffer, November 20, 1906, Albert J. Beveridge Papers. Manuscript Division, Library of Congress, Washington, DC.

28. Braeman, "Albert J. Beveridge and the First National Child Labor Law," 17–18.

29. Samuel M. Lindsay to Rev. Edgar Gardner Murphy, November 24, 1906, Edgar Gardner Murphy Papers, #1041, Southern Historical Collection, The Wilson Library, University of North Carolina at Chapel Hill.

30. Francis G. Caffey to Edgar Gardner Murphy, November 30, 1906, Murphy Papers.

31. Senator Albert J. Beveridge to President Theodore Roosevelt, November 24, 1906, Beveridge Papers.

32. Theodore Roosevelt, Sixth Annual Message, December 3, 1906. Online by Gerhard Peters and John T. Woolley, *The American Presidency Project*, http://www.presidency.ucsb.edu/ws/?pid=29547.

33. "Senator Scott on Child Labor," *Crockery and Glass Journal*, January 17, 1907, 27.

34. Albert J. Beveridge, "Child Labor and the Nation," *Annals of the American*

Academy of Political and Social Science 29 (January 1907): 115–124, at 121. This is the speech Beveridge made at that National Child Labor Committee's Annual Conference in December 1906.

35. Braeman, "Albert J. Beveridge and the First National Child Labor Law," 20.

36. Samuel McCune Lindsay, "Child Labor and the Republic," *Federation Bulletin* 5 (February 1907): 182.

37. Samuel McCune Lindsay to George Foster Peabody, January 25, 1907, Murphy Papers.

38. Beveridge, "Child Labor and the Nation."

39. Lindsay, "Child Labor and the Republic," 181.

40. Beveridge, "Child Labor and the Nation," 123.

41. "For a Child Labor Law," *New York Times*, December 21, 1906, 6.

42. Claude G. Bowers, *Beveridge and the Progressive Era* (New York: The Literary Guild, 1932), 251.

43. Edgar Gardner Murphy to Felix Adler, December 18, 1906, attached to the minutes of the fourteenth meeting of the Board of Trustees of the National Child Labor Committee, January 29, 1907, National Child Labor Committee Papers.

44. Shelley Sallee, *The Whiteness of Child Labor Reform in the New South* (Athens: University of Georgia Press, 2004), 110.

45. "Real Child Labor Reform," *New York Times*, March 15, 1907, 8.

46. President Theodore Roosevelt to Edgar Gardner Murphy, November 15, 1907, Murphy Papers.

47. Dr. B. J. Baldwin, "History of Child Labor Reform in Alabama," *Annals of the American Academy of Political and Social Science* 38 (July 1911): 111–113.

48. Braeman, "Albert J. Beveridge and the First National Child Labor Law," 22.

49. Ibid. *Report of Proceedings of the Twenty-Sixth Annual Convention of the American Federation of Labor* (Washington, DC: National Tribune, 1907): 164.

50. Senator Albert J. Beveridge to President Theodore Roosevelt, October 22, 1907, Beveridge Papers.

51. President Theodore Roosevelt to Senator Beveridge, November 12, 1907, Beveridge Papers.

52. Committee on the Judiciary, Jurisdiction and Authority of Congress over the Subject of Woman and Child Labor, H.R. Rep. No. 59-7304 (1907).

53. "Heresy from Washington," *New York Times*, February 8, 1907, 8.

54. Braeman, "Albert J. Beveridge and the First National Child Labor Law," 25.

55. The 59th Congress tackled a variety of reforms. According to the House archives, Congress granted the Interstate Commerce Commission railroad enforcement powers; charged the Agriculture Department with inspecting meatpacking facilities; passed the Pure Food and Drug Act; prohibited corporations from contributing to political campaigns; and established the Bureau of Immigration and Naturalization.

56. Bowers, *Beveridge and the Progressive Era*, 253.

57. "Senator Beveridge Declares Regulation of Child Labor a National Problem," in Grace Abbott, *The Child and the State*, vol. 1, *Legal Status in the Family Apprenticeship and Child Labor* (New York: Greenwood Press, reprinted 1968), 475.

58. *Congressional Record*, 41, Senate, 1802–1820 (1907).

59. *Congressional Record*, 41, Senate, 1805 (1907).

60. Bowers, *Beveridge and the Progressive Era*, 253.

61. William Carey Jones, "The Child Labor Decision," *California Law Review* 6, no. 6 (September 1918): 395.

62. "Beveridge Makes a Great Speech," *Aberdeen Daily American*, January 24, 1907.

63. *Congressional Record*, 41, Senate, January 28 (1907), 1807.

64. Ibid., 1808.

65. Ibid.

66. For a discussion of these issues, see Logan Everett Sawyer III, "Constitutional Principle, Partisan Calculation, and the Beveridge Child Labor Bill," *Law and History Review* (May 2013): 325–353.

67. Ibid., 341–342.

68. *Champion v. Ames*, 188 U.S. 321 (1903), 357–358.

69. *Congressional Record*, 41, 1872–1875.

70. "Children's Rights and States' Rights," *Literary Digest*, February 9, 1907, 194.

71. "Practicability of a Federal Child-Labor Law," *Literary Digest*, December 22, 1906, 930.

72. "Child Labor Laws," *New York Times*, January 28, 1907, 6.

73. "Practicability of a Federal Child-Labor Law," 930.

74. Beveridge to Theodore Roosevelt, October 22, 1907, 2–3, Beveridge Papers.

75. Ibid., 5–6.

76. *Champion v. Ames*, 188 U.S. 321 (1903).

77. Beveridge to Theodore Roosevelt, October 22, 1907, 7, Beveridge Papers.

78. President Theodore Roosevelt to Senator Beveridge, November 7, 1907, Beveridge Papers.

79. Senator Albert J. Beveridge to President Roosevelt, November 11, 1907, Beveridge Papers.

80. "Church Fights Child Labor," *Kalamazoo Gazette*, October 12, 1907.

81. McKelway, "The Evil of Child Labor," 360.

82. Senator Albert J. Beveridge to President Roosevelt, October 28, 1907, Beveridge Papers.

83. Owen R. Lovejoy to Edgar Gardner Murphy, January 6, 1908, Murphy Papers.

84. Samuel McCune Lindsay to Beveridge, November 27, 1907, Beveridge Papers.

85. Florence Kelley to son, November 10, 1907, reel 4, Florence Kelley Papers, microfilm, New York Public Library. Quoted in Sallee, *The Whiteness of Child Labor Reform in the New South*, 110.

86. Bowers, *Beveridge and the Progressive Era*, 266.

87. Robert H. Bremmer, *Children and Youth in America: A Documentary History* (Cambridge, MA: Harvard University Press, 1971), 687.

88. US Bureau of Labor, *Report on Condition of Woman and Child Wage-Earners in the United States*, 61st Cong., 2d Sess. (Washington, DC: GPO, 1910).

89. US Congress, "Special Message of the President of the United States Communicated to the Two Houses of Congress," March 25, 1908, 60th Cong., 1st Sess., Senate document 406, 1.

90. "Child Labor Bill Passed," *New York Times*, May 10, 1908, 7; "Another Child Labor Law," *Youth's Companion*, June 18, 1908, 294; "Progress in Child Labor Laws," *Zion's Herald*, January 6, 1909, 3.

91. "Senate Laughs at Crane," *New York Times*, January 12, 1909, 3.

92. Beveridge to John Lindon Smith, September 27, 1909, Beveridge Papers.

Chapter 3. Regulating Child Labor as Interstate Commerce: The Keating-Owen Act and *Hammer v. Dagenhart*

1. William J. Novak, *The People's Welfare: Law and Regulation in Nineteenth-Century America* (Chapel Hill: University of North Carolina Press, 1996), 13–16. Novak argues that prior to the Civil War, local government officials and private groups used police powers to promote a common-law vision of a "well-regulated society" based on the people's welfare. In the post–Civil War period, police powers and social and economic regulation were constitutionalized and transformed. The connection between private rights and local self-government gave way to an American liberalism that strictly separated private rights and public power in pursuit of a centralized state and individualized citizen. In the antebellum period, moral minorities also used local police powers to advance the morals of the people by promoting public observation of the Christian Sabbath, temperance, and abolitionism. See Kyle G. Volk, *Moral Minorities and the Making of American Democracy* (New York: Oxford University Press, 2014).

2. *Lawton v. Steele*, 152 U.S. 133 (1894).

3. *Slaughterhouse Cases*, 83 U.S. 16 Wall. 36 (1873), 122.

4. Matthew S. Bewig, "*Lochner v. The Journeymen Bakers of New York*: The Journeymen Bakers, Their Hours of Labor, and the Constitution," *American Journal of Legal History* 38, no. 4 (October 1994): 413–451.

5. See Paul Kens, Lochner v. New York: *Economic Regulation on Trial* (Lawrence: University Press of Kansas, 1998), 13.

6. *Lochner v. New York*, 198 U.S. 45 (1905), 58.

7. *Lochner v. New York*, Harlan dissenting, 70.

8. *Lochner v. New York*, Holmes dissenting, 75. Justice Holmes was referring to Herbert Spencer's book *Social Statics*, published in 1851. Spencer applied an extreme form of economic and social laissez faire to society, which he later called "survival of the fittest" and critics called Social Darwinism.

9. Progressive-Era critics of the *Lochner* decision took their cue from Justice Harlan's and Justice Holmes's dissenting opinions. For example, Professor Ernest Freund reiterated Justice Harlan's argument that the majority had substituted its view of policy for that of the New York legislature. Ernest Freund, "Limitation of Hours of Labor and the Federal Supreme Court," *Green Bag* 17 (June 1905): 411. Others repeated Justice Holmes's argument that the Court was enacting Spencer's *Social Statics*. Learned Hand, "Due Process of Law and the Eight-Hour Day," *Harvard Law Review* 21, no. 7 (May 1908): 495–509; Roscoe Pound, "Liberty of Contract," *Yale Law Journal* 18, no. 7 (1909): 454–487; Charles Warren, "The New 'Liberty' under the Fourteenth Amendment," *Harvard Law Review* 39, no. 4 (February 1926): 431–465. For a contemporary criticism, see David A. Strauss, "Why Was Lochner Wrong?" *University of Chicago Law Review* 70, no. 1 (Winter 2003): 373–386. Strauss argues that

the Supreme Court was correct to recognize a freedom of contract but wrong in elevating it to a fundamental right that can almost never be abrogated.

10. Benjamin Wright, *The Growth of American Constitutional Law* (Boston, MA: Houghton Mifflin published for New York: Reynal and Hitchcock, 1942). Wright identified nearly two hundred cases where the Court invalidated labor and social welfare legislation. But the Court also upheld many regulatory provisions. See Howard Gillam, *The Constitution Besieged: The Rise and Demise of Lochner Era Police Powers Jurisprudence* (Durham, NC: Duke University Press, 1993); Michael J. Phillips, *The Lochner Court, Myth and Reality: Substantive Due Process from the 1890s–1930s* (Westport, CT: Praeger, 2001). Professor Phillips concludes that the Court's substantive due process decisions were more Progressive than previously thought and that in some cases, the Court was justified in striking down legislation.

11. *In re Spencer*, 149 Cal. 396, 86 Pac. 896 (1906). See also *Ex Parte Weber*, 149 Cal. 392 (1906).

12. *State v. Shorey*, 48 Oregon 396 (1906).

13. *Inland Steel Co. v. Yedinak*, 172 Ind. 423 (1909), 430; 87 N.E. 229.

14. Louisiana, *State v. Rose*, 51 So. 496 (La. 1910); Minnesota, *Fitzgerald v. International Flax Twine Co.* 104 Minn. 138 (1908); New Jersey, *Bryant v. Skillman Hardware Co.*, 76 N.J. 45 (1908); New York, *People v. Taylor*, 192 N.Y. 398 (1908); and Oregon, *State v. Shorey*, 86 P. 881 (Ore. 1906).

15. "Child Labor Law Defied," *New York Times*, December 19, 1912, 24.

16. US Bureau of Labor, *Report on Condition of Woman and Child Wage-Earners in the United States*, vol. 1; *Cotton Textile Industry* (61st Cong., 2d Sess., Senate Doc. 645, Washington, DC, 1910), in Grace Abbott, *The Child and the State*, vol. 1, *Legal Status in the Family Apprenticeship and Child Labor* (New York: Greenwood Press, 1968), 360.

17. Russell Freedman, *Kids at Work: Lewis Hine and the Crusade against Child Labor* (New York: Clarion Books, 1994), 26.

18. Kriste Lindenmeyer, *"A Right to Childhood": The U.S. Children's Bureau and Child Welfare, 1912–1946* (Champaign: University of Illinois Press, 1997); Robyn Muncy, *Creating a Female Dominion in American Reform, 1890–1935* (New York: Oxford University Press, 1992).

19. "Opposed to Federal Children's Bureau," *New York Times*, January 28, 1912, 14.

20. Walter I. Trattner, *Crusade for the Children* (Chicago: Quadrangle Books, 1970), 119.

21. Muncy, *Creating a Female Dominion in American Reform, 1890–1935*, 38–65.

22. Samuel Gompers, "To Conserve Child Life," *American Federationist*, 20, Part 1 (1913): 306.

23. For an excellent discussion of child labor reform and birth registration, see Susan J. Pearson, "'Age Ought to Be a Fact': The Campaign against Child Labor and the Rise of the Birth Certificate," *Journal of American History* 101, 4 (March 2015): 1144–1165.

24. Hon. Theodore Roosevelt, "Purposes and Policies of the Progressive Party," before the Progressive Convention in Chicago, Illinois, August 6, 1912. Printed in 62d Cong., 2d Sess., Document No. 904, Washington, DC, August 9, 1912, 13–14.

25. "Roosevelt Hits Judiciary and Humane Laws," *Albuquerque Journal*, September 22, 1914.

26. "Wilson and Child Labor," *New York Times*, August 9, 1916, 10.

27. "Wilson Captures Social Workers," *New York Times*, January 27, 1913, 1.

28. Ibid.

29. *Hoke v. United States*, 227 U.S. 308 (1913), 317–318.

30. For a discussion of the social origins and enforcement of the Mann Act, including *Hoke v. United States*, see David J. Langum, *Crossing over the Line: Legislating Morality and the Mann Act* (Chicago: University Press of Chicago, 1994).

31. *Hoke v. United States*, 322.

32. Ibid., 323.

33. *Sturges & Burn Manufacturing Co. v. Beauchamp*, 231 U.S. 320 (1913), 324, 326.

34. David Bernstein, *Rehabilitating Lochner: Defending Individual Rights against Progressive Reform* (Chicago: University of Chicago Press, 2011).

35. Owen R. Lovejoy, "Child Labor Ten Years After," Tenth Annual Report of the General Secretary, *Child Labor Bulletin* 3, no. 3 (November 1914): Table, 8. A few states may have been omitted from the list if exemptions severely weakened the restrictions.

36. Ibid.

37. Ibid., 9.

38. Samuel McCune Lindsay, "National Child Labor Standards," Proceedings of the Tenth Annual Conference on Child Labor, *Child Labor Bulletin* 3, no. 1 (May 1914): 26.

39. Arizona, Arkansas, Illinois, Kentucky, Massachusetts, New York, Ohio, Oklahoma, and Wisconsin. US Department of Labor, Children's Bureau, Publication 10.

40. "Start Campaign to Stop Child Labor," *New York Times*, January 9, 1914, 10.

41. Raymond G. Fuller, *Child Labor and the Constitution* (New York: Thomas Y. Crowell, 1923), 237.

42. Owen R. Lovejoy, "The Federal Government and Child Labor: A Brief for the Palmer-Owen Child Labor Bill," National Child Labor Committee, Pamphlet No. 216, March 1914, 4.

43. Ibid, 13.

44. National Child Labor Committee, Report of the General Secretary to the Fortieth Meeting of the Board of Trustees (April 20, 1914), NCLC Papers, Box 7, Library of Congress.

45. Elizabeth Sands Johnson, "Child Labor Legislation," in John R. Commons et al., *History of Labor in the United States*, 4 vols., volume 3, *Working Conditions* (New York: Macmillan, 1935), 440.

46. Bart Dredge, "David Clark's 'Campaign of Enlightenment': Child Labor and the Farmers' States Rights League, 1911–1940," *North Carolina Historical Review* 91, no. 1 (January 2014): 30–62, 34.

47. "Denies Child Labor Tales," *New York Times*, January 7, 1915, 10.

48. Ibid.

49. Fuller, *Child Labor and the Constitution*, 237–238.

50. 64th US Congress, Keating-Owen Act, September 1, 1916, ch. 432, 39 Stat. 675.

51. Edward Keating, "Federal Child Labor Legislation," Proceedings of the Twelfth Annual Conference, *Child Labor Bulletin* 5 (May 1916–February 1917): 68.

52. "Ohio Adopts a Higher Standard in 1913," in Abbott, *The Child and the State*, vol. 1, 335.

53. House Report, No. 46, 64th Cong. 1st Sess., 12.

54. Ibid., 11.

55. *Congressional Record*, Hearings before the Committee on Labor on H.R. 8234, 64th Cong., 1st Sess., January 10–12, 1916, 239.

56. Ibid.

57. Senate Report, No. 358, 64th Cong. 1st Sess., 21.

58. Ibid., 16.

59. Arden J. Lea, "Cotton Textiles and the Federal Child Labor Act of 1916," *Labor History* 16, no. 4 (1975): 490.

60. "Debate Child Labor Bill: Divergent Views Advanced in Senate on Its Constitutionality," *New York Times*, August 5, 1916, 16.

61. *Congressional Record*, 64th Cong., 1st Sess. 1916, LIII, Part 12, p. 12064; Part 2, 1571.

62. "President Urges Child Labor Bill," *The Independent*, July 31, 1916, 150.

63. Committee on Interstate Commerce, US Senate, James A. Emery, Argument in Opposition to the Form and Validity of the Keating Child Labor Bill, Monday, February 21, 1916.

64. Ibid., 9.

65. "Debate Child Labor Bill," 16.

66. "Overman Opposes Child Labor Bill," *New York Times*, August 8, 1916, 5. Senator Husting voted for the Keating-Owen Act, but he was accidentally killed by his brother a year later while duck hunting.

67. Keating, "Federal Child Labor Legislation," 61.

68. "Overman Opposes Child Labor Bill," 5.

69. Keating, "Federal Child Labor Legislation," 67.

70. Arthur Stanley Link, *Wilson: Campaigns for Progressivism and Peace, 1916–1917*, vol. 5 (Princeton, NJ: Princeton University Press, 1965).

71. Beth Behn, "A Principled Shift: Woodrow Wilson and the Keating-Owen Child Labor Bill," unpublished conference paper presented at the Midwest Political Science Association annual meeting, Chicago, IL, April 3, 2008, 28.

72. "The President and the Mill-Child," *Literary Digest*, August 5 1916, 290.

73. Keating, "Federal Child Labor Legislation," 60.

74. "The Democrats' Child-Labor Law," *Literary Digest*, September 2, 1916, 547.

75. "Signs Child Labor Bill," *New York Times*, September 2, 1916, 4.

76. "The Democrats' Child-Labor Law," 547.

77. Ibid., 548.

78. Excerpts from "Administration of the First Federal Child Labor Law," US Children's Bureau Publication No. 78, Washington, DC, 1921, in Abbott, *The Child and the State*, vol. 1, 493.

79. *Hammer v. Dagenhart*, transcript of record, No. 704, October term 1917, 2.

80. "Child Labor Act Declared Invalid," *New York Times*, September 1, 1917, 11.

81. "Author of Child Labor Law Says It Will Be Held Good," *Labor Journal*, September 14, 1917, 3.

82. Brief for the Appellant, *Hammer v. Dagenhart*, 9.

83. Ibid., 10.

84. Enacted in May 1813, the Connecticut law required employers to provide some schooling in the areas of reading, writing, and mathematics. Additionally, owners were responsible for the moral instruction of their young employees, including a requirement that all working children participate in religious worship. The law, however, did not address the minimum age of the workers or their maximum hours.

85. *Hammer v. Dagenhart*, 247 U.S. 251 (1918), at 271–272.

86. Ibid., 275.

87. As reported in the *Congressional Register*: When Representative Thomas Tucker of South Carolina moved on August 18, 1789, to insert the word "expressly" into what became the Tenth Amendment, Madison "objected to this amendment, because it was impossible to confine a government to the exercise of express powers; there must necessarily be admitted powers by implication, unless the constitution descended to recount every minutiae. He [Madison] remembered the word 'expressly' had been moved in the convention of Virginia, by the opponents to the ratification, and after full and fair discussion was given up by them, and the system allowed to retain its present form." Tucker's amendment was voted down. Three days later, Elbridge Gerry made a similar motion, but he was supported by only one-fifth of the members present. Neil H. Cogan, ed., *The Complete Bill of Rights: The Drafts, Debates, Sources, and Origins* (New York: Oxford University Press, 1997), 665–683.

88. Ibid., 276.

89. *Hammer v. Dagenhart*, dissenting opinion, 280.

90. Ibid., Holmes dissenting, 280.

91. Ibid., 281.

92. "Child Labor Law Upset by the Court," *New York Times*, June 4, 1918, 14.

93. "The Child Labor Decision," *New York Times*, June 5, 1918, 10.

94. "Protecting the Little Ones," *Life*, July 25, 1918, 128.

95. Thurlow M. Gordon, "The Child Labor Law Case," *Harvard Law Review* 32, no. 45 (1918–1919): 45–67, 52.

96. Ibid., 55.

97. William Carey Jones, "The Child Labor Decision," *California Law Review* 6, no. 6 (September 1918): 395–417, 402.

98. Article III, § 2, Clause 2 of the US Constitution reads: "In all Cases affecting Ambassadors, other public Ministers and Consuls, and those in which a State shall be Party, the [S]upreme Court shall have original Jurisdiction. In all the other Cases before mentioned, the Supreme Court shall have appellate Jurisdiction, both as to Law and Fact, with such Exceptions, and under such Regulations as the Congress shall make."

99. "Dispensing with the Courts," *New York Times*, June 7, 1918, 12.

100. John A. Ryan, "The Supreme Court and Child Labor," *Catholic World* (November 1918): 222–223. Ryan believed that the closely divided opinion in *Hammer v. Dagenhart* held hope that it would soon be overturned. He based this belief on "powerful support from social thought of our times and the whole logic of events."

101. "Criticizes Supreme Court: Senator Owen Thinks It's Time to Apply the Recall," *New York Times*, July 29, 1.

102. "Opposed to Federal Children's Bureau," 14.

Chapter 4. Taxing Profits of Companies Using Child Labor: Bailey v. Drexel Furniture Company

1. The one state was not specified. See US Department of Labor, *Seventh Annual Report of the Chief*, Children's Bureau, June 30, 1919, 21; "Child Labor and the War," *Monthly Labor Review* 10 (February 1920): 174; "Child Labor Grows as Effect of War," *New York Times*, January 4, 1920, 14.

2. *Report of the Secretary of Labor*, 66th Cong., 2d Sess., House of Representatives, Doc. 422, Washington, DC, 1920, 740; "Labor Shortage Forcing Children of School Age to Work," *New York Tribune*, June 16, 1918, Sec. 3, 6.

3. "Labor Shortage Forcing Children of School Age to Work," *New York Times*, October 13, 1918, 21.

4. Ibid.

5. National Child Labor Committee, Pamphlet, "What Shall We Do for the Children in Time of War?" (February 1918).

6. "Call Children from War Plants," *New York Times*, November 24, 1918, 8.

7. "The Government and Child Labor," *Child Labor Bulletin* 7, no. 2 (August 1918): 80.

8. "New Move in Senate on Child Labor," *New York Times*, June 20, 1918, 11.

9. Minutes of the Board of Trustees, NCLC, June 7, 1918.

10. "The New Child Labor Bill," *The Independent*, September 14, 1918, 343.

11. "Child Labor and Man Power," *Outlook*, November 6, 1918, 331.

12. Stephen B. Wood, *Congressional Politics in the Progressive Era: Child Labor and the Law* (Chicago: University of Chicago Press, 1968), 194.

13. Report of the Executive Council, "Child Labor Legislation," *American Federationist* 26, no. 2 (August 1919): 724.

14. Wood, *Congressional Politics in the Progressive Era*, 204.

15. *McCray v. United States*, 195 U.S. 27 (1904).

16. The dairy industry also convinced states to ban the use of the yellow dye used in margarine. Margarine producers provided a separate packet of dye that consumers had to add to the product to make it look like butter. Several states even enacted laws requiring oleomargarine producers to dye their product an unappealing pink color to turn away customers.

17. Wood, *Congressional Politics in the Progressive Era*, 197.

18. "State Rights and the Child Labor Tax Law," *Columbia Law Review* 22, no. 7 (November 1922): 659–662.

19. *Veazie Bank v. Fenno*, 8 Wall. (U.S.) 533 (1869).

20. *United States v. Doremus*, 249 U.S. 86 (1919), 93.

21. Wood, *Congressional Politics in the Progressive Era*, 206–207. Wood credits David Clark with devising the strategy of loading the *Congressional Record*, which turned out to be an effective plan.

22. "Conscience, Congress, and the Constitution," *Child Labor Bulletin* 7, no. 4 (February 1919): 230.

23. Ibid.

24. *Congressional Record*, 65th Cong., 3d Sess., December 18, 1918, 618.

25. "Conscience, Congress, and the Constitution," 233.

26. *Congressional Record*, 65th Cong., 3d Sess., 611.

27. Ibid.

28. Ibid.

29. *Congressional Record*, 65th Cong., 3d. Sess., 3029–3033.

30. See Ajay K. Mehrotra, *Making the Modern Fiscal State: Law, Politics, and the Rise of Progressive Taxation, 1877–1929* (Cambridge, UK: Cambridge University Press, 2013).

31. "A New Weapon against Child Labor," *Literary Digest*, January 4, 1919, 14.

32. Ibid.

33. Ibid.

34. Ibid.

35. Despite the assurances from Senator Pomerene, the Labor Department was never used in the implementation of the law. The treasury secretary established a special enforcement section within the Internal Revenue Bureau to collect the tax. Although this administrative structure strengthened the view that the statute was a revenue measure, it worried opponents of child labor and ultimately failed to convince the Court.

36. "Children's Bureau Conference on Child-Welfare Standards," *Monthly Labor Review* 8 (June 1919): 216–220, 219.

37. Ibid., 220.

38. Raymond Garfield Fuller, *Child Labor and the Constitution* (New York: Thomas Y. Crowell, 1923), 222.

39. Legislative Committee Report, "Child Labor," *American Federationist* 26 (December 1919): 1146.

40. Senator Irvine L. Lenroot, "Taxing Child Labor out of Industry," *Child Labor Bulletin* 7, no. 4 (February 1919): 255.

41. Wood, *Congressional Politics in the Progressive Era*, 223.

42. *George v. Bailey*, 274 F. 639 (1921).

43. "Court Overthrows Child Labor Law," *New York Times*, August 23, 1921, 31.

44. *George v. Bailey*, at 643; "Labor Laws and Court Decisions: Federal Child Labor Law Held Unconstitutional," *Monthly Labor Review* 13 (October 1921): 191–192.

45. A.F. of L. Attacks Child Labor Ruling," *New York Times*, August 24, 1921, 7.

46. NCLC, "Judge Boyd's Decision," *American Child* 1, no. 2 (August 1919): 76.

47. *Drexel Furniture Company v. Bailey*, 276 F. 452 (WD NC), December 10, 1921.

48. Wood, *Congressional Politics in the Progressive Era*, 262–263. According to NCLC files, the cost of enforcing the child labor tax exceeded the penalties collected.

49. *Drexel Furniture*, 454.

50. "Supreme Court Brief Quotes Shakespeare," *New York Times*, March 9, 1922, 8.

51. NCLC, "Argument for Constitutionality," *American Child* 1, no. 4 (February 1920): 279.

52. *Bailey v. Drexel Furniture Company*, Supreme Court of the United States, October term 1921, Abstract of Oral Argument for the Defendant in Error, No. 657, Wm. P. Bynum, 27, 29.

53. Ibid., 42.

54. Ibid., 50. Italics in original.

55. Ibid., 47. Italics in original.

56. *Bailey v. Drexel Furniture Company,* 259 U.S. 20 (1922), 37.

57. Ibid., 38–39.

58. Ibid., 40.

59. *Atherton Mills v. Johnston,* 259 U.S. 13 (1922), 15.

60. Alexander M. Bickel, *The Unpublished Opinions of Mr. Justice Brandeis* (Cambridge, MA: Belknap Press, Harvard University Press, 1957).

61. Clyde Spillenger, "Reading the Judicial Canon: Alexander Bickel and the Book of Brandeis," *Journal of American History* 79, no. 1 (June 1992): 125–151.

62. Ibid., 139.

63. Wood, *Constitutional Politics in the Progressive Era,* 247–251.

64. Louis D. Brandeis to Norman Hapgood, June 1, 1922, quoted in Alpheus Thomas Mason, *Brandeis: A Free Man's Life* (New York: Viking Press, 1956), 558.

65. Alpheus Thomas Mason, *The Supreme Court from Taft to Warren* (Baton Rouge: Louisiana State University Press, 1968), 57–58.

66. Wood, *Constitutional Politics in the Progressive Era,* 288.

67. Samuel Gompers, "Let Us Save the Children," *American Federationist* 24 (June 1922): 413. Quoted in Bernard Mandel, *Samuel Gompers: A Biography* (Yellow Springs, OH: Antioch Press, 1963), 499–500.

68. "State Laws Sought to Aid Child Labor," *New York Times,* May 17, 1922, 6.

69. "Is There No Protection?" *Outlook,* May 31, 1922, 199.

70. *Barron's,* "Involuntary Child Servitude," 2, no. 21 (May 22, 1922): 9.

71. Thomas Reed Powell, "Child Labor and the Constitution," *Child Labor Bulletin* 7, no. 4 (February 1919): 258.

72. Edward S. Corwin, "The Child Labor Decision," *New Republic* 26, no. 397 (July 12, 1922): 179.

73. Edward S. Corwin, "Constitutional Law in 1921–1922: The Constitutional Decisions of the Supreme Court of the United States in the October Term, 1921," *American Political Science Review* 16, no. 4 (November 1922): 615.

74. Ibid., 179.

75. "Is the Supreme Court Too Supreme?" *Literary Digest,* July 1, 1922, 21.

76. Ibid.

77. Ibid.

78. Fuller, *Child Labor and the Constitution,* 246.

79. "The Child-Labor Amendment," *Literary Digest,* September 16, 1922, 12.

Chapter 5. Congress Proposes the "Children's Amendment"

1. US senator Medill McCormick, "Child Labor Must Go," *American Federationist* 24, part II (September 1922): 644–645.

2. "Child Labor," *New York Times,* May 21, 1922, 38.

3. Julie Novkov, "Historicizing the Figure of the Child in Legal Discourse: The Battle over the Regulation of Child Labor," *American Journal of Legal History* 44, no. 4 (October 2000): 394.

4. Hoover's remark was made in an address to the American Child Hygiene Association, *American Child* 2 (November 1920): 204.

5. When George Gallup asked respondents in April 1936 if they would favor an "amendment to the Constitution giving Congress the power to limit, regulate, and prohibit the labor of persons under 18," 61 percent said yes. By early February 1937, support had increased to 76 percent. George H. Gallup, *The Gallup Poll: Public Opinion*, vol. 3, 1935–1971 (New York: Random House, 1972): 31.

6. Novkov, "Historicizing the Figure of the Child in Legal Discourse," 379.

7. George Lakoff, *Don't Think of an Elephant: Know Your Values and Frame the Debate* (White River Junction, VT: Chelsea Green Publishing, 2d rev. ed., 2014).

8. The six amendments were the Sixteenth (providing for a national income tax, ratified in 1913), the Seventeenth (authorizing direct election of Senators, 1913), the Eighteenth (implementing national prohibition, 1919), the Nineteenth (providing for women's suffrage in national elections, ratified in 1920), the Twentieth (establishing January as the month in which federal elected officials took office and providing for succession, added in 1933), and the Twenty-First (repealing prohibition, effective 1933).

9. Miriam Keeler, "The Child Labor Amendment: Its History and Prospects," *Social Science* 10, no. 3 (July 1935): 257–260.

10. "Child Labor Fight Reaches Senate," *New York Times*, May 4, 1924, XX10.

11. "State Rights Row Looms: Johnson's Move for Child Labor Regulation Draws Fire," *Kansas City Star*, May 20, 1922.

12. Ibid.

13. Bernard Mandel, *Samuel Gompers: A Biography* (Yellow Springs, OH: Antioch Press, 1963); "Organizes for Law to End Child Labor: Gompers Heads New Body Seeking Amendment to the Constitution," *New York Times*, June 2, 1922, 13.

14. Walter I. Trattner, *Crusade for the Children: A History of the National Child Labor Committee and Child Labor Reform in America* (Chicago: Quadrangle Books, 1970), 163.

15. Hearing before the Committee on the Judiciary, House of Representatives, 67th Cong., 2nd Sess., on H.J. Res. 327, June 1, 1922.

16. "Organizes for Law to End Child Labor," 13.

17. Ibid.

18. Hearing before the Committee on the Judiciary, Testimony of Owen R. Lovejoy, 14.

19. Ibid., Testimony of Florence Kelley, 17.

20. National Child Labor Committee, minutes on the Child Labor Amendment, June 9 1922. NCLC papers, Box 8, 1921–1926, Library of Congress.

21. The Supreme Court would not uphold broad powers for Congress to regulate labor conditions under the Commerce Clause until *National Labor Relations Board v. Jones and Laughlin Steel Co.* (1937).

22. National Child Labor Committee, minutes on the Child Labor Amendment, Box 8.

23. Ibid.

24. Felix Frankfurter, "Child Labor and the Court," *New Republic* 31, no. 399 (July 26, 1922): 248–250.

25. "La Fallotte Lashes Federal Judiciary," *New York Times*, June 15, 1922, 1.

26. Ibid, 2.

27. Warren G. Harding, Second Annual Message to Congress, December 8, 1922. The American Presidency Project, Gerhard Peters and John T. Woolley. http://www.presidency.ucsb.edu/ws/index.php?pid=29563 (accessed July 27, 2016).

28. NCLC, "Editorial Comment on the Child Labor Amendment," *American Child* 4, no. 4 (December 1922): 3.

29. Ibid.

30. Owen R. Lovejoy, "Child Labor and the Constitution," *American Child* 5, no. 1 (January 1923): 1.

31. Ibid.

32. Richard B. Sherman, "The Rejection of the Child Labor Amendment," *Mid-America: An Historical Review* 45, no. 1 (1963): 6. See also *Hearings before a Subcommittee of the Committee on the Judiciary*, US Senate, 67th Cong., 4th Sess., Child Labor Amendment to the Constitution, January 10, 1923.

33. David E. Kyvig, *Explicit and Authentic Acts: Amending the U.S. Constitution, 1776–1995* (Lawrence: University Press of Kansas, 1996), 257. See also Josephine Goldmark, *Impatient Crusader: Florence Kelley's Life Story* (Champaign: University of Illinois Press, 1953).

34. Lela B. Costin, *Two Sisters for Social Justice: A Biography of Grace and Edith Abbott* (Champaign: University of Illinois Press, 1983), 154.

35. Lowell Mellett, quoting King Lear, "How sharper than a serpent's tooth it is to have a thankless child," *Labor*, November 17, 1923. Interview excerpted in Grace Abbott, *The Child and the State*, vol. 1, *Legal Status in the Family Apprenticeship and Child Labor* (New York: Greenwood Press, reprinted 1968), 515–517.

36. NCLC, "Child Labor Amendment Favored by Newspapers," *American Child* 5, no. 10 (October 1923): 1.

37. "Text of President Coolidge's Address to Congress on the Affairs of the Nation," *New York Times*, December 7, 1923, 4.

38. "Child Labor Laws Urged in Congress," *New York Times*, December 24, 1923, 21.

39. NCLC, "Foes of the Amendment," *American Child* 6, no. 3 (March 1924): 2.

40. James A. Emery, "An Examination of the Proposed Twentieth Amendment to the Constitution of the United States: Being the So-Called Child Labor Amendment," in a legal pamphlet by the General Counsel of the National Association of Manufacturer (New York, 1924), 10.

41. Trattner, *Crusade for the Children*, 174. Later in the campaign against the amendment, the American Farm Bureau distributed a pamphlet entitled "National Child Labor Law or Socialistic Bureaucratic Control Supplanting Parental Control of Children, Plain Politics for Parents."

42. "Ban on Child Labor Opposed by Grange," *New York Times*, November 22, 1924, 20.

43. NCLC, "The Anvil Chorus," *American Child* 6, no. 3 (March 1924): 3–4.

44. NCLC, "Several Leading Agricultural Publications Favor Child Labor Amendment," *American Child* 6, no. 10 (October 1924): 6.

45. Ibid.

46. Costin, *Two Sisters for Social Justice*, 151.

47. Ibid., 152.

48. US Senate, 68th Congress, Report No. 406, "Child Labor Amendment," Prepared by Senator Shortridge, April 1924, 39.

49. NCLC, "The First Victory," *American Child* 6, no. 5 (May 1924): 1, 7.

50. Kyvig, *Explicit and Authentic Acts*, 257.

51. Trattner, *Crusade for the Children*, 167.

52. Ibid., 168.

53. "Amendment on Child Labor Goes to State Legislatures," *New York Times*, June 22, 1924, X12.

54. Kyvig, *Explicit and Authentic Acts*, 258.

55. J. E. Hulett, Jr., "Propaganda and the Proposed Child Labor Amendment," *Public Opinion Quarterly* 2, no. 1 (1938): 105–115.

56. Trattner, *Crusade for the Children*, 167.

57. J. E. Hulett, Jr., "Propaganda and the Proposed Child Labor Amendment," 105–115; see also Edward W. Macy, "Opposition Tactics against the Child Labor Amendment," *American Labor Legislation Review* 15 (December 1924): 110–114.

58. Sherman, "The Rejection of the Child Labor Amendment," 7.

59. "The Child Labor Amendment," *Constitutional Review* 9 (1925): 44–50.

60. Ibid, 50.

61. National Child Labor Committee, minutes on the Child Labor Amendment, September 16, 1924, NCLC papers, Box 8, 1921–1926, Library of Congress.

62. National Consumers' League, Files on Child Labor and Child Labor Amendment, Letter to Jane Addams, October 15, 1924, Reel 48, Library of Congress, Manuscript Division.

63. "The Child Labor Amendment's Defeat," *New Republic* 42 (May 20, 1925): 330–331.

64. Quoted in *Manufacturers' Record*, September 4, 1924.

65. Bill Kaufman, "The Child Labor Amendment Debate of the 1920s," in *Essays in Political Economy*, published by The Ludwig von Mises Institute, No. 16, November 1992. The quote is from congressional testimony over federal child labor legislation, *Congressional Record*, 2 (February 1916): 2025.

66. Costin, *Two Sisters for Social Justice*, 155.

67. Vincent A. McQuade, O.S.A., *The American Catholic Attitude on Child Labor Since 1891* (Washington, DC: Catholic University of America, 1938); Thomas R. Greene, "The Catholic Committee for the Ratification of the Child Labor Amendment, 1935–1937: Origins and Limits," *Catholic Historical Review* 74, no. 2 (April 1988): 248; George Q. Flynn, *American Catholics and the Roosevelt Presidency, 1932–1936* (Lexington: University Press of Kentucky, 1968) 109–110.

68. Dorothy Dunbar Bromley, "Child Labor Fight at a Critical Stage," *New York Times*, January 27, 1935, E6.

69. "High Cost of Government," *Manufacturers' News*, October 3, 1925, 12. See Abbott, *The Child and the State*, vol. 1, 547.

70. Novkov, "Historicizing the Figure of the Child in Legal Discourse," 398–399.

71. Ibid.

72. "What the Child Labor Amendment Means," *Manufacturers' Record*, September 4, 1924.

73. *Congressional Record*, 68th Cong., 1st Sess., 1924, 10122.

74. NCL, Reel 48, letter from Florence Kelley to Ida Clyde Clarke of the National Arts Club, October 3, 1924.

75. Evelyn V. Petersen, "The History of the Movement for a Child Labor Amendment in the United States." MA thesis, Department of History, University of Southern California, June 1931, 147.

76. *Manufacturers' Record*, 84 (September 11, 1924): 3.

77. The league was first exposed in January 1925 in an issue of *Labor*, a publication of railroad labor organizations. Representative Israel Foster, in a speech before the House on February 17, 1925, quoted much of the article. Senator Walsh of Montana also wrote an article that was reprinted in the *Congressional Record* on March 5, 1925. The revelations had little impact, however, because the damage had already been done.

78. Bart Dredge, "David Clark's 'Campaign of Enlightenment': Child Labor and the Farmers' States' Rights League, 1911–1940," *North Carolina Historical Review* 91, no. 1 (January 2014): 58–59.

79. W. A. Robinson, "Advisory Referendum in Massachusetts on the Child Labor Amendment," *American Political Science Review* 19 (1925): 69–73.

80. Trattner, *Crusade for the Children*, 175.

81. Robinson, "Advisory Referendum in Massachusetts on the Child Labor Amendment," 71.

82. Novkov, "Historicizing the Figure of the Child in Legal Discourse," 400. Louis A. Coolidge, Radio Address: *The Child Labor Amendment: An Appeal to the Christian Men and Women of Massachusetts* (1924). The text of the address is found in Box 2, folder 14, Alexander Lincoln papers, Arthur and Elizabeth Schlesinger Library, Harvard University.

83. Catholic University of America, American Catholic History Research Center and University Archives, "Catholic Responses to Industrialization." http://cuomeka.wrlc.org/exhibits/show/industrial/background/background—catholic-responses (accessed March 30, 2017).

84. Catholic University of America, American Catholic History Research Center and University Archives, "Conservative Critics and the End of Reform: The 1920s." http://cuomeka.wrlc.org/exhibits/show/bishops/hiatus/1919hiatus-intro (accessed March 30, 2017).

85. Robinson, "Advisory Referendum in Massachusetts on the Child Labor Amendment," 71.

86. "Child Labor Ban Urged in Pulpits," *New York Times*, January 26, 1925, 19.

87. NCLC minutes, December 24, 1924, Number 4.

88. California ratified on January 8, 1925, and Arizona on January 29.

89. NCL, Reel 48, letter from Florence Kelley to Laura Williams, January 7, 1925. Kelley noted that Governor Smith has "joined hands with Wadsworth on behalf of a referendum preceding every amendment, state or federal, to any Constitution."

90. Jeremy P. Felt, *Hostages of Fortune: Child Labor Reform in New York State* (Syracuse, NY: Syracuse University Press, 1965), 208.

91. NCLC minutes, March 18, 1925.

92. Sherman, "The Rejection of the Child Labor Amendment," 3.

93. Chaim M. Rosenberg, *Child Labor in America: A History* (Jefferson, NC: McFarland, 2013), 45. The quote is taken from the Foreword to Josephine Goldmark's book *Impatient Crusader: Florence Kelley's Life Story* (Urbana: University of Illinois Press, 1953).

94. Rosenberg, *Child Labor in America: A History*, 197.

95. Frances Perkins, "Secretary Perkins Pleads for Child Labor Amendment," *New York Times*, January 28, 1934, XX3.

96. Lillian Holmen Mohr, *Frances Perkins: "That Woman in FDR's Cabinet!"* (Great Barrington, MA: North River Press, 1979), 186.

Chapter 6. The Great Depression and the Renewed Fight over the Child Labor Amendment

1. NCLC minutes, January 30, 1933, Manuscript Reading Room, Library of Congress.

2. Michael Hiltzik, *The New Deal: A Modern History* (New York: Free Press, 2011).

3. John A. Fliter and Derek S. Hoff, *Fighting Foreclosure: The Blaisdell Case, the Contract Clause, and the Great Depression* (Lawrence: University Press of Kansas, 2012).

4. David E. Kyvig, *Explicit and Authentic Acts: Amending the U.S. Constitution, 1776–1995* (Lawrence: University Press of Kansas, 1996), 307.

5. "Texas Refuses to Ratify Child Labor Amendment," *New York Times*, February 9, 1934, 13. The Texas House passed the resolution, but the amendment was voted down in the Senate 17 to 11. In several states that considered the amendment, resolutions never made it out of committee.

6. Grace Abbott, *The Child and the State*, vol. 1, *Legal Status in the Family Apprenticeship and Child Labor* (New York: Greenwood Press, reprinted 1968), 469.

7. Paul Comly French, "Children on Strike," *Nation* 136, no. 3543 (May 31, 1933): 611.

8. NCLC, "Children in Revolt," *American Child* 15, no. 5 (May 1933): 1.

9. Ibid.

10. NCLC minutes, One-Hundred Ninth Meeting of the Board of Trustees, "National Legislation," May 22, 1933.

11. Ibid.

12. National Industrial Recovery Act (1933), US National Archives and Records Administration, Washington, DC.

13. "Child Labor Rule Asked in All Codes," *New York Times*, July 20, 1933, 10.

14. "Cotton Mills Put Child Labor Ban into Textile Code," *New York Times*, June 29, 1933, 1.

15. Kyvig, *Explicit and Authentic Acts*, 307.

16. Anthony J. Badger, *The New Deal: The Depression Years, 1933–1940* (Chicago: Ivan R. Dee, 1989), 86. For a critical view of the textile codes and the NRA, see Hiltzik, *The New Deal*, 129–130.

17. Walter I. Trattner, *Crusade for the Children: A History of the National Child Labor Committee and Child Labor Reform in America* (Chicago: Quadrangle Books, 1970), 191.

18. "Child Labor's End Foreseen as Outcome of Textile Code," *New York Times*, August 13, 1933, XX2.

19. The codes did not apply to an estimated one hundred thousand children working on farms or forty thousand, mostly girls, working as domestic servants. The figures for these occupations come from the 1930 Census. See "More Child Labor Seen over Nation," *New York Times*, March 22, 1936, E10.

20. Trattner, *Crusade for the Children*, 192.

21. Ibid., 194.

22. "News Men Demand 5-Day Week in Code," *New York Times*, September 23, 1933, 8.

23. Trattner, *Crusade for the Children*, 195. Leon Whipple, "The Press Gets a Code," *Survey Graphic* 23 (April 1934): 194–195.

24. "Newspaper Code Is Signed 'Conditionally'; Child Labor Angle Thought Still Pending," *New York Times*, February 18, 1934, 1. "Texts of Order and Letter by President on New Code for Newspapers and Gen. Johnson's Comment," *New York Times*, February 19, 1934, 8.

25. "Child Labor's End Forseen As Outcome of Textile Code," *New York Times*, August 13, 1933, XX2.

26. Ibid.

27. Trattner, *Crusade for the Children*, 195; National Child Labor Committee, NCLC, "The Rise and Fall of Child Labor in 1933," *American Child* 15, no. 9 (December 1933): 6.

28. Franklin D. Roosevelt, *The Public Papers and Addresses of Franklin D. Roosevelt*, vol. 3, *The Advance of Recovery and Reform*, "Annual Message to Congress," January 3, 1934 (New York: Random House, 1938), 10.

29. Lillian Holmen Mohr, *Frances Perkins: "That Woman in FDR's Cabinet!"* (Great Barrington, MA: North River Press, 1979), 186.

30. William D. Guthrie, "The Child Labor Amendment," *American Bar Association Journal* 20 (1934): 404–406, at 405.

31. Ibid.; NCLC, "The Press and the Amendment," *American Child* 27, no. 2 (February 1935): 2.

32. *Dillon v. Goss*, 256 U.S. 368 (1921), at 374.

33. Special Committee of the ABA, "Federal Child Labor Amendment," 1934, 12–13. Excluding the Bill of Rights, the average time for ratification of amendments Eleven through Twenty-One was one year and six months. The longest period of ratification was three years and six months for the Sixteenth Amendment.

34. Edward W. Macy, "Opposition Tactics against the Child Labor Amendment," *American Labor Legislation Review* 15 (December 1924): 110–114.

35. Dorothy D. Bromley, "The Newspapers and Child Labor," *Nation* 140 (January 30, 1935): 131–32; NCLC, "Newspapers Rush to Support Amendment," *American Child* 19, no. 2 (February 1937): 2–3.

36. "The Bogus Child Labor Amendment," *Chicago Tribune*, July 16, 1936, 12, reprinted in Abbott, *The Child and the State*, vol. 1, 556.

37. Trattner, *Crusade for the Children*, 198.

38. NCLC, "Scripps-Howard Press Repudiates A.N.P.A. Stand on Child Labor," *American Child* 17, no. 4 (April 1935): 4.

39. Quoted in *Editor and Publisher*, March 30, 1935.

40. Thomas R. Greene, "The Catholic Committee for the Ratification of the Child Labor Amendment, 1935–1937," *Catholic Historical Review* 74, no. 2 (April 1988): 251.

41. Miriam Keeler, "The Child Labor Amendment: Its History and Prospects," *Social Science* 10, no. 3 (July 1935): 259.

42. "Roosevelt Appeals for Child Labor Law," *New York Times*, November 19, 1934, 26.

43. "Child Labor Foes Urge State to Act," *New York Times*, February 19, 1934.

44. "Child Labor Curb Offered by Smith," *New York Times*, March 6, 1934, 6.

45. "Child Labor Group Scorns Smith Plan," *New York Times*, March 7, 1934, 6.

46. Jeremy P. Felt, *Hostages of Fortune: Child Labor Reform in New York State* (Syracuse, NY: Syracuse University Press, 1965), 213.

47. *Panama Refining Co. v. Ryan*, 293 U.S. 388 (1935), 419.

48. "Child Labor Drive Gets New Impetus: Non-Partisan Committee Set Up," *New York Times*, January 7, 1935, 10.

49. Minutes, Conference on the Child Labor Amendment, Washington, DC, April 13, 1935.

50. *Schechter Poultry Corporation v. United States*, 295 U.S. 495 (1935). In *Humphrey's Executor v. United States*, 295 U.S. 602 (1935), the Court ruled that President Roosevelt did not have the power to remove a member of the Federal Trade Commission for political reasons. In *Louisville Bank v. Radford*, the Court invalidated the 1934 Frazier-Lemke Act, which provided mortgage relief, primarily to farmers. The Court reasoned that the law violated the Fifth Amendment just compensation clause because it denied creditors their property without due process of law.

51. *Schechter Poultry Corporation v. United States*, 295 U.S. 495 (1935), 553.

52. Ibid, 549.

53. Burt Solomon, *FDR v. the Constitution: The Court-Packing Fight and the Triumph of Democracy* (New York: Walker, 2009), 73.

54. Solomon, *FDR v. The Constitution*, 74.

55. "End of NRA," *New York Times*, June 1, 1935, E1.

56. Leo C. Rosten, "Public Opinion and the Washington Correspondents," *Public Opinion Quarterly* 1, no. 1 (January 1937): 43.

57. "Return of Child Labor Predicted by Committee," *New York Times*, May 30, 1935, 12.

58. "Child Labor Rise Found after NRA," *New York Times*, February 2, 1936, N2.

59. "NRA Review Urges Child Labor Curbs," *New York Times*, April 10, 1936, 39.

60. "More Child Labor Seen over Nation," *New York Times*, March 22, 1936, E10.

61. Memorandum from Frances Perkins, Secretary of Labor, to FDR (December 28, 1936) at 1. FDR Presidential Library, Hyde Park, NY.

62. "Roosevelt Pleads on Child Labor Act," *New York Times*, January 9, 1937, 5.

63. NCLC, "Highlights on the Amendment!" *American Child* 19, no.2 (February 1937): 1.

64. "Roosevelt Pleads on Child Labor Act," 5.

65. Ibid.

66. Gerard N. Magliocca, "Court-Packing and the Child Labor Amendment," *Constitutional Commentary* 27 (2011): 475.

67. NCLC, "President Roosevelt Endorses Amendment," *American Child* 16, no. 3 (March 1934): 1.

68. Gregory A. Caldeira, "Public Opinion and the U.S. Supreme Court: FDR's Court-Packing Plan," *American Political Science Review* 81 (December 1987): 1139–1153.

69. George Gallup, "Child Labor Amendment Approved by 76% in National Poll," in *America Speaks: The National Weekly Poll of Public Opinion*, February 21, 1937.

70. Ibid.

71. Felt, *Hostages of Fortune*, 214.

72. Franklin D. Roosevelt, *Public Papers and Addresses*, 1937 (New York: Russell and Russell, 1938–1950), Item 37.

73. Felt, *Hostages of Fortune*, 214.

74. "Child Labor Bill Dies in Assembly; Vote Is 102 to 42," *New York Times*, May 10, 1937, 8.

75. "Child Labor Bill Menaced by Shift in Assembly," *New York Times*, February 24, 1936, 1.

76. "Child Labor Bill Dies in Assembly," 8.

77. Ibid.

78. "Vandenberg Gives a New Amendment to Ban Child Labor," *New York Times*, March 28, 1937, 1.

79. Ibid.

80. Senate Judiciary Committee, 75th Cong., 1st Sess., Report No. 788, June 22, 1937.

81. "Child Labor Plans Offered in the Senate," *New York Times*, March 25, 1937, 1.

82. *Kentucky Whip and Collar Co. v. Illinois Central Railroad Co.*, 299 U.S. 334 (1937).

83. Bruce R. Trimble, "The Child Labor Problem," *Kansas City Law Review* 5 (1936–1937): 188.

84. Hearings, US Senate Committee on Interstate Commerce, May 12, 1937, 61–68. See also Grace Abbott, "Federal Regulation of Child Labor, 1906–1938," *Social Service Review* 13, no. 3 (September 1939): 409–430.

85. "Child Labor Legislation: Plan of First Federal Law Preferred," editorial response from Courtenay Dinwiddie, General Secretary, National Child Labor Committee, *New York Times*, January 2, 1938, 60.

86. Ibid.

87. Minutes, Conference on the Child Labor Amendment, Washington, DC, April 9, 1937.

88. "Results of the Referendum as to Child Labor Amendments and Legislation," Report, *American Bar Association Journal* 23 (1937): 915–919.

89. Ibid., 915.

90. *West Coast Hotel v. Parrish*, 300 U.S. 379 (1937), 391. The decision was announced March 29, 1937.

91. *Wright v. Vinton Branch of Mountain Trust Bank*, 300 U.S. 440 (1937).

92. *NLRB v. Jones and Laughlin Steel Corporation*, 301 U.S. 1 (1937), 37.

93. See William E. Leuchtenberg, *The Supreme Court Reborn: The Constitutional Revolution in the Age of Roosevelt* (New York: Oxford University Press, 1995), 176.

94. Leuchtenberg, *The Supreme Court Reborn*, 142–143; Barry Cushman, *Rethinking the New Deal Court* (New York: Oxford University Press, 1998); Laura Kalman, "The Constitution, the Supreme Court, and the New Deal," *American Historical Review* 110, no. 4 (October 2005): 1052–1080.

95. For a good discussion of Justice Owen Roberts's motives for the "switch in time," see Solomon, *FDR v. The Constitution*, 209–217.

96. "New National Labor Laws Pondered," *New York Times*, April 4, 1937, 70. See also "Bill Is Introduced: Embodies Policies of Message Calling on Congress to Act," *New York Times*, May 25, 1937, 1.

97. "The Roosevelt Proposal: President Roosevelt's Message to Congress," *New York Times*, May 25, 1937, 1, 19.

98. *Wise v. Chandler*, 271 Ky. 1 (Ky. Ct. App. 1937).

99. Kyvig, *Explicit and Authentic Acts*, 310. Also, "Ratified by 28th State: Child Labor Amendment Approved by Kansas Legislature," *New York Times*, February 26, 1937, 6. Kansas was the last state to ratify the Child Labor Amendment on February 25, 1937.

100. *Coleman v. Miller*, 307 U.S. 433 (1939).

101. *Coleman v. Miller*, Memorandum of Petitioners in Reply to Brief of Solicitor General, 8.

102. *Coleman v. Miller*, No. 796, Brief on Behalf of Respondents, 9.

103. Ibid., 17.

104. *Chandler v. Wise*, 307 U.S. 474 (1939).

105. Brief for the United States Amicus Curiae, 7.

106. Ibid., 33.

107. Brief Amicus Curiae Filed on Behalf of the State of Wisconsin, *Coleman v. Miller* and *Chandler v. Wise*, October 7, 1938, 3–4.

108. Ibid., 18.

109. *Coleman v. Miller*, 307 U.S. 433 (1939), 452.

110. Courtenay Dinwiddie, "The Present Status of Child Labor," *Social Service Review* 13, no.3 (September 1939): 431–439.

Chapter 7. The Fair Labor Standards Act and Final Victory in *United States v. Darby Lumber*

1. Frances Perkins, *The Roosevelt I Knew* (New York: Viking Press, 1946), 152. See also Jonathan Grossman, "Fair Labor Standards Act: Maximum Struggle for a Minimum Wage," *Monthly Labor Review* 101, no. 6 (June 1978): 24.

2. Perkins, *The Roosevelt I Knew*, 257.

3. Grossman, "Fair Labor Standards Act," 25.

4. "The Roosevelt Proposal: President Roosevelt's Message to Congress," *New York Times*, May 25, 1937, 1, 19.

5. Virginia Van Der Veer Hamilton, *Hugo Black: The Alabama Years* (Baton Rouge: Louisiana State University Press, 1972), 265.

6. John S. Forsythe, "Legislative History of the Fair Labor Standards Act," *Law and Contemporary Problems* 6, no. 3 (Summer 1939): 466.

7. Ibid., 474.

8. Van Der Veer Hamilton, *Hugo Black*, 265.

9. Fair Labor Standards Act of 1937, Joint Hearings before Committee on Education and Labor, US Senate, and the Committee on Labor, House of Representatives, 75th Congress, Part 1, June 2–5, 1937, testimony of Assistant Attorney General Robert H. Jackson, 2–4.

10. Ibid., 5.

11. Ibid., 6.

12. Ibid., testimony of Robert Johnson, 98.

13. "Vandenberg Fears Fascist Wage Bill," *New York Times*, June 6, 1937, 4.

14. Forsythe, "Legislative History of the Fair Labor Standards Act," 468.

15. Paul H. Douglas and Joseph Hackman, "The Fair Labor Standards Act of 1938," *Political Science Quarterly* 53, no. 4 (December 1938): 502.

16. Grossman, "Fair Labor Standards Act," 25.

17. Ibid.

18. Forsythe, "Legislative History of the Fair Labor Standards Act," 467.

19. Ibid., 468. The amount of flexibility or discretion given to a wage board or labor administrator represents a classic problem in political science and public administration. New Dealers favored giving federal administrators discretion to use their expertise to set standards. Opponents of delegated lawmaking power believe that Congress should use its legislative authority to define wage and hour standards by law.

20. Grossman, "Fair Labor Standards Act," 25–26.

21. Fair Labor Standards Act of 1937, Joint Hearings before the Committee on Education and Labor of the US Senate and the Committee on Labor in the House of Representatives, 75th Cong., 1st Sess., Part 2, June 7–June 15, 945–946.

22. Ibid., testimony of Courtenay Dinwiddie, 396.

23. Ibid.

24. Ibid., 402.

25. Ibid.

26. Fair Labor Standards Act of 1937, Joint Hearings, Part 2, testimony of Mrs. Larue Brown, 391–392.

27. Douglas and Hackman, "The Fair Labor Standards Act of 1938," 504.

28. Van Der Veer Hamilton, *Hugo Black*, 257.

29. "Southerners Rake Wage Bill As Evil to the Whole Nation," *New York Times*, July 31, 1937, 1.

30. "Wages, Hours: Congress Is Stirred by a Contentious Bill," *Pathfinder*, December 18, 1937, 5.

31. "Roosevelt Plans Face Fight by King," *New York Times*, November 9, 1937, 5.

32. Hearings on the Fair Labor Standards Act, S. 5267, 72nd Congress, 295. Quoted in Roger K. Newman, *Hugo Black: A Biography*, 2d ed. (New York: Fordham University Press, 1997).

33. Hearings on the Fair Labor Standards Act, 267.

34. Newman, *Hugo Black*, 157.

35. *Congressional Record*, 1115, 1125.

36. Newman, *Hugo Black: A Biography*, 157.

37. Forsythe, "Legislative History of the Fair Labor Standards Act," 487.

38. Douglas and Hackman, "The Fair Labor Standards Act of 1938," 507–508.

39. Franklin D. Roosevelt, "The Message to the Extraordinary Session of the Congress Recommending Legislation," November 5, 1937. In *Public Papers and Addresses*, 1937 volume, *The Constitution Prevails* (New York: Macmillan, 1941), 496–497.

40. "Wages, Hours: Congress Is Stirred by a Contentious Bill," 3.

41. Douglas and Hackman, "The Fair Labor Standards Act of 1938," 509.

42. Congress passed the Supreme Court Retirement Act on March 1, allowing justices to retire at age seventy with a full pension. On August 26, 1937, President Roosevelt signed the Judicial Procedure Reform Act, a compromise on his original reorganization plan.

43. Michael Hiltzik, *The New Deal: A Modern History* (New York: Free Press, 2011), 376.

44. Douglas and Hackman, "The Fair Labor Standards Act of 1938," 510.

45. Forsythe, "Legislative History of the Fair Labor Standards Act," 471.

46. "Vote 216 to 198: Southerners and Republicans Doom Bill for Present, at Least," *New York Times*, December 18, 1937, 6.

47. Grossman, "Fair Labor Standards Act of 1938," 26.

48. Perkins, *The Roosevelt I Knew*, 261.

49. Franklin D. Roosevelt, "Annual Message to Congress," January 3, 1938. In *Public Papers and Addresses*, 1938 volume, *The Continuing Struggle for Liberalism* (New York: Macmillan, 1941), 1.

50. "Press Comment on the President's Message on State of the Nation," *New York Times*, January 4, 1938, 17.

51. Grossman, "Fair Labor Standards Act of 1938," 26.

52. Ibid.

53. Perkins, *The Roosevelt I Knew*, 262

54. Grossman, "Fair Labor Standards Act of 1938," 27.

55. Perkins, *The Roosevelt I Knew*, 262.

56. Grossman, "Fair Labor Standards Act of 1938," 27.

57. *New York Times*, "Pepper Wins in Florida Primary, Swamping Wilcox, New Deal Critic," May 4, 1938, 1; Grossman., "Fair Labor Standards Act of 1938," 27.

58. Perkins, *The Roosevelt I Knew*, 264.

59. Howard D. Samuel, "Troubled Passage: The Labor Movement and the Fair Labor Standards Act," *Monthly Labor Review* (December 2000): 32–37, 36.

60. Roosevelt, "I Have Every Right to Speak," Fireside Chat, June 24, 1938. In *Public Papers and Addresses*, 1938 volume, *The Continuing Struggle for Liberalism* (New York: Macmillan, 1941), 391–392.

61. Ibid., 392.

62. Pub. Law No. 718, 75th Cong., 3d Sess. 52 STAT. 1060, 29 U.S.C. §§ 201–219 (Supp. 1938).

63. Perkins, *The Roosevelt I Knew*, 266.

64. David M. Kennedy, *The American People in the Great Depression: Freedom from Fear* (New York: Oxford University Press, 1999), 345.

65. Grossman, "Fair Labor Standards Act of 1938," 29.

66. NCLC, "Wages and Hours Law Now in Effect," *American Child* 20, no. 8 (November 1938), 1.

67. Katherine Du Pre Lumpkin, "The Child Labor Provisions of the Fair Labor Standards Act," *Law and Contemporary Problems* 6 (1939): 392.

68. FLSA, Section 12(a).

69. Lumpkin, "The Child Labor Provisions of the Fair Labor Standards Act," 401.

70. Ibid., 402.

71. Courtenay Dinwiddie, "The Present Status of Child Labor," *Social Service Review* 13, no. 3 (September 1939): 432.

72. "Regulations Set for Child Labor," *New York Times*, October 17, 1938, 17.

73. "Children Still Need Fair Labor Standards," *Social Service Review*, 13, no. 4 (December 1939): 697. Federal certificates were being issued in three states: Mississippi, South Carolina, and Idaho. In only two states—Louisiana and Texas—no satisfactory procedures for issuing certificates had been negotiated by 1939.

74. Ibid., 697.

75. NCLC, "Two Years of Federal Control," *American Child* 22 (December 1940): 2.

76. Bart Dredge, "David Clark's 'Campaign of Enlightenment': Child Labor and the Farmers' States' Rights League, 1911–1940," *North Carolina Historical Review* 91, no. 1 (January 2014): 30–62, 61.

77. *Myers v. State Journal Company*, C.C. H. Lab. Law Serv. Sect. 18, 290 (Mich. Cir. Ct., 1938).

78. "Newsboy Is Ruled Beyond Wage Law," *New York Times*, January 1, 1939, 7.

79. US Children's Bureau, *Application of the Child Labor Provisions of the Fair Labor Standards Act to Children Engaged in the Distribution and Delivery of Newspapers*, Washington, DC, April 12, 1939; Dinwiddie, "The Present Status of Child Labor," 434.

80. Minutes, Conference on the Child Labor Amendment, Washington, DC, March 15, 1939.

81. Transcript of Record, Supreme Court of the United States, *United States v. Darby Lumber*, May 18, 1940, 20.

82. *Gibbons v. Ogden*, 9 Wheat. 1, 194–195; *United States v. Darby Lumber Company*, October term 1940, No. 82, Brief for the United States, 11–12.

83. *United States v. Darby Lumber Company*, Brief for the United States, 13.

84. Ibid., 101.

85. Harlan Fiske Stone Papers, Library of Congress, Manuscript Reading Room, *United States v. Darby Lumber*, memo from Chief Justice Hughes to Justice Stone, January 27, 1941. Emphasis in original text.

86. Ibid., 2.

87. Harlan Fiske Stone Papers, Library of Congress, Manuscript Reading Room, *United States v. Darby Lumber*, memo from Justice Stone to Chief Justice Hughes, January 27, 1941.

88. *United States v. Darby Lumber*, 312 U.S. 100 (1941), 114.

89. Ibid.

90. Ibid., 116–117.

91. Ibid., 124.

92. Alpheus T. Mason, *Harlan Fiske Stone: Pillar of the Law* (New York: Viking Press, 1956), 553.

93. Memorandum from Noel T. Dowling to A.T.M, 1951. Quoted in Mason, *Harlan Fiske Stone*, 552.

94. Mason, *Harlan Fiske Stone*, 554.

95. *Opp Cotton Mills v. Administrator*, 312 U.S. 126 (1941).

96. William E. Leuchtenburg, *The Supreme Court Reborn: The Constitutional Revolution in the Age of Roosevelt* (New York: Oxford University Press, 1995), 224. The quote is from historian Paul R. Benson, Jr., *The Supreme Court and the Commerce Clause, 1937–70* (New York: Dunellen, 1970), 89.

97. "Federal Powers," *Washington Post*, February 5, 1941; "Constitutional Change," *Asheville Citizen*, February 4, 1941.

98. NCLC, "The Significance of the Supreme Court Decision," *American Child* 23, no. 3 (March 1941): 1.

99. "The Supreme Court and the Children," *Social Service Review* 15, no. 1 (March 1941): 119.

100. "Wage Law Upheld by Supreme Court; Old Decision Upset," *New York Times*, February 4, 1941, 1.

101. Ibid.

102. Donald Murtha, "Wage-Hour and Child Labor Legislation in the Roosevelt Administration," *Lawyers Guild Review* 5 (1945): 190.

103. *Gemsco Inc. v. Walling*, 324 U.S. 244 (1945).

104. Ibid., 249.

105. Murtha, "Wage-Hour and Child Labor Legislation," 190.

106. Ella Arvilla Merritt and Floy Hendricks, "Trend of Child Labor, 1940–44," *Monthly Labor Review* (April 1945): 756–775.

107. "Children of School Ages Deserting the Classroom," *New York Times*, October 10, 1943, E9.

108. "Six States Accused of Wage Law Fight," *New York Times*, March 10, 1944, 32.

109. "Child Labor Provisions under Fair Labor Standards Act," *Social Service Review* 18, no. 2 (June 1944): 255.

110. NCLC, "The Impact of the War on Child Labor," *American Child* 25, no. 3 (March 1943): 1.

111. NCLC, "Shall Children Work in Wartime?" *American Child* 24, no. 7 (November 1942): 1.

112. "Children of School Ages Deserting the Classroom," E9.

113. Walter I. Trattner, *Crusade for the Children: A History of the Child labor Committee and Child Labor Reform in America* (Chicago: Quadrangle Books, 1970), 216.

114. NCLC, "Jobs after School Hours," *American Child* 24 (January 1942): 2.

115. "Delinquency Rise Pictured at Forum," *New York Times*, February 5, 1943, 13.

116. Perkins, *The Roosevelt I Knew*, 374.

117. "Children of School Ages Deserting the Classroom," E9.

118. Trattner, *Crusade for the Children*, 216

119. NCLC, "A Children's Charter in Wartime," *American Child* 24 (April 1942): 2.

120. Children's Bureau Commission on Children in Wartime, "Goals for Chil-

dren and Youth as We Move from War to Peace." Statement adopted March 17–18, 1944 and first published in June 1944. *Public Welfare* Winter (1993): 7–8.

121. NCLC, "The Legislative Record—1943," *American Child* 25 (October 1943): 2.

122. In 1946, AMF introduced the automatic pinsetter, and by the early 1950s, machines produced by both AMF and Brunswick eliminated the need for children to work late hours as pinsetters.

123. Perkins, *The Roosevelt I Knew*, 375.

124. NCLC, "Basic National Policy," *American Child* 25, no. 3 (March 1943): 2.

125. "Child Labor Remains," *New York Times*, December 24, 1944, 54.

Chapter 8. Contemporary Child Labor Issues

1. "Child Labor and the Fair Labor Standards Act," *Social Service Review* 22, no. 1 (March 1948): 87–88.

2. William S. Tyson, "The Fair Labor Standards Act: A Survey and Evaluation of the First Eleven Years," *Labor Law Journal* (January 1950): 278–286.

3. "Sponsors Defend Child Labor Laws," *New York Times*, November 26, 1954, 23.

4. Ibid.

5. Gerald Mayer, "Child Labor in America: History, Policy, and Legislative Issues," *Congressional Research Service* (December 27, 2010): 12.

6. NCLC, "A Proposal by Secretary Wirtz," *American Child* 46, no. 3 (May 1964): 1–2.

7. Martin Hamburger, "Protection from Participation as Deprivation of Rights," *New Generation* 53, no. 3 (Summer 1971): 1–7; Robert Taggart III, "The Case for Less Stringent Regulations," *New Generation* 53, no. 3 (Summer 1971): 14–19.

8. Barbara Becnel, "Black Workers: Progress Derailed," *AFL-CIO American Federationist* (January 1978): 1.

9. Mayer, "Child Labor in America," 13.

10. David Shribman, "Youth Work Proposals Are Assailed at Hearing," Special to the *New York Times*, July 29, 1982, A19.

11. U.S. Congress, House Committee on Education and Labor, Subcommittee on Labor Standards, *Oversight Hearings—Proposed Changes in Child Labor Regulations*, 97th Cong., 2nd Sess., July 28 and August 3, 1982, 1–30.

12. Shribman, "Youth Work Proposals Are Assailed at Hearing," A19.

13. Ibid. See also Peter Edelman, "Child Labor Revisited," *The Nation*. August 21–28, 1982, 136–138.

14. David Shribman, "Proposed Relaxation of Child Labor Rules," Special to the *New York Times*, July 28, 1982, A19.

15. Jeffrey Newman, "Child Labor Law: Bad Time for a Shift," *New York Times*, August 1, 1982, E21.

16. Ken Rankin, "Wage-hour Reforms Raise National Furor." *Nation's Restaurant News*, February 28, 1983, 2.

17. Section 801, Public Law 99-425 (September 30, 1986).

18. Peter T. Kilborn, "Playing Games with Labor Laws: When Work Fills a Child's Hours," *New York Times*, December 10, 1989, 1, 46.

19. Michael Freitag, "Thousands of Children Doing Adults' Work," Special to the *New York Times*, February 5, 1990, A1, B1, B4.

20. Ibid.

21. Peter T. Kilborn, "Tougher Enforcing of Child Labor Law Vowed," *New York Times*, February 8, 1990, A22.

22. Ibid.

23. Janet Battaile, "Supermarket Faces Federal Complaints in Child-Labor Case," *New York Times*, November 9, 1992, A13.

24. "Labor Case to Cost Food Lion Millions," Bloomberg Business News, August 4, 1993. http://articles.sun-sentinel.com/1993-08-04/business/9301270762_1_food-lion-child-labor-labor-laws (accessed April 24, 2017).

25. "Publix Settles Child Labor Charges," Bloomberg Business News, August 17, 1993. http://articles.sun-sentinel.com/1993-08-17/business/9308170449_1_paper-balers-child-labor-labor-charges (accessed April 24, 2017).

26. "Labor Case to Cost Food Lion Millions."

27. "Going to Bat against Bureaucracy." http://savannahnow.com/stories/0702 05/3138634.shtml#.WQIJRsZOmM8 (accessed April 27, 2017).

28. "Batboy Is Called Out by Labor Officials, Who Vow a Review," *New York Times*, May 28, 1993, A10.

29. Robert B. Reich, *Locked in the Cabinet* (New York: Alfred A. Knopf, 1997), 113–116.

30. Ibid.

31. Child Labor Regulations, Orders and Statements of Interpretation. 29 CFR Part 570. *Federal Register*, 60, 73 (April 17, 1995): 19336.

32. Ibid.

33. Mayer, "Child Labor in America: History, Policy, and Legislative Issues," 16.

34. US Congress, House Committee on Economic and Educational Opportunities, *Authority for 16 and 17 Years Olds to Load Materials into Balers and Compactors*, report to accompany H.R. 1114, 104th Cong., 1st Sess., House Rept. 104-278 (Washington, DC: GPO, 1995).

35. Mayer, "Child Labor in America: History, Policy, and Legislative Issues," 17.

36. Public Law No. 105-334 (1998).

37. Christopher Klicka, "Child Labor Laws," *Home School Court Report* 22, no. 3 (May–June 2006).

38. US Department of Labor, "Agricultural Employment," https://www.dol.gov/general/topic/youthlabor/agriculturalemployment (accessed January 5, 2018).

39. Sarah Gonzalez, "Lawmakers Put Child Agricultural Labor Rules under the Microscope," Agri-Pulse.com, February 2, 2012, https://www.agri-pulse.com/articles/1538-lawmakers-put-child-agricultural-labor-rules-under-the-microscope (accessed June 12, 2017).

Postscript: Those "Truly Stupid" Child Labor Laws

1. Kevin Liptak, "Gingrich: Laws Preventing Child Labor Are 'Truly Stupid,'" CNN, November 19, 2011. http://politicalticker.blogs.cnn.com/2011/11/19/gingrich-laws-preventing-child-labor-are-truly-stupid/ (accessed April 2, 2017).

2. Liz Halloran, "Gingrich's Proposals on Child Labor Stir Attacks, but Raise Issues," NPR, December 7, 2011. http://www.npr.org/sections/itsallpolitics/2011 /12/07/143258836/gingrichs-proposals-on-child-labor-stir-attacks-but-raise-real -issues (accessed March 31, 2017).

3. "Gingrinch's History Gap," editorial, *Los Angeles Times*, November 22, 2011. http://articles.latimes.com/2011/nov/22/opinion/la-ed-history-20111122 (accessed April 2, 2017).

4. Jordan Weissmann, "Newt Gingrich Thinks School Children Should Work as Janitors," *Atlantic*, November 21, 2011. https://www.theatlantic.com/business /archive/2011/11/newt-gingrich-thinks-school-children-should-work-as-janitors /248837/ (accessed March 26, 2017).

5. Matthew Cooper, "The Tea Party's Constitutional Vision," *National Journal*, February 17, 2011.

6. Sahil Kapur, "GOP Senator: Federal Ban on Child Labor Is Unconstitutional," Monday, January 17, 2011. http://www.rawstory.com/2011/01/gop-sena tor-calls-federal-laws-child-labor-unconstitutional/ (accessed March 25, 2017).

7. Christopher Cousins, "LePage's Efforts to Remove Child Labor Barriers to Continue in January," *Bangor Daily News*, December 2, 2013. http://bangordaily news.com/2013/12/02/politics/lepages-efforts-to-remove-child-labor-barriers-to -continue-in-january/ (accessed April 4, 2017).

8. Michelle Chen, "States Attempt to Instill 'Work Ethic' by Rolling Back Child Labor Protections," *Nation*, January 12, 2012, https://www.thenation.com /article/states-attempt-instill-work-ethic-rolling-back-child-labor-protections/ (accessed April 1, 2017).

9. Gordon Lafer, "The Legislative Attack on American Wages and Labor Standards, 2011–2012," EPI Briefing Paper #364, Economic Policy Institute (October 31, 2013): 32.

10. Ibid.

11. Rep. Bruce Bickford, quoted in Amanda Terkel, "Maine GOP Legislators Looking to Loosen Child Labor Laws," May 30, 2011. http://www.huffingtonpost .com/2011/03/30/maine-gop-legislators-loo_n_842563.html (accessed March 25, 2017).

12. SB 222, Missouri Senate, "Modifies Child Labor Laws." http://www.senate .mo.gov/11info/BTS_Web/Bill.aspx?SessionType=R&BillID=4124271 (accessed March 25, 2017).

13. Rebecca Berg, "Jay Leno Makes Fun of the Missouri Senate Bill," *St. Louis Post Dispatch*, February 16, 2011. The joke: "And in Missouri, Republican state Sen. Jane Cunningham has introduced a bill that would eliminate her state's child labor laws," Leno said. "Well, yeah, I mean, why should the 10-year-olds in China be getting all the good factory jobs?"

14. "The Mean Girls & Boys Club. Our View: Missouri Legislators Champion Purely Mean Bills. OPINION." *St Louis Post-Dispatch* [MO], February 20, 2011, A22, *Infotrac Newsstand*, go.galegroup.com/ps/i.

15. Quoted in Holly Rosenkrantz, "Taking Aim at Child Labor Laws," *Bloomberg Businessweek Magazine*, January 5, 2012, https://www.bloomberg.com/news/articles /2012-01-05/taking-aim-at-child-labor-laws (accessed August 9, 2017).

16. Chen, "States Attempt to Instill 'Work Ethic.'"

17. US Department of Labor, Bureau of Labor Statistics, "Employment Projections," https://www.bls.gov/emp/ep_chart_001.htm (accessed January 3, 2018).

18. A red state is generally a conservative state, usually with a majority of registered Republican voters, and a legislature and executive controlled by the Republican Party.

19. National Conference of State Legislatures, "2014 Child Labor Enacted Legislation," December 16, 2014. http://www.ncsl.org.

20. David K. Li, "New Law Aims to Protect Underage Models," *New York Post*, October 22, 2013. http://nypost.com/2013/10/22/new-law-aims-to-protect-under age-models/ (accessed March 25, 2017). Also see "Child Model FAQs," New York State, Department of Labor. https://labor.ny.gov/workerprotection/laborstandards /secure/ChildModelFAQs.shtm (accessed March 25, 2017).

21. The TGANC issued the following statement: "TGANC does not condone the use of child labor and believes tobacco growers, and farm labor contractors should not employ workers younger than 16 years of age for work in tobacco, even with parental permission. If growers elect to employ 16- and 17-year-olds, the employee should provide express written parental permission." Chris Bickers, "Tobacco Growers Say 'No' on Child Labor," *Southeast FarmPress*, October 29, 2014, http://www.southeastfarmpress.com/tobacco/tobacco-growers-say-no-child-labor (accessed March 25, 2017).

22. Ibid.

23. *Human Rights Watch*, "Tobacco's Hidden Children: Hazardous Child Labor in United States Tobacco Farming," May 13, 2014. https://www.hrw.org/report /2014/05/13/tobaccos-hidden-children/hazardous-child-labor-united-states-tobacco -farming (accessed April 2, 2017). Another report followed in 2015.

24. Sarah Gonzalez, "Child Farm Labor Debate Resurfaces with Focus on Tobacco Farms," Agri-pulse.com, September 25, 2014. https://www.agri-pulse.com /articles/4445-child-farm-labor-debate-resurfaces-with-focus-on-tobacco-farms (accessed June 12, 2017).

25. "Bill Would 'Seriously Weaken' State's Child Labor Laws," March 7, 2017. http://weac.org/2017/03/07/bill-would-seriously-weaken-states-child-labor-laws/ (accessed March 12, 2017).

26. Kenneth Dickerman, "20 Haunting Portraits of Child Laborers in 1900s America," *Washington Post*, October 31, 2016. https://www.washingtonpost.com/news /in-sight/wp/2016/10/31/20-haunting-portraits-of-child-laborers-in-1900s-america /?utm_term=.f65a3a4bc9bb (accessed February 12, 2017).

27. Jeffrey A. Tucker, "Let the Kids Work." Foundation for Economic Education, November 3, 2016. https://fee.org/articles/let-the-kids-work/ (accessed February 12, 2017).

28. Ibid.

29. Steve Wishnia, "Trump's Education Pick Funds Child-Labor Advocates," November 30, 2016, Laborpress. http://laborpress.org/national-news/9012-trump -s-education-pick-funds-child-labor-advocates (accessed February 12, 2017).

BIBLIOGRAPHY

Books and Book Chapters

Abbott, Edith. *Women in Industry: A Study in American Economic History*. New York: D. Appleton, 1918.

———. "Child Labor in Pennsylvania in 1838." In *History of Labor in the United States*, 4 vols., John R. Commons et al. New York: Macmillan, 1935.

Abbott, Grace. *Massachusetts Legislative Files, 1825, Senate, No. 8074*. Vol. 8074. Report on Returns of Children Employed in Factories.

———. *The Child and the State: Select Documents with Introductory Notes*. Vol. 1: *Legal Status in the Family Apprenticeship and Child Labor*. University of Chicago, 1938. Reprinted by Greenwood Press, 1968.

Badger, Anthony J. *The New Deal: The Depression Years, 1933–1940*. Chicago: Ivan R. Dee, 1989.

Balkin, Jack M. *Constitutional Redemption: Political Faith in an Unjust World*. Cambridge, MA: Harvard University Press, 2011.

Barling, Julian, and E. Kevin Kelloway. *Young Workers: Varieties of Experience*. Washington, DC: American Psychological Association, 1999.

Benson, Paul R., Jr. *The Supreme Court and the Commerce Clause, 1937–70*. New York: Dunellen, 1970.

Bernstein, David. *Rehabilitating Lochner: Defending Individual Rights against Progressive Reform*. Chicago: University of Chicago Press, 2011.

Bickel, Alexander M. *The Unpublished Opinions of Mr. Justice Brandeis*. Cambridge, MA: Belknap Press, Harvard University Press, 1957.

Bowers, Claude G. *Beveridge and the Progressive Era*. New York: The Literary Guild, 1932.

Brace, Charles Loring. *The Dangerous Classes of New York*. New York: Wynkoop & Hallenbeck, 1872.

Brandeis, Elizabeth. "Section III: Labor Legislation." In *History of Labor in the U.S., 1896–1932*, ed. John R. Commons. New York: Macmillan, 1932.

Brands, H. W. *American Colossus: The Triumph of Capitalism, 1865–1900*. New York: Anchor Books, 2010.

Bremmer, Robert H. *Children and Youth in America: A Documentary History*. Cambridge, MA: Harvard University Press, 1971.

Brock, William R. *Investigation and Responsibility: Public Responsibility in the United States, 1865–1900*. Cambridge, UK: Cambridge University Press, 1984.

Campbell, Helen. *Prisoners of Poverty: Women Wage-Workers, Their Trades, and Their Lives*. Boston: Roberts Brothers, 1887.

Cogan, Neil H., ed. *The Complete Bill of Rights: The Drafts, Debates, Sources, and Origins*, 2d ed. New York: Oxford University Press, 1997.

Commons, John R., et al. *History of Labor in the United States*, 4 Vols. New York: Macmillan Co., 1935.

Cooley, Thomas M. *Constitutional Limitations*. Boston: Little, Brown, and Co., 1868.

Costin, Lela B. *Two Sisters for Social Justice: A Biography of Grace and Edith Abbott*. Champaign: University of Illinois Press, 1983.

Cushman, Barry. *Rethinking the New Deal Court*. New York: Oxford University Press, 1998.

Dickens, Charles. *Oliver Twist*. London: Richard Bentley, 1838.

———. *A Christmas Carol*. London: Chapman and Hall, 1843.

Elazar, Daniel J. *The American Partnership*. Chicago: University of Chicago Press, 1962.

Engels, Friedrich. *The Condition of the Working Class in England*. New York: Oxford University Press, 2009.

Felt, Jeremy. *Hostages of Fortune: Child Labor Reform in New York State*. Syracuse, NY: Syracuse University Press, 1965.

Fitzpatrick, John C., ed. *The Diaries of George Washington, 1748–1799*. Boston: Houghton Mifflin, 1925.

Fliter, John A., and Derek S. Hoff. *Fighting Foreclosure: The* Blaisdell *Case, the Contract Clause, and the Great Depression*. Lawrence: University Press of Kansas, 2012.

Flynn, George Q. *American Catholics and the Roosevelt Presidency, 1932–1936*. Lexington: University Press of Kentucky, 1968.

Freedman, Russell. *Kids at Work: Lewis Hine and the Crusade against Child Labor*. New York: Clarion Books, 1994.

Fuller, Raymond Garfield. *Child Labor and the Constitution*. New York: Thomas Y. Crowell, 1923. Reproduction from the Yale Law Library.

Gallup, George H. *The Gallup Poll: Public Opinion, 1935–1971*. New York: Random House, 1972.

Gillam, Howard. *The Constitution Besieged: The Rise and Demise of Lochner Era Police Powers Jurisprudence*. Durham, NC: Duke University Press, 1993.

Glasner, David, and Thomas F. Cooley, eds. *Business Cycles and Depressions: An Encyclopedia*. New York: Garland Publishing, 1997.

Goldmark, Josephine. *Impatient Crusader: Florence Kelley's Life Story*. Urbana: University of Illinois Press, 1953.

Gompers, Samuel. *Labor and the Common Welfare*. Edited by Hayes Robbins. New York: E. P. Dutton and Co., 1919.

Grozdins, Martin. *The American System*. Chicago: Rand-McNally, 1966.

Herndon, Ruth Wallis, and John E. Murry, eds. *Children Bound to Labor: The Pauper Apprenticeship System in Early America*. Ithaca, NY: Cornell University Press, 2009.

Hiltzik, Michael. *The New Deal: A Modern History*. New York: Free Press, 2011.

Hindman, Hugh D. *Child Labor: An American History*. New York: M. E. Sharpe, 2002.

Honeyman, Katrina. *Child Workers in England, 1780–1820*. Aldershot, England: Ashland, 2007.

Humphries, Jane. *Childhood and Child Labour in the British Industrial Revolution.* New York: Cambridge University Press, 2011.

Johnson, Elizabeth Sands. "Child Labor Legislation." In *History of Labor in the United States*, 4 vols., John R. Commons et al. Vol. 3: *Working Conditions.* New York: Macmillan, 1935.

Kasson, John F. *Civilizing the Machine: Technology and Republican Values in America, 1776–1900.* New York: Grossman Publishers, 1976.

Kaufman, Stuart B., Peter J. Albert, and Grace Palladino, eds. *The Samuel Gompers Papers*, vol. 4: *A National Labor Movement Takes Shape, 1895–1898.* Urbana: University of Illinois Press, 1991.

Kennedy, David M. *The American People in the Great Depression: Freedom from Fear.* New York: Oxford University Press, 1999.

Kens, Paul. *Lochner v. New York: Economic Regulation on Trial.* Lawrence: University Press of Kansas, 1998.

Kilpatrick, James J., ed. *The Constitution of the United States and Amendments Thereto.* Richmond, VA: Virginia Commission on Constitutional Government, 1961.

Kirby, Peter. *Child Labour in Britain, 1750–1870.* New York, NY: Palgrave Macmillan, 2003.

Kyvig, David E. *Explicit and Authentic Acts: Amending the U.S. Constitution, 1776–1995.* Lawrence: University Press of Kansas, 1996.

Lakoff, George. *Don't Think of an Elephant: Know Your Values and Frame the Debate*, 2d rev. ed. White River Junction, VT: Chelsea Green Publishing, 2014.

Langum, David J. *Crossing over the Line: Legislating Morality and the Mann Act.* Urbana: University of Chicago Press, 1994.

Leuchtenburg, William E. *The Supreme Court Reborn: The Constitutional Revolution in the Age of Roosevelt.* New York: Oxford University Press, 1995.

Lindenmeyer, Kriste. *"A Right to Childhood": The U.S. Children's Bureau and Child Welfare, 1912–1946.* Urbana: University of Illinois Press, 1997.

Link, Arthur Stanley. *Wilson: Campaigns for Progressivism and Peace, 1916–1917.* Vol. 5. Princeton, NJ: Princeton University Press, 1965.

Mandel, Bernard. *Samuel Gompers: A Biography.* Yellow Springs, OH: Antioch Press, 1963.

Mason, Alpheus Thomas. *Brandeis: A Free Man's Life.* New York: Viking Press, 1956.

———. *Harlan Fiske Stone: Pillar of the Law.* New York: Viking Press, 1956.

———. *The Supreme Court from Taft to Warren.* Baton Rouge: Louisiana State University Press, 1968.

McLaurin, Melton Alonza. *The Knights of Labor in the South.* Westport, CT: Greenwood Press, 1978.

McQuade, Vincent A., O.S.A. *The American Catholic Attitude on Child Labor since 1891.* Washington, DC: Catholic University of America, 1938.

Mehrotra, Ajay K. *Making the Modern American Fiscal State: Law, Politics, and the Rise of Progressive Taxation, 1877–1929.* Cambridge, UK: Cambridge University Press, 2013.

Mintz, Steven. *Huck's Raft: A History of American Childhood.* Cambridge, MA: Harvard University Press, 2004.

Mohr, Lillian Holmen. *Frances Perkins: "That Woman in FDR's Cabinet!"* Great Barrington, MA: North River Press, 1979.

Morrison, Elting E., John M. Blum, and John J. Buckley, eds. *The Letters of Theodore Roosevelt*, 8 vols. Cambridge, MA: Harvard University Press, 1951.

Muncy, Robyn. *Creating a Female Dominion in American Reform, 1890–1935*. New York: Oxford University Press, 1992.

Murphy, Edgar Gardner. *Problems of the Present South*. New York: Macmillan, 1904.

National Research Council Institute of Medicine. *Protecting Youth at Work: Health, Safety, and Development of Working Children and Adolescents in the United States*. Washington, DC: National Academy Press, 1998.

Newman, Roger K. *Hugo Black: A Biography*, 2d ed. New York: Fordham University Press, 1997.

Novak, William J. *The People's Welfare: Law and Regulation in Nineteenth-Century America*. Chapel Hill: University of North Carolina Press, 1996.

Novkov, Julie. "Our Towering Superstructure Rests on a Rotten Foundation: *Hammer v. Dagenhart* (1918)." In *Creating Constitutional Change: Clashes Over Power and Liberty in the Supreme Court*, Ivers, Gregg and Kevin T. McGuire, eds. Charlottesville: University Press of Virginia, 2004.

Ogburn, William F. *The Progress and Uniformity of Child Labor Legislation*. Vol. 48, part 2. New York: Columbia University Studies, 1912.

Painter, Nell Irvin. *Standing at Armageddon: A Grassroots History of the Progressive Era*. New York: W. W. Norton, 2008.

Pearson, Susan J. *The Rights of the Defenseless: Protecting Animals and Children in Gilded Age America*. Chicago: University of Chicago Press, 2011.

Pennington, Shelley, and Belinda Westover. *A Hidden Workforce: Homeworkers in England, 1850–1985*. London: Macmillan Education Ltd., 1989.

Perkins, Frances. *The Roosevelt I Knew*. New York: Viking Press, 1946.

Phillips, Michael J. *The Lochner Court, Myth and Reality: Substantive Due Process from the 1890s–1930s*. Westport, CT: Praeger, 2001.

Reich, Robert B. *Locked in the Cabinet*. New York: Alfred A. Knopf, 1997.

Robertson, David Brian. *Capital, Labor, and the State: The Battle for American Labor Markets from the Civil War to the New Deal*. Lanham, MD: Rowman and Littlefield, 2000.

Roosevelt, Franklin. *Public Papers and Addresses*. Vol. 7. New York: Random House, 1937.

Rosenberg, Chaim M. *Child Labor in America: A History*. Jefferson, NC: McFarland, 2013.

Rosenberg, Gerald N. *The Hollow Hope: Can Courts Bring about Social Change?*, 2d ed. Chicago: University of Chicago Press, 2008.

Sallee, Shelley. *The Whiteness of Child Labor Reform in the New South*. Athens: University of Georgia Press, 2004.

Schmidt, James D. *Industrial Violence and the Legal Origins of Child Labor*. New York: Cambridge University Press, 2010.

Schultz, David A., ed. *Leveraging the Law: Using Courts to Achieve Social Change*. New York: Peter Lang, 1998.

Solomon, Burt. *FDR v. the Constitution: The Court-Packing Fight and the Triumph of Democracy.* New York: Walker, 2009.

Trattner, Walter I. *Crusade for the Children: A History of the National Child Labor Committee and Child Labor Reform in America.* Chicago: Quadrangle Books, 1970.

Van Der Veer Hamilton, Virginia. *Hugo Black: The Alabama Years.* Baton Rouge: Louisiana State University Press, 1972.

Van Vorst, Elizabeth. *The Cry of the Children: A Study of Child-Labor.* New York: Moffat, Yard, 1908.

Volk, Kyle G. *Moral Minorities and the Making of American Democracy.* New York: Oxford University Press, 2014.

Wade, Rufus R. *First National Convention of Factory Inspectors.* Columbus, OH: Myers Brothers, 1887.

Whittaker, William G. *Child Labor in America: History, Policy, and Legislative Issues.* Hauppauge, NY: Nova Science Publishers, 2004.

Wilson, Woodrow. *Constitutional Government in the United States.* New York: Columbia University Press, 1908.

Witt, John Fabian. *The Accidental Republic: Crippled Workingmen, Destitute Widows, and the Remaking of American Law.* Boston: Harvard University Press, 2006.

Wood, Stephen B. *Constitutional Politics in the Progressive Era: Child Labor and the Law.* Chicago: University of Chicago Press, 1968.

Wright, Benjamin. *The Growth of American Constitutional Law.* Boston: Houghton Mifflin published for New York: Reynal and Hitchcock, 1942.

Zipf, Karin L. *Labor of Innocents: Forced Apprenticeship in North Carolina 1715–1919.* Baton Rouge: Louisiana State University Press, 2005.

Journals

Abbott, Edith. "Summary of the Report on Conditions of Woman and Child Wage-Earners in the United States." *U.S. Bureau of Labor Statistics Bulletin* (1916): 246.

Abbott, Grace. "Federal Regulation of Child Labor, 1906–38." *Social Service Review* 13, no. 3 (1939): 409–430.

Baldwin, B. J. "History of Child Labor Reform in Alabama." *Annals of the American Academy of Political and Social Science* 38 (July 1911): 111–113.

Behn, Beth. "A Principled Shift: Woodrow Wilson and the Keating-Owen Child Labor Bill." Unpublished conference paper presented at the Midwest Political Science Association annual meeting, Chicago, IL, April 3, 2008.

Beveridge, Albert J. "Child Labor and the Nation." *Annals of the American Academy of Political and Social Science* 29 (January 1907): 115–124.

Bewig, Matthew S. "*Lochner v. The Journeymen Bakers of New York:* The Journeymen Bakers, Their Hours of Labor, and the Constitution." *American Journal of Legal History* 38, no. 4 (October 1994): 413–451.

Braeman, John. "Albert J. Beveridge and the First National Child Labor Bill." *Indiana Magazine of History* 60, no. 1 (March 1964): 1–36.

Brinton, Jasper Yeates. "The Constitutionality of a Federal Child Labor Law." *University of Pennsylvania Law Review and America Law Register* 62, 7 (1914): 487–503.

Caldeira, Gregory A. "Public Opinion and the U.S. Supreme Court: FDR's

Court-Packing Plan." *American Political Science Review* 81 (December 1987): 1139–1153.

"The Child Labor Amendment." *Constitutional Review* 9 (1925): 44–50.

"Child Labor and the Fair Labor Standards Act." *Social Service Review* 22, 1 (March 1948): 87–88.

"Child Labor: Conditions and Attempted Legislation before 1840." *American Economic Association* 9, no. 3 (October 1908): 5–7.

"Child-Labor in England." *American Economic Association* 5, no. 2 (March 1890): 13–17.

"Child Labor in the United States." *American Economic Association* 5, no. 2 (March 1890): 25, 29.

"Child Labor in the United States." *American Economic Association* 8, no. 3 (August 1907): 1.

"Child Labor Provisions under Fair Labor Standards Act." *Social Service Review* 18, no. 2 (June 1944): 253–255.

"Children Still Need Fair Labor Standards." *Social Service Review* 13, no. 4 (December 1939): 696–698.

Corwin, Edward S. "Constitutional Law in 1921–1922: The Constitutional Decisions of the Supreme Court of the United States in the October Term, 1921." *American Political Science Review* 16, no. 4 (November 1922): 612–639.

Crawford, Ruth. "Development and Control of Industrial Homework." *Monthly Labor Review* 58, no. 6 (1944): 1145–1158.

Dinwiddie, Courtenay. "The Present Status of Child Labor." *Social Service Review* 13, no. 3 (September 1939): 431–439.

Douglas, Paul H., and Joseph Hackman. "The Fair Labor Standards Act of 1938." *Political Science Quarterly* 53, no. 4 (December 1938): 491–515.

Dredge, Bart. "David Clark's 'Campaign of Enlightenment': Child Labor and the Farmers' States Rights League, 1911–1940." *North Carolina Historical Review* 91, no. 1 (January 2014): 30–62.

Felt, Jeremy. "The Child Labor Provisions of the Fair Labor Standards Act." *Labor History* 11, no. 4 (1970): 467–481.

Forsythe, John S. "Legislative History of the Fair Labor Standards Act." *Law and Contemporary Problems* 6, no. 3 (Summer 1939): 464–490.

Freund, Ernest. "Limitation of Hours of Labor and the Federal Supreme Court." *Green Bag* 17 (June 1905): 411.

Gordon, Thurlow M. "The Child Labor Law Case." *Harvard Law Review* 32, no. 45 (1918–1919): 45–67.

Graffenried, Miss Clare de. "Child-Labor." *American Economic Association* 5, no. 2 (March 1890): 71.

Greene, Thomas R. "The Catholic Committee for the Ratification of the Child Labor Amendment, 1935–37." *Catholic Historical Review* 74, no. 2 (April 1988): 248–269.

Grossman, Jonathan. "Fair Labor Standards Act of 1938: Maximum Struggle for a Minimum Wage." *Monthly Labor Review* 101, no. 6 (1978): 22–30.

Guthrie, William D. "The Child Labor Amendment." *American Bar Association Journal* 20 (1934): 404–406.

Hand, Learned. "Due Process of Law and the Eight-Hour Day." *Harvard Law Review* 21, no. 7 (May 1908): 495–509.

Hulett, J. E., Jr. "Propaganda and the Proposed Child Labor Amendment." *Public Opinion Quarterly* 2, no. 1 (1938): 105–115.

Jones, William Carey. "The Child Labor Decision." *California Law Review* 6, no. 6 (September 1918): 395–417.

Kalman, Laura. "The Constitution, the Supreme Court, and the New Deal." *American Historical Review* 110, no. 4 (October 2005): 1052–1080.

Kaufman, Bill. "The Child Labor Amendment Debate of the 1920s." *Essays in Political Economy*, The Ludwig von Mises Institute. Number 16, November 1992.

Keeler, Miriam. "The Child Labor Amendment: Its History and Prospects." *Social Science* 10, no. 3 (July 1935): 257–260.

Klarman, Michael J. "Rethinking the Civil Rights and Civil Liberties Revolutions." *Virginia Law Review* 82, no. 1 (1996): 1–67.

Klicka, Christopher. "Child Labor Laws." *Home School Court Report* 22, no. 3 (May–June 2006).

Lafer, Gordon. "The Legislative Attack on American Wages and Labor Standards, 2011–2012." *Economic Policy Institute Briefing Paper* #364, October 21, 2013.

Lea, Arden. "Cotton Textiles and the Federal Child Labor Act of 1916." *Labor History* 16, no. 4 (1975): 485–494.

Leuchtenburg, William E. "The Origins of Franklin D. Roosevelt's 'Court-Packing Plan.'" *Supreme Court Review* (1966): 347.

Lovejoy, Owen R. "Child Labor in the Coal Mines." *Annals of the American Academy of Political and Social Science* (March 1906): 35–41.

———. "Child Labor in the Glass Industry." *Annals of the American Academy of Political and Social Science* (March 1906): 42–53.

Lumpkin, Katherine Du Pre. "The Child Labor Provisions of the Fair Labor Standards Act." *Law and Contemporary Problems* 6 (1939): 391–405.

Macy, Edward W. "Opposition Tactics against the Child Labor Amendment." *American Labor Legislation Review* 15 (December 1924): 110–114.

Magliocca, Gerard N. "Court-Packing and the Child Labor Amendment." *Constitutional Commentary* 27 (2011): 455–486.

McKelway, Alexander J. "Child Labor in Southern Industry." *Annals of the American Academy of Political and Social Science* (May 1905): 431.

———. "Child Labor in the Southern Cotton Mills." *Annals of the American Academy of Political and Social Science* (March 1906): 1–11.

———. "The Child Labor Problem: A Study in Degeneracy." *Annals of the American Academy of Political and Social Science* (May 1906): 135–147.

Merritt, Ella Arvilla, and Floy Hendricks. "Trend of Child Labor, 1940–44." *Monthly Labor Review* (April 1945): 756–775.

Moskowitz, Seymour. "Dickens Redux: How American Child Labor Law Became a Con Game." Legal Studies Research Paper Series, Valparaiso University School of Law. April 2010.

Murtha, Donald. "Wage-Hour and Child Labor Legislation in the Roosevelt Administration." *Lawyers Guild Review* 5 (1945): 185–191.

Novkov, Julie. "Historicizing the Figure of the Child in Legal Discourse: The Battle over the Regulation of Child Labor." *American Journal of Legal History* 44, no. 4 (October 2000): 369–404.

Parsons, Alzina. "Child Slavery in America: The Child, the Factory, and the State." *The Arena* 10, no. 1 (June 1894): 177–122.

Pearson, Susan J. "'Age Ought to Be a Fact'": The Campaign against Child Labor and the Rise of the Birth Certificate." *Journal of American History* 101, no. 4 (March 2015): 1144–1165.

"The Political Economy of Child Labor." *American Economic Association* 5, no. 2 (March 1890): 41, 48.

Pound, Roscoe. "Liberty of Contract." *Yale Law Journal* 18, no. 7 (1909): 454–487.

———. "The Scope and Purpose of Sociological Jurisprudence." *Harvard Law Review* 25, no. 6 (April 1912): 489–516.

"Results of the Referendum as to Child Labor Amendments and Legislation." Report. *American Bar Association Journal* 23 (1937): 915–919.

Robinson, W. A. "Advisory Referendum in Massachusetts on the Child Labor Amendment." *American Political Science Review* 19 (1925): 69–73.

Rosten, Leo C. "Public Opinion and the Washington Correspondents." *Public Opinion Quarterly* 1, no. 1 (January 1937): 36–52.

Samuel, Howard D. "Troubled Passage: The Labor Movement and the Fair Labor Standards Act." *Monthly Labor Review* (December 2000): 32–37.

Sanders, Frederic W. "Hull House Maps and Papers." *Political Science Quarterly* 11, no. 2 (June 1896): 340, 342.

Sawyer, Logan Everett, III. "Constitutional Principle, Partisan Calculation, and the Beveridge Child Labor Bill." *Law and History Review* (May 2013): 325–353.

Schoenfeld, Margaret H. "Analysis of the Labor Provisions of N.R.A. Codes." *Monthly Labor Review* 40, no. 3 (1935): 574–603.

Sherman, Richard B. "The Rejection of the Child Labor Amendment." *Mid-America: An Historical Review* 45, no. 1 (1963): 6.

Smith, James Barclay. "A Child Labor Amendment Is Unnecessary." *California Law Review* 27:1 (1938): 15–47.

"Social Aspects of Child-Labor." *American Economic Association* 5, no. 2 (March 1890): 59.

Social Dynamite: The Report of the Conference on Unemployed, Out-of-School Youth in Urban Areas. Washington, DC: National Committee for Children and Youth, 1961.

Spillenger, Clyde. "Reading the Judicial Canon: Alexander Bickel and the Book of Brandeis." *Journal of American History* 79, no. 1 (June 1992): 125–151.

"State Rights and the Child Labor Tax Law." *Columbia Law Review* 22, no. 7 (November 1922): 659–662.

Storrs, Landon R.Y. *Civilizing Capitalism: The National Consumers' League, Women's Activism, and Labor Standards in the New Deal Era.* Chapel Hill: University of North Carolina Press, 2000.

Strauss, David A. "Why Was Lochner Wrong?" *University of Chicago Law Review* 70, no. 1 (Winter 2003): 373–386.

"The Supreme Court and the Children." *Social Service Review* 15, no. 1 (March 1941): 116–119.

Trimble, Bruce R. "The Child Labor Problem." *Kansas City Law Review* 5 (1936–1937): 184–191.

Tyson, William S. "The Fair Labor Standards Act: A Survey and Evaluation of the First Eleven Years." *Labor Law Journal* (January 1950): 278–286.

Waite, Edward F. "The Child Labor Amendment." *Minnesota Law Review* 9, no. 3 (1925): 179–210.

Walker, Roger. "The A.F.L. and Child-Labor Legislation: An Exercise in Frustration." *Labor History* 11, no. 3 (1970): 323–340.

Warren, Bentley W. "The Proposed Child Labor Amendment: Its Implications and Consequences." *Virginia Law Review* 11, no. 1 (1924): 1–20.

Warren, Charles. "The New 'Liberty' under the Fourteenth Amendment." *Harvard Law Review* 39, no. 4 (February 1926): 431–465.

Yellowitz, Irwin. "The Origins of Unemployment Reform in the United States." *Labor History* 9, no. 3 (1968): 338–360.

Newspapers and Magazines

"A.F. of L. Attacks Child Labor Ruling." *New York Times*, August 24, 1921, 7.

"Amendment on Child Labor Goes to State Legislatures." *New York Times*, June 22, 1924, X12.

"Another Child Labor Law." *Youth's Companion*, June 18, 1908, 294.

"Article 13." *Christian Nation* 34, no. 2 (September 23, 1886): 2.

"Author of Child Labor Law Says It Will Be Held Good." *Labor Journal*, September 14, 1917, 3.

"Ban on Child Labor Opposed by Grange." *New York Times*, November 22, 1924, 20.

"Batboy Is Called Out by Labor Officials, Who Vow a Review." *New York Times*, May 28, 1993, A10.

Battaile, Janet. "Supermarket Faces Federal Complaints in Child-Labor Case." *New York Times*, November 9, 1992, A13.

Berg, Rebecca. "Jay Leno Makes Fun of the Missouri Senate Bill." *St. Louis Post Dispatch*, February 16, 2011.

"Beveridge Makes a Great Speech." *Aberdeen Daily American*, January 24, 1907.

"Bill Is Introduced: Embodies Policies of Message Calling on Congress to Act." *New York Times*, May 25, 1937, 1.

"Boys Employed in Coal Mines." *New York Times*, July 19, 1885, 3.

Bromley, Dorothy Dunbar. "Child Labor Fight at a Critical Stage." *New York Times*, January 27, 1935, E6.

———. "The Newspapers and Child Labor." *Nation* 140 (January 30, 1935): 131–132.

"Call Children from War Plants." *New York Times*, November 24, 1918, 8.

Campbell, Helen. "Prisoners of Poverty." *New York Tribune*, October 1886.

———. "Child Labor and Some of Its Results." *The Chautauquan: A Weekly Magazine* 10, no. 1 (October 1889): 22–23.

"Child Labor." *The Chautauquan: A Weekly Magazine* 7, no. 10 (July 1887): 631.

"Child Labor." *The Independent* (August 21, 1902): 2032.

"Child Labor." *New York Times*, May 21, 1922, 38.

"Child Labor Act Declared Invalid." *New York Times*, September 1, 1917, 2.

"The Child-Labor Amendment." *Literary Digest*, September 16, 1922, 12.

"The Child Labor Amendment's Defeat." *New Republic* 42 (May 20, 1925): 330–331.

"Child Labor and Man Power." *Outlook*, November 6, 1918, 331.

"Child Labor and the Consumers' League." *Friends' Intelligencer*, February 24, 1906, 124.

"Child Labor and the War." *Monthly Labor Review* 10 (February 1920): 174.

"Child Labor Ban Urged in Pulpits." *New York Times*, January 26, 1925, 19.

"Child Labor Bill Dies in Assembly; Vote Is 102 to 42." *New York Times*, May 10, 1937, 8.

"Child Labor Bill Menaced by Shift in Assembly." *New York Times*, February 24, 1936, 1.

"Child Labor Bill Passed." *New York Times*, May 10, 1908, 7.

"Child Labor Curb Offered by Smith." *New York Times*, March 6, 1934, 6.

"The Child Labor Decision." *New York Times*, June 5, 1918, 10.

"Child Labor Drive Gets New Impetus: Non-Partisan Committee Set Up." *New York Times*, January 7, 1935, 10.

"Child Labor Fight Reaches Senate." *New York Times*, May 4, 1924, XX10.

"Child Labor Foes Urge State to Act." *New York Times*, February 19, 1934.

"Child Labor Group Scorns Smith Plan." *New York Times*, March 7, 1934, 6.

"Child Labor Grows as Effect of War." *New York Times*, January 4, 1920, 14.

"Child Labor Law Defied." *New York Times*, December 19, 1912, 24.

"Child Labor Laws." *New York Times*, January 28, 1907, 6.

"Child Labor Laws Urged in Congress." *New York Times*, December 24, 1923, 21.

"Child Labor Law Upset by the Court." *New York Times*, June 4, 1918, 14.

"Child Labor Plans Offered in the Senate." *New York Times*, March 25, 1937, 1.

"Child Labor Remains." *New York Times*, December 24, 1944, 54.

"Child Labor Rise Found after NRA." *New York Times*, February 2, 1936, N2.

"Child Labor Rule Asked in All Codes." *New York Times*, July 20, 1933, 10.

"Child Labor's End Foreseen as Outcome of Textile Code." *New York Times*, August 13, 1933, XX2.

"The Children at Work." *The Catholic World: A Monthly Magazine of General Literature and Science* 43 (August 1886): 619.

"Children of School Ages Deserting the Classroom." *New York Times*, October 10, 1943, E9.

"Children's Bureau Conference on Child-Welfare Standards." *Monthly Labor Review* 8 (June 1919): 216–220.

"Children's Labor in Factories." *New York Times*, January 1, 1887, 1.

"Children's Rights and States' Rights." *Literary Digest*, February 9, 1907, 194.

"Church Fights Child Labor." *Kalamazoo Gazette*, October 12, 1907.

Compton, Stephen C. "Edgar Gardner Murphy and the Child Labor Movement." *Historical Magazine of the Protestant Episcopal Church* 52, no. 2 (June 1983): 181–194.

Cooper, Matthew. "The Tea Party's Constitutional Vision." *National Journal*, February 17, 2011.

Corwin, Edward S. "The Child Labor Decision." *New Republic* 26, no. 397 (July 12, 1922): 179.

"*The Cosmopolitan*'s Readers Agree That This Disgrace Must Go." *The Cosmopolitan*, November 1906, 109.

"Cotton Mills Put Child Labor Ban into Textile Code." *New York Times*, June 29, 1933, 1.

"Court Overthrows Child Labor Laws." *New York Times*, August 23, 1921, 31.

"Criticizes Supreme Court: Senator Owen Thinks It's Time to Apply the Recall." *New York Times*, July 29, 1911, 1.

"Debate Child Labor Bill: Divergent Views Advanced in Senate on Its Constitutionality." *New York Times*, August 5, 1916, 16.

"Delinquency Rise Pictured at Forum." *New York Times*, February 5, 1943, 13.

"The Democrats' Child-Labor Law." *Literary Digest*, September 2, 1917, 547.

"Denies Child Labor Tales." *New York Times*, January 7, 1915, 10.

Dinwiddie, Courtenay. "Child Labor Legislation: Plan of First Federal Law Preferred." *New York Times*, January 2, 1938, 60.

"Dispensing with the Courts." *New York Times*, June 7, 1918, 12.

Edelman, Peter. "Child Labor Revisited." *Nation*. August 21–28, 1982, 136–138.

"Education the Remedy." *New York Times*, January 17, 1887, 3.

"The Employment of Children in Factories." *New York Times*, October 1, 1871, 4.

"End of NRA." *New York Times*, June 1, 1935, E1.

"Evils of Child Labor." *New York Times*, April 23, 1888, 2.

"Evils of Child Labor." *New York Observer and Chronicle* 83, no. 9 (March 2, 1905): 280.

"Evils of Child Labor: Prof. Adler Calls Attention to a Menacing Danger." *New York Times*, January 10, 1887, 8.

"Factories of New York: Annual Report of State Inspector O'Leary." *New York Times*, January 18, 1897, 3.

"Factory Children: Their Condition in This City." *New York Times*, January 25, 1871, 5.

"Factory Report." *New York Times*, February 1, 1894, 3.

"For a Child Labor Law." *New York Times*, December 21, 1906, 6.

Frankfurter, Felix. "Child Labor and the Court." *New Republic* 31, no. 399 (July 26, 1922): 248–250.

Freitag, Michael. "Thousands of Children Doing Adults' Work." Special to the *New York Times*, February 5, 1990, A1, B1, B4.

French, Paul Comly. "Children on Strike." *Nation* 136, no. 3543 (May 31, 1933): 611.

Gallup, George. "Child Labor Amendment Approved by 76% in National Poll." *America Speaks: The National Weekly Poll of Public Opinion*, February 21, 1937.

"Georgia for Child Labor: A Bill to Restrict It Killed Because of Its New England Backing." *New York Times*, November 10, 1897, 1.

Goldmark, Pauline. "Child Labor in Canneries." *Annals of the American Academy of Political and Social Science*, 35, Suppl.: *Child Employing Industries* (March 1910): 152–154.

"Heresy from Washington." *New York Times*, February 8, 1907, 8.

Humphreys, Mary G. "The Consumers' League Holds an Annual Meeting." *Harper's Bazaar*, June 21, 1890, 23, 25.

"The Investigation Mania." *New York Times*, September 7, 1883, 4.

"Involuntary Child Servitude." *Barron's*, 2, 21 (May 22, 1922): 9.

"Is There No Protection?" *Outlook*, May 31, 1922, 199.

"Is the Supreme Court Too Supreme?" *Literary Digest*, July 1, 1922, 21.

"It's Work for Women: The Consumers' League Holds an Annual Meeting." *New York Times*, February 13, 1896, 10.

Kilborn, Peter T. "Playing Games with Labor Laws: When Work Fills a Child's Hours." *New York Times*, December 10, 1989, 1, 46.

———. "Tougher Enforcing of Child Labor Law Vowed." *New York Times*, February 8, 1990, A22.

"Labor Laws and Court Decisions: Federal Child Labor Law Held Unconstitutional." *Monthly Labor Review* 13 (October 1921): 191–192.

"Labor Shortage Forcing Children of School Age to Work." *New York Times*, October 13, 1918, 21.

"Labor Shortage Forcing Children of School Age to Work." *New York Tribune*, June 16, 1918, Section 3, 6.

"La Follette Lashes Federal Judiciary." *New York Times*, June 15, 1922, 1.

"The Little Slaves of Capital." *New York Times*, January 29, 1871, 4.

"The Little Slaves of Capital." *New York Times*, January 26, 1873, 4.

McKelway, Alexander J. "The Evil of Child Labor: Why the South Should Favor a National Law." *Outlook*, February 16, 1907, 360.

"More Child Labor Seen over Nation." *New York Times*, March 22, 1936, E10.

"National Effort to Solve Child Labor Problem." *New York Times*, November 27, 1904, SM8.

"The New Child Labor Bill." *The Independent*, September 14, 1918, 343.

Newman, Jeffrey. "Child Labor Law: Bad Time for a Shift." *New York Times*, August 1, 1982, E21.

"New Move in Senate on Child Labor." *New York Times*, June 20, 1918, 11.

"New National Labor Laws Pondered." *New York Times*, April 4, 1937, 70.

"Newsboy Is Ruled Beyond Wage Law." *New York Times*, January 1, 1939, 7.

"News Men Demand 5-Day Week in Code." *New York Times*, September 23, 1933, 8.

"Newspaper Code Is Signed 'Conditionally'; Child Labor Angle Thought Still Pending." *New York Times*, February 18, 1934, 1.

"A New Weapon against Child Labor." *Literary Digest*, January 4, 1919, 14.

"New York Cigar Makers." *Scientific American*, February 23, 1889, 113.

"NRA Review Urges Child Labor Curbs." *New York Times*, April 10, 1936, 39.

"Opinions about Labor." *New York Times*, August 28, 1883, 3.

"Opposed to Federal Children's Bureau." *New York Times*, January 28, 1912, 14.

"Organizes for Law to End Child Labor." *New York Times*, June 2, 1922, 13.

"Overman Opposes Child Labor Bill." *New York Times*, August 8, 1916, 5.

"Pepper Wins in Florida Primary, Swamping Wilcox, New Deal Critic." *New York Times*, May 4, 1938, 1.

Perkins, Frances. "Secretary Perkins Pleads for Child Labor Amendment." *New York Times*, January 28, 1934, XX3.

"A Plea for Reform in Child-Labor Laws." *Literary Digest*, October 20, 1906, 537.

"Powderly Gives Advice: Child Labor, Labor-Saving Machinery, and Education Discussed." *New York Times*, December 16, 1887, 3.

"Practicality of a Federal Child-Labor Law." *Literary Digest*, December 22, 1906, 930.

"The President and the Mill-Child." *Literary Digest*, August 5, 1916, 290.

"President Urges Child Labor Bill." *The Independent*, July 31, 1916, 150.

"Press Comment on the President's Message on State of the Nation." *New York Times*, January 4, 1938, 17.

"Proceedings of the New England Convention of Farmers, Mechanics, and other Working Men." *Workingman's Advocate* (October 20, 1832): 4.

"Progress in Child Labor Laws." *Zion's Herald*, January 6, 1909, 3.

"Protecting the Little Ones." *Life*, July 25, 1918, 128.

Rankin, Ken. "Wage-hour Reforms Raise National Furor." *Nation's Restaurant News*, February 28, 1983, 2.

"Ratified by 28th State: Child Labor Amendment Approved by Kansas Legislature." *New York Times*, February 26, 1937, 6.

"Real Child Labor Reform." *New York Times*, March 15, 1907, 8.

"Regulations Set for Child Labor." *New York Times*, October 17, 1938, 17.

"Return of Child Labor Predicted by Committee." *New York Times*, May 30, 1935, 12.

"Roosevelt Appeals for Child Labor Law." *New York Times*, November 19, 1934, 26.

"Roosevelt Hits Judiciary and Humane Laws." *Albuquerque Journal*, September 22, 1914.

"Roosevelt Plans Face Fight by King." *New York Times*, November 9, 1937, 5.

"Roosevelt Pleads on Child Labor Act." *New York Times*, January 9, 1937, 5.

"The Roosevelt Proposal: President Roosevelt's Message to Congress." *New York Times*, May 25, 1937, 1, 19.

Ryan, John A. "The Supreme Court and Child Labor." *Catholic World* (November 1918): 212–223.

"The Senate Committee." *New York Times*, October 14, 1883, 2.

"Senate Laughs at Crane." *New York Times*, January 12, 1909, 3.

"Senator Scott on Child Labor." *Crockery and Glass Journal*, January 17, 1907, 27.

Shribman, David. "Proposed Relaxation of Child Labor Rules." Special to the *New York Times*, July 28, 1982, A19.

———. "Youth Work Proposals Are Assailed at Hearing." Special to the *New York Times*, July 29, 1982, A19.

"Signs Child Labor Bill." *New York Times*, September 2, 1916, 4.

"Six States Accused of Wage Law Fight." *New York Times*, March 10, 1944, 32.

"Southerners Rake Wage Bill As Evil to the Whole Nation." *New York Times*, July 31, 1937, 1.

Spahr, Charles B. "Child Labor in England and the United States." *The Chautauquan: A Weekly Newsmagazine*, 30, no. 1 (October 1899): 41.

"Sponsors Defend Child Labor Laws." *New York Times*, November 26, 1954, 23.

"Start Campaign to Stop Child Labor." *New York Times*, January 9, 1914, 10.

"State Laws Sought to Aid Child Labor." *New York Times*, May 17, 1922, 6.

"State Rights Row Looms: Johnson's Move for Child Labor Regulations Draws Fire." *Kansas City Star*, May 20, 1922.

"Supreme Court Brief Quotes Shakespeare." *New York Times*, March 9, 1922, 8.

"Sweating-System Evils." *New York Times*, January 21, 1893, 10.

"Sweating-System Inquiry." *New York Times*, April 14, 1892, 3.

"Texas Refuses to Ratify Child Labor Amendment." *New York Times*, February 9, 1934, 13.

"Text of President Coolidge's Address to Congress on the Affairs of the Nation." *New York Times*, December 7, 1923, 4.

"Texts of Order and Letter by President on New Code for Newspapers and Gen. Johnson's Comment." *New York Times*, February 19, 1934, 8.

"Vandenberg Fears Fascist Wage Bill." *New York Times*, June 6, 1937, 4.

"Vandenberg Gives a New Amendment to Ban Child Labor." *New York Times*, March 28, 1937, 1.

Van Vorst, Elizabeth. "The Cry of the Children." Lead article of series. *Saturday Evening Post*, March 10, 1906, 1–3, 28–29.

"Vote 216 to 198: Southerners and Republicans Doom Bill for Present, at Least." *New York Times*, December 18, 1937, 6.

"Wages, Hours: Congress Is Stirred by a Contentious Bill." *Pathfinder*, December 18, 1937, 5.

Whipple, Leon. "The Press Gets a Code." *Survey Graphic* 23 (April 1934): 194–195.

"Wilson and Child Labor." *New York Times*, August 9, 1916, 10.

"Wilson Captures Social Workers." *New York Times*, January 27, 1913, 1.

"Wisconsin Children at Work: Their Condition More Serious Than in Any Other State of the Union." *New York Times*, June 17, 1895, 8.

Wood, Lewis. "Wage Law Upheld by Supreme Court; Old Decision Upset." *New York Times*, July 4, 1941, 1.

Bulletins, Newsletters, and Pamphlets

Becnel, Barbara. "Black Workers: Progress Derailed." *AFL-CIO American Federationist* (January 1978): 1.

"Child Labor." Legislative Committee Report. *American Federationist*, 26 (December 1919): 1146.

"Conscience, Congress, and the Constitution." *Child Labor Bulletin* 7, no. 4 (February 1919): 230.

Coolidge, Louis A. "The Child Labor Amendment: An Appeal to the Christian Men and Women of Massachusetts" (radio address) (1924). The text of the address is found in Box 2, folder 14, Alexander Lincoln papers, Arthur and Elizabeth Schlesinger Library, Harvard University.

Emery, James A. "An Examination of the Proposed Twentieth Amendment to the Constitution of the United States: Being the So-Called Child Labor Amendment." National Association of Manufacturers, New York City, 1924.

Gompers, Samuel. "To Conserve Child Life." *American Federationist* 20, no. 1 (1913): 306.

———. "Let Us Save the Children." *American Federationist* 24 (June 1922): 413.

"The Government and Child Labor." *Child Labor Bulletin* 7, no. 2 (August 1918): 80.

Hamburger, Martin. "Protection from Participation as Deprivation of Rights." *New Generation* 53, no. 3 (Summer 1971): 1–7.

"High Cost of Government." *Manufacturers' News*, October 3, 1925, 12.

Hoover, Herbert. "Address to the American Child Hygiene Association." *American Child* 2 (November 1920): 204.

Keating, Edward. "Federal Child Labor Legislation." Proceedings of the Twelfth Annual Conference. *Child Labor Bulletin* 5 (May 1916–February 1917): 60–68.

Kelley, Florence. "Wanted: A New Standard Child Labor Bill." *Child Labor Bulletin* 7 (May 1917): 32.

Lenroot, Irvine L. (US Senator). "Taxing Child Labor out of Industry." *Child Labor Bulletin* 7, no. 4 (February 1919): 255.

Lindsay, Samuel McCune. "The National Child Labor Meetings." *Federation Bulletin* (February 1906): 221–222.

———. "Child Labor and the Republic." *Federation Bulletin* 5 (February 1907): 182.

———. "National Child Labor Standards." Proceedings of the Tenth Annual Conference on Child Labor. *Child Labor Bulletin* 3, no. 1 (May 1914): 26.

Lovejoy, Owen R. "The Federal Government and Child Labor: A Brief for the Palmer-Owen Child Labor Bill." National Child Labor Committee, Pamphlet 216 (March 1914).

———. "Child Labor Ten Years After." Tenth Annual Report of the General Secretary. *Child Labor Bulletin* 3, no. 3 (November 1914): 8–29.

Manufacturers' Record 86 (September 11, 1924): 3.

McCormick, Medill (US Senator). "Child Labor Must Go." *American Federationist* 24, no. 2 (September 1922): 644–645.

National Child Labor Committee (NCLC). "Judge Boyd's Decision." *American Child* 1, no. 2 (August 1919): 76.

———. "Argument for Constitutionality." *American Child*, 1, no. 4 (February 1920): 279.

———. "Editorial Comment on the Child Labor Amendment." *American Child* 4, no. 4 (December 1922): 3.

———. "Child Labor and the Constitution." *American Child* 4, no. 5 (January 1923): 1.

———. "Child Labor Amendment Favored by Newspapers." *American Child* 5, no. 10 (October 1923): 1.

———. "The Anvil Chorus." *American Child* 6, no. 3 (March 1924): 3–4.

———. "Foes of the Amendment." *American Child* 6, no. 3 (March 1924): 2.

———. "The First Victory." *American Child* 6, no. 5 (May 1924): 1–7.

———. "Children in Revolt." *American Child* 15, no. 5 (May 1933): 1.

———. "The Rise and Fall of Child Labor in 1933." *American Child* 15, no. 9 (December 1933): 6.

———. "President Roosevelt Endorses Amendment." *American Child* 16, no. 3 (March 1934): 1.

———. "The Press and the Amendment." *American Child* 17, no. 2 (February 1935): 2.

———. "Scripps-Howard Press Repudiates A.N.P.A. Stand on Child Labor." *American Child* 17, no. 4 (April 1935): 4.

———. "Highlights on the Amendment!" *American Child* 19, no. 2 (February 1937): 1.

———. "Newspapers Rush to Support Amendment." *American Child* 19, no. 2 (February 1937): 2–3.

———. "Wages and Hours Law Now in Effect." *American Child* 20, no. 8 (November 1938): 1.

———. "Two Years of Federal Control." *American Child* 22, no. 8 (December 1940): 2.

———. "The Significance of the Supreme Court Decision." *American Child* 23, no. 3 (March 1941): 1.

———. "Jobs after School Hours." *American Child* 24, no. 1 (January 1942): 2-3.

———. "A Children's Charter in Wartime." *American Child*, 24, no. 4 (April 1942): 2.

———. "Shall Children Work in Wartime?" *American Child* 24, no. 7 (November 1942): 1.

———. "Basic National Policy." *American Child* 25, no. 3 (March 1943): 2.

———. "The Impact of the War on Child Labor." *American Child* 25, no. 3 (March 1943): 1.

———. "The Legislative Record—1943." *American Child* 25, no. 6 (October 1943): 2.

———. "President Roosevelt on Child Labor." *American Child* 27, no. 4 (April 1945): 1, 4.

———. "A Proposal by Secretary Wirtz." *American Child* 46, no. 3 (May 1964): 1-2.

Powell, Thomas Reed. "Child Labor and the Constitution." *Child Labor Bulletin* 7, no. 4 (February 1919): 258

Report of Proceedings of the Twenty-Sixth Annual Convention of the American Federation of Labor. Washington, DC: National Tribune, 1907.

Report of the Executive Council. "Child Labor Legislation." *American Federationist* 26, no. 2 (August 1919): 724.

"Several Leading Agricultural Publications Favor Child Labor Amendment." *American Child* 6, no. 10 (October 1924): 6.

Taggart, Robert, III. "The Case for Less Stringent Regulations." *New Generation* 53, no. 3 (Summer 1971): 14-19.

"What Shall We Do for the Children in Time of War?" *National Child Labor Committee* (February 1918).

"What the Child Labor Amendment Means." *Manufacturers' Record*, National Association of Manufacturers, Baltimore, Maryland. September 4, 1924.

Wright, Frances. "Lecture on Existing Evils". New York, 1829, 13.

Government Publications and Reports

Code of Federal Regulations, 29 chapter V, subchapter B, 779.505.

Congressional Record, 41, Senate, 1802-1820 (1907).

Congressional Record, Hearings before the Committee on Labor on H.R. 8234, 64th Cong., 1st Sess., January 10-12, 1916, 239.

Congressional Record, 65th Cong., 3d Sess., 611.

Eighth Biennial Report of the Bureau of Labor and Industrial Statistics. State of Wisconsin, 1897-1898: 491.

Emery, James A. "Argument in Opposition to the Form and Validity of the Keating Child Labor Bill." Monday, February 21, 1916, Committee on Interstate Commerce, US Senate.

Fair Labor Standards Act of 1937, Joint Hearings before Committee on Education and Labor, US Senate, and the Committee on Labor, House of Representatives, 75th Congress, Part 1, June 2-5, 1937.

Fair Labor Standards Act of 1937, Joint Hearings before Committee on Education and Labor, US Senate, and the Committee on Labor, House of Representatives, 75th Congress, Part 2, June 7–15, 1937.

Foster, Israel M. "Proposing Child Labor Amendment to the Constitution of the United States." House of Representatives, 67th Congress, Report No. 1694.

Hamilton, Alexander. *Report on the Subject of Manufacturers*. Philadelphia, December 5, 1791, Section III.

Hearing before the Committee on the Judiciary, House of Representatives, 67th Congress, 2nd Sess., on H.J. Res. 327, June 1, 1922. Washington, DC: GPO.

Hearings, US Senate Committee on Interstate Commerce, May 12, 1937, 61–68.

Hearings before a Subcommittee of the Committee on the Judiciary, US Senate, 67th Cong., 4th Sess., Child Labor Amendment to the Constitution, January 10, 1923.

Hearings on the Fair Labor Standards Act, S. 5267, 72nd Congress.

Mayer, Gerald. "Child Labor in America: History, Policy, and Legislative Issues." *Congressional Research Service* (December 27, 2010): 1–33.

Office of Child Labor, Forced Labor, and Human Trafficking. *2015: Findings on the Worst Forms of Child Labor*. Bureau of International Labor Affairs, US Department of Labor, 2016.

Pub. Law No. 718, 75th Cong., 3rd Sess. 52 STAT. 1060, 29 U.S.C. §§ 201–219 (Supp. 1938).

Report of the Secretary of Labor, 66th Cong., 2d Sess., House of Representatives, Doc. 422, Washington, DC, 1920, 740.

Report on Conditions of Woman and Child Wage-Earners in the United States, vol. 6. Senate Document No. 645. Washington, DC, 1910, 52–53.

Roosevelt, Theodore. "Purposes and Policies of the Progress Party." Before the Progressive Convention in Chicago, Illinois, August 6, 1912. Printed in 62d Cong., 2d Sess., Document No. 904, Washington, DC, August 9, 1912.

Second Annual Report of the Factory Inspectors of the State of New York. December 1, 1887, 50.

Second Annual Report of the Inspector of Factories and Workshops of the State of New Jersey, Trenton, NJ, 1884.

"Second Report New Jersey Inspector of Factories and Workshops." Orange, NJ, 1884, 14–18.

"Second Report New Jersey Inspector of Factories and Workshops." *American Economic Association* 5, no. 2 (March 1890): 59.

Senate Judiciary Committee, 75th Cong., 1st Sess., Report No. 788, June 22, 1937.

Sixty-Fourth Congress of the United States of America; At the First Session. *Keating-Owen Child Labor Act of 1916: An Act to Prevent Interstate Commerce in the Products of Child Labor, and for Other Purposes*. Washington DC: GPO, 1916.

Third Biennial Report of the Bureau of Labor Statistics of the State of Colorado, 1891–1892. Excerpted in Grace Abbott, *The Child and the State*. Vol. 1: *Legal Status in the Family Apprenticeship and Child Labor*. New York: Greenwood Press, 1968.

Transcript of Record, Supreme Court of the United States, *United States v. Darby Lumber*. May 18, 1940, 20.

US Bureau of Labor, *Report on Condition of Woman and Child Wage-Earners in the*

United States, 61st Cong., 2d Sess., 1910 (a Bureau of Labor study published in 19 volumes).

US Bureau of Labor, *Report on Condition of Woman and Child Wage-Earners in the United States*. Vol. 1: Cotton Textile Industry (61st Cong., 2d Sess., Senate Doc. 645, Washington, DC, 1910. In Grace Abbott, *The Child and the State*. Vol. 1: *Legal Status in the Family Apprenticeship and Child Labor*. New York: Greenwood Press, 1968.

US Children's Bureau, *Application of the Child Labor Provisions of the Fair Labor Standards Act to Children Engaged in the Distribution and Delivery of Newspapers*. April 12, 1939.

US Congress, "Special Message of the President of the United States Communicated to the Two Houses of Congress," March 25, 1908, 60th Cong., 1st Sess., Senate Document, 406.

US Congress, House Committee on Economic and Educational Opportunities, *Authority for 16 and 17 Years Olds to Load Materials into Balers and Compactors*, report to accompany H.R. 1114, 104th Cong., 1st Sess., House Report 104-278 (Washington, DC: GPO, 1995).

US Congress, House Committee on Education and Labor, Subcommittee on Labor Standards, *Oversight Hearings—Proposed Changes in Child Labor Regulations*, 97th Cong., 2nd Sess., July 28 and August 3, 1982, 1–30.

US Congress, House of Representatives, 69th Cong., 1st Sess., *Statement of Status of Proposed Child Labor Amendment*, transmitted by secretary of state, February 10, 1926. Washington, DC: GPO.

US Department of Commerce and Labor, Bureau of Labor, *Laws Relating to the Employment of Women and Children in the United States*, chapter 564, "Employment of Children in Mines, Enacted March 3, 1891." Washington, DC: GPO, July 1907, 145.

US Department of Labor, *Seventh Annual Report of the Chief*, Children's Bureau, June 30, 1919.

US Department of Labor, Bureau of Labor Statistics, "Employment Projections," https://www.bls.gov/emp/ep_chart_001.htm. (accessed January 3, 2018).

US Department of Labor, Bureau of Labor Statistics, *Record of the Discussion before the U.S. Congress on the FLSA of 1938*, I. Washington, GAO, 1938.

US Department of Labor, Bureau of Labor Statistics, *Summary of the Report on Conditions of Woman and Child Wage Earners in the United States*, US Bureau of Labor Statistics Bulletin No. 175. Washington, DC: GPO, 1916.

US Department of Labor Wage and Hour Division, *The Fair Labor Standards Act of 1938, As Amended*. Washington DC: GPO, 2011.

US House of Representatives, 52nd Cong., 2d Sess., January 20, 1893, Report of the Committee on Manufactures on the Sweating System, Report No. 2309.

US Industrial Commission, Final Report. Washington, DC: GPO, 1902, vol. 19, 917–919.

US Senate, *Report on Condition of Woman and Child Wage-Earners in the United States*. Washington, DC: GPO, 1910–1913.

US Senate, 68th Congress, Report No. 406, "Child Labor Amendment," prepared by Senator Shortridge, April 1924, 39.

Paper Collections

Albert J. Beveridge Papers. Manuscript Division, Library of Congress, Washington, DC.

Alexander Jeffrey McKelway Papers, 1814–1942. Manuscript Division, Library of Congress, Washington, DC.

Edgar Gardner Murphy Papers, #1041, Southern Historical Collection, The Wilson Library, University of North Carolina at Chapel Hill.

Felix Frankfurter Papers, Containers 129 and 150. Manuscript Division, Library of Congress, Washington, DC.

Harlan Fiske Stone Papers. Manuscript Division, Library of Congress, Washington, DC.

National Child Labor Committee Papers. Manuscript Division, Library of Congress, Washington, DC.

National Consumers' League Records, 1882–1986. Manuscript Division, Library of Congress, Washington.

Presidential Letters and Speeches

Harding, Warren G. *Second Annual Message to Congress*, December 8, 1922. The American Presidency Project, http://www.presidency.ucsb.edu/ws/index.php?pid =29563 (accessed July 27, 2016).

Roosevelt, Franklin D. *The Public Papers and Addresses of Franklin D. Roosevelt*. Vol. 3: *The Advance of Recovery and Reform*. "Annual Message to Congress," January 3, 1934, 10.

———."Letter to Governors Urging Ratification of the Child Labor Amendment to the Constitution," January 7, 1937. Online by Gerhard Peters and John T. Woolley, *The American Presidency Project*, http://www.presidency.ucsb.edu/ws/?pid =15338 (accessed August 9, 2017).

———. *Public Papers*, vol. 6, "Message to Congress Recommending Legislation," November 5, 1937.

———. "Annual Message to Congress, January 3, 1938."*Public Papers and Addresses*, 1938. New York: Macmillan, 1941.

———. *Public Papers and Addresses*, 1937. New York: Russell and Russell, 1938–1950.

Roosevelt, Theodore. "Fourth Annual Message to Congress," December 6, 1904. *The American Presidency Project*, Gerhard Peters and John T. Woolley, http://www.presidency.ucsb.edu/ws/index.php?pid=29545 (accessed March 26, 2017).

———. "Sixth Annual Message to Congress." December 3, 1906.

Thesis

Petersen, Evelyn V. "The History of the Movement for a Child Labor Amendment in the United States." MA Thesis, Department of History, University of Southern California, June, 1931.

Online Resources

Bickers, Chris. "Tobacco Growers Say 'No' on Child Labor." *Southeast FarmPress*, October 29, 2014. http://www.southeastfarmpress.com/tobacco/tobacco-grow ers-say-no-child-labor (accessed March 25, 2017).

"Bill Would 'Seriously Weaken' State's Child Labor Laws." Wisconsin Education

Association Council, March 7, 2017. http://weac.org/2017/03/07/bill-would-se riously-weaken-states-child-labor-laws/ (accessed March 12, 2017).

"Catholic Responses to Industrialization." Catholic University of America, *American Catholic History Research Center and University Archives*. http://cuomeka.wrlc.org /exhibits/show/industrial/background/background—catholic-responses (accessed March 30, 2017).

Chen, Michelle. "States Attempt to Instill 'Work Ethic' by Rolling Back Child Labor Protections." *Nation*, January 12, 2012. https://www.thenation.com/article /states-attempt-instill-work-ethic-rolling-back-child-labor-protections/ (accessed April 1, 2017).

"Child Model FAQs." New York State Department of Labor. https://labor.ny.gov /workerprotection/laborstandards/secure/ChildModelFAQs.shtm (accessed March 25, 2017).

"Conservative Critics and the End of Reform: The 1920s." Catholic University of America, *American Catholic History Research Center and University Archives*. http:// cuomeka.wrlc.org/exhibits/show/bishops/hiatus/1919hiatus-intro (accessed March 30, 2017).

Cousins, Christopher. "LePage's Efforts to Remove Child Labor Barriers to Continue in January." http://bangordailynews.com/2013/12/02/politics/lepages-ef forts-to-remove-child-labor-barriers-to-continue-in-january/ (accessed April 2, 2017).

Dickerman, Kenneth. "20 Haunting Portraits of Child Laborers in 1900s America." *Washington Post*, October 31, 2016. https://www.washingtonpost.com/news/in -sight/wp/2016/10/31/20-haunting-portraits-of-child-laborers-in-1900s-america /?utm_term=.f65a3a4bc9bb (accessed January 12, 2017).

"Employment Projections." US Department of Labor. March 15, 2016. https:// www.bls.gov/emp/ep_chart_001.htm (accessed April 2, 2017).

"Gingrich's History Gap." *Los Angeles Times*, editorial, November 22, 2011. http:// articles.latimes.com/2011/nov/22/opinion/la-ed-history-20111122 (accessed April 2, 2017).

"Going to Bat against Bureaucracy." http://savannahnow.com/stories/070205/313 8634.shtml#.WQIJRsZOmM8 (accessed April 27, 2017).

Gonzalez, Sarah. "Lawmakers Put Child Agricultural Labor Rules under the Microscope." Agri-Pulse.com, February 2, 2012. https://www.agri-pulse.com/arti cles/1538-lawmakers-put-child-agricultural-labor-rules-under-the-microscope (accessed June 12, 2017).

———. "Child Farm Labor Debate Resurfaces with Focus on Tobacco Farms." Agri-pulse.com, September 25, 2014. https://www.agri-pulse.com/articles/4445-child -farm-labor-debate-resurfaces-with-focus-on-tobacco-farms (accessed June 12, 2017).

Halloran, Liz. "Gingrich's Proposals on Child Labor Stir Attacks, but Raise Issues." NPR, December 7, 2011. http://www.npr.org/sections/itsallpolitics/2011 /12/07/143258836/gingrichs-proposals-on-child-labor-stir-attacks-but-raise -real-issues (accessed March 31, 2017).

Kapur, Sahil. "GOP Senator: Federal Ban on Child Labor Is Unconstitutional." Monday, January 17, 2011. http://www.rawstory.com/2011/01/gop-senator -calls-federal-laws-child-labor-unconstitutional/ (accessed March 25, 2017).

"Labor Case to Cost Food Lion Millions." Bloomberg Business News, August 4, 1993. http://articles.sun-sentinel.com/1993-08-04/business/9301270762_1_food -lion-child-labor-labor-laws (accessed April 24, 2017).

Li, David K. "New Law Aims to Protect Underage Models." *New York Post*, October 22, 2013. http://nypost.com/2013/10/22/new-law-aims-to-protect-under age-models/ (accessed March 25, 2017).

Library of Congress. National Child Labor Committee Collection. Lewis Hine photos. http://www.loc.gov/pictures/collection/nclc/ (accessed April 11, 2017).

Liptak, Kevin. "Gingrich: Laws Preventing Child Labor Are 'Truly Stupid.'" CNN, November 19, 2011. http://politicalticker.blogs.cnn.com/2011/11/19/gingrich -laws-preventing-child-labor-are-truly-stupid/ (accessed April 2, 2017)

"The Mean Girls & Boys Club. Our View: Missouri Legislators Champion Purely Mean Bills. OPINION." *St Louis Post-Dispatch* [MO], February 20, 2011, A22. http://go.galegroup.com.er.lib.k-state.edu/ps/retrieve.do?tabID=T004&resultList Type=RESULT_LIST&searchResultsType=SingleTab&searchType=Advanced SearchForm&currentPosition=44&docId=GALE%7CA249542828&docType =Editorial&sort=Relevance&contentSegment=&prodId=STND&contentSet =GALE%7CA249542828&searchId=R4&userGroupName=ksu&inPS=true *Infotrac Newsstand* (accessed April 2, 2017).

National Conference of State Legislatures. "2014 Child Labor Enacted Legislation." December 16, 2014. http://www.ncsl.org/research/labor-and-employment /2014-child-labor-enacted-legislation.aspx (accessed March 25, 2017).

"Publix Settles Child Labor Charges." *Bloomberg Business News*, August 17, 1993. http://articles.sun-sentinel.com/1993-08-17/business/9308170449_1_paper-bal ers-child-labor-labor-charges (accessed April 24, 2017).

Rosenkrantz, Holly. "Taking Aim at Child Labor Laws." *Bloomberg Businessweek Magazine*, January 5, 2012. https://www.bloomberg.com/news/articles/2012 -01-05/taking-aim-at-child-labor-laws (accessed August 9, 2017).

S.B. 222. Missouri Senate. "Modifies Child Labor Laws." http://www.senate.mo.gov /11info/BTS_Web/Bill.aspx?SessionType=R&BillID=4124271 (accessed March 25, 2017).

Semuels, Alana. "How Common Is Child Labor in the United States?" *Atlantic* (December 14, 2015). https://www.theatlantic.com/business/archive/2014/12/how -common-is-chid-labor-in-the-us/383687/ (accessed January 5, 2018).

Sunde, Joseph. "Work Is a Gift Our Kids Can Handle." Acton Institute Powerblog, November 3, 2016. http://blog.acton.org/archives (accessed March 25, 2017).

Terkel, Amanda. "Maine GOP Legislators Looking to Loosen Child Labor Laws." May 30, 2011. http://www.huffingtonpost.com/2011/03/30/maine-gop-legisla tors-loo_n_842563.html (accessed March 25, 2017).

"Tobacco's Hidden Children: Hazardous Child Labor in United States Tobacco Farming." Human Rights Watch, May 13, 2014. https://www.hrw.org/report /2014/05/13/tobaccos-hidden-children/hazardous-child-labor-united-states-to bacco-farming (accessed April 2, 2017).

Tucker, Jeffrey A. "Let the Kids Work." Foundation for Economic Education, November 3, 2016. https://fee.org/articles/let-the-kids-work/ (accessed February 12, 2017).

Tuttle, Carolyn. "Child Labor during the British Industrial Revolution." August 14,

2001. *EH.Net Encyclopedia*, edited by Robert Whaples, 2001. http://eh.net.ency clopedia/child-labor-during-the-british-indudtrial-revolution/.

US Department of Labor. "Agricultural Employment." https://www.dol.gov/gen eral/topic/youthlabor/agriculturalemployment (accessed January 5, 2018).

US Department of Labor. "Factory Inspection Legislation." 2001. https://www.dol .gov/general/aboutdol/history/mono-regsafepart02 (accessed December 12, 2016).

US Department of Labor, Bureau of Labor Statistics. "Employment Projections." Educational attainment influences earnings and unemployment rates. https:// www.bls.gov/emp/ep_chart_001.htm. (accessed January 3, 2018).

Walsh, Joan. "The Right's Crusade to Repeal the 20th Century." March 14, 2014. http://www.alternet.org/tea-party-and-right/rights-crusade-repeal-20th-century (accessed March 25, 2017).

Weissmann, Jordan. "Newt Gingrich Thinks School Children Should Work as Jan-itors." *Atlantic*, November 21, 2011. https://www.theatlantic.com/business/ar chive/2011/11/newt-gingrich-thinks-school-children-should-work-as-janitors /248837/ (accessed March 26, 2017).

Wishnia, Steve. "Trump's Education Pick Funds Child-Labor Advocates." November 30, 2016, Laborpress. http://laborpress.org/national-news/9012-trump-s-edu cation-pick-funds-child-labor-advocates (accessed January 12, 2017).do?p=ST ND&sw=w&u=ksu&v=2.1&id=GALE%7CA249542828&it=r&asid=a3fb-4f70798e31de2b8d391005c65489 (accessed April 2, 2017).

INDEX

Abbott, Grace, 87, 127, 134–135, 141,
    146, 148, 172, 192
  on Child Labor Amendment, 139–140
  federal child labor legislation and,
    159
  prison-goods theory and, 181
Acheson, Dean, 117
Acton Institute, 9, 238
Adams, Winston, 111
Addams, Jane, 4, 47, 55, 75, 130, 145
Adkins v. Children's Hospital (1923), 127,
    193–194
Adler, Felix, 32, 45–46, 51, 55
Alabama, 41, 189, 197
Alabama Child Labor Committee, 44,
    57
Aldrich, Nelson, 60
Alger, George W., 131
Amalgamated Clothing Workers of
    America, 195
America (Catholic weekly), 145
American Association for Labor
    Legislation, 100
American Association of University
    Women, 143
American Bar Association, 82, 102, 164–
    165
  Vandenberg amendment and, 182–
    183
American Child, The, 47, 133
American Constitutional League, 143
American Cotton Manufacturers'
    Association, 97, 111, 161
American Farm Bureau Federation, 5–6,
    138, 143, 153–154, 170
American Federationist, 31
American Federation of Labor (AFL), 5,
    31, 44, 57, 81, 111, 132, 195, 198

Beveridge-Parsons bill and, 57
  Child Labor Tax Law and, 111
  on Fair Labor Standards Act, 195,
    198, 202
  NRA codes of fair competition and,
    161
  Palmer-Owen bill and, 81
American Federation of Teachers, 134
American Institute of Public Opinion,
    177
American Legion, 143
American Medical Association, 81
American Newspaper Publishers'
    Association (ANPA), 162
Andrews, John, 100
"Anti-Sweating" bill, 34–35
apprenticeship system, 14–15
  in America, 19
  pauper apprenticeship and, 15
Arizona, 152
Arkansas, 152
Arkwright, Richard, 14
Article V, US Constitution, 123–124,
    140–141, 165, 187–189
Ashby, Irene, 28–29
Ashurst-Sumners Act, 181
Atherton Mills, 110
Atherton Mills v. Johnston (1922), 116

Bailey v. Drexel Furniture Company (1922),
    10, 114–116, 118–120, 132
  reaction to, 118–122
Bankhead, William, 200
Barkley, Alben, 182
Barrett, William H., 209
Barron's, 120
Beck, James M., 113
Berger, Victor L., 148

Beveridge, Albert J., 7, 50–51, 62–65, 78, 85–87
  Beveridge bill and, 52, 55, 58–65
  child labor reforms and, 50–51, 58–60
  electoral defeat of, 67
  Theodore Roosevelt and, 51–52, 67
Beveridge-Parsons bill, 55–56, 58, 83
  labor opposition and, 57–58
Bickel, Alexander, 116–117
Bickford, Bruce, 234
birth registration, 75–76
Bitter Cry of the Children, The, 49–50, 59
Bituminous Coal Conservation Act, 173
Black, Hugo, 158, 192, 210
  debate on FLSA and, 197–198
  Supreme Court appointment and, 198
Black-Connery bill, 192–194, 201
Black Monday, 170
Blair, Emily Newell, 134
Boer War, 86
Bolshevik Revolution, 105
Borah, William, 85, 180
Borchardt, Selma, 134
Boston Pilot, The, 152
Boyd, James E., 88–89, 109–112, 116
  Bailey decision and, 112–113
Brace, Charles Loring, 29
Bradley, Joseph, 70–71
Braeman, John, 50
Brandeis, Louis, 91, 116–118, 167, 171–172, 188
breaker boys, 27
Brooklyn Eagle, 121
Brooks, William C., 226
Brown, Larue, 176, 196
Browning, Gordon, 175–176
Bryan, William Jennings, 64
Bureau of Labor, 73, 100, 230
Burlingham, Charles C., 169–170
Burns, David, 233
Bush, George W., 229
Butler, Nicholas Murray, 168
Butler, Pierce, 167, 189
Byrnes, James F., 210

Caffey, Francis G., 51, 131
California, 72, 152, 236
Camp Fire Girls, 143
Cardozo, Benjamin, 167, 171, 188

Carr, Charlotte, 217
Carter v. Carter Coal Co. (1936), 173–174
Catholic Church, Roman, 126, 150–152, 178–179
Census, US, 2, 25, 29, 35, 40, 74, 127, 137, 146, 231
Champion v. Ames (1903), 61, 63, 90. *See also* Lottery Case
Chandler, Albert B., 175
Chandler, Walter, 129
Chandler v. Wise (1939), 187, 208
Charlotte Observer, 81
Chicago Record-Herald, 62
Chicago Tribune, 92, 216
child labor, 2, 24, 26, 159
  age minimums and, 6, 69, 73–74, 82, 107
  age verification and, 41–42, 75–76
  British reforms and, 15–16, 58
  child slavery and, 24, 58
  congressional investigations and, 34–36, 65, 83
  definition of, 2–3, 106, 222
  delinquency and, 216, 222
  evils of, 24, 59, 74, 83
  illiteracy and, 24, 103
  injuries and deaths and, 27–29, 89, 215–216
  maximum hours and, 22, 107
  number of children employed and, 25, 29, 74
  occupations and, 23, 27, 29, 36
  religious views and, 12–13
  southern states and, 40–41, 43–44, 73–74
  standards and, 21, 107–108
  sweatshops and, 33–35
  World War I and, 96–97
  World War II and, 215–219
Child Labor Amendment (1924), 3, 10, 124, 140, 146–149, 188–189, 208
  agricultural support for, 139
  American Bar Association and, 164–165
  arguments against, 140, 143, 146–149
  Catholic opposition to, 146, 151–152, 166, 178–179
  farm opposition and, 138–139, 148–149

Great Depression and, 157–159
House vote and, 140
Massachusetts ratification and, 149–150
newspapers and, 137, 165–166
New York ratification and, 178–179
public opinion and, 158, 177
ratification campaign and, 142–145, 158–159, 189–190
sectional differences and, 126
Senate vote and, 141
text of, 141–142, 155
Child Labor Bulletin, 47
child labor laws, 37, 40, 43–44, 69, 79
Clinton administration and, 226–229
contemporary attacks on, 9, 232–235
enforcement issues and, 37–38, 79
hazardous occupations and, 228–230
NRA codes of fair competition and, 161–163, 171
Reagan administration and, 224–225
southern states and, 73–74, 126
unemployed youth and, 222–223
wartime experience and, 216–219
Child Labor Tax Law, 106, 110, 113–117, 119, 127
Children's Aid Society, 29
Children's Bureau, 7, 74, 87–88, 95–96, 107, 127, 157, 187, 196–197, 208
birth registration and, 75
Child Labor Division of, 99–100
Child Labor Tax Law and, 127
establishment of, 7, 74–75
Fair Labor Standards Act and, 206–207
Keating-Owen Act and, 95
World War II and, 217–219
Children's Code, 107–108
children's strike, 159
Children's Year, 96
Christmas Carol, A, 186
Citizens' Committee to Protect Our Homes and Children, 150, 153
Clark, Bennett Champ, 181
Clark, David, 81, 108–110, 134, 143, 148–149, 207
Farmers' States' Rights League and, 149
Southern Textile Bulletin and, 81, 134

Clark Distilling Co. v. Western Maryland Railway Co., 90
Clarke, John H., 91, 116
Clinton administration, 226–229
Cohen, Benjamin V., 192
Coleman v. Miller (1939), 186–190, 208
Collier's, 144
Colorado, 36–37
Colt, LeBaron, 139
Combest, Larry, 229
Commerce Clause, 60, 67, 91, 171, 174, 197, 209–211
arguments in *Hammer*, 89
Hoke v. United States and, 77–78
Commission on Children in Wartime, 217–218
Compton, Carl T., 170
compulsory school attendance laws, 4, 22–23, 43, 107, 238, 241
Cone, Fred P., 175
Congress, 188
Congress of Industrial Organizations (CIO), 195, 199
Connecticut, 6, 20, 22, 40, 170, 177, 241
Connery, William, 192
constitutional amendment, 123–124, 133
Constitutional Government in the United States, 76–77
Constitutional Limitations, 70
Constitutional Revolution of 1937, 183, 189
Cooley, Thomas, 70
Coolidge, Calvin, 125, 137, 179
Coolidge, Louis A., 143, 150
Copeland, Royal, 168
Copley, Ira C., 79–80
Corcoran, Thomas G., 171, 192
Corwin, Edward S., 120–121
Cosmopolitan, 47
Costigan, Edward P., 135, 139
cotton textile mills, 17, 28, 41, 73–74, 81, 108
Council for Burley Tobacco, 236
Court-packing plan, 176–177, 180, 184, 210
Craig, Larry, 229
Crane, Winthrop, 66
Cummings, Homer, 172

Cunningham, Jane, 234
Curely, James M., 150, 152

Dagenhart, Reuben, 136–137
Dagenhart, Roland H., 88–89
Darby, Fred W., 208–209
Davis, George H., 194
Day, William Rufus, 71, 90–91, 101
Debs, Eugene, 148
De Forest, Robert W., 54, 64
Delaware, 189
Democratic Party, 77, 81, 84, 142, 179
DeVos, Betsy, 9, 238
Dickens, Charles, 15, 58, 186
Digest of Manufacturers, 20
Dillon v. Goss (1921), 165, 186
Dinwiddie, Courtenay, 167, 176, 181–182, 195–196, 205
District of Columbia, 52, 65–66, 83, 96, 108
Dockweiler, John, 200
Dodds, Harold W., 170
Dole, Elizabeth, 226
Donahue, Thomas, 224
Donovan, Raymond, 224
Douglas, William O., 188, 210
Dowling, Noel T., 158, 212
Drexel Furniture Company, 112, 114
Drexel Furniture Company v. Bailey (1921), 112–113. *See also* Boyd, James E.
Dubinsky, David, 195

Economic Policy Institute, 233
Editor and Publisher, 165
Edmunds, Sterling E., 166
Eighteenth Amendment, 126, 131. *See also* prohibition
El Paso Times, 106
Emery, James A., 40, 85, 143, 194
Emporia Gazette, 166, 170
Ewing, Thomas, 229
Exceptions Clause, 94
Executive Committee of Southern Cotton Manufacturers, 88, 109

Factory Act of 1802, 15
factory inspectors, 38–39

Fair Labor Standards Act (1938), 7–8, 10, 158, 190, 192, 237
agricultural exemptions and, 230
batboys and batgirls and, 227–228
child labor provisions and, 193, 204–205, 231–232
congressional testimony and, 194–195
Darby Lumber decision and, 210–211
industrial home work and, 214–215
labor unions and, 195, 198, 202
1949 amendments and, 221–222
violations of, 225–227
wage and hour provisions of, 204–205
Farm and Fireside, 139
Farmers' Educational and Co-operative Union of America, 81
Farmers' States' Rights League, 149. *See also* Clark, David
Farm Journal, 138–139
FDR v. The Constitution (book), 171–172
Federal Council of Churches of Christ in America, 81, 128
federalism, 8, 34
cooperative, 8, 121
dual, 8, 34, 59, 66, 91, 114, 146–147
Feldman, Justin, 235
Fidelity Manufacturing Company, 88, 136
Field, Stephen, 70
Fitzgerald, Roy G., 128
Food Lion, 226–227
Foster, Israel Moore, 134, 140, 144
Foundation for Economic Education, 237
Four Horsemen, 168, 174, 189, 198, 210
Fourteenth Amendment's Due Process Clause, 70
substantive due process, 70–72
France, Joseph, 103
Frankfurter, Felix, 97, 131–132, 139, 155–156, 188, 210
Freund, Ernst, 139
Fuller, Raymond Garfield, 122, 251n8
Fulton, Charles, 60–61

Gallup, George, 177, 188, 201
Gard, Warren, 105
Gemsco, Inc. v. Walling (1945), 214
General Court of Massachusetts, 149–150

General Federation of Women's Clubs,
43, 64
George v. Bailey (1921), 112
Georgia, 41, 73, 144, 152
Gerry, Elbridge T., 75
Gibbons, Edmund F., 178
Gibbons v. Ogden (1824), 62, 89, 210–211
Gilded Age, 23
Gingrich, Newt, 231–232
Glennon, John J., 166
Golodner, Linda F., 226
Gompers, Samuel, 28, 31–32, 111, 119,
128–129, 145
on Beveridge-Parsons bill, 57
Child Labor Amendment and, 128–
129
child labor views of, 31–32
reaction to *Bailey v. Drexel Furniture
Company*, 119
Good Housekeeping, 144
Gordon, Thurlow M., 93
Gorton, Slade, 229
Grange, 138, 143, 179
Great Atlantic & Pacific Tea Company
(A&P), 227
Great Depression, 155
Great Recession, 233, 235
Green, William, 161, 195, 199–200, 204
Greenback Party, 26
Griswold, Glenn, 200
Guthrie, William D., 165, 168, 185

Hall, George, 169
Hamilton, Alexander, 13–14
Hammer, William C., 88
Hammer v. Dagenhart (1918), 10, 89–94,
98, 102, 104–105, 109, 181, 185,
193, 233
Bailey v. Drexel Furniture Company
and, 116
Child Labor Tax Law and, 112–114
Dagenhart brief in, 89–90
Darby Lumber and, 209–213
dissenting opinion and, 91, 185
impact of, 95, 136–137
reaction to, 92–94
US government brief in, 89
Hand, Learned, 167
Hapgood, Norman, 117

Harding, Warren G., 113, 125, 132–133,
137
Hardwick, Thomas W., 84, 102, 107
Harkin, Tom, 236
Harlan, John, 61, 71
Harrison Narcotics Tax Act (1914), 101
Harvard Law Review, 93
Hay, Alice, 140
Hayes, Cardinal Patrick, 153, 178
hazardous occupations, 228–230
Heflin, J. Thomas, 201
Helvering v. Davis (1937), 183
Hersey, Ira G., 130
Hill, Lister, 201
Hillman, Sidney, 195
Hindman, Hugh D., 2, 17
Hine, Lewis W., 1, 44, 74, 236–237
photo collection, 1, 74
Hippolite Egg Company v. United States, 90
Hoar, George F., 34
Hoboken conference, 76, 86
Hoke v. United States (1913), 77–78, 90,
93, 121
Holmes, Oliver Wendell, 71–72, 90, 105,
116–118, 167, 185
dissent in *Hammer*, 91
vote in *Bailey*, 118
Home School Legal Defense Association,
229
Homeschool Non-Discrimination Act,
230
Hoover, Herbert, 125, 175, 179
Hormel, Jay C., 194
House Labor Committee, 83, 98, 202
Hughes, Charles Evans, 167, 171, 183–
184, 189, 211
Hull House settlement, 4, 75, 148, 217
Human Rights Watch, 236
Humphreys, Benjamin G., II, 105
Humphreys, David, 20
Husting, Paul, 85

Idaho, 233
Illinois Bureau of Labor Statistics (BLS),
27, 38
Industrial Commission, 35–36
Industrial Revolution, 14, 16–18, 23
early American (Market Revolution),
17–18

Inland Steel Co. v. Yedinak (1909), 72
In re Spencer (1906), 72
International Child Welfare League, 79,
   81

Jackson, Robert H., 187, 193
Jenkins, Thomas A., 145
Johnson, Edwin O., 181
Johnson, Hiram, 128
Johnson, Hugh S., 160
Johnson, Robert, 194
Johnston, Eugene T., 110
Johnston, John W., 110, 116
Jones, William Carey, 93

Kansas, 152, 185–186, 189
Kapenga, Chris, 236
Keating, Edward, 82, 85, 94, 98
Keating-Owen Act, 10, 86–87, 91–92,
   97–98, 101, 110, 114, 182, 206
   implementation of, 88, 95
   provisions of, 87
Keating-Owen bill, 82–83, 101
   opposition to, 84–85
Keeler, Miriam, 127
Kelley Wischnewetzky, Florence, 32–33,
   45, 65, 75, 79, 130, 134–135, 141–
   142, 147–148, 153–154
   chief inspector of Illinois's BLS and,
     33, 38
   on Child Labor Amendment, 141,
     145, 147–148, 153
   death of, 155–156
   as general secretary of the National
     Consumers' League, 48
   NCLC trustee and, 65
Kellog, Frank B., 102–103
Kennedy, Edward M., 225
Kentucky, 185–186
Kentucky Whip and Collar Co. v. Illinois
   Central Railroad Co. (1937), 181,
   193
Kenyon, William S., 80, 94, 97, 99
King, William H., 197
Kirkland, Lane, 224
Kitchen, Claude, 105
Kitchin, William W., 83
Kleinfeld resolution, 178
Knights of Labor, 30–31

Knox, Philander, 60–61
Kreidler, Mike, 229
Ku Klux Klan, 151, 198
Kuldell, R. C., 194
Kyvig, David, 126, 135

Labor, 135–137
Labor, US Department of, 37, 225–228,
   230
Lafer, Gordon, 233
La Follette, Robert, 121–122, 125, 132
LaGuardia, Fiorello, 168
laissez faire, 126–127, 212
Landon, Alf, 174
Lane, Franklin K., 92
Lasson, James F., 129
Lathrop, Julia, 75, 98, 131, 134, 145
Lawton v. Steele (1889), 70
League of Women Voters, 132
Lee, Mike, 9, 233
Lehman, Herbert H., 168–169, 177–
   178
Lenroot, Irvine, 99, 108
LePage, Paul, 233
Lewis, John L., 195
Lewis, William Draper, 98, 131, 134
liberty of contract doctrine, 70–72, 78,
   127, 173, 183, 210. See also
   Lochner v. New York (1905)
Lindsay, John D., 75
Lindsay, Matilda, 129
Lindsay, Samuel McCune, 45, 47, 54–55,
   64–65, 98, 130–131, 154
   on Beveridge-Parsons bill, 55, 64–
     65
   Child Labor Amendment and, 154
Lindsay, William M., 185
Link, Arthur, 86
Literary Digest, 144
Lochnerism, 72
Lochner v. New York (1905), 71–72, 78
Lodge, Henry Cabot, 52–53, 103–104,
   107, 125, 149
Lord Ashley (Anthony Ashley Cooper),
   16
Los Angeles Times, 232
Lottery Case, 61, 63, 90
Loudenbeck, Amy, 236
Louisville Courier-Journal, 163

Lovejoy, Owen R., 45, 64, 78–79, 81,
  100, 119, 129–130, 144, 148, 154
  Child Labor Amendment and, 133–
  135, 154
Lowell, A. Lawrence, 143, 150
Lowell, Francis Cabot, 18–19
Lowell, Josephine, 47
Lowell mills, 18–20

Macy, V. Everit, 98
Madison, James, 91
Maginnis, Edward J., 145
Magliocca, Gerard N., 176
Maine, 23, 233
Mann Act, 77–78, 90
  Hoke v. United States and, 77–78
Mansfield, Joseph, 199
Manufacturers' Record, 144–145, 147
Market Revolution, 18
Markham, Edwin, 47, 53
Marshall, John, 67, 106, 114, 210
Martin, Clarence E., 164
Martin, George, 139
Mason, Alpheus T., 118, 212
Massachusetts, 7, 35, 37, 20, 22, 149–150,
  152, 241
  Child Labor Amendment and, 149–
  152
Match Act (Esch-Hughes Act) (1912),
  100
Maverick, Maury, 184
Mayo, Leonard W., 217
McConnell, Beatrice, 208
McCormick, Medill, 123, 134
McCorsey, James, 144
McCoy, Tommy, 227–228
McCray v. United States (1904), 100, 102,
  113, 115
McCulloch v. Maryland (1819), 114–115
McDaid, Hugh, 226
McKelway, Alexander J., 45, 64, 74
  testimony on Keating-Owen bill, 83–
  84
McKenna, Joseph, 77–78, 91, 93
McReynolds, James Clark, 90, 92, 167,
  189
Meat Inspection Act, 50, 53–54
Mellett, Lowell, 135
Meredith, E. T., 139

Michigan, 233, 235
Miller, George, 225
Milwaukee Sentinel, 62
Minnesota, 235
Mississippi, 73, 189
Missouri, 166–167, 235
Moderation League, 138
Morehead v. New York ex rel. Tipaldo
  (1936), 173
Muller v. Oregon (1908), 116
Munn v. Illinois (1877), 173
Murphy, Edgar Gardner, 44–46, 56–57,
  79
  Alabama reforms and, 57
Myers, Mac, 207

Napier, Viola, 144
Nash v. United States (1913), 211
Nation, 144
National Association of Manufacturers
  (NAM), 5, 39–40, 85, 143–145,
  148–149, 153
  Fair Labor Standards Act and, 194,
  202
National Association of Wood
  Manufacturers, 194
National Association Opposed to Woman
  Suffrage, 140
National Catholic Welfare Council, 129,
  151
National Child Labor Committee
  (NCLC), 5, 10, 44, 67, 78–79, 81,
  96, 112, 172, 219
  agenda of, 46, 67, 78–79
  Bailey v. Drexel Furniture Company
  and, 119
  on Beveridge-Parsons bill, 51, 56, 64–
  65
  Board of Trustees of, 51, 54, 64, 98,
  130–131, 158–160
  Child Labor Amendment and, 130–
  131, 137
  Child Labor Tax Law and, 112
  Fair Labor Standards Act and, 214
  formation of, 44–46
  Lewis Hine and, 74
  NRA codes and, 160–161, 163, 172
  on Palmer-Owen bill, 80–81
  United States v. Darby Lumber and, 213

National Child Labor Committee
(NCLC), *contiuned*
World War I and, 96, 98
World War II and, 217
National Civic Federation, 63
National Committee for the Protection
of Child, Family, School and
Church, 166
National Committee on the Employment
of Youth, 223
National Consumers' League, 5, 39, 47–
48, 182, 226
National Council of Catholic Women,
151
National Federation of Teachers, 143
National Federation of Women's Clubs, 5
National Grocers Association, 229
National Industrial Recovery Act
(NIRA), 159–160, 167
Schechter Poultry and, 169–172
National Labor Relations Act, 183
National Labor Relations Board, 207
National League of Women Voters, 196
National Parent Teacher Association
(PTA), 228
National Publishers Association, 194
National Recovery Administration
(NRA), 160
codes of fair competition, 160–161
live poultry code and, 169–172
newspaper code, 162–163, 165
textile code, 161
National Trades' Union, 21
National Women's Trade Union League,
129
Nebraska, 190
Neill, Charles P., 49, 55, 98
New Deal, 158, 160, 169, 171–173, 183,
203, 214
New Generation, 223
New Jersey, 22, 177
Newman, Jeffrey, 224
New Orleans Times-Picayune, 86, 106
New Outlook, 168
New Republic, 145
New York Bakeshop Act (1895), 71
New York Call, 121
New York City, 33
New York Evening Mail, 122

New York Globe, 88, 121, 133
New York Herald Tribune, 165
New York Post, 133
New York Society for the Prevention of
Cruelty to Children, 29, 75
New York State, 23, 73, 168, 170, 177–
179, 235–236
Child Labor Amendment ratification
and, 152–154
New York State Committee Opposing
Ratification, 168
New York Sun, 62, 165
New York Times, 24–25, 34, 56, 62, 92, 94,
179, 201, 219
Child Labor Amendment and, 177
evils of child labor and, 24–25
Wheeler-Johnson bill and, 181
New York Tribune, 62, 133
New York World, 106, 121–122
New York World-Telegram, 166
Nineteenth Amendment, 126, 131
*NLRB v. Jones and Laughlin Steel
Corporation* (1937), 183, 193, 209
Non-Partisan Committee for
Ratification, 169–170
North Carolina, 73, 109, 152, 170, 172,
188, 213
North Carolina Tobacco Growers
Association, 236
Northern Baptist Convention, 143
Norton, Mary T., 193, 199
Novkov, Julie, 125

Obama administration, 230
O'Connell, Cardinal William Henry, 151
O'Conner, John J., 202
Ohio, 38
Oklahoma, 152
Oleomargarine Act (1886), 100
Oliver Twist, 15
*Opp Cotton Mills, Inc. v. Administrator
Wage and Hour Division* (1940),
209, 212
oppressive child labor, 2–3, 222, 238
Osgood, Irene, 100
Otter, William, 224
Outlook, 119–120
Overman, Lee S., 81–82, 102, 104, 128
Owen, Robert L., 80, 94

Palmer, A. Mitchell, 80
Palmer-Owen bill, 80–82
Panama Refining Company v. Ryan (1935), 169
Panic of 1873, 26
parens patriae, 72, 125
Parsons, Herbert, 52
Peckham, Rufus, 71
Peel, Sir Robert, 15
Pence, Mike, 235, 238
Pennsylvania, 22, 159
Pepper, Claude, 203
Pepper, George Wharton, 135, 141
Perkins, Frances, 156, 164, 167–168, 174–175, 191, 215
    Fair Labor Standards Act and, 200–202
    World War II and, 217
Permanent Conference for the Abolition of Child Labor, 129–130, 134–135, 142
Peterson, Dutton S., 179
Philadelphia Inquirer, 88
Philadelphia Public Ledger, 106
phosphorus necrosis, 100
Pierce v. Society of Sisters (1925), 151
Pinchot, Gifford, 159
Pitney, Mahlon, 90
Poindexter, Miles, 79–80
police powers, 66, 69–70
Pomerene, Atlee, 97, 99, 103, 123
Pomerene Amendment, 100–105, 108
Poole, Rufus, 201
Portland Maine Press-Herald, 122
Pound, Roscoe, 7, 139, 170
Powderly, Terence V., 30
Powell, Thomas Reed, 120
prison-goods theory, 181–182, 196, 198. *See also* Wheeler-Johnson bill
Progressive coalition, 124, 138, 154
Progressive Party, 67, 81, 128, 132
Progressive Period, 37, 44, 68, 86, 124
    reform spirit of, 47
prohibition, 138
Prohibition Party, 25
Publix, 227
Pure Food and Drug Act, 50, 90

Quayle, Dan, 225

Ramspeck, Robert, 202
Raushenbush, Elizabeth Brandeis, 117
Reagan administration, 221, 224–225
Recent Social Trends, 155
Red Scare, 148
Reed, Stanley, 210
Reich, Robert B., 227
Reilly, Gerard D., 201, 214
Republican Party, 51, 76, 81, 103, 142, 179, 232, 239
Revenue Act (1919), 106
Reynolds, James, 49
Rice, William G., 117
Rhode Island, 20–22, 177, 190
Roberts, Owen, 167, 173, 183–184
Robinson, Joe, 200
Rogers, John Jacob, 132
Roosevelt, Eleanor, 216–217
Roosevelt, Franklin D., 125, 156, 161, 200–202
    Child Labor Amendment and, 167, 175–176
    Court-packing plan and, 176–177
    election of 1936 and, 174
    on fair labor standards, 191–192
    Fair Labor Standards Act and, 200–201, 204
    National Industrial Recovery Act and, 160
    reaction to *Schechter Poultry*, 172
    success of NRA codes and, 163–164
    on wages and hours legislation, 185, 199
    World War II and, 218
Roosevelt, Theodore, 48–49, 52, 64–66, 76, 128
    on Beveridge-Parsons bill, 56, 58
    investigation of child labor, 65–66
    Progressive or Bull Moose Party and, 76
Roosevelt recession, 200
Root, Elihu, 168
Rural New Yorker, 148
Ryan, John A., 94, 129, 151, 170

Sacramento Bee, 122
Sallee, Shelley, 5
Saturday Evening Post, 144
Sawyer, Logan E., III, 61

Schechter Poultry Corporation v. United States (1935), 170–172
Schescke, Kent, 230
Schmidt, James D., 251–252n8
Scott, Nathan, 53
Searl, Kelly S., 207–208
Senate Committee on Interstate Commerce, 84
Sentinels of the Republic, 143, 150, 153, 166
Sheppard-Towner Act, 131, 138
Shortridge, Samuel, 137
Silver, Gray, 138
Sinclair, Upton, 49, 234
Slater, Samuel, 18
Slaughterhouse Cases (1873), 70
Smith, Alfred E., 5, 153, 168–169
Smith, Ellison DuRant "Cotton Ed," 84, 104, 197
Socialist Party, 148
Social Service Review, 213
Social Statics, 72
sociological jurisprudence, 7
Solomon, Burt, 171
South Carolina, 73, 119–120, 152, 188
Southern Agriculturalist, 139
Southern Textile Bulletin, 144, 148, 207
Southern Textile Committee, 5
Spargo, John, 49–50, 59
Spencer, Herbert, 72
Spooner, John C., 58, 60–61
Starr, Ellen Gates, 4
state labor bureaus, 37–38
Steinberg, Laurence E., 224
Stephens, Hubert D., 148
St. Louis Post-Dispatch, 165, 234
St. Louis Republic, 88
Stodghill, H. W., 163
Stone, Harlan Fiske, 167, 211–212
Sturges and Burn Manufacturing Co. v. Beauchamp (1913), 78
substantive due process, 70–73. See also *Lochner v. New York* (1905)
Successful Farming, 139
Sunde, Joseph, 238
Supremacy Clause, 134, 147
Supreme Court, US, 169, 188–189, 213–214
    attacks on judicial review, 121–122, 132

composition of, 167–168, 188, 210
Constitutional Revolution of 1937 and, 183–184, 210
"switch in time that saved nine," 183–184, 191
Sutherland, George, 167, 174
sweating system, 33–35
Swift, Wiley H., 142

Taft, William Howard, 50, 75, 100, 112, 114–117
    Bailey v. Drexel Furniture Company and, 114–117
Taney, Roger, 120
Tea Party, 9–11, 232, 236
tenement work, 33
Tenth Amendment, 34, 58–59, 69–70, 90–91, 111, 210, 212
Texas, 152
textile industry code, 161–162
Tillman, Benjamin, 60, 87
Trattner, Walter I., 3, 138, 146, 161, 251n8
Trump, Donald, 9, 236, 238
Tucker, Jeffrey, 237–238

United Mine Workers of America, 195
United States v. Butler (1936), 173
United States v. Darby Lumber (1941), 7–8, 208–209
    majority opinion and, 210–212
    significance of, 213
United States v. Doremus (1919), 101
United States v. E. C. Knight Co. (1895), 89
Unpublished Opinions of Mr. Justice Brandeis, 116–117
US Chamber of Commerce, 194

Vandenburg, Arthur, 180, 197
Vandenburg amendment, 180, 182
Van Devanter, Willis, 90, 167, 198
Veazie Bank v. Fenno (1869), 100–101
Venable, William, 105–106
Vivian Spinning Mills, 110

Wadsworth, James W., 140, 152
Wagner, Robert F., 168
Wald, Lillian D., 74

Wallace, Henry A., 169
Walling, L. Metcalfe, 215
Walsh, David I., 149, 152
Walsh, Thomas J., 141
War Labor Policies Board, 97–98
War Manpower Commission, 218–219
Warner, John De Witt, 34
Washington, George, 13
Washington Post, 213, 236
Watkins, Vincent G., 226
Watson, E. O., 128
Webb, Edwin Yates, 84
Webb-Kenyon Act, 97
West Coast Hotel v. Parrish (1937), 183–184
Wheeler, Burton K., 181
Wheeler, Everett P., 134
Wheeler-Johnson bill, 181, 198, 206
White, Edward Douglas, 71, 90, 110, 117
White, William Allen, 166, 170
White Slave Traffic Act (Mann Act), 77–78, 90
Wilcox, J. Mark, 203
Williams, John, 73

Wilson, Woodrow, 68, 76–77, 80–81, 84, 91–92, 99, 106, 154
  Child Labor Tax Law and, 99, 106
  early views on child labor, 76–77
  on Keating-Owen bill, 86–87
  on Palmer-Owen bill, 81
  World War I and child labor, 96, 98
Wirtz, W. Willard, 223
Wisconsin, 37, 152, 187–188, 233, 236
Wise v. Chandler (1937), 185
Woman Patriots, 143
Wood, Stephen B., 118, 251n8
Working Men's Party, 25
Works, John D., 85
World War I, 85, 95, 98, 146
Wright, Frances "Fanny," 17
Wright v. Vinton Branch of Mountain Trust Bank (1937), 183

Young Women's Christian Association, 143
youth unemployment, 223

Zimmand, Gertrude, 177